Fig. 1   Class J38 No. 1442 on a coal train from one of the Lothian pits to Granton, passing Craigentinny, c. 1927.

LOCOMOTIVES OF THE L.N.E.R.

Part 6A

TENDER ENGINES – CLASSES J38 to K5

Published by
THE RAILWAY CORRESPONDENCE AND TRAVEL SOCIETY
1982

ISBN 0 901115 53 3

CONTENTS

————

INTRODUCTION

A total of 684 engines of the 0-6-0 and 2-6-0 wheel arrangements feature in this Part of "Locomotives of the L.N.E.R.". The story of the 0-6-0 type, begun in Part 5 of this series, is completed here with the remaining four classes, all put into stock after Grouping. Classes J38 and J39 were new designs by Gresley and were amongst the largest 0-6-0's built in this country. The other two classes (J40 and J41) were of Midland Railway design and entered L.N.E.R. service in 1936 when the locomotive stock of the Midland & Great Northern Joint system was absorbed.

The 2-6-0 wheel arrangement was favoured by Gresley for mixed-traffic duties. His first design, with two cylinders, was introduced in 1912 on the G.N.R., and became class K1 on the L.N.E.R. Developed from this was a version with a larger boiler, known as K2 on the L.N.E.R., and then in 1920 there appeared the impressive three-cylinder type with a 6-foot diameter boiler. This became class K3 on the L.N.E.R. and was chosen as a Group Standard design and multiplied further. There were also the six three-cylinder K4 engines, specially designed for work on the steeply-graded West Highland line. An order for seventy more 2-6-0's, based on this latter design, but with only two cylinders, was placed by Peppercorn in 1947. Classified K1, they did not appear until after nationalisation of the railways had taken place.

In this work the complete history of each engine owned by the L.N.E.R., or built to its design, is given. Dimensions are quoted as well as full lists of detail alterations and dates of building, rebuilding, renumbering and withdrawal. Illustrations are generally confined to the post-Grouping period.

Most of the information has been obtained from official sources and it will be noted that in several instances it is at variance with previously published accounts, including such classical works as those by E. L Ahrons. In every case the greatest possible care has been taken to have the details verified and the authors are confident that the version now presented is authentic. Records kept at the various L.N.E.R. locomotive works and elsewhere were not on a uniform basis, particularly of course in the pre-Grouping period, and this has prevented full documentation of some of the detail variations in certain classes.

Acknowledgements will be found in Part 1, The Preliminary Survey, to firms, organisations and, not least, British Railways, for their assistance in providing material for this Part. In addition, readers are referred to Part 1 for full details of the L.N.E.R.'s history and its policy regarding locomotive construction, classification of engines and boilers, diagrams, numberings, naming, liveries, brakes, tenders, route restrictions and load and power classifications. A full list of locomotive classes and their subdivision into class parts is also included therein.

The individual class articles in this series have been arranged on a uniform basis, each class being divided under sub-headings. This method was preferred by the authors to a chronological history as it facilitates reference, but some unavoidable repetition does occur. The following notes on these sub-headings are offered to assist the reader:—

ENGINES AT GROUPING (or at subsequent date of absorption). – For convenience the locomotive numbers quoted are wherever possible on an L.N.E.R. basis. In some instances, however, locomotives were withdrawn without actually receiving new L.N.E.R. numbers.

STANDARD L.N.E.R. DIMENSIONS. – These are on a uniform basis for each class and have generally been taken from the first engine diagram issued by the L.N.E.R. for the class concerned, unless otherwise stated. The pitch of the boiler is its centre line height above rail level. Boiler diagram numbers refer to those brought into use from 1928 onwards by the L.N.E.R. These numbers have also been used for locomotive classes which became extinct before that date where the particular boiler type survived in use on some other class at 1928 and thus received a diagram number.

REBUILDING. – Generally this section is confined to major rebuilding, or reboilering with a different type of boiler. All other variations appear under other headings, e.g. "Details" and "Brakes".

ENGINE DIAGRAMS. – The diagrams issued by the L.N.E.R. are listed under this heading. Generally the diagrams were prepared at the end of the year quoted and issued early in the following year. In certain classes an indication is given of major variations not recognised by the issue of a diagram.

SUMMARY. – (i) Engine Numbers: An L.N.E.R. number shown in brackets indicates that it was never actually borne. Dates of re-numbering are given, except in the case of many of the 1924 L.N.E.R. numbers where the relevant information is not uniformly available. (ii) Rebuilding and other alterations: As this work is primarily a history from Grouping to the present day, the Summary normally lists only alterations that occurred after 1923. Alterations made in pre-Grouping days are therefore generally confined to the body of the article on each class, except that, where a particular alteration to a class was initiated before Grouping and continued by the L.N.E.R., complete details will be given in the Summary.

Dates of building, rebuilding and detail alterations are on the basis customarily employed by the various companies before Grouping. For the L.N.E.R. and B.R. periods they are "to traffic", i.e. when the locomotive took up revenue earning work. Differences may thus occur between these and previously published information where, for instance, "ex-works" or "official" rebuilding dates may have been quoted. "Ex-works" frequently meant the date an engine emerged from the erecting shop; a further period then elapsed during which time it ran one or more trial trips and was painted and varnished. Rebuilding dates were often recorded when a new boiler was allotted to or installed on an engine then under repair and could precede the date the engine returned to traffic by several months. From about 1929, ex-works dates ceased to be quoted in L.N.E.R. records, dates to traffic being solely used thereafter.

0-6-0 CLASSES

SUMMARY OF J38-J41 CLASS TOTALS

		31st December																			
Class	Rly.	1926	1927	1928	1929	1930	1931	1932	1933	1934	1935	1936	1937	1938	1939	1940	1941	1942	1943	1944	1945
J38	L.N.E.	35	35	35	35	35	35	35	35	35	35	35	35	35	35	35	35	35	35	35	35
J39	L.N.E.	17	44	74	114	123	132	146	148	160	199	224	234	271	271	271	289	289	289	289	289
J40	M.G.N.												8*	7	7	7	5	4	4		
J41	M.G.N.												3*	3	2	2	2	1			

	31st December																					
Class	1946	1947	1948	1949	1950	1951	1952	1953	1954	1955	1956	1957	1958	1959	1960	1961	1962	1963	1964	1965	1966	1967
J38	35	35	35	35	35	35	35	35	35	35	35	35	35	35	35	35	33	31	25	21	3	
J39	289	289	289	289	289	289	289	289	289	289	289	289	289	241	178	128						

* Five further 0-6-0's (four class J40 and one class J41) were taken over from the M. & G.N. but were not added to L.N.E.R. stock.

0-6-0 CLASSES J38 TO J41

Apart from the engines brought into stock by the absorption of the M. & G.N., only two entirely new classes of 0-6-0 were introduced after Grouping. Both came out during Gresley's period in office and it is worth noting that they were considerably heavier than any of the comparable 0-6-0 designs produced by the other three major companies.

To deal with heavy goods and mineral trains on the difficult main lines, and often very steeply graded branches of the N.B. Section, thirty-five class J38 engines were designed and built at Darlington in 1926. They had 4ft. 8in. diameter wheels, 20in. × 26in. cylinders and a boiler of 5ft. 6in. diameter. This was the first entirely new Group Standard class on the L.N.E.R. to be produced in quantity, having been preceded only by the solitary class U1 Garratt locomotive and the two class P1 2-8-2 mineral engines.

No further J38's were built as the J39 class that followed immediately afterwards was more generally useful all over the L.N.E.R. system, and was adopted as standard. Although otherwise similar to class J38, the wheels of class J39 were 6in. larger and the distance between tubeplates of the boiler was 6in. shorter. The first engines were turned out in late 1926 and additions to stock of this most versatile class were made every year until 1938. A final batch came out during 1941, when the class totalled

3

289. Withdrawal began in 1959 and proceeded rapidly over a period of only four years. Class J38, however, remained intact until 1962 and did not become extinct until 1967.

On 1st October 1936 the L.N.E.R. took over the working of the M. & G.N. Joint lines. Among the hitherto separately-maintained locomotive stock were sixteen 5ft. 3in. 0-6-0 engines built in 1896-99. When constructed they were of standard M.R. design, by S. W. Johnson, and had 4ft. 3in. diameter boilers with round-topped firebox. By the time that the L.N.E.R. took them over, four of these engines were running with 4ft. 9½in. boilers with Belpaire firebox standard with the class C

Rebuilt 4-4-0's that became class D54 on the L.N.E.R. Only eleven of the sixteen 0-6-0's were actually taken into L.N.E.R. book stock, the others being regarded as worn out. At first the two varieties continued to be known by their M. & G.N. classifications, D and D Rebuilt, but in July 1942 the survivors were classified J40 and J41 respectively. They became extinct in 1944 and 1943 respectively.

A statistical analysis of the four classes of 0-6-0 dealt with in this book is given above. For a full analysis of all the L.N.E.R.'s engines of this wheel arrangement the reader is referred to Part 5 of this series.

CLASS J38

GRESLEY 4ft. 8in. ENGINES

ENGINES BUILT AFTER GROUPING (1926): 1400/1/3-11/3-7/9-24/6/7/8/34/7/40-7. TOTAL 35.

When the 1925-26 building programme was discussed at the meeting of the Joint Traffic & Locomotive Committee on 30th October 1924, reference was made to 103 0-6-0 goods engines. The intended distribution was forty-eight to the Southern Area, twenty to the N.E. Area and thirty-five to the Scottish Area. A month later approval was given to the purchase of forty-eight ex-R.O.D. 2-8-0's (class O4) for the Southern Area instead, and the 0-6-0 authority was correspondingly reduced. On 4th March 1925 Gresley signed the general construction order for fifty-five new engines, referred to as "J27 Modified". On 12th June the twenty engines intended for the N.E. Area were deleted and on 16th June the Darlington Works order was issued for one batch of thirty-five engines, which appeared during the first half of 1926.

They were despatched to Scotland where they were used on main line goods work and on short distance mineral haulage from the Fife and Lothian coalfields to the Scottish east coast ports and the industrial belt between Edinburgh and Glasgow.

No further J38's were built and future construction was of the later J39 class, which had larger diameter wheels making it more versatile. Although the J38 was a comparatively small class, dating back to the early days after Grouping, it had the distinction of being the last L.N.E.R. steam engine class to remain intact, until December 1962 when Nos. 65923/8 were withdrawn. The class became extinct in April 1967 with the withdrawal of Nos. 65901/29 and these were the last Gresley steam engines in service on B.R.

L.N.E.R. Renumbering

In 1946 the engines were renumbered 5900-34 in sequence according to their original numbers.

4

Cylinders (2 inside)	..	..	..	..	..	$20'' \times 26''$
Motion	..	..	..	..	..	Stephenson with 8″ piston valves
Boiler:						
Max. diam. outside	..	..	..	..	..	5′ 6″
Barrel length	..	..	..	..	..	11′ 4⅝″(a)
Firebox length outside		..	..	..	..	9′ 0″ (b)
Pitch	..	..	..	..	..	8′ 9½″
Diagram No.	..	..	..	..	..	97A 97

Heating surface:							
Firebox	..	..	..	..	..	171.50 sq.ft.	171.50 sq.ft.
Tubes (177 × 1¾″)	..	..	..	..	..	912.25 sq.ft.	871.75 sq.ft.
Flues (24 × 5¼″)	..	..	..	..	..	371.00 sq.ft.	354.53 sq.ft.
Total evaporative	..	..	..	..		1454.75 sq.ft.	1397.78 sq.ft.
Superheater (24 × 1⁷⁄₃₂″)	..	..	..	..		289.60 sq.ft.	271.80 sq.ft.
Total	..	..	..	..	..	1744.35 sq.ft.	1669.58 sq.ft.
Grate area	..	..	..	..	..	26 sq.ft.	
Boiler pressure	..	..	..	..	..	180 lb./sq.in.	
Coupled wheels	..	..	..	..	..	4′ 8″	
Tractive effort (85%)	..	..	..	..	..	28,414 lb.	
Wheelbase (engine)	..	..	..	..	..	$8' 0'' + 9' 0'' = 17' 0''$	
Weight (full):							
Engine	..	..	..	..	..	58T	19C
Max. axle load	..	..	..	..	..	20T	6C

Leading particulars applicable to tenders fitted:

						New	From 1931
Wheel diameter	..	..	..	..	..	3′ 9″	3′ 9″
Wheelbase	..	..	..	..	..	7′ 3″ + 6′ 3″	7′ 0″ + 6′ 0″
						= 13′ 6″	= 13′ 0″
Total wheelbase (engine and tender)		..	..	..		41′ 3″	40′ 5″
Length over buffers							
(engine and tender)	..	..	..	..	..	56′ 0″	54′ 3¾″
Weight (full)	..	..	..	..	..	51T 10C	44T 4C
Water capacity	..	..	..	..	..	4,200 gallons	3,500 gallons
Coal capacity	..	..	..	..	..	7T 10C	5T 10C

(a)   11′ 4¹¹⁄₁₆″ from 6/1931 for replacement fireboxes.
(b)   8′ 11⅞″ from 6/1931 for replacement fireboxes.

Development

The J38's were the first entirely new Group Standard class and the detail design work was carried out in the Darlington drawing office. Although referred to in the general construction order as "J27 Modified", this is misleading. As one contemporary draughtsman at Darlington afterwards commented, the last thing Gresley wanted was a design based on the J27, and about the only point of similarity was the wheel arrangement! The 4ft. 8in. diameter of the coupled wheels

was the Doncaster standard size for goods engines and not the 4ft. 7½in. diameter hitherto used by Darlington for this type of work. The axle journals were 8in. diameter and 9in. long instead of 7½in. by 8in. on class J27. The diameter of the cylinders was 20in. and their layout followed Gorton practice, with dished piston heads. The steam chest however followed Doncaster practice, with 8in. diameter piston valves having 1½in. steam lap – features of the class K3 2-6-0's which Darlington was then building. The Stephenson link motion again followed Gorton practice though adjustments were incorporated to lengthen the valve travel. Steam operated reversing gear was provided, which was a Darlington feature.

The Stephenson valve gear arrangement was virtually identical with that of the original class A5 4-6-2T's, having 4ft. 8in. eccentric rods, but with a valve travel of $5\frac{5}{8}$in. at 75 per cent cut-off compared with $4\frac{1}{8}$in. in the original G.C. arrangement. For example the throw of the eccentrics was increased to $7\frac{1}{2}$in. and the proportions of the rocking shaft arms were altered: the lower arm connected to the expansion link was $9\frac{7}{16}$in. between pin centres, whilst the upper arm connected to the piston valve spindle via the intermediate valve rod was $10\frac{7}{16}$in. The first J38 drawing was for the cylinders and this appeared at Darlington on 30th December 1924, followed three days later by the valve events table. The J38 arrangement of cylinders, piston valves and motion was then incorporated by Gorton in the improved A5's which in fact appeared before the J38's. The arrangement was afterwards employed in class J39 and in addition it formed the basis for the layout in several classes which were afterwards rebuilt both by Gresley (see Part 3B class D11 and Part 3C class D16/3) and Thompson (Part 4 class D and Part 5 class J11/3).

Compared with class J27, the engine wheelbase was lengthened by 6in. between the second and third axles in order to accommodate a longer firebox, 9ft. instead of 7ft. The grate area was increased from 20 to 26 sq.ft. The diameter of the boiler barrel was 5ft. 6in., as in class J27, but was pitched $8\frac{1}{2}$in. higher in order to clear the piston valves. This feature, together with the raised running plate above the wheels, gave the J38's an appearance quite different from the J27's.

There was an all-round increase in the heating surface figures, giving the J38's greater boiler power. The working pressure was kept at 180 lb. per sq. in. but because of the larger cylinders the tractive effort was raised from 24,642 lb. to 28,414 lb. Class J38 weighed 9 tons 9 cwt. more than the latest version of class J27 and had a maximum axle load of 20 tons 6 cwt.

The firebox had a sloping throatplate (not externally obvious as the clothing plate had a vertical front edge) and a sloping cab faceplate. These were Doncaster features found in the Diagram 96 boiler (see class K3). However, the firehole was circular, following Darlington practice, and not oval as in the later class J39 boilers; the firehole door was the square N.E.R. pattern. The front end of the firebox had a drop grate section. The rodding which operated it

passed along the right-hand side of the firebox and there was a complicated arrangement of bell cranks and balance weights, partly hidden under a semi-circular shaped cover (fig. 2). In 1930 the mechanism was altered. The bell cranks and balance weights were replaced by a coil spring and the rodding dropped down at a steeper angle than before (fig. 3). The semi-circular shaped cover was removed.

The firebox had two hand holes at each side, high up above the boiler handrails (fig. 2). Due to boiler changes, examples latterly appeared of Diagram 97 boilers (see later) having four wash-out plugs at each side instead (fig. 4). From 1931 extra inspection doors were provided in the firebox sides below the boiler centre line (fig. 3) to combat trouble caused by the build-up of incrustations in the water space, resulting in deterioration of the copper fireboxes and the need for new plates every four years or so. The inner fireboxes were constructed of $\frac{5}{8}$in. thick copper plate except for the tubeplate which was $1\frac{3}{16}$in. Replacement fireboxes from 1931 had $\frac{9}{16}$in. plate instead of $\frac{5}{8}$in. (see also under class J39).

The details for the Robinson superheater header with $1\frac{1}{2}$in. outside diameter elements based on standard Doncaster practice, were prepared at Darlington in March 1925. However the engine diagram originally showed the inside diameter of the elements as $1\frac{3}{32}$in., which was the standard Darlington dimension for the Schmidt type, and the surface area as 257.5 sq.ft. (Similar particulars appeared in the first published information for classes J38, J39 and D49). In December 1927 the engine diagram was corrected to read $1\frac{7}{32}$in. and 289.6 sq.ft. respectively. When the L.N.E.R. boiler classification system was introduced in 1928, the J38 boilers were allotted Diagram 97A. The somewhat similar boilers introduced in September 1926 for class J39 became Diagram 97.

In December 1932 No. 1406 was provided with a Diagram 97 boiler and thus a spare boiler became available for class J38. The alteration to No. 1406 was not dramatic. The respective barrel lengths were identical so that there was no change where the front end of the barrel was attached to the cylinders. However, in the Diagram 97 boiler the front of the barrel was cut away at a slant above its centre line and the tubeplate was recessed 6in. further into the barrel. The reduction in heating surface is shown under "Standard L.N.E.R. Dimensions". The smokebox was lengthened from 4ft. $2\frac{1}{4}$in. to 4ft.

8¾in. and the rearwards extension beyond the smokebox saddle was noticeable (cf. figs. 3 and 4). The chimney and anti-vacuum valve were also set back 6in.

In 1935 Nos. 1410/3/5 were also given Diagram 97 boilers. From 1940 conversions became more common, particularly with the gradual scrapping of the original boilers which commenced in 1942, but there were also reversions to the original pattern. From 1941 the two varieties of class J38 were accorded separate part numbers: Part 1 for the engines with original boilers and Part 2 for the altered engines. Class J38 had previously been segregated into two parts, in 1931-33, with a quite different significance (see Tenders). The only engine to be withdrawn with a Diagram 97A boiler was No. 65928 in December 1962, and the last boiler of this type was scrapped in November 1963 when No. 65918 was reboilered.

In accordance with the practice adopted in 1925 by the L.N.E.R., the engines were arranged for left-hand drive, i.e. the automatic steam brake valve, vacuum ejector, steam reversing gear levers, cylinder drain cocks lever and leading sanding gear lever were all on that side of the cab. The regulator handle was the double pull-out type though Darlington recorded that six engines instead had the N.E. "bull's horn" (or cow horn) variety, so named from its shape.

The steam reversing gear (fig. 5) was ideal for tedious shunting movements involving frequent reversal, but its efficient operation depended on good maintenance and skilled manipulation. The cataract cylinder had to be kept topped up and the glands kept tight, or the gear would not stay set in an early cut-off position. Care had to be taken in "notching up" to avoid inadvertent complete reversal of the gear, or the dislocation of the cataract valve arm on the side of the boiler, again resulting in the failure of the gear to remain in the selected position. In these circumstances the coal consumption increased especially under wartime conditions, and so between February 1945 and June 1948 the gear was removed from the entire class and replaced by screw reverse. A small piece had to be cut out of the top of the frame on the left-hand side where it would otherwise have fouled the reversing rod (fig. 6). In an attempt to hold the steam reversing gear in position, some drivers used to wedge a firebar between the cut-off pointer and the faceplate (a trick handed down by old North Eastern men), but this often resulted in distortion of the indicator mechanism.

Details

The cab footboards extended well back over the space between the engine and tender and the fall plate was hinged on the tender front. The arrangement was altered in the mid-forties: the cab footboards were shortened, tender footboards were provided which projected forward over the gap and the fall plate was then hinged on the cab footboards.

The whistle was originally connected to the steam manifold valve and the stem passed through the cab front plate. From March 1931 the whistle was repositioned on top of the firebox, just behind the safety valves. Darlington fitted their style of circular cover around the base of the safety valves on the Diagram 97A boilers (fig. 2). With the widespread use of Diagram 97 boilers on the class, many latterly had no cover at all (fig. 4). Others had a rectangular or square-shaped cover, fitted at one of the Scottish works (fig. 7).

The chimney was 1ft. 3¼in. high, and the height above rail level to the top was 13ft. 0in. The heights above rail level to the tops of the dome, safety valves and cab roof were respectively 12ft. 10¾in., 12ft. 7¼in. and 12ft. 11 1/16 in., all within the L.N.E.R. Composite Load Gauge.

The smokebox door was of Darlington design, 4ft. 5¼in. diameter and dished to a radius of 11ft. 0in. Similar doors were later used in other classes, for example J39, D49 and B17. The boiler handrail circled the top of the smokebox front plate and the upper lampiron was originally fitted at the top of the smokebox, both being features of the latest N.E.R. 0-6-0's (fig. 2). However, the door was secured by the Doncaster twin-handle arrangement, though at a later date No. 1442 acquired the N.E. type of wheel and handle – probably at its February 1932 visit to Darlington Works. As the engines went through shops from March 1930 the upper lampiron was transferred to the smokebox door (fig. 4), but this modification was only completed when No. 65929 was so altered in November 1949.

It is reported that ash ejectors were fitted to Nos. 1414/21 in March 1928 and to No. 1411 at an unrecorded date. No further details are available and no photographic evidence has been located.

The sanders were gravity fed, in front of the leading coupled and behind the trailing coupled wheels. This arrangement was similar to class J27.

A Wakefield No. 7 mechanical lubricator was mounted on the right-hand side running plate and this provided oil for the axleboxes. The drive for this lubricator was taken from a return crank attached to the crank pin on the centre axle. A Eureka D four-feed hydrostatic sight-feed lubricator in the cab on the fireman's side fed oil to the cylinders and valves. Two sloping feed pipes ran along each side of the boiler. At each side of the smokebox, one of the feeds split into two before entering the steam chest. The other feed went directly into the cylinder below it. In February 1939 No. 1416 received a similarly acting Detroit type in exchange for the Eureka.

Spencer's double-case buffers, 1ft. 6in. long, were provided of the type fitted to certain K3's and O2's. With this type of buffer there was one spring in front of the bufferbeam and one behind it, each in its own case. By comparison the J39's had 2in. longer Group Standard buffers, the springs for which were in front of the bufferbeam. The J38's had G.S. drawgear, originally with three-link couplings (fig. 5), but most if not all latterly had the screw adjustable type (fig. 6) which was mainly fitted from the late thirties, though there were some temporary fittings noted earlier. About 1930-31 Nos. 1401/37 had steam heat connections at both ends and No. 1400 had it at the tender end only. This was at the period when Thornton was using J38's on passenger trains, particularly in the summer months. This practice does not appear to have been officially encouraged with the result that in June 1931 one of the Thornton engines, No. 1437, had its vacuum brake ejector specially removed at Cowlairs Works (see Brakes).

Brakes

Steam brakes were provided on engine and tender. The brake cylinder on the engine was 11in. diameter and located under the cab. A vacuum ejector was also provided for train braking. The vacuum pipe at the front end was fitted below the bufferbeam following N.E. practice (fig. 2) but swan-neck stand-pipes were generally substituted in the thirties (fig. 4), though Nos. 5901/7/10/4/28 at least still had the original arrangement in 1946-47 but were altered later. Others were noted in B.R. days with the pipe occasionally absent to facilitate the fitting of a small snow plough.

There was a small hole in the vacuum ejector exhaust pipe, for drainage purposes, inside the smokebox. This prevented water collecting in the pipe, but the continual dripping caused corrosion of the main steam pipe instead. From August 1930 a drain pipe was connected to this hole, which then passed through the smokebox side, downwards and through the running plate to discharge where it could do no harm (fig. 5).

It was only occasionally that the vacuum brake equipment on these engines was put to good use, for example on 2nd January 1930 when Thornton shed turned out a J38 to work an eight-coach passenger train to Edinburgh and back. The vacuum brake equipment was also required on the occasions when these engines were commandeered as passenger station pilots, in particular at Aberdeen, or to work fast goods trains. In June 1931 No. 1437 had its vacuum brake equipment removed at Cowlairs Works, only to have it restored at Darlington Works in the following February. The vacuum brake equipment was also removed from No. 1427, this time permanently, in January 1932. This was a Dundee engine and the story told at the time was that it was regularly employed on a lodging turn to Bathgate and the vacuum brake was removed to make sure the engine was not misappropriated for passenger work. The 3,500-gallon tender, which was attached to this engine in June 1933, had a vacuum hose pipe at the rear end and more than one running shed foreman was deceived by this when looking round his shed for extra passenger power. The vacuum hose pipe was certainly removed from the front of the engine and the vacuum ejector exhaust pipe was absent from the boiler side.

On the N.B. section it was customary to control heavy loose-coupled trains descending steep gradients by pinning down as many wagon brakes as the driver considered necessary and then relying on the tender hand brake. This method of operation enabled the engine brake to be kept in reserve for emergency use. When the J38's were introduced it was found that the small brake blocks fitted to their tenders were unsuitable for this purpose and, following complaints from the Scottish Area, Doncaster issued an instruction in January 1927 that standard tenders would henceforward be fitted with engine brake blocks, when operating in Scotland.

Another difficulty encountered with the J38 tender brakes was that the hand-operated mechanism was of the type discarded by the N.B.R. forty years previously (but still to be found on Wheatley engines such as class J31, usually known as the "plunger" type. This worked in a vertical pillar of circular section, the die-block (attached to the shaft arm) working on a screw thread on the bottom end of the hand brake spindle. When the power brake was applied, the lifting of the brake shaft arm lifted up the die-block and with it the hand brake

Fig. 2   Class J38 No. 1440 at Gorgie, July 1926.

Original drop grate arrangement, circular cover around base of safety valves, two hand holes on firebox above handrail, lampiron at top of smokebox, vacuum hose connection below bufferbeam, 4,200-gallon tender with stepped-out coping plate.

Fig. 3   Class J38/2 No. 1400 at Eastfield shed, March 1934.

Diagram 97A boiler, additional hand hole low down towards front of firebox, simplified drop grate arrangement and semi-circular cover removed, 3,500-gallon tender with separate coping plate.

Fig. 4   Class J38/2 No. 1417 at St. Margaret's shed, May 1946.

Diagram 97 boiler with 6 in. longer smokebox, chimney and anti-vacuum valve set 6 in. further back, four wash-out plugs in place of upper firebox hand holes, no cover around base of safety valves, lampiron on smokebox door, swan-neck vacuum brake stand-pipe.

Fig. 5   Class J38 No. 1403 at Eastfield shed, October 1932.
Steam reversing gear, drain from vacuum ejector exhaust pipe low down on smokebox side, three-link coupling.

Fig. 6   Class J38/1 No. 5928 at Thornton shed, April 1947.
Screw reversing gear with piece cut out of frame top, screw coupling, wartime letters ''N E'' on tender.

Fig. 7   Class J38/2 No. 65911 at Thornton shed, August 1960.
Square cover around base of safety valves, 3,500-gallon tender with high
front plate.

Fig. 8   Class J38 No. 1447 on a Kirkcaldy-Glasgow special at Inverkeithing, c. 1927.

Fig. 9   Class J38 No. 1417 on a Berwick to Portobello goods passing Drem, 1928.

Fig. 10   Class J38 No. 1423 on a down class A goods at Gorgie, July 1926.

Fig. 11   Class J38/1 No. 1424 on a westbound class A goods at Saughton, March 1945.

Fig. 12   Class J38/1 No. 5919 on coal empties at Morrison's Haven, April 1948.

Fig. 13   Class J38/2 No. 65914 at Kinneil, April 1966.

Fig. 14   Class J39 No. 1452 at York, c. 1927.

Westinghouse brake with hose connection below bufferbeam, original drop grate arrangement, mechanical lubricator for axleboxes, sight feed lubricator with feed to cylinder low down on smokebox saddle and divided feed higher up to each end of steam chest, wide support plate for cab footsteps, lampiron at top of smokebox, two hand holes on firebox above handrail, 3,500-gallon tender with stepped-out coping plate and short handrails.

Fig. 15   Class J39 No. 1275 at Doncaster shed, July 1929.

Steam reversing gear, no external drain from vacuum ejector exhaust pipe, sight-feed lubricator pipes lower down on left-hand side than on right, 3,500-gallon tender with stepped-out coping plate and short handrails.

Fig. 16   Class J39/1 No. 1459 at Neville Hill shed, March 1938.

Altered from steam to screw reversing gear, additional hand hole low down towards front of firebox, Westinghouse brake removed, lampiron on smokebox door.

spindle, which rose up a little out of the pillar at the top, where the operating handle was attached. When the power brake was released, the die-block and spindle were lowered. If the brake was screwed on tight with the power brake applied it could not be released again by hand. In the later standard N.B. type, as subsequently used on the J38 tenders, a short screwed spindle and die-block were mounted in a slotted frame on the tender front, and two long links extended downwards to couple the die-block to the brake shaft arm. The bottom ends of the long links were slotted to allow the power brake to operate the brake shaft and arms without lifting the die-block or screw spindle – an arrangement which gave very good hand control on the brake.

Between August 1960 and February 1961 the following engines were fitted with the standard A.W.S. equipment: Nos. 65909/10/2/6/7/8/ 20/2/6/9/30/1/3/4.

Tenders

The tenders originally attached to the J38's were the Group Standard 4,200-gallon type with stepped-out copings (fig. 2). Water pick-up apparatus was fitted though there were no troughs in the Scottish Area.

Between 1931 and 1933 the J38's received new Group Standard 3,500-gallon tenders in exchange. They were shorter in length, had straight sides and no water pick-up apparatus (fig. 3). Twelve of these tenders were constructed at Doncaster and hauled to the Scottish sheds where they were exchanged. The larger tenders were then sent to Doncaster for attaching to new class O2 engines Nos. 2954-61, 2430-3. Darlington constructed the remaining small tenders, seven of which were exchanged in Scotland whilst sixteen were attached at Darlington Works during the course of repairs to the engines concerned (see also under Maintenance). The displaced tenders were taken for fifteen D49's (see Part 4 of this series) and eight new J39's (Nos. 2977-80, 1453/69/71/80). During the period when these exchanges were taking place, Part 1 was allocated to the engines with 3,500-gallon tenders and Part 2 to the remaining engines of the class.

In the fifties there were instances of tenders transferred from other classes. These were usually similar 3,500-gallon tenders from J39's, but the following exceptions are worthy of note:-

65916 9/53 – 10/53   4,125-gallon N.E.-type tender, ex-class J39 (formerly with Raven

Pacific class A2). See class J39 for details.

65902 8/55 – 10/55   Same type of tender as fitted to No. 65916 in 1953, see above.

65911 5/60 – 10/66   3,500-gallon tender, ex-class K4. High-front type with longer coping plate (fig. 7). This tender was then attached to No. 65922, which was withdrawn later that month.

65919 9/61 – wdl.   4,200-gallon type, ex-class K3. Welded tank.

Descriptions of the 3,500-gallon and 4,200-gallon tenders will be found under classes J39 and K3 respectively.

Maintenance

Throughout their lives the engines were allocated to Scottish Area sheds and normally visited Cowlairs Works for repairs. In 1931-33 however, twenty-four engines received a general repair at Darlington Works instead, including two engines, Nos. 1434/46, which visited Darlington twice for this purpose during this period. In addition, No. 1427 received a light repair at this works in June 1933. During the course of these repairs, Darlington exchanged the tenders in sixteen instances from the 4,200-gallon to the 3,500-gallon variety. No. 1417 visited Darlington Works for a general repair from December 1941 to March 1942. It was back in again for a non-classified repair the following day after being recorded ex-works and finally returned to traffic in the following June.

Towards the end of their career, Inverurie Works took a hand in the repairing of J38's, commencing with No. 65903 in February 1955, followed soon afterwards by Nos. 65917/24. Odd ones then appeared over the next few years, for example No. 65906 in 1956. From October 1959 they were shopped there regularly until November 1965 (No. 65925) when this works ceased the repair of steam engines.

British Railways

The entire class was taken over at nationalisation and by August 1950 all the engines had had 60,000 added to their running numbers. Cowlairs did not always repaint the tender when an engine was renumbered, hence Nos. 65900/21/3/8 ran thus numbered with the letters "N E" on their tenders, whilst Nos. 65906/19/29/31/3 for example had the letters

"L N E R". They all eventually acquired the first B.R. emblem, and when the new style crest was introduced, No. 65928 was the first engine to acquire one at Cowlairs Works in June 1957.

Allocation and Work

The initial allocation of the J38's was as follows:-

Dunfermline – Nos. 1400/6/10/9/20/8/34/7/45 (9).
Thornton – Nos. 1401/4/8/9/13/5/24/7 (8).
Dundee – Nos. 1403/5/11/26/41 (5).
St.Margaret's – Nos. 1407/14/6/7/21/2/3/40/2 (9).
Stirling – Nos. 1443/4 (2).
Eastfield – Nos. 1446/7 (2).

There were a small number of early transfers. In December 1926 Stirling's two went to Dunfermline (No. 1443) and Dundee (No. 1444). Then in June 1928 Nos. 1434/45 left Dunfermline for Thornton, whilst No. 1427 moved from Thornton to Dundee, and the Eastfield pair replaced Nos. 1434/45 at Dunfermline. Consequently, the allocation at the beginning of 1929 was Dunfermline 10, Thornton 9, St.Margaret's 9 and Dundee 7. The last-mentioned shed also covered Ferryhill (Aberdeen) for which there was then no separate allocation, and from about mid-1930 to mid-1934 No. 1427 was stationed there. No further moves took place until the War, during which No. 1407 was shedded at Haymarket from 1940 until 1944 (when it returned to St.Margaret's), and Dundee's allocation of J38's was divided between Thornton (Nos. 1403/5/11/44) and Dunfermline (1426/7/41) in December 1943.

Post-nationalisation transfers were those of Nos. 65909/17 from Dunfermline to Polmont (1949), Nos. 65916/22/34 from Dunfermline to St.Margaret's (1954), Nos. 65900/5 from Dunfermline to Thornton (1956), No. 65903 from Thornton to Dunfermline, No. 65906 from St.Margaret's to Dunfermline and No. 65916 from St.Margaret's to Thornton (all in 1961), and No. 65931 from Thornton to Dunfermline (1962). On the closure of Polmont shed in 1964, Nos. 65909/17 went to nearby Grangemouth (ex-L.M.S.) shed for a few months before moving on to Thornton and Dunfermline respectively. In that same year, another old Caledonian shed acquired two J38's when Nos. 65912/20 went from St.Margaret's to Dalry Road, but again their stay was short-lived, and these two engines were transferred to Dunfermline. The remainder

of the St.Margaret's J38's had been moved away to Thornton and Dunfermline during 1962-65 and by the beginning of 1966 the remaining twenty-one engines of the class were located entirely in Fife, and this proved to be the final distribution:-

Dunfermline – Nos.   65903/12/7/8/20/30/1/4 (8).
Thornton – Nos.   65901/5/7/9/10/1/4/5/21/2 /5/9/32 (13).

It will be noted that not only was the J38 class allocated throughout its existence entirely to the Scottish Area/Region, but apart from short periods the class belonged to only four sheds. These were Dunfermline, Thornton, Dundee and St.Margaret's, and of these Dundee only kept engines of the class for roughly half their lifespan. Eight of the class remained allocated throughout their lives to the sheds to which they went when new; these were Nos. 65901/7/8/11/3 (ex-1401/8/9/13/5) at Thornton, No. 65919 (ex-1422) at St.Margaret's and Nos. 65924/6 (ex-1428/37) at Dunfermline.

When the J38's first came to St.Margaret's they replaced J37's on main line goods working, each engine being rostered for a regular driver. A typical duty at that time was the 9-0 p.m. Leith Walk to Aberdeen, a lodging turn worked alternate days by Ferryhill. In the same link, to give the men a day-shift job, was the 10-40 a.m. Portobello to Berwick (better known as the "Berwick Local"), a pick-up goods train which · took 7 hours 35 minutes to complete its journey of 54½ miles. This was also a "book-off" (worked alternately by Tweedmouth), although as in the case of other moderate-distance lodging turns, the men usually travelled to and from their home station in their own time. With the advent of K2's and J39's at St.Margaret's, the J38's were taken off regular long-distance work and were then chiefly employed on local coal trains. In the 1930's the Coal Train Link at St.Margaret's consisted of forty-four sets of men rostered for short distance working and, as the name of the link implied, most of the duties were concerned with the working of trains of coal from the pits in the Lothian coalfield to the marshalling yards and docks in the Edinburgh district. In those days, besides the large quantity of coal required for domestic use, considerable amounts of coal were exported from Leith, and the needs for ships' bunkers at Leith and Granton had also to be met. Granton gasworks and Portobello power station also required daily supplies, not to mention the L.N.E.R.'s own requirements. At the beginning of the shift, the engine would proceed to Granton, South Leith or Portobello, and pick up a train of empty wagons, taking these to Morrison's Haven or Prestonpans on the East Coast main line, Smeaton or Woodhall on the branch from Monktonhall Junction (also on the Berwick main line), or Arniston or Newbattle on the Carlisle line. Many of these duties were day-shift turns (a number being double-shifted), and the J38's were employed on night goods work to obtain maximum utilisation (e.g. to Sighthill, Selkirk, Thornton, Stirling or Perth), and during the War even to Aberdeen and Newcastle (both by then worked on a change-over basis). Having got as far as Heaton, they were then liable to be used on southbound workings, and so in 1940, No. 1416 was noted at York, No. 1403 at Doncaster, and No. 1423 at Retford. The last-named was seen on a down goods train, so had presumably been as far as Grantham, or more probably Peterborough. The St.Margaret's engines also appeared on Waverley Route goods workings to Carlisle, with St.Margaret's and Carlisle men changing en route. Included in the Coal Train and goods links at St.Margaret's were a number of conditionals, which were worked by various classes, including the J38's. This class was also frequently used on engineer's trains, there being three daily "ballasts" (with often an extra one as well) booked from Portobello. Each of the three Main Line Goods links at St.Margaret's had one of these ballast trains, which were all double shifted, thus giving the goods men a share of day-shift working. The relief men travelled by train to the station nearest the scene of operations, but in later years, following the drastic curtailment of passenger services, it was common practice for the men to proceed by bus. If the location of the engineering work was not readily accessible by road, as for example Winchburgh tunnel, a light engine would be booked for the ballast men to "work their passage" from and to St.Margaret's. During the War, the J38's were used to work the heavy ammunition trains to and from the Ministry of Supply "dump" at Macbie Hill, on the erstwhile Dolphinton branch. St.Margaret's did not favour the J38 class for passenger train working, but in October 1947 No. 5933 was noted on the Polton branch, and from time to time a J38 would be called on to work a passenger train in an emergency, such as No. 5931 on a down East Coast express into Waverley after the failure of an A2 at Drem on 27th March 1948.

At Dunfermline the J38's were used on main line goods trains from Townhill yard to Perth, Dundee, Bathgate, Cadder and Niddrie, and in the early days of the class they were allotted to regular drivers in the Main Line Goods Link (known as "The Big Link"). They were also employed throughout their career on the local coal trains (manned by "West of Fife" Link), which covered workings to Whitemyre, Kelty, Blairhall, Oakley and Kinglassie, bringing the coal from the pits to the marshalling yard at Townhill. Between these two links there was another link which was responsible for seven daily conditional trains (five from Dunfermline and two from Kelty), which were mainly concerned with the movement of coal, to supplement the regular booked trains.

The duties of the Thornton J38's were broadly similar to those of the class shedded at Dunfermline. Main line goods trains were worked to Portobello, Perth, Dundee and Cadder, and local coal trains from the collieries such as Lochgelly, Glencraig and Dundonald to the yards at Thornton and Kirkland, as well as the docks at Methil, from which a considerable quantity of coal was exported or shipped to other parts of Great Britain. These two classes of traffic were manned by the "Long Road Goods" link and the "Short Road Goods" link respectively, between which were two spare links, with the "Conditional" link sandwiched between. There were thirteen conditional trains starting from Thornton, and these were primarily concerned with transport of coal, covering seasonal variations and special requirements not met by the normal booked services. A typical Thornton J38 local duty was what was unofficially known as the "Glencraig Pilot" – a treble-shifted job, starting with the 6-10 a.m. empties from Thornton. The engine then shunted the sidings at Glencraig, Bowhill, Minto and Dundonald collieries and towards the end of each shift brought a load of coal into Thornton Yard. The Dundonald branch was on a gradient of 1 in 40, a J38 being allowed to bring down thirty wagons of coal; to control such a train on the descent sometimes entailed pinning down the brakes of every wagon. Both at Dunfermline and Thornton, the J38's were used on busy summer Saturdays on passenger trains, usually to Edinburgh, but also to Glasgow (fig. 8).

The two engines allocated to Stirling were intended for turns to Thornton and Glasgow, but their stay was short-lived as the foreman at the time did not want J38's and it is understood that he would not use them, resulting in their early transfer to other sheds. On the other hand, the pair at Eastfield were assigned to regular drivers working the 12-15 a.m. Cadder to Stirling via the Forth Bridge, working alternate days and rostered to lodge at Stirling. This train loaded up with empty coal wagons, and the return working (7-15 p.m. ex-Stirling), although a class B goods train, conveyed mainly coal from Manor Powis (depart 8-45 p.m.) for the Glasgow area.

Dundee made use of their J38's on the 10-25 p.m. to Sighthill (lodging turn worked alternate days by Eastfield) and the 6-30 p.m. to Bathgate via Townhill (worked alternate days by Bathgate), as well as turns to Edinburgh and Aberdeen.

No. 1407 was shedded at Haymarket during the War, its usual job being the 3-5 a.m. Craigentinny to Whifflet. This was one of the iron ore trains which ran from the Southern Area (Highdyke and Tibshelf Town) to the Clydeside steel works served by the L.M.S. These trains were staged in Craigentinny Down Loop and worked forward via Bathgate. To obtain maximum usage, Haymarket also employed No. 1407 on the 4-30 p.m. Niddrie to Polmont, returning on the 8-30 p.m. Grahamston to Carlisle, the engine coming off the train at Niddrie. When the "Austerity" 2-8-0's came new to Haymarket, No. 1407 was returned to its former home at St.Margaret's.

After nationalisation, Polmont acquired a pair of J38's, two typical duties of the period being the 3-45 p.m. Bo'ness to Clydebridge Steelworks (with coal from Kinneil Colliery) returning with empties to Polmont at 8-8 p.m. and the 3-30 a.m. empties Grangemouth to Oakley via Alloa, thence 7-45 a.m. to Clydesmill Electricity Works, conveying coal from Comrie Pit. The Bo'ness train ran via the Garngaber branch, joining the former L.M.S. line at Gartsherrie Junction, whilst the Oakley train proceeded via Alloa, Throsk and Greenhill Junction (an ex-L.M.S. line over which the L.N.E.R. had always exercised running powers), continuing thence on the former L.M.S. line westwards.

The early days of the J38's were not happy. The pull-out regulator, N.E.R. pattern steam reverse, and inadequate tender brakes took some time to master, and for some time the mortality rate among wagon couplings and draw-bars was high. Eventually, however, these difficulties were overcome and the J38's became highly regarded as very strong engines. Their coal consumption was always relatively high, but in view of their free steaming and tremendous haulage capacity, this was considered tolerable. In 1932, for example, the coal consumption of this class was far and away the highest of all L.N.E.R. 0-6-0 engines. The average for class J38 was 85.83 lb. per mile, the average for all 0-6-0 classes being 57.91 lb. per mile and for the three main ex-N.B.R. 0-6-0 classes (J35, J36 and J37) the average figure was 64.29 lb. per mile. These figures are purely coal consumption returns and take no account of quality of coal used, trains hauled, or gradients encountered. The J38's were invariably hardworking engines, very often double-shifted, and allowed little time on shed before being sent out on another duty. At St.Margaret's for instance, crews on the incoming goods trains from Fife and the north would be relieved, the engine reconditioned, and immediately sent out on local coal train working, and thus a typical St.Margaret's driver's record of engines used includes all except two of the class (both Thornton engines). Main line loads quoted under class K3 on p. 137 show the rated haulage capacity of the J38's in relation to classes J37, J39, K2 and K3 for the N.B. Section. Loads were of course given for many branch lines, and the J38 class also figured in special tables of "Through loads to ports" which gave loads from the colliery districts to the docks on the former N.B. system.

The J38's, having a maximum axle load of 20 tons 6 cwt. as against 19 tons 13 cwt. for the J39's, became R.A.8 whereas the J39's were only R.A.6. When the Route Availability tables were drawn up for publication in 1947, it was realised that a great many of the lines in Scotland were not up to R.A.8 standard, and as the native J37 class was also in this category a special dispensation had to be given to allow the J37 and J38 classes to run on eighty-eight sections of R.A.6 track, and twenty-two of R.A.7! In this connection it may be remarked that the Running Department was not always over-scrupulous in its observance of the "R.A." rules, and J38's were even known to work on the Lochty branch, which was R.A.4!

Engine Diagrams

Section L.N.E., 1926. Superheater element diameter shown as $1\frac{3}{3}$in. and heating surface as 257.5 sq.ft. Corrected 12/1927 to $1\frac{7}{3}$in. and 289.6 sq.ft. respectively. Class Part 1 added, for 4,200-gallon tender, 12/1931. Diagram deleted 12/1933.

Section L.N.E., 1931. Part 2. New engine diagram for engines with 3,500-gallon tenders. Empty weight of tender altered from 22T 12c to 23T 1c, 12/1936. Alternative boiler wrapper plate thickness of $\frac{9}{16}$in. added, 12/1937. Diagram deleted 12/1938.

Section L.N.E., 1938. New engine diagram, no class parts. Superheater element diameter shown as 1.244in. Diagram deleted 12/1941.

Section L.N.E., 1941. New composite engine diagram showing Part 1 engines with original Diagram 97A boiler and Part 2 with Diagram 97 boiler.

Classification: Route availability 8; B.R. power class 6F.

Summary of J38 Class

B.R. No.	1946 No.	Orig. No.	Built Darlington	3500-gal. Tender Attached	Alt. to Screw Reverse	Diag. 97 Boiler Carried	Withdrawn
65900 10/49	5900 9/46	1400	1/1926	12/31	7/47	9/61-wdl.	11/63
65901 3/50	5901 9/46	1401	1/1926	12/31	3/45	4/52-wdl.	4/67
65902 12/49	5902 5/46	1403	1/1926	-/31 (a)	2/45	11/57-wdl.	12/63
65903 2/50	5903 6/46	1404	1/1926	-/31	11/46	11/46-5/52, 1/56-wdl.	11/66
65904 2/49	5904 8/46	1405	1/1926	1/32	6/46	6/59-wdl.	7/64
65905 6/48	5905 10/46	1406	1/1926	-/31	6/48	12/32-12/39, 12/50-wdl.	5/66
65906 4/50	5906 11/46	1407	2/1926	1/32	7/47	6/41-11/52, 8/57-wdl.	8/65
65907 12/48	5907 9/46	1408	3/1926	-/31	3/45	12/48-8/58, 4/63-wdl.	8/66
65908 1/50	5908 10/46	1409	2/1926	6/32	2/45	2/45-1/50, 8/55-wdl.	9/64
65909 11/49	5909 7/46	1410	2/1926	-/31	4/45	7/35-4/41, 11/55-wdl.	11/66
65910 8/48	5910 9/46	1411	3/1926	-/31	11/45	5/50-wdl.	7/66
65911 1/49	5911 11/46	1413	3/1926	-/33	4/45	5/35-12/40, 6/52-wdl.	3/67
65912 12/49	5912 9/46	1414	3/1926	2/32	9/47	8/52-wdl.	11/66
65913 7/48	5913 10/46	1415	3/1926	-/31	11/45	10/35-5/41, 3/52-wdl.	8/64
65914 8/48	5914 9/46	1416	3/1926	-/31	10/46	10/46-5/53, 3/62-wdl.	11/66
65915 9/48	5915 9/46	1417	3/1926	1/32	6/46	8/44-wdl.	11/66
65916 5/49	5916 7/46	1419	3/1926	10/32 (a)	11/45	11/60-wdl.	10/65
65917 5/48	5917 9/46	1420	3/1926	-/32	4/46	4/40-5/44, 1/53-1/58, 4/63-wdl.	11/66
65918 1/49	5918 9/46	1421	3/1926	2/32	8/45	3/41-10/46, 11/63-wdl.	11/66
65919 4/50	5919 9/46	1422	3/1926	12/31 (b)	12/45	2/55-wdl.	8/64
65920 4/50	5920 9/46	1423	3/1926	12/31	5/47	4/50-wdl.	11/66
65921 5/49	5921 9/46	1424	3/1926	6/32	5/45	10/50-11/56, 5/60-wdl.	11/66
65922 8/50	5922 9/46	1426	3/1926	12/33	9/45	8/50-wdl.	10/66
65923 8/48	5923 11/46	1427	3/1926	6/33	7/47	8/56-wdl.	12/62
65924 1/50	5924 11/46	1428	4/1926	12/33	11/46	4/58-wdl.	6/64
65925 8/49	5925 9/46	1434	4/1926	8/33	6/46	11/57-wdl.	11/66
65926 12/49	5926 9/46	1437	4/1926	2/32	4/47	5/41-10/44, 6/59-wdl.	2/65
65927 7/50	5927 9/46	1440	4/1926	6/33	3/48	6/47-wdl.	12/64 (c)
65928 3/50	5928 9/46	1441	4/1926	-/32	5/45	3/53-6/57	12/62
65929 7/48	5929 4/46	1442	4/1926	2/32	12/46	1/53-wdl.	4/67
65930 5/48	5930 9/46	1443	5/1926	6/33	11/45	8/53-wdl.	9/66
65931 6/49	5931 9/46	1444	4/1926	5/32	10/45	1/57-wdl.	9/66
65932 2/49	5932 3/46	1445	5/1926	4/32	9/46	4/59-wdl.	3/66
65933 4/48	5933 4/46	1446	5/1926	8/33	2/46	2/51-wdl.	4/65
65934 6/50	5934 4/46	1447	5/1926	9/33	4/46	6/50-wdl.	12/66

(a) 4,125-gallon N.E.-type tenders ran with Nos. 65902 (8/55 – 10/55) and 65916 (9/53 – 10/53).

(b) A 4,200-gallon G.S. tender was re-attached to No. 65919 from 9/61 to withdrawal.

(c) Although withdrawn on 30/12/64, No. 65927 was included in the B.R. 1965 Statistical Year.

CLASS J39

GRESLEY 5ft. 2in. ENGINES

ENGINES BUILT AFTER GROUPING (1926-41): 1233/55/9/63/5-70/2-5/7/81/2/6/7/9/90/5/6/8, 1412/8/25/9/36/48-60/3-98, 1504/5/6/8/9/32-48/51/8/60/3/77/80/4-7, 1803/4/8/13/24/8/35/54/6/7/62/3/9/70/5/80/94/6/8, 1903/22/6/7/8/30/3/40/2/3/52/65/71/4/7/80/4/96/7, 2691-2742/70-88, 2941-53/62-99, 3000/81-98. TOTAL 289.

The first new Group Standard class was the J38, but after the initial order was completed in the early part of 1926 no more were built. Instead future construction of 0-6-0 goods engines was concentrated on a version with larger wheels which appeared later in 1926 and which was multiplied in such quantities that within fifteen years the total stood at 289, making it the most numerous Gresley class. (By coincidence, the numerically largest L.N.E.R. pre-Grouping

class, the J15, also reached 289 at its peak though it took thirty years to achieve this figure).

The initial outline diagram for the J39 was produced at Darlington in September 1925 and the first engine, No. 1448, appeared exactly one year later in September 1926. The design closely followed that for class J38 and displayed very little Doncaster influence. Apart from a batch of twenty-eight engines supplied by Beyer, Peacock & Co. in 1936-37, all the J39's were built at Darlington. The construction of the class is summarised in the accompanying table.

From December 1930 class J39 was divided into Parts according to the type of tender which was attached. Parts 1 and 2 comprised the engines with Group Standard 3,500 and 4,200-gallon capacity tenders respectively. Part 3 was introduced in 1934 and covered the remaining engines with miscellaneous tenders of N.E.R. (mostly) and

Engine Nos.	Maker	Date Ordered	No. Built	Date
1448-52/4-9/81/4/92-8, 1233/55/9/63/5-70/2-5/ 7/81/2/6/7/9/90/5/6/8	Darlington	November 1925	44	1926-27
2691-2742	,,	August 1927	52	1928-29
2770-85, 1418/25/9/66/70/87/9/91, 2786/7/8	,,	December 1928	27	1929-30
2962-80, 1453/69/71/80/2/3	,,	December 1929	25	1931-33
1412/63/7/8/72/5-9/88/90	,,	December 1933	12	1934
2941-53/81-94, 1436/60/4/5/73/4/85/6, 1504/5/ 6/84	,,	December 1934	39	1935
2995-3000	,,	September 1935	6	1936
1803/13/24/8/54/6/7/69/70	Beyer, Peacock (a)	October 1935	9	1936
1532/3/4/6/9/40/3/4/5/7	,, (b)	October 1935	10	1936
1563/77/80/5/6/7, 1875/80/94	,, (c)	October 1935	9	1937
1508/9/35/7/8/41/2/6/8/51/8/60, 1804/8/35/62/ 3/96/8, 1903/22/6/7/8/30/3/40/2/3/52/65/ 71/4/7/80/4/96/7	Darlington	November 1936	38	1937-38
3081-98	,,	January 1940	18	1941

(a) Order No. 1529, Works Nos. 6802-10
(b) Order No. 1531, Works Nos. 6811-20
(c) Order No. 1532, Works Nos. 6821-9

G.C.R. origin. Latterly the number of random exchanges of tender increased and the class Parts were discontinued from December 1952. The only other notable division within the class was the type of power brake employed. The first twelve engines had Westinghouse brake for the engine, tender and train with vacuum brake for alternative train braking and these engines were originally employed in the N.E. Area. Twenty engines (Nos. 2711-30) built in 1928-29 for the G.E. Section were similarly equipped, but otherwise those built up to 1934 had steam brake for the engine and tender and vacuum brake for the train. The engines built from 1935 had vacuum brake only. The Westinghouse engines in the N.E. Area were altered to steam brake in the thirties but those on the G.E. Section (one of which had been exchanged for an N.E. Area engine) retained their Westinghouse equipment to the end.

In Thompson's 1941 standard engine proposals class J39 was shown to replace all other 0-6-0's having an axle load in excess of 18 tons, though it was not anticipated that the need for new building would be great once the standard 4-6-0 (class B1) had become established. There was a proposal in April 1946 to fit the J39's with Diagram 115 boilers, pressed to 225 lb. per sq. in., as fitted to class L1 No. 9000 (see Appendix drawing 1). The smaller diameter boiler would have reduced the weight in working order from 57 tons 17 cwt. to 54 tons 10 cwt. The cylinders would have been lined up to 17 in. to keep the tractive effort down to comparative proportions, i.e. 23,178 lb. Nothing came of the proposal though it was not finally endorsed "no action" until February 1949.

The J39's were primarily goods engines but appearances on passenger trains became increasingly frequent in the thirties, more so in some areas than others. The class remained intact until 1959 but by the end of 1962 the last one had been withdrawn, though No. 64747 survived at Woodford shed until October 1964 performing stationary boiler duties after its withdrawal from traffic.

Standard L.N.E.R. Dimensions

Cylinders (2 inside)	..	..	..	..	$20'' \times 26''$
Motion ..	..	..	..	..	Stephenson with 8″ piston valves
Boiler:					
Max. diam. outside ..	..	..	..	..	5′ 6″
Barrel length ..	..	..	..	..	11′ $4\frac{5}{8}''$ (a)
Firebox length outside	..	..	..	..	9′ 0″ (b)
Pitch ..	..	..	..	..	8′ $9\frac{1}{2}''$
Diagram No. ..	..	..	..	..	97
Heating surface:					
Firebox ..	..	..	..	..	171.50 sq.ft.
Tubes ($177 \times 1\frac{3}{4}''$) ..	..	..	..	..	871.75 sq.ft.
Flues ($24 \times 5\frac{1}{4}''$) ..	..	..	..	..	354.53 sq.ft.
Total evaporative ..	..	..	..	..	1397.78 sq.ft.
Superheater ($24 \times 1\frac{7}{32}''$)	..	..	..	..	271.80 sq.ft.
Total ..	..	..	..	..	1669.58 sq.ft.
Grate area ..	..	..	..	..	26 sq.ft.
Boiler pressure ..	..	..	..	..	180 lb./sq.in.
Coupled wheels ..	..	..	..	..	5′ 2″
Tractive effort (85%) ..	..	..	..	..	25,664 lb.
Wheelbase (engine) ..	..	..	..	..	$8' 0'' + 9' 0'' = 17' 0''$
Weight (full):					
Engine ..	..	..	..	..	57T 17C
Max. axle load	..	..	..	..	19T 13C

Leading particulars applicable to tenders fitted:

	L.N.E.R. Part 1	L.N.E.R. Part 2	ex-N.E.R. Part 3(c)
Wheel diameter	3' 9"	3' 9"	3' 9¼"
Wheelbase	7' 0" + 6' 0" = 13' 0"	7' 3" + 6' 3" = 13' 6"	6' 4" + 6' 4" = 12' 8"
Total wheelbase (engine and tender)	40' 5¼"(d)	41' 3¼"	40' 5⅛"
Length over buffers (engine and tender)	54' 0"	55' 8⅜"	54' 10⅛"

	Part 1	Part 2	ex-A2,C7	ex-B13	ex-D17	ex-D21
Weight (full)	44T 4C	52T 0C	46T 12C	44T 0C	42T 17C	46T 8C
Water capacity (gall.)	3,500	4,200	4,125	3,940	3,650	4,125
Coal capacity	5T 10C	7T 10C	5T 10C	5T 0C	5T 0C	5T 0C

(a) 11' 4¹¹⁄₁₆" from 6/1931 for new boiler construction.
(b) 8' 11¼" from 6/1931 for new boiler construction.
(c) Diagram not issued for Part 3 engines with ex-G.C.R. tenders.
(d) 40' 5¼" from 12/1946.

L.N.E.R. Renumbering

Originally, more than half of the class J39 engines had taken blank numbers between 1200 and 2000 in the N.E.R. numbering series using whichever numbers happened to be available at the time. Usually the numbers chosen for each batch of new engines were in ascending order. Gradually a few long sequences were built up, e.g. Nos. 1463-98, though a number by itself gave no indication of the engine's series and therefore individual characteristics. Despite the seemingly random choice of numbers, it may be observed that there was some system in so far as the 12XX series of engines were all destined for Southern Area sheds, whereas the N.E. Area received the 14XX (other than eight of the first batch built in 1927 which went to the Southern Area) and 15XX series. All the 18XX and 19XX series went to the Southern Area except for a few of the former, which went to the Scottish Area. The remaining engines were all allocated to the Southern and Scottish Areas and took spare numbers outside the N.E.R. series and here it was possible to allocate long sequences at the time of construction, e.g. Nos. 2691-2742. The last eighteen engines took spare numbers 3081-98 in the G.N.R. series.

Under the 1946 scheme the J39's received numbers 4700-4988 in construction order based on the calendar month of entering traffic, except where two batches appeared simultaneously and it was desirable to keep them apart. For instance, Nos. 4853/4 were taken by 1488/90, built in December 1934, although Nos. 4855-9 had been turned out during October-December of that year. However, these latter engines were Part 3 whereas Nos. 4853/4 were Part 1 and more conveniently followed Nos. 4848-52 built during March 1934. Similarly, Nos. 4860-71 were allotted to the 14XX and 15XX Part 1 engines built in October-December 1935 and preceded Part 2 engines 4872-98 turned out during June-October of that year as Nos. 2941-53/81-94. This allowed the 1936-built Part 2 engines (Nos. 2995-3000) to follow on. Nos. 4943/4 (1558/60), built in April 1938, preceded Nos. 1804/8, built in March, as it was preferred to keep the 15XX and 18XX series turned out that year separate from each other.

Development

With a total of 289 engines it is not surprising that some changes were made to the details of the design during the period of fifteen years over which they were constructed. Reference has already been made to changes in the braking arrangements and to the type of tender attached and these are more fully recounted on pages 22 to 28. Other alterations are detailed in the pages that follow but it is convenient to list briefly in chronological order the more important of these.

The first forty-four engines were given steam reversing gear, mechanical lubrication for their axleboxes, sight-feed lubrication for the cylinders, a pair of live steam injectors and hand holes on the firebox casing (fig. 14). Most had vertical slide regulators operated by twin handles, but the Howard and Owen patterns were fitted to several engines.

On the next fifty-two engines, built in 1928-29, there was a change to screw reverse (fig. 20) and this feature was used on all further construction, as was the use of exhaust steam injector in place of one of the live steam type. A pair of mechanical lubricators supplied the axleboxes and the cylinders (fig. 22). This arrangement persisted on engines built up to 1934. Owen regulators were fitted to all fifty-two engines.

The third series of engines (i.e. commencing with No. 2770) had an improved pattern of slide regulator but operated by the N.E.R. type of bull's horn handle, and this arrangement was used on further engines built to the end of 1934. From 1931 onwards a revised mechanism for the drop grate was used (fig. 22). Wash-out plugs replaced the hand holes on the firebox casing (fig. 22), but from April 1933 there was a reversion to hand holes. From October 1934 the steam chests had removable front covers.

On engines built in 1935 and thereafter the lubrication of the axleboxes was by means of a Fountain sight-feed lubricator (fig. 25), whilst the pattern of regulator was changed again, to a new type of slide operated by twin handles.

Details

FRAMES AND RUNNING GEAR

The frames were 29ft. 3in. long, 1¼in. thick and spaced 4ft. 1¼in. apart. They were therefore 6in. shorter than those of class J38 notwithstanding the use of larger diameter wheels. The height above rail level to the underside of the running plate alongside the boiler was 5ft. 0in., as in the J38's. Consequently the J39's had 6in. deep splasher casings which readily distinguished them from the earlier engines, which did not have splashers.

In place of the Spencer double-case type of buffer on the J38 class, Group Standard buffers, 2in. longer at 1ft. 8in., were fitted though Nos. 1296 and 2964 at least had non-standard buffers at one time (fig. 21). The height above rail level to buffer centre was reduced from the original 3ft. 6in. to 3ft. 5½in. on the engines which were built from 1928 onwards. At the same time the thickness of the front bufferbeam was increased from 1in. to 1⅛in., though the resulting extra

overhang at the front end was not shown on all subsequent engine diagrams.

The class was arranged for left-hand drive. The first forty-four engines originally had steam-operated reversing gear (figs. 15 and 18), which was mounted between the frames and was partly visible behind the middle left-hand splasher. A horizontal rod ran from the cab to the valve on the left-hand side of the boiler which when operated allowed steam into the reversing pump. At the same time the vertical rodding which led down from this steam valve opened the oil valve on the cataract cylinder. This allowed oil to flow between the opposite ends of the cylinder according to which way the cataract piston moved. A second horizontal rod ran from the cab to the pump and was used by the driver to set the gear in the desired position. When the new position was obtained, the driver then operated the first rod again to cut off steam to the reversing pump and simultaneously close the oil valve. This locked the gear in position. A third horizontal rod ran from the reversing gear back to the cab indicator plate to inform the driver of the setting.

The gear proved troublesome in service and was removed from the engines in the N.E. Area between April 1935 and May 1937 and conventional screw reversing gear substituted (fig. 16). A start was also made in 1935 removing the steam reversing equipment from the engines in the Southern Area, but the process was not completed until about 1946. Not all the removal dates have been traced; those which are known are set out in the Summary.

The coupled wheel axle journals were 8in. diameter and 9in. in length, as on class J38. The engines which were built up to the end of 1934 had a Wakefield No. 7 mechanical lubricator for the axleboxes. This was mounted on the running plate on the right-hand side (fig. 14). Following satisfactory results on B17's and D49's, the engines built from 1935 onwards had instead a Wakefield Fountain six-feed lubricator. This was mounted inside the cab on the fireman's side, with the feeds taken almost horizontally alongside the boiler on both sides of the engine. A distinctive feature of this system was the U-shaped bend in the feed pipe above the driving wheels, incorporating an air inlet which revealed any blockage in the pipe at the axlebox end by emitting oil. The feed pipes were higher up at first but commencing with, it is believed, No. 2993 they were 10in. lower on the later engines (figs. 25 and 26). From October 1943 the air inlet was dispensed with, the feed pipes sloped down alongside the firebox (fig. 33) and test valves were provided close to the axleboxes between the frames.

As was usual with inside cylinder engines, the coupling rod throws on opposite sides of the engine were at 90 degrees to one another. Also, as the coupling rod throws at 180 degrees to the adjacent connecting rod cranks, the twisting effect on the axleboxes of such powerful engines resulted in heavy maintenance. In June 1938 the Mechanical Engineer at Darlington drew Gresley's attention to the fact that more trouble was experienced with overheating of right-hand axleboxes than for those of the left. Gresley said he had noticed this for some time on inside cylinder six-coupled engines, whose axleboxes on the right-hand side appeared to be subject to greater pressure than those on the left.

Modified axleboxes of one sort or another were tried out from time to time with little or no improvement. The possibility of reducing the loading on the axleboxes by placing the coupling rod throws on the same centres as the adjacent connecting rod cranks was also considered in 1946. In a further attempt to reduce the incidence of hot axleboxes, it was decided in November 1947 to fit twenty engines at Gorton Works with divided axleboxes. No. 64879 was fitted first, in September 1948, followed by Nos. 64736, 64829/35/7, 64951 during 1949. It was decided in May 1950 to fit no more and to remove the divided axleboxes from these six engines at their next shopping. The experiment was concluded in February 1951.

The cylinders, which were integral with the smokebox saddle, were similar to those fitted to the J38's and were based on the pattern which was fitted to the G.C.R. 4-6-2T's (L.N.E.R. class A5). The engines which were built in 1926-27 had a Eureka D four-feed sight-feed lubricator for the cylinders and valves. This was mounted inside the cab on the fireman's side. The feed pipes from the cab sloped down along both sides of the boiler, noticeably lower down on the left side (because of the additional slope of the feed pipes across the firebox backplate from the fireman's side to the driver's side, figs. 14 and 15). The engines built from 1928 onwards had a second Wakefield No. 7 mechanical lubricator, also mounted on the running plate on the right-hand side (fig. 22). On each side of the smokebox saddle there was one feed to the cylinder and a divided feed higher up to each end of the steam chest.

From October 1940 steam anti-carbonisers were provided on the engines which had

mechanical lubricators for the cylinders (fig. 29). At the same time the two feeds to the steam chest were replaced by a single feed, higher up on the smokebox saddle and feeding into the steam pipe instead. Afterwards, new cylinders had no provision for lubricating the valves direct. Meanwhile engines with sight-feed lubricators continued to have their valves lubricated direct, so that when they were fitted with new cylinders it was usual to convert them to mechanical feed at the same time. No. 1495 was the first one to be altered, in October 1945. However, No. 4708 retained its sight-feed lubricator when new cylinders were fitted in June 1947, with the oil then fed into the steam pipe instead of the steam chest by way of a single feed higher up on the smokebox saddle (fig. 30), as in the latest arrangement for mechanical lubrication. Another change recorded about this time was from Eureka to Detroit feed on No. 64728 in April 1949 – probably when new cylinders were fitted though this has not been confirmed.

Commencing with No. 1475, new in October 1934, removable front covers were provided on the steam chests for the cylinders. Afterwards earlier engines were altered similarly when new cylinders were provided (figs. 17 and 27).

As with class J38, the drive for the operation of the mechanical lubricators was taken from a return crank specially fitted for the purpose on the middle right-hand crank pin (fig. 14). The lubrication arrangements for class J39 may be summarised as follows:-

Engines Built	Axleboxes	Cylinders
1926-27	Mechanical	Sight-feed*
1928-34	Mechanical	Mechanical
1935-41	Sight-feed	Mechanical

* Some engines later had mechanical lubricators substituted.

BOILERS

The boiler barrel was made of one ring 11ft. 3½in. long and ⅝in. thick. The smokebox tubeplate was ⅞in. thick and recessed into the barrel so that the distance between the tubeplates was 10ft. 9in. The boiler and firebox were stayed together in the usual manner. Six longitudinal stays tied the top of the barrel to a tee-bar riveted to the smokebox tubeplate, four similar stays tied the top of the barrel to a tee-bar riveted to the firebox backplate and eight palm stays secured the firebox tubeplate to the bottom of the barrel. All the seams and joins were riveted in the traditional manner with no welds, except for three boilers built in 1938 (see page 21).

Compared with the class J38 boilers, the firebox was $2\frac{1}{2}$ in. shallower at the rear end to enable the ashpan to clear the rear axle of the larger diameter coupled wheels.

The boilers constructed from June 1931 onwards had $\frac{9}{16}$ in. plate for the inner and outer fireboxes instead of $\frac{5}{8}$ in. which had been carried forward from N.E.R. practice, as for example in class J27 boilers. Certain dimensions were therefore altered slightly, though it was some time before some of these were noted on the engine diagrams. These differences were as follows:-

	As built	From 6/1931
Length of boiler barrel	11′ 4$\frac{5}{8}$″	11′ 4$\frac{11}{16}$″
Firebox casing:		
Length outside	9′ 0″	8′ 11$\frac{7}{8}$″
Length at bottom	8′ 6″	8′ 5$\frac{7}{8}$″
Width at bottom	4′ 0$\frac{1}{2}$″	4′ 0$\frac{3}{8}$″
Firebox grate:		
Length on slope	7′ 9$\frac{1}{2}$″	7′ 9$\frac{5}{8}$″
Width	3′ 4″	3′ 4$\frac{1}{4}$″

Although Darlington built most of the J39's, it should be noted that a number of these engines were fitted when new with boilers supplied by contractors, a practice noted on other classes built after Grouping at Darlington, e.g. B17, D49, K3 and W1. Twenty boilers were supplied by Armstrong Whitworth & Co. for the first batch of J39's and fitted initially to Nos. 1233/63/5-9/72-5/7/81/6/9, 1492/4-7. R. Stephenson & Co. supplied thirty-five boilers in 1931-33 of which twenty-six went to new J39's Nos. 1412/53/69/71/80/2/3, 2962-80, five went to new D49's and four were used as replacements on J38's and J39's.

With the exception of No. 1270 (see later) Robinson long return bend superheaters were standard. (There is an unconfirmed note that Nos. 1804/8/35/62/3/96 may have had ball-jointed elements when new). The elements were 1$\frac{1}{4}$in. outside diameter, following Doncaster practice but the first engine diagram, prepared at Darlington, erroneously assumed the outside diameter to be 1$\frac{3}{8}$in., following N.E.R. practice with Schmidt-type superheaters. The elements were probably 10 S.W.G. thick on the earlier engines as they would have been ordered before Gresley's instruction in July 1926 to employ 9 S.W.G. elements in future. The thickness reverted once more to 10 S.W.G. from December 1932 (1.244 in. inside diameter) and finally back to 9 S.W.G. from (officially) November 1944 (1.212 in. inside diameter).

No. 1270 when new had a Cruse-Gray superheater, supplied by Bolton's Superheater & Pipe Works. In this design there were twenty-four elements, in eight columns of three. Each element comprised an outer cylindrical tube, 4$\frac{3}{8}$in. outside diameter, which was shrunk during manufacture over an inner elliptical tube. The two tubes, which were 9ft. 9in. long, were welded together at the firebox end. The space between the tubes was therefore divided into two parts, upper and lower, which served for the flow and return of the steam being superheated. Eight pipes left the top superheater header, each being connected in turn to three elements, the superheated steam being finally collected in a common horizontal pipe below the superheater. Evidence suggests that when originally fitted to No. 1270, the bottom row of eight elements was omitted altogether, with their flue tubes blanked off, so that steam then passed through two elements in turn instead of three (fig. 17). This may have been tried out to avoid throttling the steam by having too many passes through a constricted space. Reports showed that the arrangement provided about 100 degrees Fahr. higher superheat than with the conventional type, with a maximum temperature of around 820 degrees, or around 700 to 750 when working hard. Gresley was sufficiently impressed to consider in October 1929 its application to ten new D49's. In January 1930 Bolton's quoted for ten sets, with the full twenty-four elements, but no orders followed and the one fitted to No. 1270 was removed in August 1931.

The first J39, No. 1448, was provided with a Howard combined regulator and steam separator. No other information is available of this fitting other than that it was removed from this engine in June 1929. The remaining engines built in 1926-27, with six exceptions referred to later, had J38-type vertical slide regulators in their domes and operated in the cab by twin pull-out handles. This arrangement had been introduced in 1920 by Gresley for his three-cylinder 2-6-0's (see class K3 p.94) and was a simple combination, though stiff to operate. The initial $\frac{3}{8}$in. lift ($\frac{1}{4}$in. from June 1927) raised the first slide, which uncovered two 3in. wide by $\frac{1}{2}$in. deep apertures (the pilot valve) in the second slide. The final $\frac{5}{8}$in. lift raised both slides together, which uncovered two 6$\frac{1}{2}$in. wide by 1$\frac{1}{4}$in. deep ports (the main valve) in the regulator head.

Six of the engines which appeared during 1927, Nos. 1270/82/90/5/6/8, were provided instead with Owen double-beat regulators, also operated by pull-out handles. The valve had two separate seatings with the base of the top valve sliding inside the cylinder of the bottom valve in the manner of a piston and a steamtight fit was provided by cast-iron packing rings. Little effort was needed to open the bottom (pilot) valve first and after $\frac{1}{8}$in. lift the top (main) valve then opened to give a further $\frac{1}{8}$in. lift. Owen regulators were also fitted to Nos. 2691-2742 which appeared in 1928-29.

Meanwhile, the vertical slide type of regulator was giving trouble. Not only was it stiff to operate but during 1927 Cowlairs found that the operating rod in one of the J38 boilers had become bent, possibly as the result of force being applied to close it. In November 1927 Gresley agreed to try a slide regulator based on N.B.R. practice. The pilot valve had 2$\frac{1}{8}$in. wide apertures instead of 3in., the main valve had 1$\frac{1}{8}$in. deep port openings instead of 1$\frac{1}{4}$in. and the total lift was 2$\frac{1}{8}$in. instead of 1$\frac{1}{8}$in. Six J39's were fitted with this arrangement at their home sheds during 1928, though the actual dates are not recorded: Nos. 1266 (Stratford), 1275 (Lincoln), 1449/50/5 (Newport), 1498 (Gorton). The original pull-out handle was unsuitable on account of the longer lift needed and the Darlington-style bull's horn handle was fitted instead. This could also be manipulated from either side of the cab so that it retained to some extent the flexibility of operation which was associated with the pull-out type. With this bull's horn type, the operating rod inside the boiler was rotated instead of pulled and pushed. The valves which were fitted to Nos. 1266/75 failed within a few days of one another due to weakness in design and the whole lot was speedily replaced by strengthened ones, after which there was no further trouble. In addition to these six J39's, six J38's were similarly fitted by Cowlairs.

Another problem with the original slide type of regulator was that of excessive wear. Following the discovery of a badly worn valve, Gateshead Works fitted an experimental type to No. 1458 in February 1929. The initial $\frac{1}{2}$in. lift opened the pilot valve (two 5in. wide $\frac{1}{4}$in. deep apertures) and the final $\frac{1}{2}$in. lift opened the main valve (two 6$\frac{1}{2}$in. wide by 1$\frac{1}{4}$in. deep ports). The total lift was only 1$\frac{1}{32}$in. so that the original pull-out handles were refitted. After this engine had run 6,000 miles since being fitted it was reported in July 1929 that it was a distinct improvement on the original type and was easier to operate, though it was said to be heavy.

The relative merits of the Darlington bull's horn handle versus the Doncaster twin pull-out type were evaluated in the early part of 1929. The Scottish Area reported a preference, based on experience with the J38's, for the two-handle type as drivers could keep a constant lookout for hand signals during shunting and at the same time comfortably handling the regulator. The N.E. Area preferred the bull's horn type as drivers could keep a lookout from the side window when shunting or setting back against a train whilst at the same time manipulating the handle. The Southern Area reported that whilst handles at each side of the firebox were convenient to reach, the bull's horn handle was generally more popular as it worked less stiffly. The result was two to one in favour of the bull's horn type, which was hardly conclusive. The issue was swayed when the Mechanical Engineer at Darlington pointed out that the improved regulator which had been fitted during 1928 to the six J39's could not be operated by the pull-out handle because of the increased lift which was necessary. The sixty-four engines built between September 1929 and the end of 1934 were accordingly provided with this improved type of valve and operated by the bull's horn handle.

Meanwhile the prototype J39, No.1448, lost its Howard regulator in June 1929 and was fitted instead with a slide regulator which was similar to that fitted at Gateshead to No. 1458 but was of lighter construction. This too was designed to be operated by the existing pull-out handles to avoid the expense of replacing them. The result was satisfactory and in September 1929 it was agreed that all the early J39's which still had the original type of slide regulator should be similarly altered as they passed through shops for repair.

As an experiment, in March 1929 No. 1459 was provided with a Joco combined regulator and drifting valve, retaining the existing pull-out handles. Class K3 No. 17 was similarly fitted at the same time and the operation of this regulator is described on p. 99. The Joco regulator was removed from No. 1459 in February 1934. In March 1930 No. 1457 was provided with a N.B. Locomotive Co. patent balanced single-beat regulator. Class K3 Nos. 39, 52/3 were similarly fitted at the same time, but no technical details are available. The removal date is not recorded for No. 1457.

The J39's built from 1935 onwards had a new type of vertical slide regulator, which had been designed for the last batch of class D49 4-4-0's. The initial $\frac{1}{2}$in. lift opened the pilot valve (four 2$\frac{1}{4}$in. wide by $\frac{1}{4}$in. deep apertures) and the final

¾in. lift opened the main valve (two 8in. wide by 1⅛in. deep ports). The 1¼in. total lift was suitable for the twin pull-out handles, so that these reappeared once more on the new J39's.

On the early boilers the whistle was originally connected to the steam manifold on the top of the firebox just inside the cab, with the stem passing horizontally through the cab front plate. From mid-1929 new boilers had their whistle fitted directly on top of the firebox behind the safety valves and older boilers were afterwards brought into line.

The safety valves on the first forty-four engines had a shallow circular cover around the base, following Darlington practice. These boilers changed around among other engines of the class, when the covers were usually removed or in some cases transferred to more modern boilers. For example No. 64861, with a 1929 boiler in B.R. days, had one of these circular covers (fig. 33), whilst Nos. 64703/95, 64978 were noted with rectangular or square-shaped covers, as fitted at Cowlairs and Inverurie Works.

The fireboxes had drop grate sections. To operate these, on the engines up to No. 2788 new in February 1930, there was a complicated system of bell cranks at first, with the rodding on the right-hand side of the firebox. There was also a semi-circular casing above the running plate which protected the screwed end of the operating rod (fig. 14). In March 1930 Gresley asked for the new operating arrangement, as tried out for example on class D49, to be applied also to the J39's as he wanted to abolish the balance weights and bell cranks. Nos. 2962 onwards had the new arrangement in which the rodding passed down at a steeper angle alongside the firebox and a large coil spring was fitted to balance the weight of the drop grate section (fig. 22). The earlier engines were gradually brought into line and the semi-circular casing was usually removed, though not in every case, Nos. 64772 and 64811 still having them in the early fifties whilst No. 64780 carried one until withdrawal in January 1960 (cf. figs. 30 and 47).

Prior to 1930 there was no standard arrangement on L.N.E.R.-designed engines of wash-out plugs on the firebox sides. The J39's for example, followed Darlington practice and had hand holes above the handrails, which made it easier to get at the top of the copper firebox to remove deposits which formed. On the other hand other classes from Doncaster had ordinary wash-out plugs instead. In November 1930 Gresley issued instructions that new fireboxes should have wash-out plugs in place of hand holes, as a result of which fifty Diagram 97 boilers put to work in 1931-34 were so arranged (cf. figs. 14 and 22). These boilers comprised thirty-five built by R. Stephenson and fifteen at Cowlairs Works, shared between classes D49, J38 and J39. From August 1931 an extra hand hole was provided in new and existing fireboxes, towards the front below the boiler centre line (fig. 16). This was introduced because this part of the firebox became so frequently encrusted that the inner fireboxes deteriorated and needed new plates after only four years or so in service. In April 1933 Gresley reversed his November 1930 instruction and ordered hand holes to be fitted instead of wash-out plugs in all new boilers. As far as Diagram 97 was concerned this was simply a reversion to previous Darlington practice.

The first forty-four engines had two 10mm. live steam injectors under the footplate. Later engines had a 9mm. exhaust steam injector on the right-hand side in place of the live steam one. On the post-1935 engines, which had two large vacuum brake cylinders below the cab, the exhaust steam injector was located in front of the bottom cab footstep (fig. 25). It was decided in December 1942 that exhaust steam injectors were no longer needed on J39's and they were gradually replaced by live steam injectors as they passed through shops (fig. 29) or simply had the exhaust steam supply blanked off. American injectors were fitted to some J39's, e.g. Nos.1273 (March 1946), 2742 (May 1946), 64964 (September 1948).

The first all-welded steel boiler was placed in service on a Delaware & Hudson 2-8-0 in 1934. In this year too Gresley made arrangements with Babcock & Wilcox for them to construct three welded boilers for class J39. Because of production delays, the first boiler was not put into service until early 1938 (No. 1509 to traffic 25th January) so that the Southern Railway narrowly had the distinction of being the first British main line company to put a welded boiler into service (class Q 0-6-0 No. 530 to traffic 10th January) thanks to their new C.M.E., O.V.S. Bulleid, who had been Gresley's assistant. The J39 boiler barrel was made of 23/32in. plate, instead of ⅝in., and was welded along the horizontal join. A flanged tubeplate was butt-welded to the front of the barrel, and a dummy-ring was welded to the front end to give the necessary length for attaching the boiler to the cylinders and smokebox. An ordinary firebox was riveted to the barrel in the conventional manner.

Longitudinal staying was achieved by means of eight 1¼in. diameter round bars, running horizontally from the firebox backplate (into which they were screwed) to the smokebox tubeplate, where the ends were secured by nuts. These welded boilers were originally carried by Nos. 1509/35/7 but rotated amongst other J39's in the normal way. They were finally condemned in 1961-62. One of them was also carried by a J38, No. 65907, from July 1954 to August 1958.

GENERAL

The cab proportions were similar to those of class J38, with a typical N.E.R. appearance which was retained throughout the life of the class. The cab seats were a simple affair at first, on boxes (which incorporated the sandboxes) above the trailing coupled wheels. The position of the seats made it difficult to fill these sandboxes and from 1937 new engines had what were termed piano stool seats. From about 1947 tip-up seats were gradually fitted to the J39's. (Padded seats with backs were considered then rejected as being undesirable with so much tender-first working). One Starbeck engine latterly had comfortable seats, retrieved from a local motor car scrap yard and fitted by an enterprising driver! Similar considerations to the J38's applied regarding the cab footboards and fall plate between engine and tender. The fall plate was transferred to the cab footboards from the tender front plate in the forties.

There were differences in the arrangement of the cab footsteps and support plate. On the first forty-four engines the support plate was 2ft. 0in. wide (fig. 14). On later engines this plate was 1ft. 3in. wide with a different profile, though the widths of the steps were the same (fig. 21). However on the post-1935 engines, which had vacuum brakes, the bottom step on the right-hand side was 3in. shorter to clear the exhaust steam injector and the support plate on this side had a different profile (fig. 25).

The smokebox was 5ft. 9½in. diameter and 4ft. 8¼in. long, six inches more than in class J38. The smokebox door was identical to the J38 pattern. The door rim had a flat surface which fitted flush against the asbestos seal in the front plate door ring (fig. 17). In later Group Standard classes the rim was usually rounded, following Doncaster practice, to provide a better airtight joint. As far as is known, the J39 doors were not brought into line in this respect.

The upper lampiron was originally located at the top of the smokebox on the engines built up to 1930 (figs. 14 and 17). In December 1929 attention was drawn to difficulties encountered on the G.E. Section, with its lower headroom, where the light was liable to be blown out when passing under a bridge. It was agreed in March 1930 to transfer this lampiron to the smokebox door and the engines were altered accordingly (fig. 16). Engines built from 1931 onwards had the lampiron at the new height when built.

The maximum height above rail level was that to the top of the chimney, 13ft. 0in., which was the same as in class J38. The various other maximum heights were as follows: dome cover nut 12ft 10⅜in., safety valves 12ft. 7⅛in., whistle (later style) 12ft. 9¾in., cab roof ventilator 12ft. 11 1/16 in.

The minimum radius curvature the engines could negotiate was 5 chains.

Brakes

The first twelve engines were allocated to the N.E. Area and had Westinghouse brakes with the 8in./8½in. air compressor mounted on the right-hand side of the firebox (fig. 14). An 18in. diameter brake cylinder was located under the cab, with a 10in. diameter by 11in. long brake valve reservoir cylinder inside the cab in front of the driver. The main air reservoir was at the back of the tender. A vacuum ejector was provided for alternative train braking.

There were two brake pipe connections at the front of the engine. The drawings showed the vacuum stand-pipe on the left-hand side of the draw-hook (facing) with the Westinghouse stand pipe on the right-hand side. This is confirmed by the official photograph of No. 1448 when new, but at an early date the Westinghouse pipe was transferred to a union below the bufferbeam in accordance with usual Darlington practice. It is believed that the other engines of this batch had this altered arrangement before they entered traffic (fig. 14).

The next fifty-two engines were allocated to the Southern Area and had steam brake. An 11in. diameter brake cylinder was located under the cab and the usual vacuum ejector was provided for train braking.

The following twenty engines, Nos. 2711-30, were ordered for the G.E. Section and had Westinghouse brakes like the first batch. The brake pipes were similarly arranged but it was found that the position of the Westinghouse connection was awkwardly placed for G.E.R. stock (fig. 39). It was not until January 1933 that Gresley authorised the substitution of a vertical stand-pipe, on the same side of the draw-hook as the vacuum brake stand-pipe (fig. 30). The engines were then quickly altered; but Nos. 2712/5, at least, had their Westinghouse stand-pipes fitted on the wrong side of the draw-hook, i.e. conforming in fact with the original intention as applied to No. 1448 when new.

A further seventy-six engines were constructed between 1929 and 1934 and these all had steam brakes and vacuum ejectors, making a total of 128 J39's built with this arrangement. Nos. 2731-42/86/7/8, 2977-80 in the Scottish Area differed in having larger brake blocks for all coupled wheels (fig. 22) and tender wheels. Those for the coupled wheels were afterwards replaced by the standard pattern, probably in the thirties.

In 1931-33 ten of the Westinghouse-braked engines operating in the N.E. Area were converted to steam brake (still with vacuum ejector) in accordance with the Unification of Brakes programme, begun in 1928. Two other engines in the N.E. Area, Nos. 1457/9, missed out on the modification at this time because they were sent to Gorton Works in February 1934 for general repair instead of to Darlington. In October 1935 one of the Westinghouse-braked J39's on the G.E. Section, No. 2725, was converted to steam brake at Darlington Works by mistake. The error was rectified by transferring this engine to the N.E. Area in exchange for No. 1457. The Running Department at Stratford then offered to exchange other steam-braked J39's for any more Westinghouse-braked engines in the North East. By then there was only one possible candidate, No. 1459, but the transfer was not agreed and this engine was converted to steam brake in May 1936 (fig. 16). The twenty Westinghouse-braked engines remaining on the G.E. Section (Nos. 1457, 2711-24/6-30) were never converted. Conversion dates for the other engines are given in the Summary.

The vacuum ejector exhaust pipe ran along the left-hand side of the boiler. There was a drain pipe fitted just in front of the cab to deal with water condensate and, additionally, inside the smokebox a small hole was provided in the U-bend of the pipe before it joined the chimney cone (fig. 17). It was found that water dripping from this hole caused corrosion of the main steam pipe from the header and from August 1930 a drain pipe was connected to this hole too. This pipe ran downwards and left the smokebox at the side just above the saddle, then passed through the running plate to discharge on to the track. The existing engines were gradually fitted

with this arrangement and new engines built from 1931 had it when new.

On 31st January 1933 a mishap at Loughborough occurred when a passenger train, hauled by class B2 No. 5423, collided with a goods train which was being shunted out of its way into a siding, propelled by No. 2781. The following day a report was prepared relative to the brake pressure of the J39, though the ensuing official accident report made no reference at all to this engine. Tests were made at Doncaster Works on 24th March 1933 with another J39, No. 2703, to measure the time interval from the application of the driver's brake valve to full application of the brake blocks against the wheels. This was found to vary from instantaneous to six seconds (engine) or eight seconds (tender), depending upon the lapse of time since the previous brake application, as it was affected by condensation in the brake cylinders. A comparison was also made between the application of the driver's steam brake valve and the vacuum ejector, the response to the latter being generally half a second slower. Comparative tests were also made with the inside diameter of the steam pipe from the brake valve to the brake cylinder $\frac{1}{2}$in. (as standard), then $\frac{7}{8}$in. and finally $\frac{1}{4}$in., though these produced no significant differences. (Gorton Works then made similar tests with class B2 No. 5427, which showed a similar relationship between the delay in full application and the lapse of time since a previous brake application).

Meanwhile Gresley had stated on 14th March 1933 that he did not wish to fit the steam brake to any more engines, but that he intended instead to adopt the vacuum brake as standard on passenger engines and on goods engines which might be called upon to work passenger trains, though not on shunting engines. For the time being, the J39's were seen as purely goods engines and the next batch was ordered with steam brake and vacuum ejector.

The 129 engines which were built between 1935 and 1941 had vacuum brakes for engine, tender and train. There were two 27in. diameter brake cylinders side by side below the shallow portion of the frame under the cab. In October 1953 there was a proposal to alter the vacuum-braked J39's to steam brake with vacuum ejector, but this was not implemented.

One of the engines with steam brake, No. 4791 (ex-2738), was noted in August 1947 working a No. 2 express goods, with the vacuum brake stand-pipe absent at the front end (fig. 44). Two of the engines with Westinghouse brake, Nos.

64781/3 (ex-2728/30) were recorded as having had their vacuum ejectors removed in December 1956.

The engines which worked over the East Coast main line in the N.E. Area were equipped with Raven's cab signalling apparatus. This was dispensed with from October 1933. Many J39's were fitted with A.W.S. equipment in B.R. days, though the exact number is not known. Engines were still being fitted as late as 1961 when inroads had already been made into the class. Nos. 64790/5, for example, were equipped in March of that year at Cowlairs and Inverurie Works respectively.

Tenders

The class was divided into three parts according to the type of tender which was attached. Parts 1 and 2 comprised the engines with Group Standard tenders, 3,500 and 4,200 gallon capacities respectively. Part 3 covered the remaining engines with miscellaneous tenders of N.E.R. or, in two cases, G.C.R. origin.

Before describing in detail the allocation of tenders to the class, it will be helpful to summarise the initial distribution pattern when the engines were constructed. The first J39's were turned out with 3,500-gallon tenders. These were specially designed for the class and were a smaller version of the previous Group standard 4,200-gallon type. Up to the end of 1934, 3,500-gallon tenders were attached to all the J39's built for use in the Southern and North Eastern Areas, except for four engines constructed in 1932 for the N.E. Area which received second-hand 4,200-gallon tenders (though these were changed later) and five engines, also for the N.E. Area, turned out in 1934 with second-hand ex-N.E.R. tenders. The Scottish Area authorities preferred larger tenders and nineteen J39's (Nos. 2731-42 built in 1929, 2786/7/8 in 1930 and 2977-80 in 1932) sent there were specially attached to the 4,200-gallon type.

From 1935 onwards the Southern Area also chose 4,200-gallon tenders for their new construction of J39's, but those for the N.E. Area continued to be given the small pattern. The Scottish Area received three more J39's in 1937 and these were exceptional in being attached to the small variety. The six engines (Nos. 1804/8/35/62/3/96) allocated there during 1938 had the customary 4,200-gallon type.

Finally, during wartime, the last eighteen J39's were turned out coupled to second-hand ex-N.E.R. tenders. Four were sent to Scotland and the remainder to the Southern Area.

There were instances of changes of tender type in later years and these are recorded below. Individual dates are given in the Summary.

PART 1. – This tender was of 3,500-gallons capacity and was a smaller version of the 4,200-gallon type. The main and well tanks were 2ft. 2in. and 6ft. 2in. shorter respectively. The coal space was also smaller and held 5½ tons of coal instead of 7½ tons. The coping plate was considerably shorter towards the rear end of the tender, affording an easy means of identification. The tenders which were attached to the engines built in 1926-27 had flared (or stepped-out) coping plates (fig. 14) but, commencing with No. 2691, later tenders had separate coping plates overlapping the side sheets (straight-sided) (fig. 21). The tenders which were built by Beyer, Peacock & Co. had all-welded tanks (coping plate integral with the sides) which presented a smoother appearance (fig. 27).

The vertical handrails on the tender sides were 2ft. 10½in. long prior to December 1932 (fig. 21). Later tenders had 3ft. 9½in. handrails (fig. 27) and the earlier engines were quickly brought into line.

The front of the 3,500-gallon tender was redesigned in 1937 so that future construction was intended to have high front plates, 1ft. 8in. further forward than before and incorporating coal gates which provided access into the bunker space for the fireman. This modification came too late to affect the J39's which appeared in 1938 and the only high-front tender which appeared on this class (No. 64971 from May 1958) came from class V4 No. 61701 after its withdrawal.

Nos. 2726-30 had Goodall articulated draw-bar between engine and tender though it was removed from No. 2730 in March 1941. Fifteen D49's had been similarly fitted until 1941-45 (see Part 4, p.99), after which the spare serviceable parts were sent to Gorton Works as stock for maintaining Nos. 2726-9.

The brake details were the same as in the corresponding 4,200-gallon tenders, except that on those with steam brakes the thirty-two tenders which appeared with the J39's built in 1926-27 had 9in. diameter brake cylinders. Later steam-braked tenders had 8½in. diameter cylinders with altered leverage that increased the brake power. The 4,200-gallon tenders (which were heavier) did not need this modification.

Standard 3,500-gallon tenders were attached at one time or another to the following Gresley classes:- J38, J39, K4 and V4.

Fig. 17   Class J39 No. 1270.

Smokebox layout with Cruse-Gray superheater, vacuum ejector
exhaust pipe with U-bend to trap condensed water, front plate
with asbestos door sealing ring, door rim with flat edge, handrail
circling front plate with lampiron at top, footsteps on each side of
door opening, steam chest fronts protruding through vertical fall
plate below smokebox.

Fig. 18   Class J39 No. 1448.

Steam reversing gear, sloping sight-feed lubricator pipes to
cylinders, two hand holes on firebox casing, circular cover around
base of safety valves.

Fig. 19   Class J39 Nos. 2728 and 2712 at Southend shed, August 1929.

Adjacent Westinghouse and vacuum brake stand-pipes at rear of No. 2712's tender. No. 2712 with original style of number on tender with small
"L N E R" lettering. No. 2728 with later style of number on cab and large "L N E R" lettering on tender.

Fig. 20   Class J39/2 No. 2731 at Eastfield shed, August 1932.

Screw reversing gear, 4,200-gallon tender with separate coping plate and short handrails.

Fig. 21   Class J39/1 No. 2964 at Parkeston shed, c. 1933.

Narrow support plate for cab footsteps, parallel shank buffers, no cover around base of safety valves, drains from vacuum ejector exhaust pipe both in front of cab and low down on smokebox side, 3,500-gallon tender with separate coping plate and short handrails.

Fig. 22   Class J39/2 No. 2980 at Eastfield shed, May 1937.

Simplified drop grate arrangement, four wash-out plugs in place of upper hand holes on firebox, twin mechanical lubricators for cylinders (front) and axleboxes (rear), larger brake blocks, 4,200-gallon tender with stepped-out coping plate (from class J38).

Fig. 23   Class J39/3 No. 1471 at West Hartlepool shed, c. 1938.

3,940-gallon ex-N.E. tender (from class B13).

Fig. 24   Class J39/3 No. 1471 at Darlington shed, June 1939.

4,125-gallon ex-N.E. tender (from class C7).

Fig. 25   Class J39/2 No. 2989 at Stratford shed, c. 1936.

Vacuum-braked engine, mechanical lubricator for cylinders, Fountain lubricator for axleboxes with pipes on boiler side with U-bends, exhaust steam injector in front of bottom cab footstep which has straight rear edge, 4,200-gallon tender with vacuum reservoir behind coping plate and long handrails.

Fig. 26   Class J39/2 No. 1803.
Fountain lubricator for axleboxes with pipes low down on boiler side and with U-bends, 4,200-gallon tender of welded construction.

Fig. 27   Class J39/1 No. 1532 at Neville Hill shed, May 1939.
Removable front covers on steam chests (cf. fig. 17), 3,500-gallon tender with coping plate integral with side sheet, longer handrails
(cf. fig. 21) and no vacuum reservoir on left-hand side.

Fig. 28   Class J39/3 No. 3084 at Darlington Works, March 1941.
3,650-gallon ex-N.E. tender (from class D17).

Fig. 29   Class J39/2 No. 1896 at Newport shed, c. January 1945.

Exhaust steam injector replaced by live steam injector below cab footstep, anti-carboniser fitting at rear of smokebox saddle
for mechanical lubricator oil feeds to cylinders, wartime lettering "N E".

Fig. 30   Class J39/1 No. 4708 at Stratford shed, June 1947.

Adjacent Westinghouse and vacuum brake stand-pipes, altered drop grate arrangement with original semi-circular cover
removed, sight-feed lubrication retained with new cylinders fitted and with single feed high up on smokebox saddle into steam
pipe for valves, "L N E R" lettering restored.

Fig. 31   Class J39/3 No. 4978 at Darlington shed, August 1947.

4,125-gallon ex-N.E. tender (from class D21).

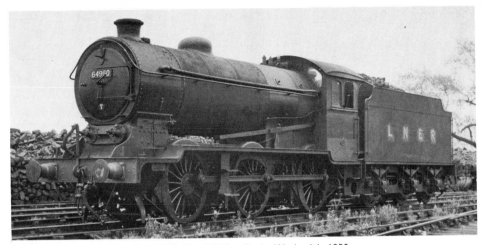

Fig. 32   Class J39/2 No. 64960 at Derby Works, July 1950.

After overhaul but before being repainted with B.R. number on cab side and emblem on tender, 4,200-gallon tender with high front and coping plate extended forward (cf. fig. 20).

Fig. 33   Class J39/1 No. 64861 at Eastfield shed, c. May 1948.

Circular cover around base of safety valves, Fountain lubricator for axleboxes with pipes from cab sloping down steeply in front of drop grate rodding and no U-bends, 3,500-gallon tender with vacuum reservoir behind coping plate, lettered "BRITISH RAILWAYS".

Fig. 34   Class J39 No. 64910 at York shed, August 1959.

4,200-gallon tender with coal division plate further forward and made higher.

Fig. 35   Class J39 No. 1255 on a down coal train at Sheffield Victoria station, May 1929.

Fig. 36   Class J39 No. 1272 at Nottingham Victoria station, c. 1927.

Fig. 37   Class J39/2 No. 1974 with an engineer's brake van near Peascliffe, July 1946.

Fig. 38   Class J39/2 No. 3000 shunting fruit vans at Spalding, 1937.

PART 2. – The 4,200-gallon tender was the first Group Standard design and was introduced in 1924 for class K3. It is appropriately described in more detail under that class. Between 1929 and 1938 ninety-two J39's appeared with this type of tender, of which there were several distinct varieties.

The earliest variety had stepped out coping plates. Eight were provided for the Part 2 engines which appeared in 1932, (Nos. 2977-80 and 1453/69/71/80, fig. 22). These were second-hand, having been originally attached to class J38 Nos. 1417/22/3/09/42/1/19/28, in that order. In 1937-38 four new V2's, Nos. 4777, 4804/5/14, received the stepped-out tenders from Nos. 1471/80/69/53 respectively. These J39's in turn acquired second-hand N.E.R. tenders and were transferred to Part 3 (see later). No. 4777 afterwards lost its stepped-out tender, when it was temporarily loaned in April 1938 to class J39 No. 1560, whose allotted 3,500-gallon G.S. tender was not ready. The latter was eventually provided in November 1938 and No. 1560 was transferred to Part 1. The stepped-out tender was afterwards used for class V2 No. 4813.

The remaining Part 2 engines which were built at Darlington between 1929 and 1936 had tenders with straight sides. These were of riveted construction, and the join of the coping plate to the sides was clearly visible (fig. 20). The first thirteen Part 2 engines built in 1938, numbered between 1804 and 1930, had similar tenders which are of interest as having been constructed from material originally ordered for class V2 Nos. 4791-4803, before a change was made in the design of the front plate which resulted in fresh material being ordered for these V2's. The nine Part 2 engines which were built in 1936 by Beyer, Peacock had tenders of all-welded construction with the coping plate integral with the sides (fig. 26).

The thirteen Part 2 engines numbered between 1933 and 1997 had straight sided tenders of riveted construction with a new style of front plate, as introduced with class V2 No. 4791. This plate was 1ft. 8in. further forward than before and $11\frac{1}{16}$in. higher at its centre to provide room for an access door (or gate) leading into the coal space. The coping plate was extended forward at the front end (fig. 32) and the tool boxes were provided lower down on the footplate, recessed into the tank. The coal gate was of slatted construction, with 2in. spaces between the horizontal bars – adequate to hold back large pieces of coal but a source of complaint when wartime conditions brought about a deterioration in the size of the coal. From November 1940 the coal gates were gradually replaced on these high-fronted tenders by solid doors which prevented coal spillage on the footplate and also acted as wind breaks when running tender first.

In the mid-fifties the division plate at the back of the coal space was sometimes raised in height and repositioned 1ft. $10\frac{1}{2}$in. further forward to prevent coal spillage around the water filler hole. Tenders so altered include that attached to No. 64910 (fig. 34).

Standard 4,200-gallon tenders were attached at one time or another to the following Gresley classes:-B17, D49, J38, J39, K3, O2 and V2.

PART 3, N.E.R. TYPE. – Nos. 1475-9 when new in 1934 received second-hand 4,125-gallon tenders from the Raven Pacifics (see Part 2A, p.141). These tenders were the most modern N.E.R. type, with self-trimming bunkers holding $5\frac{1}{2}$ tons of coal, wide tanks and coal rails which curved downwards towards the back (fig. 45). The cab entrance between engine and tender was less on these particular J39's because the tender sides were 2in. nearer to the front of the frame (see later). These tenders were numbered 8901-5 in the 1938 tender numbering scheme. Each tender changed allocation several times subsequently, as follows:-

Tender No.	Removed from	
8901	A2 2402	1475/64855 new-7/53, 64758 7/53-8/53, J38 65916 9/53-10/53, 64758 10/53-wdl.
8902	A2 2401	1476/4856 new-10/49, 64816 11/49-?11/51, 64819 ?11/51-6/60.
8903	A2 2404	1477/4857 new-by 4/49, 64845 by 4/49-4/53, 64778 4/53-wdl.
8904	A2 2403	1478/64858 new-2/50, 64817 3/50-2/51 and 6/51-wdl.
8905	A2 2400	1479/4859 new-12/46, 4851 1/47-2/51, 64846 2/51-8/55, J38 65902 8/55-10/55, 64846 10/55-wdl.

In 1937-38 Nos. 1453/69/71/80 running in the N.E. Area received second-hand N.E.R. tenders, releasing 4,200-gallon tenders for more profitable employment on class V2. Two were spare 4,125-gallon tenders, which had previously been attached to class C7 Nos. 718 and 2166 (see Part 3A, p. 107). These were distinguished from those taken from the A2's by having their coal rails cut short at the back end of the self-trimming bunker (fig. 24). The other two tenders were of 3,940 gallons capacity and came from withdrawn B13's Nos. 726/75. These had ordinary bunkers holding 5 tons of coal, and were distinguished by their coal rails being extended back and round the rear of the tender (fig. 23). In addition, their tanks were 5 in. narrower so that the cab entrance between engine and tender, when attached to class J39, was less restricted because the gap was at an angle. These four tenders were numbered 8906-9 in the 1938 scheme. Their allocations were as follows:-

Tender No.	Removed from	
8906	B13 775	1471 8/37-8/38,
		1453/64842 12/38-2/51,
		64849 2/51-7/52,
		64700 8/52-5/60,
		64701 5/60-6/60.
8907	B13 726	1469/64843 9/37-11/54,
		64704 11/54-4/60.
8908	C7 2166	1471/64844 9/38-wdl.
8909	C7 718	1480/4845 7/37-by
		4/49, 64857 by
		4/49-wdl.

The final batch of J39's, Nos. 3081-98, all received second-hand N.E.R. tenders as part of a wartime scheme to save steel in new construction (figs. 28 and 31). Eight tenders came from D17's, mainly withdrawn, whilst ten came from class D21 which acquired second-hand G.N.R. tenders instead (see Part 3C, p. 99). The D17 tenders dated back to 1893-97 and were originally quoted as having 3,940 gallons capacity, like the B13 tenders mentioned earlier. However, the well tank between the frames, originally 13ft. 6in. long, was shortened to provide room for the vacuum brake cylinders, which had to be located behind the front axle. The capacity of No. 3081's tender was calculated as being 3,617 gallons, after weighing it first empty and then full of water. This was rounded up to 3,650 gallons when entered on the engine diagram. These tenders were already numbered between 8584 and 8598

according to their 1938 allocation, plus 8921/2/4 which were at that time spare. Their allocations were as follows:-

Tender No.	Removed from	
8921	D17 1632	3081/64971 new-5/58.
8597	D17 1907	3082 new-3/46,
		4974 5/46-2/59,
		64983 2/59-wdl.
8922	D17 1638	3083/64973 new-wdl.
8587	D17 1636	3084 new-3/46,
		4984 5/46-wdl.
8598	D17 1908	3085/64975 new-wdl.
8924	D17 1901	3086/64976 new-10/58,
		64983 10/58-2/59,
		64974 2/59-wdl.
8584	D17 1621	3087/64977 new-6/59,
		64959 6/59-wdl.
8593	D17 1902	3089/64979 new-wdl.

The D21 tenders were early examples of the 4,125-gallon type. Compared with the former A2 and C7 types mentioned earlier, the coal bunkers held 5 tons of coal, the tanks were 5in. narrower, the coal rails were extended back and round the rear of the tenders and the frame lightening holes were D-shaped instead of oval. Although the official capacity was 4,125 gallons, after No. 3088's tender was weighed empty and then full of water it was calculated that it actually held 4,200 gallons. These tenders were already numbered 8686-95 according to their 1938 allocation on class D21. Their allocations were as follows:-

Tender No.	Removed from	
8689	D21 1240	3088/64978 new-wdl.
8688	D21 1239	3090/64980 new-wdl.
8692	D21 1243	3091/64981 new-wdl.
8695	D21 1245	3092/64982 new-1/50,
		64926 1/50-11/59.
8687	D21 1238	3093/64983 new-9/58,
		64988 9/58-wdl.
8693	D21 1244	3094 new-3/46,
		4972 4/46-wdl.
8690	D21 1241	3095/64985 new-wdl.
8686	D21 1237	3096/64986 new-1/62.
8694	D21 1246	3097/64987 new-wdl.
8691	D21 1242	3098/64988 new-9/58,
		64983 9/58-10/58,
		64976 10/58-wdl.

The restricted cab entrance space on the tenders with self-trimming tenders, whose tank width was the same as the cab width, was a source of complaint, particularly when the engine was standing on a curve. Remedial action was taken in at least one instance. A Starbeck engine, No. 64845, had its tender side sheets shortened by about 2in. at the front by cutting away a vertical piece. The date is not recorded but it is thought to have been in the early fifties. It was said at the time that the engine was sent specially to the Wagon Works at Shildon for the work to be carried out.

If other self-trimming tenders were also altered this may explain the temporary absence between February and May 1951 of No. 64817's ex-A2 tender, during which time the engine was temporarily paired with yet another ex-N.E.R. tender, No. 8679, which was an oddity. It too had a self-trimming bunker holding $5\frac{1}{2}$ tons of coal and the water capacity was also 4,125 gallons. It originally had cut-short coal rails, like Nos. 8908/9, but in 1921 it was temporarily altered to carry fuel oil and had extended coal rails added behind its bunker. These rails curved down in the manner of the later tenders though

they were noticeably longer (see Part 3A, p. 107 and fig. 107). This tender had latterly been attached to class B1 No. 1038 from new in December 1947 to June 1949.

It will have been noticed that the water capacity was exactly the same (4,125 gallons) in both the non-self trimming (ex-D21) and self trimming (ex-A2 and C7) varieties according to the engine diagrams, though doubt was cast on the D21-type following No. 3088's tender weighing referred to above. Then in November 1952 discrepancies were observed between the empty and loaded weights. It was decided to accept the empty weights as correct and adjust the loaded weights accordingly on the engine and tender record cards, on the assumption that they held 4,125 gallons of water (though this itself was suspect) and the appropriate amount of coal. The amended weights (without water scoop gear) were as follows:-

Non-self trimming   45T   4C
Self-trimming   45T 12C

The various N.E.R.-type tenders are summarised as follows:-

Tender No. range	Coal capacity	Water capacity	Previous allocation (class)	Remarks
8584-98, 8921-4	5T	3,650 gall.	D17	Full length coal rails.
8906/7	5T	3,940 gall.	B13	Full length coal rails.
8686-95	5T	4,125 gall.	D21	Full length coal rails.
8908/9	$5\frac{1}{2}$T	4,125 gall.	C7	Short coal rails, self-trimming bunker, wide tank.
8679	$5\frac{1}{2}$T	4,125 gall.	B1	As 8908/9 except curved coal rails at rear, extra long.
8901-5	$5\frac{1}{2}$T	4,125 gall.	A2	As 8679 except shorter curve in coal rails at rear.

PART 3, G.C.R. TYPE.—There was a proposal in June 1940 to transfer thirty-five ex-G.C.R. tenders to twenty-nine D49's and six J39's in order to release Group Standard tenders for new V2's on order. This was slightly modified a month later to twenty-eight and seven respectively after the Running Department had pointed out that one of the nominated D49's had Goodall articulated draw-gear between engine and tender which made a straightforward exchange impossible. In June 1941 it was decided after all to attach new tenders to the V2's and share the Group Standard tenders from the D49's and J39's between twenty-five new O2's

on order and the ten K3's which still had G.N.R. tenders (Nos. 32, 80, 91, 184/6/8/91/5, 200, 4007). The tenders were changed on the twenty-eight D49's as planned and shared between the new O2's and Nos. 80, 91 and 4007. The scheme to transfer seven J39 tenders to class K3 was dropped and when class J39 No. 2731 acquired a G.C.R. 4,000-gallon tender on 13th May 1942 this was by mistake. This was corrected on the 28th of the month when it received back its former tender. Another G.C.R. tender found its way on to class J39 when No. 1496 (later 4718) acquired one in September 1945 from class J11 No. 5993. This remained with No. 4718 until March 1948 when it reverted to Part 1.

No engine diagram was issued to cover this variety of Part 3 and the following details have been prepared by comparison with class D49 (see Part 4 of this series).

Wheel diam.	4′ 4″
Wheelbase	6′ 6″ + 6′ 6″
	= 13′ 0″
Total wheelbase	
(engine and tender)	40′ 4½″
Length over buffers	
(engine and tender)	54′ 7½″
Weight (full)	47T 6C
Water capacity	4,000 gallons
Coal capacity	6T 0C

WATER PICK-UP APPARATUS.—This was not provided on the tenders which were attached to Scottish Area J39's, where the absence of water troughs rendered this fitting pointless. The original 4,200-gallon G.S. tenders attached to the J38's, however, did have this equipment so that after their transfer to other classes in the thirties, including J39, it could be put to use. Its use on goods engines was of questionable utility and in March 1946 it was decided to dispense with the equipment on the J39's, in company with certain other classes (see Part 1, p. 69).

Maintenance

With close on three hundred engines allocated to sheds all over the system, it is not surprising that their repairs were undertaken by all the main L.N.E.R. workshops, at Stratford, Doncaster, Gorton, Darlington, Gateshead, Cowlairs and Inverurie. Additionally, from 1st May 1950 maintenance of all 180 engines then in Eastern Region stock was transferred to the former L.M.S. works at Derby (fig. 32), but only 159 received repairs there before maintenance reverted to Eastern Region workshops from 1st January 1953. There was also one repair at Bow Works, No. 64918 having a nine-day visit there in March 1952 for a casual repair during the time it was working from Cricklewood shed.

Until Gateshead Works was closed at the start of 1933, it had shared fully with Darlington in the repair of North Eastern Area J39 class engines. Darlington continued with such shoppings until August 1943; subsequent maintenance of N.E. Area, later N.E. Region, engines was then undertaken mainly by Cowlairs. As a wartime measure, Gateshead Works was reopened in June 1944 and remained operative until March 1959, but during this period it only carried out casual light repairs to J39's.

All the engines allocated to the Scottish Area (later Region) normally went to Cowlairs for repairs, the only exception in L.N.E.R. days being No. 2786 (of Dundee shed) which had a light repair at Inverurie in February 1945. During October-December 1951 Inverurie gave intermediate repairs to Nos. 64792, 64843, 64933/75, whilst No. 64975 was there again for a casual light repair in August 1955. Heavy repairs there began with No. 64822 in December 1959, whilst in 1960 Nos. 64794, 64852 and 64921 received them. No. 64794 also visited Inverurie, in September 1960, for the fitting of A.W.S. equipment. During 1961 general repairs were made to Nos. 64812/75, 64917 (April-June) and, finally, to No. 64786 in November.

Out of the forty-four engines of the first batch thirty-two went to Southern Area sheds and all of these except for two, Nos. 1255/89, had their first general repairs at Doncaster in 1929-30. No others were repaired there until September 1938, between when and October 1943 forty-eight engines were repaired, most of them receiving a general. These were all Southern Area engines with one exception, No. 1534 from Hull Dairycoates (the first to be done) in September 1938 and thus probably an aberration as no other N.E. Area J39's followed it to Doncaster. Otherwise J39 maintenance was carried out by Gorton and Stratford, almost equally shared.

Life mileages are recorded for a number of engines, ranging from 343,271 for No. 64979 to 900,097 for No. 64706. The first engine of the class, No. 64700, achieved 854,264 miles.

Liveries

The whole class ran in black livery throughout its existence. New engines up to No. 2720 originally had their numbers on the tender. No. 2721, new from Darlington in March 1929, was the first to have cab numbering. The whole class also originally had "L N E R" lettering on their tenders.

Until the economy instruction issued in June 1928 single red lining had been applied, but No. 2691 and subsequent engines to No. 3000 (built August 1936) were unlined. The forty-four earlier engines also had the lining omitted at their next general repair, except for No. 1481 which was repainted with lining. It was ex-Darlington after a general repair in May 1928, but was unlined when next out in February 1930. No. 1295 was the last one of these to have red lining – until it went into Gorton Works in April

1930. For the twenty-eight ordered from Beyer, Peacock, new in September 1936 onwards, Doncaster provided them with a painting drawing which included vermilion lining, and No. 1803 onwards were so treated. This evidently spurred Darlington into responding similarly because the remaining engines they built, from No. 1508 in December 1937 to No. 3098 in August 1941, had red lining when they were new.

During the period that the number was carried on the tender it was surmounted by "L N E R" in $7\frac{1}{2}$ inch shaded transfer lettering. This became 12 inch lettering as standard when the number was moved to the cab side (fig. 19), but for a while Cowlairs (only) continued to use $7\frac{1}{2}$ inch letters on at least some of the J39's of the 2731-42/86/7/8 batch. No set pattern as to the operative period for this deviation has been determined. No. 2731 which had a general repair at Cowlairs in March 1931 still had large letters when seen on 4th August 1932, as had No. 2733 in May 1937, and No. 2735 also had them in June 1935, having had a general repair in November 1934, but on 21st June 1936 No. 2734 had the smaller letters, its previous general repair being in December 1935, No. 2737 had small letters on 16th June 1935, its previous general having been in May 1934. No. 2786 also had small lettering but the photograph showing these is undated.

From July 1942, tenders which needed a fresh coat of paint carried "N E" only but still in large shaded transfer letters and "L N E R" was restored from January 1946 (cf. figs. 29 and 30). From December of that year some of the workshops had exhausted their stocks of shaded transfers and for the last year of the L.N.E.R. a gradual changeover to modified Gill Sans numbers and letters took place, applied in yellow paint and without any shading.

The general renumbering which began in January 1946 had, in a great many cases, to be done at running sheds over a weekend and often recourse had to be made to local labour. The consequent renumbering on J39 class took many unusual (indeed unseemly) forms. On some, e.g. Nos. 4937/65, the new numbers were stencilled on in white paint and were only 6 inches high. Although renumbered on 23rd November 1946 whilst under repair at Gorton Works, No. 4969 received 9 inch shaded transfer numbers, by no means matching the standard 12 inch shaded letters on the tender. These are just some examples which happened to be photographed and doubtless there were other "freaks".

In the early months of 1948, there was also some variation in the size of painted lettering

for "BRITISH RAILWAYS". Whilst this was normally $7\frac{1}{2}$ inches high (fig. 33), Gorton and Stratford turned out some examples on which only 6 inch lettering was used. From October 1949 to April 1957 the emblem of wheel surmounted by the lion was standard, but here again there was variation. Although the larger size was customary, some of those repaired by Derby in 1951 received the smaller version.

The change of number in 1946, and the addition of 60,000 to it beginning in March 1948, was concurrent with changes from "N E" to "L N E R" (in shaded block, and then unshaded Gill Sans), to "BRITISH RAILWAYS" and then to the emblem, all taking place in less than four years. It is thus to be expected that different combinations would be commonplace, especially as Cowlairs frequently did not repaint engines and tenders even following a general repair. The following examples will serve to show their extent on J39 class:-

No. 64944 unlined modified Gill Sans painted numbers, and "L N E R" in shaded transfers.

No. 64930 with similar but smaller numbers and "L N E R" in unlined Gill Sans.

No. 64851 with standard Gill Sans numbers, but "L N E R" in shaded transfers.

No. 64700 with numbers like No. 64930, but only "N E" on the tender.

No. 64978 with still smaller standard style numbers and "L N E R" in Gill Sans.

It could be that some of these combinations resulted from a change of tender, but they were all observations from engines in traffic.

British Railways

The 289 engines of the class were taken over at nationalisation and duly acquired numbers in the 60,000 series.

Allocation and Work

The decision by the Board of Directors of the newly formed L.N.E.R. to divide for most purposes the conduct of the Company's affairs into three Areas, Southern, North Eastern and Scottish, had a lasting effect upon locomotive allocations. Each of the Areas kept its own book stock of engines and new construction was decided on and allocated in accordance with decisions taken at meetings of the Joint Traffic & Locomotive Committee.

The 1926 building programme included the first forty-four engines. These were originally allocated to the Southern Area but this was later amended to twelve for the N.E. Area followed by thirty-two for the Southern Area. These engines appeared in 1926-27. Fifty-two J39's were included in the 1928 building programme. These were turned out in 1928-29 and were allocated to the Southern Area (40) and Scottish Area (12). The 1929 building programme included twenty-seven engines which appeared in 1929-30 and were allocated as follows: Nos. 2770-85 (Southern Area), eight engines numbered in the 1400 series (N.E. Area), 2786/7/8 (Scottish Area).

In the 1930 building programme there were thirty-five J39's allocated to the Southern Area (15), N.E. Area (12) and Scottish Area (8). Nos. 2962-76 for the Southern Area were built well behind schedule in 1931-32, by which time the L.N.E.R. was suffering from the effects of the depression in industry. On 29th June 1932 the orders for the N.E. and Scottish Areas were each halved, and these were completed in 1932-33. The entire 1931 building programme was abandoned for the same reason, though at the time of its announcement in September 1930, it had included no fewer than fifty-six J39's, destined as follows: Southern Area (25), N.E. Area (25), Scottish Area (6). The 1934 building programme was announced to the Mechanical Engineers on 5th October 1933 by which time industry was beginning to recover from the recession. Only twelve J39's were included, all of which were for the N.E. Area and intended to replace a similar number of ex-H. & B.R. J23's. Darlington reported that as a result of earlier cancelled orders, it had "4½ sets of material" on hand, including frames, wheels, axles, springs, boiler plates and fireboxes. Darlington Works was therefore able to complete the first five J39's in March 1934, after which there was a delay of seven months before the remaining seven engines began to appear.

The 1935 building programme provisionally included thirty-nine J39's which were actually built in that year, twenty-seven going to the Southern Area and the rest to the N.E. Area. A further thirty-four engines were later added to this programme, which was then referred to as the combined 1935-36 building programme. The additional engines, of which twenty-eight came from Beyer, Peacock & Co., were turned out in 1936-37 and were allocated as follows: Southern Area (15), N.E. Area (16), Scottish Area (3). The 1937 building programme contained thirty-eight J39's allocated as follows: N.E. Area (12), Scottish Area (6), Southern Area (20). These engines came out in 1937-38. The final batch of J39's were on the 1940 building programme and appeared in 1941, distributed as follows: Southern Area (14), Scottish Area (4).

Once an engine had been delivered to a particular Area, only in exceptional circumstances did it subsequently move to a shed outside that Area. Usually there was a balancing transfer in order not to disturb the book totals of the Areas concerned, even where the transfer was of a temporary nature. This was particularly noticeable in a numerically large standard class (such as J39) distributed over all three operating Areas.

As recorded under Details, No. 1270 had an experimental superheater when it was built. This engine was allocated to the Southern Area but for the first nine months it operated in the N.E. Area fròm Newport shed. The Southern Area received in temporary exchange No. 1448 for the duration of the trials. The next transfer took place in November 1935 and resulted from Darlington Works removing the Westinghouse brake equipment from No. 2725 (of Stratford). To rectify this mistake this engine was exchanged for No. 1457 (of Darlington) which was still Westinghouse fitted.

In June 1938 four K3's were loaned to the Southern Area for the summer traffic, two each from the North Eastern and Scottish Areas. To balance these moves, Nos. 1259 (of March) and 1942 (new) were transferred to Carlisle (though they in fact worked from Edinburgh sheds) and Nos. 1290 (of Retford) and 2783 (of Sheffield) went to York. Afterwards No. 1942 took up its intended residence at Sheffield and the other seven engines returned to their former sheds.

With the closure of Berwick marshalling yard in March 1939, Tweedmouth lost most of its large engines (see also under class K3) and received in part exchange Nos. 2735/6 from St. Margaret's. Their tenders had large brake blocks and no water scoops, conforming to Scottish Area requirements, and the engines afterwards returned to the Scottish Area (Carlisle) in October 1940 in exchange for two Beyer, Peacock engines, Nos. 1835/96.

During the 1939-45 War, Area changes were necessitated by varying demands and engine shortages. In June 1943 a start was made implementing a scheme to transfer

N.B.-designed engines not required for special purposes back to the Scottish Area. As part of this scheme Darlington received five J39's from Scotland in exchange for class J36 and J37 engines. The J39's concerned were Nos. 1804/80, 2738/87/8. The tenders attached to the last three engines had large brake blocks and no water scoops, and No. 2788 was returned to Scotland in November 1943 in exchange for No. 3088. This scheme led to Alnmouth shed receiving its first J39 in September 1943 (No. 1563) where it replaced class J36 No. 9172. In October-November 1943 two class A5 4-6-2T's were loaned to the Southern Area, which in turn sent Nos. 1273 and 2780 to Darlington. The four engines concerned were exchanged back again early in 1945. In April 1944 class J24 No. 1895 was sent from Newport to the Scottish Area for use on the Carmyllie branch and in the following month No. 3092 was transferred from St. Margaret's to Darlington. In June 1944 new class B1 No. 8310, intended for the Southern Area, was retained in the North Eastern Area to carry out coal consumption tests working from Leeds, and to balance the books No. 1539 was permanently sent to the Southern Area (to Gorton) in its place. In the following month Nos. 1450 and 1538 were transferred from Darlington to Lincoln in exchange for two class Q1 0-8-0T engines, of which No. 5044 went to Selby and No. 5087 to Hull (Dairycoates). Then in January 1945 class B1 Nos. 8309/10 from Leeds were sent to Parkeston in the Southern Area to work British Army of Liberation leave traffic and two balancing J39's, Nos. 2703 and 2993 (of Stratford), went to Darlington.

In 1947 eleven Scottish J39's with steam brake, Nos. 4784/5/7/8/9/93, 4820/38-41, were exchanged for a like number of Southern Area (Eastern Section) J39's with vacuum brake, Nos. 4875/7/80/4/8/92/5/9, 4912/63/4, which resulted in sixteen vacuum-braked J39's being concentrated at Carlisle. The position at nationalisation on 1st January 1948 was as follows:-

Eastern Region	180
North Eastern Region	85
Scottish Region	24

Subsequent changes to these totals were brought about by inter-Regional transfers, in particular the changes to the Regional boundaries that took place from time to time. In November 1948 control of the former Cheshire Lines sheds was taken over by the L.M. Region which gained the J39 allocations of Trafford Park (3) and Liverpool Brunswick (1). There were occasional exchanges between these and other sheds on the former C.L.C., whilst in the early part of 1951 Nos. 64727/33 were transferred from Stockport (Heaton Mersey) to Carlisle (Canal), which was at that time also under L.M. Region control. The last three J39's at former C.L.C. sheds were transferred to the Eastern Region in October 1952.

In December 1950 and January 1951 Nos. 64732, 64918/66 were transferred from the Eastern Region to the former Midland shed at Cricklewood, where they were used mainly on goods transfer traffic to and from Feltham via the North & South Western Junction lines. They also occasionally worked special boat trains from St. Pancras to Tilbury, as on 12th January 1950 when No. 64732 appeared. All three left Cricklewood in March 1952 for Ardsley.

In September 1951 there was a large-scale transfer of eight-coupled engines (classes O1, O4 and W.D. 2-8-0) from the North Eastern to the Eastern Region, in exchange for six-coupled engines (classes B1, J39 and K3). As part of these changes nine J39's were distributed between Leeds, Hull, Darlington and Heaton.

In 1956 the West Riding District was transferred to the North Eastern Region, and with it the J39 allocations of Ardsley (22), Bradford (3) and Copley Hill (1), which subsequently led to the appearance of this class at a former L.Y.R. shed, Low Moor. In 1958 the G.C. system in the Manchester area and the main lines south of Heath (near Chesterfield) were taken over by the L.M. Region, which gained the J39 allocations of Gorton (12) and Annesley (4). At the same time Carlisle Canal, with fifteen J39's, returned to L.M. Region control from the Scottish Region. (This former N.B.R. shed had previously been under L.M. Region control from June 1948 to July 1951). There were no further inter-Regional transfers, but within the L.M. Region J39's occasionally moved around between Carlisle, Gorton, Annesley and Woodford.

Not until after nationalisation were J39's used on the M. &. G.N. Section. This first occurred in 1949 when four Norwich-based engines, Nos. 64731/61/84, 64968, were at work between Melton Constable and South Lynn. Then for brief periods in 1954-55 and again in 1957-58 Melton Constable shed housed a few of the class; the longest spell was by No. 64802 from January to October 1957. Their use is believed to have been confined to goods trains.

Following its transfer to the Eastern Region in 1952, the former Midland Railway shed at Peterborough (Spital Bridge) received L.N.E.R. classes in replacement for L.M.S. types returned to the L.M. Region. Amongst the new arrivals were nine J39's (Nos. 64719/23/89, 64883, 64901/2/51/4/65) obtained from various sheds. These were joined by others up to 1957-58 when they began moving away. The last two, Nos. 64789 and 64901, left in January 1960. Their duties from Spital Bridge took them over former L.M.S. lines to Northampton, Nottingham, Leicester (fig. 47), Birmingham and Rugby. A most unusual working occurred on 21st April 1953 when No. 64901 passed Ashby-de-la-Zouch with a coal train from Coalville, reputedly the first ex-L.N.E.R. engine seen there, possibly as a result of failure by an L.M. Region engine working into Peterborough.

The former L.T.S. section of the L.M.S. became part of the Eastern Region at nationalisation and during mid-1957 Plaistow received six J39's, Nos. 64951-4/6/7, which were joined by Nos. 64958/62/5/8 a year later. Their use was mainly on the numerous goods and oil trains to other Regions across London such as to Acton, Feltham and Hither Green via Dalston and Willesden or the Tottenham & Hampstead Joint line. All ten were re-allocated to Tilbury in October 1959 when Plaistow was closed but it is doubtful whether they ever worked from Tilbury shed.

The J39's were powerful and versatile engines and served well the needs of the L.N.E.R. Their weakness was undoubtedly the rather heavy wear in the axleboxes which showed up in the higher than average maintenance costs for the class, this fact eventually leading to the decision by B.R. to withdraw them over a relatively short period of time. As late as June 1958 a decision to place twelve G.N. Section unserviceable J39's into store, instead of giving them a general repair, was delayed for several months when the Traffic Department conceded that they were "useful machines for working the additional holiday passenger services". The last engine in the Eastern Region, No. 64901, was withdrawn from March shed in October 1961, but it was not until December 1962 that the class became extinct. In that month forty-six engines were withdrawn, thirty-eight in the North Eastern Region and eight in Scotland. The accompanying table shows the number of J39's at each shed at selected dates. Details of the duties of the class follow.

Allocation at 31st December	1930	1939	1947	1958
New England	–	–	6	–
Boston	–	2	–	7
Colwick	–	12	23	12
Lincoln	5	3	11	18
Doncaster	5	5	17	13
Immingham	6	2	–	–
Retford	–	–	11	8
Sheffield	4	12	9	8
Barnsley	–	–	–	2
Ardsley	7	19	13	20
Copley Hill	1	–	1	1
Bradford	1	3	–	–
Low Moor	–	–	–	7
Leicester	2	3	–	–
Annesley	5	8	–	4
Gorton	12	15	18	15
Trafford Park	–	6	3	–
Liverpool (Brunswick)	1	1	2	–
Stratford	28	44	30	18
Colchester	–	2	–	–
Parkeston	7	3	4	2
Cambridge	–	–	–	2
March	2	18	–	8
Norwich	–	2	14	4
Ipswich	2	5	17	12
Lowestoft	–	–	–	1
Yarmouth	–	–	1	–
Plaistow	–	–	–	10
Peterborough (Spital Bridge)	–	–	–	2
York	2	5	–	–
Selby	–	–	–	2
Malton	–	–	–	3
Neville Hill	–	3	–	13
Starbeck	–	3	12	12
Hull (Dairycoates)	–	4	2	7
Darlington	–	8	37	–
Middlesbrough	2	7	–	–
Newport	6	20	–	–
Haverton Hill	–	4	–	–
West Hartlepool	3	5	–	–
West Auckland	–	–	–	7
Sunderland	–	–	–	2
Borough Gardens	–	–	–	8
Tyne Dock	–	2	–	–
Consett	–	3	–	–
Gateshead	–	–	–	4
Heaton	–	4	–	13
Blaydon	7	10	31	7
Alnmouth	–	–	3	–
Tweedmouth	–	2	–	7
St. Margaret's	3	3	–	–
Dalry Road	–	–	–	4
Eastfield	5	10	–	–

Parkhead	2	–	–	–
Dundee	1	2	5	5
Aberdeen (Ferryhill)	2	2	3	2
Carlisle (Canal)	2	9	16	12

SOUTHERN AREA

The Southern Area was sub-divided into the Western Section (former G.N.R. and G.C.R. lines) and the Eastern Section (G.E.R. territory). On the Western Section the ex-G.C.R. shed at Immingham was the first to receive J39's after the initial twelve engines had been allocated to the N.E. Area: the remaining five (Nos. 1484/92-5) of this first batch of seventeen were allocated to Immingham during November-December 1926. Thirteen more new J39's arrived there during May-August 1927, displacing G.C.R. class J10 and J11 engines, mostly sent to Gorton. However in October, after only a few months at Immingham, five of the J39's were moved to Stratford where the need was more urgent and a like number of J11's took their place at Immingham. After a period of nine months on loan to the N.E. Area at Newport, No. 1270 went in December 1927 to New Holland but moved to Immingham two months later. Progressive reductions were made in the Immingham stock of J39's until the last one departed in December 1945, though the class was again represented here between December 1946 and April 1947. The longest serving engine was No. 1494 which remained from December 1926 until September 1945 with two intervening short spells at Lincoln. The class was never again allocated to Immingham where, together with the indigenous class B5 4-6-0's, they were regarded as maids of all work, available for the full range of goods and mineral duties covered by the shed. These included heavy coal traffic from the Yorkshire pits around Wath and Doncaster for both export from Immingham and bunkering the large coal-fired fleet of fishing vessels based on Grimsby. Local pick-up goods were a daily feature with trips to New Holland, Lincoln and Retford. In the winter months sugar beet traffic to the refinery at Brigg necessitated intensive working. Though not used on the heaviest coal trains, usually handled by Robinson eight-coupled types, the all-round capability of the J39's was a considerable asset, particularly in the summer when they were called upon to work excursion and relief passenger trains as well. By far the most demanding tasks sometimes undertaken by Immingham J39's were trains conveying fish and butter from Grimsby to Manchester, hitherto the preserve of class B7 4-6-0's. The 5-10 p.m. fish from Grimsby to Manchester ran every weekday, often headed by a J39 which returned next day with the 2-20 p.m. Ashburys-Grimsby goods after the men had lodged. The butter trains conveying imports from Denmark ran on Mondays and Thursdays and operated on a lodging basis with return as required. Towards the end of the 1930's this practice ceased and Immingham men went to Sheffield only.

Gorton took delivery of twelve new J39's in 1927-28, Nos. 1233/55/63, 1496/7/8, 2691-6, together with No. 1298 which had first spent several months at Immingham. No. 1497 was at once sent to Liverpool (Brunswick) for use on a night lodging goods duty to Ardsley, alternating with engines and men from the latter place. Thereafter up to 1950, at least one J39 was stationed at Brunswick but individual engines changed frequently with Gorton. Another Manchester shed supplied from Gorton was Trafford Park where up to seven J39's were based at various times, working over the Cheshire Lines (fig. 42) and to Colwick with the erstwhile G.N. braked goods turn on alternate nights. More J39 engines arrived at Gorton over the years and from 1935 a stud of fifteen or more was usually there, employed on a wide variety of work, sometimes in place of the class B7 4-6-0's, to destinations in the West Riding, Grimsby, Retford and on one particularly interesting diagram to Lincoln. This duty commenced with the 5-25 a.m. stopping passenger train to Sheffield, thence to Doncaster on the 7-48 a.m. and forward from there at 11-32 a.m. all stations to Lincoln, where the men lodged before working home at 3-10 a.m. next morning on a goods to Manchester. On summer Saturdays Gorton used J39's on some expresses to East Coast resorts including the through train from Manchester to Clacton, taken to Lincoln and return. As late as August 1959, after Gorton had passed into London Midland Region control, No. 64875 was seen at Southport (Lord Street) on an excursion.

Early in 1927 the pioneer J39 No. 1448 was on loan from the N.E. Area (in exchange for No. 1270 mentioned above) at work on G.C. Section coal trains from Annesley to Woodford. In July of that year newly built No. 1287 was allocated to Leicester and put to work on the 9-50 p.m. fast goods to Manchester and Liverpool, alternating with Gorton engines and men on a lodging basis. This particular engine was regarded as sluggish and its steam reversing gear was not popular. It was joined by No. 2710 in August 1929 to work the 9-25 p.m. class A goods from Leicester to Banbury, with shunting duties at either Loughborough or Lutterworth on return from Banbury. At peak times the J39's were used on local passenger duties and specials to Lincoln, Cleethorpes and Skegness (via Nottingham and the L.D.E.C. line) on which they were often loaded to twelve bogies. A third engine No. 2975 (again newly built) arrived in April 1932 and three years later No. 1287 left for Annesley. About that time the Manchester goods train ceased to run and was replaced by one at the same departure time going to Ardsley on which J39's were used also on a lodging basis. By August 1943 all the J39's had moved away from Leicester.

It was in the West Riding District that J39's were first put to work from G.N. Section sheds. In the West Riding, and on the G.C. Section, these engines were known as "Standards". Commencing in May 1927, Ardsley received Nos. 1259/89/90/5/6 (though the last two were soon transferred to Stratford) and Copley Hill No. 1286. During 1928 Nos. 2697/8, 2700/1 were also delivered to Ardsley, whilst No. 2699 went to Bradford. Thereafter the class saw service in the West Riding right up to the time it became extinct in 1962. As the District headquarters, Ardsley always had the largest number, varying from seven in 1928 to twenty-five in 1953, using them on a variety of goods duties both vacuum fitted and unfitted. One such was the 9-30 p.m. Ardsley-Bishopsgate braked goods worked by an Ardsley J39 to Doncaster, where a Copley Hill K3 took over for the next stage to Whitemoor. It was customary for additional engines to be loaned to Ardsley temporarily during August to cover greatly increased passenger traffic generated by the annual Bowling Tide holidays. During these periods class J39 engines undertook many passenger turns. For instance, on 17th August 1929 No. 1494 was seen on a Cleethorpes-Bradford, No. 2700 on a Bridlington-Bradford relief, No. 2708 on a Yarmouth-Halifax and No. 2709 on a Cleethorpes-Queensbury train. In earlier years these trains would have been worked by G.N.R. 0-6-0's of classes J3, J4 and J6. At times, J39's from Copley Hill often appeared on stopping passenger trains to Doncaster and return as did those from Bradford on through portions of London expresses as far as Wakefield. One Bradford duty in the 1930's commenced each weekday with the 4-40 p.m. Bradford-Leeds, then 5-50 p.m. slow to Doncaster whence the

8-53 p.m. express (5-45 p.m. ex-King's Cross) was taken through to Halifax, return to Bradford being with the 11-15 p.m. goods SX, or light engine SO. No. 2701 went new to Ardsley in August 1928 and remained at that shed until withdrawn in November 1962, one of the two members of the class with only one allocation during its lifetime (No. 1862 of Carlisle being the other).

Doncaster received Nos. 2702-8 new in 1928 and thenceforth retained a small stud until the end of the War, after which numbers increased to a maximum of twenty-one by the end of 1946. Their duties were on local goods or coal trains, together with main line turns to Colwick, Harby & Stathern (on the G.N. & L.N.W. Joint line), Lincoln and Whitemoor. They also worked stopping passenger trains to Sheffield, Lincoln and March.

In 1928-29 five new J39's were sent to Annesley (Nos. 2709/10/79/80/1) and by 1942 the stock there had risen to eleven. They found use on a variety of duties ranging from express goods to coal trains and summer excursions. The enginemen regarded them as sturdy and reliable. In its early years the class worked beer trains from Burton-on-Trent, running light from the shed via Bulwell Common on to the G.N. lines to Burton and after arrival back at Annesley handing the trains over to N.E. engines for the continuation to York. Mostly the summer excursion traffic from Nottingham was handled by Colwick's ample stud of 2-6-0 and 0-6-0 classes, helped out by class B7 and B8 4-6-0's from Annesley, but it is on record that No. 2709 once took a Sunday evening excursion starting from Arkwright Street to Cleethorpes. Extra stock was added at Victoria Station to accommodate the 900 passengers. The route was via the L.D. & E.C. line to Lincoln and No. 2709 made the return to Nottingham in the early hours of Monday morning. During the War, Annesley J39's were seen regularly at Neasden. Between August 1943 and July 1944 seven different engines were noted there but otherwise the class was rarely seen south of Woodford.

Sheffield first obtained J39's in 1929 when Nos. 2782-5 arrived. Incidentally, No. 2782 remained in the Sheffield district until withdrawn in February 1961, its only move from the parent shed being to Staveley for eight months in 1937-38. More J39's arrived at Sheffield over the years from 1932 until the total allocation reached fourteen in 1942. One of these (No. 2947) spent a short while running in at Doncaster and then had an unbroken spell of twenty-six years at Sheffield from August 1935 until withdrawal in February 1961. Heavy traffic generated by local steel and associated industries kept the J39's busy for many years, but in 1957 a decline in trade meant that six were put into store.

Lincoln received its first J39's in June 1929 and, after some changes, by mid-1930 Nos. 1272/3/5/81, 2703 had settled down there. They were joined by No. 1493 in June 1931 and were used on the G.C. routes to Sheffield and Immingham and on the G.N. & G.E. Joint line to Doncaster and March. Here also their versatility was fully realised in the height of the summer season when week-end reliefs over the Joint line were numerous. During the war years Lincoln's stud was reduced to three but rose again afterwards until a maximum of eighteen was reached in 1958.

Colwick nominally received its first J39's in November 1929 when new engines Nos. 2780/1 were allocated there for only a few days before going to Annesley (as recorded earlier), but in March 1932 No. 2976 went new to Colwick and remained. Up to 1936 others were stationed at Colwick for short periods and late in that year Nos. 1828/54/6/7 arrived as permanent replacements for withdrawn G.N.R. 0-6-0's. Nos. 1898, 1903 joined the other J39's in 1938 and all seven settled down to intensive work on local and medium distance goods turns which took them to Doncaster, York, Grantham, Derby and Leicester (Belgrave Road). At times they appeared on stopping passenger trains and in the summer months on the frequent excursions or week-end reliefs to East Coast resorts at Skegness, Mablethorpe and Cleethorpes. In July 1938 Nos. 1828/54/98 were all seen at Cleethorpes on such duties. The class also took turns on the Colwick-Manchester (Deansgate) braked goods trains. During the War, the Colwick engines were also seen at Neasden. The York turn was operated week-nights on a lodging basis alternating with York J39's and men. Once, when the duty was amended at a holiday period, the crews changed over at Doncaster and the Colwick men were somewhat concerned when they were unable to locate the reversing lever on the York engine they had taken over. This engine was one of the steam reverse variety, completely unknown to Colwick men, resulting in the journey back to Nottingham being run in full gear.

No. 1277 was allocated to Retford in December 1934, joined in August 1935 for about six months by No. 2941. Duties on which No. 1277 appeared included passenger trains at 7-19 a.m. from Retford to Bardney, 10-38 a.m. Bardney-Lincoln and 12-30 p.m. thence to Retford, then 3-2 p.m. Retford-Lincoln, 4-15 p.m. Lincoln-Skegness and 6-20 p.m. return, finally reaching Retford on the 9-3 p.m. ex-Lincoln. This sole member left in August 1939 and it was 1946 before the class again began to return.

Boston acquired three J39's in 1938 and retained two (Nos. 2693/5) until April 1945. These were principally used on the night lodging goods to Doncaster but also stood in for passenger engines in summer months on extra trains between Skegness and Nottingham, Leicester and Derby, until war caused these to cease. Apart from short stays by engines replacing those in shops, no more J39's were at Boston until the winter of 1958-59 when eight from Lincoln and Colwick moved there, possibly for storage. One (No. 64728) remained until withdrawn in February 1960 but the others went back into traffic at Colwick, Lincoln and Doncaster during 1959.

In February 1940 Nos. 1952 and 2982 moved to New England from Ardsley thus initiating regular use of standard 0-6-0's up the Great Northern main line to London. Previously the only known appearance was in 1927 when No. 1272 visited King's Cross for official inspection. Although twenty-four different engines were allocated to New England over a period of sixteen years, the maximum there at any one time was seven. Through the war years J39's were a common sight in the G.N. London area on the lighter goods trains, not only those from New England but others from further afield. On 13th January 1941 No. 2782 of Sheffield was at Hornsey on an up goods; No. 2990 of Ipswich was on a down goods at Ferme Park on 4th January 1945 as was No. 1268 of Colchester on 25th May 1945. More unusual was No. 2965 of Norwich seen on Hornsey shed on 1st May 1945 and at Wood Green on the 4-8 p.m. stopping passenger train from Cambridge on 27th October 1945 – probably the first time a J39 worked a passenger train into King's Cross. During the war years Stratford-based J39's were frequent visitors to Hornsey but it was very unusual to see No. 3092 of Darlington at Wood Green on 11th July 1945. In later years there were other isolated passenger workings by J39 engines; No. 2695 (New England) took the 5-34 p.m. King's Cross-Baldock on 15th August 1946; No. 64820 (Ipswich) the 5-25 p.m. Royston-Welwyn Garden City and 8-46 p.m. Hitchin-Cambridge on 6th July 1949; No. 64969 (New England) the 5-34 p.m. King's Cross-Baldock on 26th September 1949. By June 1950 New England had lost all its J39's and the class was seldom seen south of Peterborough until 1953 when several Ardsley engines appeared on the 10-22 p.m. Leeds-King's Cross unfitted goods and 9-15 p.m. return braked goods, normally a V2 duty. In May Nos. 64749 and 64806 appeared on these trains and No. 64898 on 1st September. Doncaster J39's were also seen on the 2-15 a.m. Doncaster-King's Cross goods and 7-40 p.m. parcels return: No. 64885 on 4th July; No. 64956 on 31st July and No. 64721 on 5th September. From Colwick J39's appeared at times in place of K3's on the fast goods due in London at 12-10 a.m. returning the same day at 9-50 p.m. In 1956 five J39's were once more allocated to New England for some six months and were seen in the London area; No. 64874 was on the 7-12 p.m. Hitchin-Ferme Park goods on 17th April 1957 and next day No. 64873 worked the Henlow-King's Cross R.A.F. leave train.

For one month in 1940 No. 2970 was at Grantham; then in May-June 1941 newly-built engines 3089/90/1/3/4 went there but none remained very long. Up to 1947 frequent changes occurred but there were generally five J39's at Grantham working on local and branch goods trains with occasional passenger turns to Derby. Although in 1941-42 they were seen on the Highdyke-Stainby ironstone line, it would appear that they were unsuitable for that branch and Gresley 2-8-0's took over these duties in 1942.

Some other sheds housed small numbers of J39's at various times, mostly for short periods. In October 1946 eight arrived at Barnsley for use on goods and coal trains in the area. Barnsley enginemen had been familiar with the class from the 1930's when working Gorton-based engines on the Manchester route, and with Ardsley engines working in with South Kirkby-Stairfoot traffic, changing footplates en route. The Ardsley J39's had replaced Ivatt "Long Tom" 0-8-0's on these turns and were sometimes used by Barnsley shed on banking duties to assist coal trains from Wath travelling westwards over Woodhead. The eight Barnsley-based engines remained there for only about eight months and it was almost ten years before others of the class were allocated to the shed. From 1957-60 Nos. 64828 and 64902 were at Barnsley, during which time they were known to have worked summer excursions to Cleethorpes and Scarborough. Nearby Mexborough had little association with J39 engines; after running in at Doncaster in

1935 Nos. 2982/3 moved to the former shed but both had left by January 1937. Until January 1960 the class did not figure on Mexborough's allocation again; then Nos. 64828 and 64902 moved over from Barnsley for only about six weeks prior to withdrawal. The former L.D. & E.C. shed at Tuxford was not usually a place to house engines of L.N.E.R. origin, until September 1953 when no fewer than eleven J39's arrived for work on coal traffic, followed shortly afterwards by two more. Most of them spent sixteen months at this small shed before moving away. Further south on the G.C. Section it was well after nationalisation before J39's were stationed at Woodford. In April 1950 Nos. 64798 and 64838 spent six months there but it was not until 1960 that further examples were allocated there in the period when Woodford came under L.M.R. control.

After nationalisation, many boundary revisions occurred, and certain former L.N.E.R. sheds were transferred to the L.M.R. In the Liverpool area and Cheshire Lines this made little difference to the work of engines concerned as was also the case in later years when parts of the G.C. line were transferred to L.M.R. control, notably Gorton, Annesley and Woodford. There were a few sheds which received J39's under L.M.R. auspices which had never had them before, notably Stockport and Northwich for short periods; Bidston also acquired a couple for a few weeks in 1949-50.

The first J39's allocated to the G.E. Section were Nos. 1265-9/95/6, 1484 which arrived at Stratford in October 1927 after they had initially been sent new to Immingham and Ardsley. At Stratford all were immediately given to the regular crews in the main line goods link which, amongst other duties, included four night lodging turns (with return workings on the following nights) as follows: 11-5 p.m. Spitalfields-Yarmouth (South Town) and return with 8-25 p.m. fish to Goodmayes; 11-35 p.m. Spitalfields-Norwich (Victoria) and 9-0 p.m. return; 11-45 p.m. Thames Wharf-Bury St. Edmunds and return at 4-25 p.m. to Spitalfields; 1-15 a.m. Goodmayes-Lowestoft returning with the 8-15 p.m. fish to Spitalfields. In all cases the Stratford engines worked through daily but it appears that the crew on the Yarmouth turn were relieved at Ipswich and returned by taking over their engine there the following evening. On the Bury lodge turn an Ipswich crew took the return working as far as Ipswich, where they were relieved by the Stratford men who had travelled passenger from Bury by a later service. On these duties the engines were quickly appreciated for their good pulling and braking power but the steam reversing gear fitted to this particular batch gave trouble causing some delays. With these eight engines fully occupied on the duties mentioned and working mostly at night, their initial advent on the Great Eastern attracted little attention from observers.

Towards the end of 1928 a further ten new J39's (Nos. 2711-20) were allocated to Stratford after running-in at York. Nos. 2719/20 soon moved on to Parkeston where they were joined early in 1929 by Nos. 2721-4. A further six (Nos. 2725-30) went to Stratford and one of them was usually outstationed at Southend. All twenty of this batch were equipped with Westinghouse brake and vacuum ejector enabling them to work both air and vacuum braked trains, a very useful adjunct on the G.E. Section at that time. At Stratford there was plenty of work, not only on the normal goods duties, but also at busy times on passenger relief or excursion trains to Cambridge, Ipswich and Southend, though their extensive use on these only developed a few years later. From Parkeston there were heavy trains of bacon to Stratford, where the stock was divided into smaller loads for onward transmission to East Smithfield by 0-6-0T's. There were also relief Scandinavian boat expresses from Parkeston Quay to Liverpool Street, often worked by Stratford J39's off down empty van specials from Spitalfields or Goodmayes.

Later in 1929 a further nine engines (not Westinghouse-braked) were allocated as follows:-Parkeston (No. 2770), Ipswich (Nos. 2771/2), Stratford (Nos. 2773-8). Most of the Stratford engines of the 2711-30 series were put on the turns which might involve emergency passenger duties, hitherto covered by dual-fitted J15's, such as the Romford Pilot and night goods trains to Brentwood, Southend and Clacton. In the event of an engine failure at Romford on a down express, the pilot was substituted, taking the train forward with its own crew. Only two days after a J39 was first put on the pilot duty an Ipswich engine had to come off at Romford. With their J39 the pilot crew arrived at Ipswich late with several overheated bearings. There was then immediate pessimism over the suitability of the J39's for passenger work. However the redoubtable District Locomotive Superintendent at Stratford, L.P. Parker, would not agree and caused trials to be undertaken, culminating with a successful run on the 8-15 a.m. express to Ipswich and 12-23 p.m. return. After that there was no question as to the capabilities of the

class – in fact during later years Stratford drivers used to ask for J39's to work Lowestoft or Yarmouth non-stop reliefs. The travelling public, however, was not so enamoured of them as they induced a very unpleasant surging oscillation in the leading vehicles. The engines were not balanced for high speed running and for some reason those having Group Standard 4,200-gallon tenders seemed worse than those having the smaller 3,500-gallon variety.

The timely arrival of J39's at Stratford coincided with expansion of week-end relief coastal and excursion traffic thus making them in demand, together with K2's, for the extra Southend and Clacton trains, releasing class B12, B17 and D16 engines for longer distance work. Even so this did not prevent increasing numbers of class N7 0-6-2T's having to be used on the Southend service at week-ends to make J39's available for Ipswich and Cambridge trains. Westinghouse stock continued in use and for several years there were few passenger engine diagrams which did not need engines capable of working both Westinghouse and vacuum fitted stock. Therefore the vacuum-only J39's were given little passenger work at the time and it was almost unthinkable to diagram steam reverse members of the class for passenger work. Receipt of these twenty-seven J39's enabled a like number of G.C. 0-6-0's of classes J10 and J11 to be returned to their parent section from G.E. Section country sheds where they in turn were replaced by G.E. 0-6-0's displaced by J39's at the main sheds.

There was a heavy flow of seaborne coal from the Tyne to London (Victoria Dock) whence it was conveyed by rail to the Lea Valley and there were many loads of coke from Beckton gas works to Angel Road, Edmonton. On a foggy morning in January 1931 No. 1265 was working a heavy coal train from the docks to Brimsdown over the goods line under permissive block regulations. The J39 was travelling too fast for the poor visibility conditions prevailing and ran into the rear of a stationary engine (class J69 No. 7364) and brakevan which were standing behind another train, at Northumberland Park. The impact crushed the brakevan, drove No. 7364 into the van of the front train, destroying it and setting fire to a tank of petrol. Five railwaymen lost their lives and the J69 had to be scrapped.

Another accident involving a J39 occurred on Whit Monday 1938 when working the 7-7 p.m. express from Ipswich to Liverpool Street. Efforts to trace details of engine number, load and speeds have failed because it appears that no

Ministry of Transport report was published. Approaching Witham at speed, a big-end strap collapsed due to bolt fracture. The engine and most of the train became derailed and only the station platform prevented the engine from overturning and causing more serious damage. An immediate decision was made to replace forthwith the iron big-end bolts on the class by new steel ones. Inevitably questions were raised about the suitability of the J39's for such a duty and to satisfy the requirements of the Inspecting Officer a detailed report was prepared setting out all duties undertaken by the regular Stratford express engines, and work done by the substitute engines. On such occasions as Bank Holidays and high-summer week-ends a shortfall of thirty express engines to cover all requirements was not unusual. The difference was made up by use of 2-6-0, 0-6-0 and for the Southend line 0-6-2T engines. The analysis for that Whit Monday easily proved that the most judicious allocation of locomotives had on the whole been made. The express classes had been employed all day on fast trains and the diagram for the J39 in question had consisted of slow trains both morning and afternoon, culminating with the express concerned. It was demonstrated that the J39 class was habitually called upon to run at speeds equal to the Ipswich express, e.g. on Southend excursions.

Reference to Part 9A of this series under classes N7 (pp. 115-6) and N2 (pp. 71-2) will provide details concerning the difficulties encountered with these 0-6-2T engines working the arduous 6-0 p.m. passenger train turn from Liverpool Street to Buntingford. Substitution in 1931 of standard L.N.E.R. bogie vehicles for the lighter G.E.R. six-wheel carriages meant that the train then weighed 385 tons. This heavy train was timed to cover the 17 miles from Liverpool Street to Broxbourne in 27 (later 28) minutes, with the three rear coaches being slipped at Waltham Cross (12.8 miles), leaving 300 tons to be taken on to Broxbourne. Various suggestions were put forward to improve the punctuality of this train, including the use of class B12 4-6-0's, but this was rejected because they could not be turned at Buntingford or Hertford and the operating authorities refused to allow scheduled tender-first running on the return working as, except for a few weeks in summer, it would be in the hours of darkness. The Buntingford portion (front coaches) was patronised by several influential personages from the City, including Mr. Montagu Norman, Governor of the Bank of England, all of whom would raise strong objections if the destination or formation was altered to allow revised locomotive workings, as had occurred in the temporary remarshalling with the Bishops Stortford portion in front in January 1932 (see page 71, Part 9A). Finally, it was found that class J39 could, if carefully balanced on the turntable, be turned at Hertford East and from 1st January 1933 the 6-0 p.m. was placed in the hands of Stratford N7 men with J39 engines, the locomotive being detached at St. Margaret's and replaced by a branch engine on the Buntingford portion with the J39 then being reattached to the remaining coaches for the run to Hertford. Henceforth no difficulty was experienced in timekeeping and the diagram remained in force until the outbreak of war in September 1939, though with the winter timetable of 1936-37 a stop at Waltham Cross was substituted for slipping consequent on the withdrawal of the old G.E.R. slip brake vans. The return working to London latterly was with the 9-11 p.m. Hertford East-Liverpool Street, calling only at Broxbourne and Waltham Cross and loaded to one four-coach Quad set. The diagram was confined to the 2711-30 series of J39's because the engine for the 6-0 p.m. train worked in tender first to Platform 8 at Liverpool Street from Tottenham on the empty stock for the 5-39 p.m. to Epping, which was a Westinghouse-braked suburban set.

Over the six-year period to September 1939 twenty-three different J39's were timed on 139 occasions hauling loads exceeding 275 tons between Liverpool Street and Broxbourne, either on the 6-0 p.m. or on Cambridge expresses (mainly the 6-30 p.m. down, also referred to on page 84 under class K2). Their average speed over the 5.3 miles from Brimsdown to Wormley Box was 50.6 m.p.h. with a best average of 64 m.p.h. On the gradient rising at 1 in 731 for two miles from Cheshunt to Wormley an average of 550 drawbar horsepower was calculated with a maximum of 825 d.b.h.p. Such figures amply demonstrate the ability of these standard 0-6-0's to perform exacting passenger train duties when necessary and underline the extent to which Stratford shed realised their full potential. On their express duties on the G.E. Section, particularly the Colchester line, their success was due to the switchback nature of the road; a high *average* speed could be maintained by good uphill running without recourse to excessive downhill speeds.

As fresh batches entered service over the years 1935-38, more engines were allocated to G.E. sheds, until at the end of 1939 seventy-four were at work on the Section, representing 27.3 per cent of the class then in service. Of this number no fewer than forty-four were at Stratford (16.2 per cent of the whole class) – a figure not approached by any other L.N.E.R. shed until March 1943 when Darlington briefly housed fifty. Observations in the summer of 1938 illustrate the use made of Stratford J39's at peak times. On Saturday 13th August, of four consecutive down expresses arriving at Ipswich destined for Norwich and Yarmouth, three were hauled by that class (Nos. 1940, 2776 and 2969) none being over three minutes late. On other Saturdays Nos. 1933/40 were in evidence on Clacton trains whilst No. 1984 saw duty on empty coaches to and from Liverpool Street and the stabling points. It was customary for one to be yard pilot at Northumberland Park each weekday evening, thus covering the fitted goods trains for March and beyond.

During the 1939-45 War the G.E. Section stock of J39's was progressively reduced. At the end of 1947 sixty-one remained of which thirty were at Stratford and fourteen at Norwich where numbers had risen as a result of greatly increased traffic in East Anglia. To relieve congestion at Whitemoor yard and on the route via Cambridge to Temple Mills, a number of goods and coal trains from the East Midlands and South Yorkshire commenced running via the G.N. main line to Langley Junction, thence Hertford North and the improved connection installed in 1944 at Bounds Green to Palace Gates, to South Tottenham and then Temple Mills. J39's were frequently seen on these trains together with classes J17, J20, K2, K3, O2 and O4. In the first half of 1945 Stratford-based J39's Nos. 1269/77, 1824/70, 1965, 2724/6 and 2995 were all seen, together with Nos. 2721/71 from Parkeston and 2965 from New England. As traffic declined after the War this route fell into disuse except for emergency working.

The advent of standard class B1 4-6-0's from 1946 onwards meant that passenger duties by J39's became less common but a crisis in 1951 when all the B.R. Britannia Pacifics had to be taken out of service led to the use of J39's on stopping trains, leaving the expresses to classes B1, B12 and B17 4-6-0's. Two years later on 13th June 1953, No. 64959 of Stratford was seen working the 3-51 p.m. Ipswich-Liverpool Street passenger train.

For working trains of Continental wagons over the former L.N.W.R. line to Bletchley, Cambridge acquired five J39's in August 1955 (Nos. 64729/51, 64803/90, 64958). They remained for three years during which time they made occasional forays to Hitchin on local goods and passenger turns.

Out of the initial batch of seventeen J39's built between September and December 1926, the North Eastern Area received the first twelve. They were allocated to Newport (Nos. 1448/9/50/5/6/7), Hull Dairycoates (Nos. 1451/2/4) and West Hartlepool (Nos. 1458/9/81). The Newport and West Hartlepool engines were used on the main goods workings to York and Newcastle, with the Hull engines on similar workings to York, Leeds and Doncaster. The Newport engines also worked local mineral trips in the area. After a year, in November 1927, the three Hull engines were transferred to Blaydon for working goods trains on the Carlisle line, but they also appeared at York on similar workings from Tyneside. These first twelve J39's had the Westinghouse brake (ultimately replaced by steam, except on No. 1457) and vacuum ejectors, but all subsequent members of the class allocated to the N.E. Area were without Westinghouse equipment.

There was a gap of three years before any more J39's were allocated to the N.E. Area, consequently for the first few years in the southern part of the Area most of those observed were visitors from Southern Area sheds working goods trains to Hull and York, with extensive use on passenger trains to Bridlington and Scarborough in the summer months, particularly with the 1928 series of engines stationed in the West Riding of Yorkshire.

Between December 1929 and February 1930 eight new J39's were sent to N.E. Area sheds, allocated to Blaydon (Nos. 1418/25/9/66), York (Nos. 1470/87) and Newport (Nos. 1489/91). The two sent to Newport displaced Nos. 1448/9 to Middlesbrough. Shortly after its transfer, No. 1448 came to grief in September 1930 at the foot of the embankment after collecting a load of iron ore at Lumpsey Mines. Due to slump conditions, deliveries of new J39's were slow and only thirty were built for the N.E. Area in the years 1932-35, bringing the total there to fifty. Thirteen of the new engines were allocated to sheds already having J39's, but the other seventeen went to Neville Hill (Nos. 1436/53/60/4/9), Darlington (Nos. 1471/4/80/5), Heaton (Nos. 1482/3, 1504/5), Ferryhill (Nos. 1488/90) and Sunderland (Nos. 1465/73).

It was in the first half of the 1930's that increased use was made of J39's on passenger trains, particularly on Tees-side, where they proved very capable engines for well-loaded trains of day-trippers bound for the seaside at Redcar and Saltburn from the mining districts of central Durham, especially if a Bank Holiday week-end turned out to be hot and sunny and extra trains had to be put on at short notice. The traffic was so heavy at times that special permission was given for the trains to run on the goods lines east and west of Middlesbrough under the absolute block regulations instead of the usual permissive block. Nor was it unknown for Middlesbrough shed to use J39's on stopping trains to Newcastle and return.

The versatility of the J39's, and their proven capability on passenger trains, came in useful in 1934 when they were hurriedly pressed into service on the Middlesbrough to Scarborough service. Since the opening of the Scarborough & Whitby Railway in 1885 the service along the coast had been between Saltburn and Scarborough, but in 1933 it was changed to Middlesbrough to Scarborough via Nunthorpe and Loftus. The increase in passenger traffic was amazing and in the first summer of operation over the new route the line was unable to cope, so that at times trains were running hours late. This was due to much of the route being single line and the inability of the class A6 4-6-2T engines to handle the traffic. For the 1934 season, therefore, various alterations were made, including a new platform at Scarborough, and better motive power was promised in the shape of class A8 engines.

By the time the increased service commenced on 1st June 1934 only sixteen A8's were available and as many as could be spared from other duties were pressed into use on the coast line as the traffic continued to increase. In the meantime the rebuilding of the other twenty-nine from H1 4-4-4T's was continued at Darlington Works. Consequently J39 engines were specially authorised by the Civil Engineer to work over the coast route and they put in some extremely good work on the line, which abounded in sharp curves and steep gradients and where power rather than speed was the criterion – the usual time for the 58-mile journey being $2\frac{3}{4}$ hours, an average speed of 21 m.p.h. By July 1937 the traffic had increased to such an extent that the coast line could not carry any more trains and a relief service between Middlesbrough and Scarborough was introduced, running via Eaglescliffe, Northallerton, Gilling and Malton (where a double reversal was necessary) also worked by J39 engines from Tees-side sheds.

Thus it was possible to leave the east end of Middlesbrough station at 9-15 a.m. and arrive at Scarborough (via Whitby West Cliff) at 11-57 a.m. or to leave the west end at 9-10 a.m. and arrive at Scarborough (via Gilling) at 12-1 p.m.! However, on 9th August 1937 No. 1449 was derailed at Prospect Hill (Whitby) by spreading the track and that put a sudden stop to the use of J39's on the coast line, although they continued to appear on the service via Gilling.

One could also meet with J39's on express duties on the Leeds – Newcastle service via Harrogate, Northallerton and the Coast Road. A journey in 1937 by one of the authors from Leeds behind a D49 was rostered to change engines at Harrogate for a Stockton D20. However, a J39 from that shed took over and gave good running through to Newcastle. As on the G.E. Section, a high average speed could be maintained with quick acceleration and good uphill work without excessive speeds.

By April 1938 the total of J39's in the N.E. Area had reached seventy-eight with the steady delivery of new engines from October 1936 onwards. At this period J39 transfers became more numerous, two sheds receiving the class for the first time being Consett (No. 1465 from Sunderland in exchange for class J26 No. 1676 in June 1936) and Haverton Hill (No. 1472 from Middlesbrough in October 1936). The engine at Haverton Hill was rostered to work the 11-45 p.m. SX class A goods from Port Clarence to York. Starbeck received its first J39 (No. 1460 from Leeds) in July 1937, in this case to work the 9-38 p.m. class B goods to Blaydon, and it was joined by No. 1464 three months later. New engines built in 1937 gave Tyne Dock its first J39's (Nos. 1577 and 1580) and Stockton its first (No. 1586). In 1937-38 Dairycoates received J39's again after an absence of ten years, these being Nos. 1470/87 from York which, together with new engines Nos. 1508/9, were often used for passenger trains on the Hornsea and Withernsea branches. The two older engines were transferred specifically to replace ex-Hull & Barnsley class J28 0-6-0's, and No. 1470 became a regular performer on the 4-5 a.m. Hull to Scarborough (Gallows Close) No.2 express goods, returning at 8-50 a.m. from Scarborough (Washbeck) on a similar train, which had once been the preserve of class J28 No. 2408. Ferryhill added No. 1563 when new in July 1937 to its existing pair (Nos. 1488 and 1490) but Nos. 1488 and 1563 departed for Blaydon in August 1938, followed by No. 1490 (to Darlington) in November 1938 on the closure of the shed.

Fig. 39   Class J39 No. 2726 on an up coal train leaving Audley End tunnel, May 1930.

Westinghouse brake with hose connection below bufferbeam.

Fig. 40   Class J39/2 No. 2991 on a Cambridge-Liverpool Street express near Trumpington, 1945.

Fig. 41

Class J39/2 No. 2943 on an up excursion train at Nottingham Victoria station, c. July 1935.

Fig. 42   Class J39/1 No. 2963 on a Chester train near Brooklands, M.S.J. & A. line, August 1945.

Fig. 43   Class J39/2 No. 2742 on an up goods at Cadder, August 1931.

Fig. 44   Class J39/2 No. 4791 on an up goods at Eryholme, August 1947.

No vacuum brake stand-pipe at front end.

Fig. 45   Class J39/3 No. 4857 on an up goods near Darlington, August 1947.

4,125-gallon ex-N.E. tender (from Raven class A2).

Fig. 46   Class J39 No. 64782 departing from Norwich on a goods train to Bishopsgate, July 1955.

Fig. 47   Class J39 No. 64736 on a Leicester (Midland) – Peterborough goods passing Melton Junction, July 1958.

Altered drop grate arrangement but retaining original semi-circular cover.

Fig. 48   Class J40 M. & G.N. No. 59 at Norwich shed.

M. & G.N. type chimney without raised lip, Deeley smokebox door, M.R. arrangement of vacuum brake with large ejector on smokebox, original pattern steel-faced wooden bufferbeam with curved ends, boiler date plate on front end frames below smokebox, tender with two coal rails.

Fig. 49   Class J40 No. 065 at South Lynn shed, May 1938.

M. & G.N. type chimney with raised lip, steam pipe running below platform to front end carriage warming hose, steel bufferbeam with straight ends, tablet catcher on tender.

Fig. 50   Class J41 No. 062 at South Lynn shed, May 1939.

Original length smokebox with Deeley dished door and Deeley 2ft. $2\frac{7}{8}$ in. chimney.

Ferryhill was another depot which found its J39's very useful on passenger turns at times of pressure.

With the closure of Berwick marshalling yard in March 1939, Tweedmouth lost most of its large engines and received J39's Nos. 2735/6 from the Scottish Area: they were joined by No. 1467 from Newport in June 1939, but in July No. 2735 moved south to Malton. A week later No. 2736, without water scoop, went to Consett and was replaced by No. 1585 from Sunderland, which had a water scoop. No. 2735 did not stay very long at Malton but went on to Starbeck in September 1939, only to go to York two months later, displaced from Starbeck by the only wartime reinstated B15, No. 824.

Under the N.E. Area re-allocation scheme of 1938, the general aim of which was to concentrate engines of a class at certain sheds, Selby received its first J39 in June 1939 (No. 1534 from Newport) followed by No. 1477 (also from Newport) in July, but both departed for York in October; these engines returned to Selby in February 1940, together with Nos. 1535/60, 2735, all from York, for use on extra coal trains and war traffic. However, in July 1940 Nos. 1477, 1535/60 were surplus at Selby due to a decrease in traffic and they were transferred to Starbeck, where the shed had been allocated three extra mineral turns.

In October 1940 Nos. 2735 and 2736 were returned to the Scottish Area in exchange for two other J39's: No. 1896 was received at Consett from Carlisle to replace No. 2736, but Selby's replacement for No. 2735 did not arrive until January 1941 in the shape of No. 1835, also from Carlisle.

Otherwise few transfers took place in the war years to 1942, but 1943 saw a dramatic change in the situation. By the end of that year the N.E. Area had a stock of eighty-seven J39's concentrated at Starbeck (17), Darlington (30) and Blaydon (36), the remainder being at Alnmouth (1) and Tweedmouth (3). Blaydon's marked increase from eleven at the end of 1942 to thirty-six at the end of 1943 was due to replacements being required to cover the loss of fourteen Q6's to Newport and fifteen K3's to Gateshead and Heaton for increased traffic on the main line brought about by the War. As a result of the general reshuffle on 28th March 1943, Darlington had received no fewer than forty-four J39's, making a total of fifty at this shed. This build-up was at the expense of losing five B16's, eighteen J21, J24, J25 and J26 engines and fifteen 0-8-0's of classes Q5, Q6 and Q7. By

August 1943 Darlington had lost ten of these J39's to Starbeck and seventeen to Blaydon, though this was partly offset by five new arrivals from the Scottish Area and two from the Southern Area. In 1944 Starbeck was using its J39's on coal and coke trains originating in the Durham area to Colne (where the traffic was handed over to the L.M.S.) via Ilkley and Skipton, returning with empties. Heavy loads required two engines and an interesting combination seen on 17th February 1944 was class J39 No. 1532 + L.M.S. class 4F No. 4102. A more unusual pairing was seen on the 4-15 p.m. Newcastle – Liverpool express on 27th September 1949 when it left Ripon behind No. 64818 + class A3 No. 60074.

Workings throughout the War proved the mixed traffic capabilities of the J39's and they appeared on almost any class of train in the N.E. Area, except for main line expresses. They did even appear occasionally on main line semi-fasts, such as the 5-30 p.m. Newcastle to York, a Heaton working, on which No. 1545 was noted on 14th September 1942.

By January 1947 their distribution in the N.E. Area was little changed with the bulk of the class still being at Darlington, Blaydon and Starbeck. However, later in the year a general redistribution commenced and over the next three years many were at sheds which had housed them prior to the 1943 re-allocation scheme (see table). Sheds receiving J39's for the first time were Alston (No. 4851 from January 1949); Scarborough (Nos. 64861, 4919, 64935 from September 1949), whilst Borough Gardens' first was No. 4936 in February 1948.

Typical duties at this time were as follows: West Auckland engines ran to Newport and also worked the Wearhead pick-up and the Waterhouses branch to East Hedley Hope colliery. Dairycoates engines were employed on the Hornsea Bridge pick-up Tuesdays, Thursdays and Saturdays only, the Withernsea pick-up, on the Beverley shunt until 8-40 p.m. and on the Scarborough goods. The latter engine was used by Scarborough for the Malton goods during the day. Starbeck J39 duties were to Neville Hill and return and then on the Boroughbridge and Brafferton pick-up, the Newport goods, a further turn to Neville Hill and return, followed by a trip to Bilton Sidings for the Harrogate gasworks railway and then the Otley and Ilkley pick-up. Some N.E.R. sheds made frequent use of the class on excursions, particularly to race meetings. On Whit Monday

1952 three were seen at Redcar and five arrived at Wetherby on 6th April 1953 from various points.

By 1954 further N.E. Region sheds to get J39's were Northallerton (Nos. 64817, 64910/78) and Malton (Nos. 64867, 64928/47). The Northallerton engines were used on the Hawes branch goods and mineral trains, whilst the Malton engines were employed chiefly on the Burdale-Malton and Malton-Thirsk stone trains conveying limestone for use at steelworks in the Middlesbrough area. About this time Neville Hill had a turn involving a J39 working to Bilton, Gascoigne Wood, York and Darlington, with the engine leaving the shed at 8-40 a.m. and not getting back until 4-0 p.m. the following day, having been manned by Leeds, Starbeck and Darlington men. Neville Hill had four other goods workings involving double-shifted J39's, although a lot of their time was taken up by assisting through goods trains to and from Newport between Neville Hill and Bilton, usually over the hilly Wetherby route.

Starbeck engines also had a number of turns involving assisting goods trains between Bilton and Neville Hill, and they also worked the Thirsk and Otterington pick-up, the Ripon pilot and Masham branch (where the first set of men returned from Ripon to Harrogate by bus!) and between Haverton Hill and Skipton on I.C.I. tanker trains. A Gateshead J39 was booked to work the Ponteland branch goods, and Tweedmouth engines were rostered for goods to Kelso, St. Boswells and Duns.

By 1954 Alnmouth was responsible for three turns involving J39's – the Amble branch goods, Tweedmouth pick-up, and a complicated roster involving goods and passenger trains between Alnwick and Alnmouth, with shunting duties at each end as and when required.

December 1962 saw the end of the J39's and in that month thirty-two were withdrawn from former North Eastern sheds. Throughout the fifties, as branches closed and many services were taken over by diesel units, B1's became available for goods workings and J39's were supplanted, or reduced to working local trip traffic, particularly in the Hull and Newcastle areas. However, during 1962 J39's were still booked for Newcastle-Stockton, Newcastle-Darlington and Darlington-Shildon goods turns, and although Alnmouth shed still had the Amble branch, Tweedmouth pick-up and the Alnwick-Alnmouth mixed working, the three J39's concerned, Nos. 64869/97 and 64917, were condemned on 3rd December. The last North Eastern Region engines to go were Nos. 64934/5

of Neville Hill and Nos. 64940/3 of Dairycoates, all on 17th December 1962.

The Scottish Area did not receive its first J39's until mid-1929, though it must be remembered that in 1926 all thirty-five of the new class J38 engines had been sent there. The initial allocation of J39's was twelve engines, stationed at Eastfield (Nos. 2731/2/8), Parkhead (Nos. 2733/4), St.Margaret's (Nos. 2735/6/7), Carlisle (Nos. 2739/40), Dundee (No. 2741) and Aberdeen (No. 2742). No. 2741 joined No. 2742 at Aberdeen after only three weeks at Dundee. All were attached to 4,200-gallon tenders (J39/2) and were the first of the class to be so equipped. Three more Part 2 engines were delivered to Scotland in February 1930 (No. 2786 Dundee, Nos. 2787/8 Eastfield), followed by another four in May-June 1931 (Nos. 2977-80 Eastfield), making a total of nineteen.

No more J39's were allocated to the Scottish Area until May 1937 when Nos. 1875/80/94 went new to Carlisle. These were Part 1 engines, having the then normal 3,500-gallon type of tender. During March-April 1938 a further six Part 2 engines arrived, Nos. 1804 (St.Margaret's) and 1808/35/62/3/96 (Carlisle). Four of the final batch of Part 3 engines, Nos. 3085/8/93/6, were sent new to St.Margaret's in 1941.

Until 1939 there were few transfers of J39's between sheds in the Scottish Area. In October 1931 the two at Parkhead, Nos. 2733/4, went to Eastfield, the latter moving on to Dundee in November 1933. Carlisle lost No. 2739 to St.Margaret's in January 1935 and No. 2740 temporarily to Eastfield from November 1931 to February 1933.

In pre-war days the St.Margaret's J39's were employed on night goods trains, usually the 7-45 p.m. Leith Walk – Perth; 10-5 p.m. Leith Walk – Aberdeen (both lodging turns balanced by a J37 from Perth and a J39 from Aberdeen respectively); 10-32 p.m. Waverley – Cadder; 11-55 p.m. South Leith – Thornton (both out and home turns). During daytime these engines were often utilised for local coal trains and special passenger work, such as Sunday School trips on summer Saturdays to Roslin (on the Glencorse branch). Of the two engines on loan in 1938 from the Southern Area and working from Edinburgh sheds, No. 1259 worked daily on a St. Margaret's duty involving a stopping passenger train to Dundee via the main line, whilst No. 1942 was regularly employed on a similar turn to

Dundee via Crail (a Haymarket job). One summer, No. 2736 in tandem with a K2, worked the "Northern Belle" cruise train on a trip through the Border country.

At Parkhead before the War there was a lodging turn each night to Dundee, requiring two J39's weekly because it was exclusively worked by one shed. In October 1931 this duty was transferred to Eastfield, together with the two J39's. Eastfield also had a second goods turn to Dundee worked by a J39 and this class also ran to Aberdeen, Niddrie, Tweedmouth and Fort William. The engines were regularly employed on the same duties with regular men. The Niddrie turn was out and home but the others involved lodging. The corresponding duties from Tweedmouth and Fort William were usually worked by J37's, but Aberdeen used a J39 on their Cadder turn. In September 1938 an Eastfield J39 was observed at Fort William on the 4-5 p.m. Restaurant Car express to Glasgow.

Dundee engines usually worked to Carlisle and those from the latter shed had night goods lodging turns to Dundee and Thornton (also worked by K3's), together with a share of the busy goods service to and from Edinburgh over the Waverley route (usually operated on a change-over basis), and to Newcastle.

During the War, the maximum number of Scottish Area engines was reached in 1942 when thirty were divided between six sheds. The St.Margaret's engines were used on goods work over all the main lines from Edinburgh, including the service introduced between Meadows and Low Fell via Hawick and the Border Counties route to relieve the East Coast main line. On these duties the men changed over en route as they did by that time on the Aberdeen, Perth and main line Newcastle trains, thus avoiding the need to lodge away from home. North Eastern Area J39's worked into Edinburgh for a short period over the Border Counties line and were also seen regularly during the War on the East Coast main line into Edinburgh.

At the end of the L.N.E.R. period the total number of J39's in the Scottish Area had fallen to twenty-four, most of them at Carlisle with Dundee and Aberdeen still having a share.

However in March 1948 St.Margaret's regained three J39's (Nos. 4946/63/86) followed by No. 64794 in November 1949. From 1948 onwards duties in Scotland were more local in character and mainly on goods trains, but No. 64946 (deputising for the regular branch engine, class C16 No. 67496) had the melancholy distinction of working the last passenger trains over the Longniddry–Haddington branch on 3rd December 1949. The Carlisle engines were employed to a considerable extent on short distance work, including passenger and goods trains on the Langholm and Silloth branches, pick-up goods to Hawick and Haltwhistle, ballast trains, and as trip pilots exchanging traffic between the various yards around Carlisle. The Silloth branch was R.A.7, with J37 and J38 additionally permitted, so the J39's were well within this category. However, on 23rd October 1950 No. 64880 was working the 1-15 p.m. passenger train from Carlisle to Silloth when it became derailed and overturned between Drumburgh and Kirkbride. There were no fatalities among the passengers, but the driver and fireman were killed. Evidence given at the enquiry suggested that the permanent way had been defective. Despite this accident the class continued to be used on the Silloth line.

In February 1958 Carlisle Canal shed and its engines were transferred to the L.M.R., which left only eleven J39's in Scottish Region stock. In August 1958 Nos. 64794 and 64946/63/86 moved across Edinburgh to the former L.M.S. shed at Dalry Road where they remained for up to three years before passing back to former N.B.R. sheds. From 1959 onwards moves were made to Thornton, where Nos. 64790/2/4 and 64986 ended their days, and Dunfermline which housed Nos. 64795 and 64946/63 for short periods. Dawsholm, another former L.M.S. shed, had No. 64975 from August 1960 until withdrawn in December 1962. At times of pressure, Eastfield shed occasionally used J39's just ex-shops from Cowlairs on excursion trains. There were two noteworthy instances of this during 1960 when No. 64818 (of Thornaby) worked a train from Kirkintilloch to Ayr and No. 64865 (a Gateshead engine) a similar special from Balloch to Girvan.

Section L.N.E., 1926.J39   3,500-gallon tender. Superheater element diameter corrected from $1\frac{3}{32}$in. to $1\frac{7}{32}$in. and superheater heating surface from 246.1 sq.ft. to 271.8 sq.ft., 12/1927. Class Part 1 added, 12/1930. Alternative boiler wrapper plate thickness of $\frac{9}{16}$in. added, 12/1937. Diagram replaced 12/1938.

Section L.N.E., 1929.J39   4,200-gallon tender; steam brake and vacuum ejector; engine front overhang 8ft. $3\frac{1}{8}$in. instead of 8ft. 3in. Class Part 2 added, 12/1930. "or vacuum brake" added, 12/1935. Alternative boiler wrapper plate thickness of $\frac{9}{16}$in. added, 12/1937. Diagram replaced 12/1938.

Section L.N.E., 1934.J39/3 4,125-gallon ex-N.E.R. tender with $5\frac{1}{2}$ tons coal capacity; engine front overhang erroneously 8ft. 3in. Alternative boiler wrapper plate thickness of $\frac{9}{16}$in. added, 12/1937. Tender capacity amended to 3,940 gallons, 12/1940. Diagram replaced 12/1941.

Section L.N.E., 1938.J39/1 3,500-gallon tender; vacuum brake, or steam brake and vacuum ejector, or Westinghouse brake and vacuum ejector. Inner firebox plates amended from $\frac{5}{8}$in. to $\frac{9}{16}$in. and length of grate on the slope amended from 7ft. $9\frac{3}{4}$in. to 7ft. $9\frac{5}{8}$in., 12/1941. Diagram replaced 12/1946.

Section L.N.E., 1938.J39/2 4,200-gallon tender; steam brake with vacuum ejector. Alternative boiler wrapper plate thickness of $\frac{9}{16}$in. added; inner firebox plates amended from $\frac{5}{8}$in. to $\frac{9}{16}$in.; length of grate on the slope amended from 7ft. $9\frac{3}{4}$in. to 7ft. $9\frac{5}{8}$in.; width of grate amended from 3ft. 4in. to 3ft. $4\frac{1}{4}$in.; "or vacuum brake" added, 12/1941. Class part discontinued and diagram deleted 12/1952.

Section L.N.E., 1941.J39/3 N.E.R.-type tenders; alternative weights for 4,125, 3,940 and 3,650-gallon varieties; latest dimensions for firebox and boiler, including wrapper plate thickness $\frac{9}{16}$in.; overall length of firebox casing 8ft. $11\frac{1}{4}$in. (8ft. $5\frac{1}{8}$in. at the bottom), width of firebox at the bottom 4ft. $0\frac{3}{8}$in.; engine front overhang still 8ft. 3in.; height to top of dome 12ft. $10\frac{3}{8}$in. instead of 12ft. $10\frac{1}{4}$in.; steam brake and vacuum ejector, or vacuum brake. Class part discontinued and diagram deleted 12/1952.

1946.   J39/1 3,500-gallon tender; front engine overhang 8ft. $3\frac{1}{8}$in.; distance between trailing coupled wheels and leading tender wheels reduced from 10ft. $5\frac{1}{4}$in. to 10ft. $5\frac{1}{8}$in., and total engine and tender wheelbase reduced similarly; height to top of dome 12ft. $10\frac{3}{8}$in. Class part discontinued and diagram deleted 12/1952.

1952.   J39   3,500-gallon tender; engine front overhang 8ft. $3\frac{1}{8}$in.

1952.   J39   4,200-gallon tender; engine front overhang 8ft. $3\frac{1}{8}$in.

1952.   J39   N.E.R.-type tenders; engine front overhang still 8ft. 3in.

Classification: Southern Area load class 5; Route availability 6; B.R. power class 4F, altered to 5F in May 1953.

Summary of J39 Class

B.R. No.		1946 No.		Orig. No.	Maker	Built	Class Part (Tender Type) (a) 1, 3(5/60), 2(6/60), 1(12/60), 2(2/62)	Brake W + VE, S + VE	Steam to Screw Reverse	Withdrawn
64700	8/49	4700	11/46	1448	Darlington	9/1926	1, 3(8/52), 1(5/60)	(6/32)	11/36	4/61
64701	6/48	4701	11/46	1449	,,	10/1926	1	,, (11/32)	4/37	11/62
64702	11/48	4702	12/46	1450	,,	10/1926	1	,, (2/32)	4/36	9/59
64703	9/49	4703	2/46	1451	,,	10/1926	1	,, (2/32)	5/37	3/62
64704	5/50	4704	1/46	1452	,,	10/1926	1	,, (3/33)	4/35	12/62
64705	5/49	4705	6/46	1454	,,	10/1926	1, 3(11/54), 2(4/60)	,, (2/33)	7/35	3/62
64706	12/49	4706	6/46	1455	,,	10/1926	1	,, (12/32)	4/36	3/62
64707	5/48	4707	6/46	1456	,,	10/1926	1	,, (5/32)	8/35	8/61
64708	8/51	4708	8/46	1457	,,	11/1926	1	,, (10/31)	12/35	8/60
64709	11/48	4709	6/46	1458	,,	11/1926	1	S + VE (4/33)	4/35	11/62
64710	10/49	4710	5/46	1459	,,	11/1926	1	,, (5/36)	5/36	4/61
64711	11/49	4711	4/46	1481	,,	11/1926	1	,, (12/32)	10/36	5/62
64712	12/48	4712	8/46	1484	,,	11/1926	1		10/46	2/60
64713	8/48	4713	6/46	1492	,,	12/1926	1	S + VE	11/45	4/62
64714	2/51	4714	6/46	1493	,,	12/1926	1	,,	9/35	5/59
64715	3/49	4715	6/46	1494	,,	12/1926	1	,,	9/46	5/59
64716	5/50	4716	6/46	1495	,,	12/1926	1	,,	6/42	4/61
64717	2/49	4717	4/46	1270	,,	3/1927	1	,,	7/36	8/60
64718	12/50	4718	6/46	1496	,,	4/1927	1, 3(9/45), 1(3/48)	,,	by 7/40	2/62
64719	3/50	4719	9/46	1497	,,	4/1927	1	,,	4/45	11/62
64720	1/50	4720	7/46	1498	,,	4/1927	1	,,	11/40	9/61
64721	10/50	4721	4/46	1233	,,	5/1927	1	,,	10/35	2/60
64722	10/50	4722	4/46	1255	,,	5/1927	1	,,	11/35	2/60
64723	1/49	4723	4/46	1263	,,	5/1927	1	,,	7/44	3/61
64724	7/48	4724	6/46	1259	,,	5/1927	1, 2(9/43), 1(5/48)	,,	3/36	2/60
64725	2/49	4725	3/46	1265	,,	5/1927	1	,,	8/36	10/61
64726	5/48	4726	4/46	1266	,,	5/1927	1	,,	4/40	11/60
64727	10/48	4727	4/46	1267	,,	5/1927	1	,,	6/40	10/62
64728	3/51	4728	4/46	1272	,,	5/1927	1	,,	5/36	2/60
64729	4/48	4729	4/46	1273	,,	5/1927	1	,,	9/35	3/61
64730	4/48	4730	3/46	1268	,,	5/1927	1	,,	4/48	11/62
64731	7/48	4731	3/46	1269	,,	5/1927	1	,,	12/39	7/59
64732	11/49	4732	5/46	1274	,,	5/1927	1	,,	3/36	8/61
64733	11/48	4733	4/46	1277	,,	6/1927	1	,,	7/45	10/61
64734	12/48	4734	4/46	1275	,,	6/1927	1	,,	4/40	5/59
64735	7/48	4735	4/46	1281	,,	6/1927	1	,,	—	8/59
64736	5/48	4736	3/46	1282	,,	6/1927	1	,,	6/41	7/61
64737	10/50	4737	4/46	1286	,,	6/1927	1	,,	6/45	8/59
64738	4/50	4738	5/46	1287	,,	6/1927	1	,,	4/39?	10/60
64739	6/49	4739	5/46	1289	,,	6/1927	1	,,	12/35	11/62
64740	9/49	4740	5/46	1290	,,	7/1927	1	,,	10/35	9/62
64741	8/49	4741	5/46	1295	,,	7/1927	1	,,	7/44	7/60
64742	7/49	4742	5/46	1296	,,	8/1927	1	,,	by 7/49	7/62
64743	12/48	4743	5/46	1298	,,	9/1927	1	,,	5/36	1/61

Summary of J39 Class (continued)

B.R. No.		1946 No.		Orig. No.	Maker	Built	Class Part (Tender Type) (a)	Brake	Withdrawn
64744	10/48	4744	12/46	2691	Darlington	7/1928	1	S+VE	3/62
64745	5/48	4745	1/47	2692	"	7/1928	1	"	11/61
64746	10/48	4746	10/46	2693	"	7/1928	1	"	2/61
64747	8/48	4747	12/46	2694	"	8/1928	1	"	11/61
64748	3/49	4748	1/47	2695	"	8/1928	1	"	7/61
64749	11/50	4749	12/46	2696	"	8/1928	1	"	11/62
64750	11/48	4750	10/46	2697	"	8/1928	1	"	11/59
64751	8/48	4751	9/46	2698	"	8/1928	1	"	11/59
64752	4/48	4752	9/46	2699	"	8/1928	1	"	12/59
64753	5/48	4753	4/46	2700	"	8/1928	1	"	6/59
64754	3/50	4754	8/46	2701	"	8/1928	1	"	8/59
64755	5/48	4755	10/46	2702	"	8/1928	1	"	11/62
64756	6/49	4756	11/46	2703	"	8/1928	1	"	8/59
64757	12/49	4757	8/46	2704	"	9/1928	1, 3(7/53)	"	12/62
64758	1/50	4758	11/46	2705	"	9/1928	1	"	11/62
64759	1/49	4759	8/46	2706	"	9/1928	1	"	3/60
64760	7/48	4760	5/46	2707	"	9/1928	1	"	11/62
64761	3/50	4761	8/46	2708	"	9/1928	1	"	11/59
64762	11/48	4762	8/46	2709	"	9/1928	1	"	6/59
64763	2/49	4763	11/45	2710	"	9/1928	1	"	6/59
64764	10/49	4764	8/46	2711	"	10/1928	1	"	10/60
64765	8/49	4765	11/46	2712	"	10/1928	1	"	8/60
64766	4/48	4766	11/45	2713	"	11/1928	1	W+VE	9/59
64767	7/48	4767	8/46	2714	"	11/1928	1	"	1/61
64768	8/51	4768	11/46	2715	"	11/1928	1	"	1/60
64769	1/49	4769	11/46	2716	"	11/1928	1	"	5/59
64770	10/48	4770	10/46	2717	"	11/1928	1	"	10/60
64771	10/48	4771	11/46	2718	"	11/1928	1	"	2/60
64772	10/49	4772	8/46	2719	"	12/1928	1	"	7/61
64773	7/51	4773	11/46	2720	"	12/1928	1	"	8/59
64774	12/49	4774	12/46	2721	"	3/1929	1	"	3/60
64775	5/48	4775	8/46	2722	"	4/1929	1	"	8/60
64776	2/50	4776	10/46	2723	"	4/1929	1	"	8/59
64777	4/49	4777	12/46	2724	"	4/1929	1, 3(4/53)	S+VE(10/35)	1/60
64778	12/48	4778	11/46	2725	"	4/1929	1	"	9/60
64779	8/49	4779	11/46	2726	"	4/1929	1	"	9/61
64780	3/48	4780	10/46	2727	"	4/1929	1	"	1/60
64781	8/48	4781	3/46	2728	"	5/1929	1	W(12/56)	3/60
64782	12/50	4782	5/46	2729	"	5/1929	1	"	3/60
64783	2/51	4783	5/46	2730	"	5/1929	2, 3(5/42), 2(5/42)	W(12/56)	11/60
64784	9/48	4784	3/46	2731	"	5/1929	2	S+VE	8/60
64785	11/50	4785	5/46	2732	"	6/1929	2	"	6/59
64786	2/50	4786	12/46	2733	"	6/1929	2	"	12/62
64787	10/48	4787	10/46	2734	"	6/1929	2	"	6/59
64788	6/48	4788	11/46	2735	"	6/1929	2, 1(4/51)	"	6/59
64789	9/48	4789	11/46	2736	"	6/1929	2	"	7/60
64790	7/48	4790	4/46	2737	"	6/1929	2	"	12/62
64791	7/48	4791	5/46	2738	"	7/1929	2, 1(3/61)	"	11/62
64792	11/49	4792	3/46	2739	"	7/1929	2	"	1/62
64793	5/48	4793	4/46	2740	"	7/1929	2	"	11/59
64794	5/48	4794	6/46	2741	"	7/1929	2	"	8/62
64795	11/50	4795	8/46	2742	"	7/1929	2	"	12/62

BR No.	Date	No.	Date	Orig. No.	Darlington	Built	Repairs	S + VE	Withdrawn
64796	12/48	4796	9/46	2770	"	8/1929	1	"	12/62
64797	3/48	4797	1/47	2771	"	9/1929	1, 2(4/51)	"	9/59
64798	7/49	4798	10/46	2772	"	9/1929	1	"	9/62
64799	2/50	4799	10/46	2773	"	9/1929	1	"	7/59
64800	6/51	4800	9/46	2774	"	9/1929	1	"	1/60
64801	2/51	4801	11/46	2775	"	10/1929	1	"	11/62
64802	6/50	4802	12/46	2776	"	10/1929	1	"	7/60
64803	6/49	4803	12/46	2777	"	10/1929	1	"	9/59
64804	9/48	4804	6/46	2778	"	10/1929	1	"	4/61
64805	12/48	4805	9/46	2779	"	11/1929	1	"	10/59
64806	8/48	4806	12/46	2780	"	11/1929	1	"	5/62
64807	12/49	4807	6/46	2781	"	11/1929	1	"	4/60
64808	11/51	4808	10/46	2782	"	12/1929	1	"	2/61
64809	11/49	4809	11/46	2783	"	12/1929	1	"	1/62
64810	5/49	4810	11/46	2784	"	12/1929	1	"	6/61
64811	4/49	4811	11/46	2785	"	12/1929	1	"	3/62
64812	12/48	4812	12/46	1418	"	1/1930	1	"	12/62
64813	1/50	4813	6/46	1425	"	1/1930	1	"	12/62
64814	11/49	4814	8/46	1429	"	1/1930	1, 3(11/49), 1(11/51)	"	11/62
64815	3/50	4815	11/46	1466	"	1/1930	1, 3(3/50)	"	8/61
64816	6/49	4816	1/47	1470	"	1/1930	1	"	12/61
64817	1/51	4817	1/47	1487	"	1/1930	1, 3(10/52), 2(6/60)	"	3/62
64818	6/50	4818	12/46	1489	"	1/1930	1	"	12/62
64819	7/48	4819	10/46	1491	"	1/1930	2	"	9/62
64820	5/49	4820	3/46	2786	"	2/1930	2, 1(9/43)	"	5/62
64821	6/50	4821	10/46	2787	"	2/1930	2, 1(4/52)	"	11/62
64822	7/48	4822	11/46	2788	"	2/1930		"	12/62
64823	3/49	4823	12/46	2962	"	9/1931	1	"	1/61
64824	6/51	4824	10/46	2963	"	9/1931	1	"	3/60
64825	4/49	4825	11/46	2964	"	9/1931	1	"	11/61
64826	4/50	4826	1/47	2965	"	10/1931	1, 2(5/48)	"	2/60
64827	7/50	4827	12/46	2966	"	12/1931	1, 2(3/53)	"	2/60
64828	8/48	4828	1/47	2967	"	10/1931	1	"	3/60
64829	9/48	4829	9/46	2968	"	11/1931	1	"	5/59
64830	1/50	4830	1/47	2969	"	12/1931	1	"	2/60
64831	3/48	4831	12/46	2970	"	12/1931	1	"	6/61
64832	6/48	4832	8/46	2971	"	1/1932	1	"	9/59
64833	8/49	4833	11/46	2972	"	1/1932	1	"	11/62
64834	8/48	4834	8/46	2973	"	2/1932	1	"	11/59
64835	10/49	4835	11/46	2974	"	2/1932	1	"	12/62
64836	1/49	4836	11/46	2975	"	3/1932	1	"	4/62
64837	2/49	4837	8/46	2976	"	3/1932	1	"	11/61
64838	12/49	4838	12/46	2977	"	5/1932	1	"	1/60
64839	5/48	4839	11/46	2978	"	6/1932	1	"	10/61
64840	2/49	4840	11/46	2979	"	6/1932	2, 1(2/53)	"	10/61
64841	12/50	4841	8/46	2980	"	6/1932	2	"	11/62
64842	1/49	4842	12/46	1453	"	8/1932	2	"	12/62
64843	3/49	4843	2/46	1469	"	10/1932	2, 3(12/38), 1(2/51)	"	4/62
64844	10/48	4844	10/46	1471	"	10/1932	2, 3(9/37), 1(11/54)	"	3/62
64845	5/48	4845	9/46	1480	"	11/1932	2, 3(8/37)	"	12/62
64846	7/50	4846	1/47	1482	"	5/1933	2, 3(7/37), 1(4/53)	"	7/61
64847	9/48	4847	1/47	1483	"	5/1933	1, 3(2/51), 1(8/55), 3(10/55)	"	11/62

Summary of J39 Class (continued)

B.R. No.		1946 No.		Orig. No.	Maker	Built	Class Part (Tender Type) (a)	Brake S+VE	Withdrawn
64848	10/48	4848	5/46	1412	Darlington	3/1934	1, 3(3/51), 1(7/52)	,,	12/62
64849	7/48	4849	11/46	1463	,,	3/1934	1	,,	11/62
64850	11/49	4850	11/46	1467	,,	3/1934	1	,,	12/62
64851	6/49	4851	11/46	1468	,,	3/1934	1, 3(1/47), 1(2/51)	,,	12/62
64852	5/48	4852	11/46	1472	,,	3/1934	1	,,	12/62
64853	3/48	4853	10/46	1488	,,	12/1934	1	,,	12/62
64854	5/48	4854	12/46	1490	,,	12/1934	1	,,	12/62
64855	5/48	4855	10/46	1475	,,	10/1934	3, 1(7/53)	,,	8/62
64856	4/50	4856	10/46	1476	,,	10/1934	3, 1(4/50), 2(3/52)	,,	10/62
64857	9/50	4857	11/46	1477	,,	10/1934	3	,,	12/62
64858	6/49	4858	5/46	1478	,,	11/1934	3, 1(2/50)	,,	3/62
64859	3/49	4859	10/46	1479	,,	11/1934	3, 1(12/46)	,,	12/62
64860	8/48	4860	8/46	1436	,,	10/1935	1	V	12/62
64861	5/48	4861	10/46	1460	,,	11/1935	1	,,	12/62
64862	4/48	4862	1/47	1464	,,	11/1935	1	,,	10/61
64863	5/49	4863	10/46	1465	,,	11/1935	1	,,	1/62
64864	8/48	4864	10/46	1473	,,	11/1935	1	,,	12/62
64865	5/50	4865	11/46	1474	,,	11/1935	1	,,	12/62
64866	3/50	4866	6/46	1485	,,	11/1935	1	,,	9/62
64867	10/48	4867	11/46	1486	,,	12/1935	1	,,	2/62
64868	5/50	4868	10/46	1504	,,	12/1935	1	,,	4/62
64869	11/48	4869	9/46	1505	,,	12/1935	1	,,	12/62
64870	10/49	4870	6/46	1506	,,	12/1935	1	,,	1/62
64871	2/49	4871	12/46	1584	,,	12/1935	1	,,	10/62
64872	9/48	4872	12/46	2941	,,	6/1935	2	,,	11/62
64873	11/48	4873	11/46	2942	,,	6/1935	2	,,	10/62
64874	8/49	4874	12/46	2943	,,	6/1935	2	,,	5/59
64875	9/48	4875	12/46	2944	,,	6/1935	2	,,	4/61
64876	12/49	4876	7/46	2945	,,	6/1935	2	,,	10/62
64877	4/48	4877	12/46	2946	,,	6/1935	2, 1(9/52)	,,	9/59
64878	8/49	4878	12/46	2947	,,	7/1935	2	,,	10/62
64879	9/48	4879	11/46	2948	,,	7/1935	2	,,	2/61
64880	3/48	4880	10/46	2949	,,	7/1935	2	,,	11/62
64881	9/49	4881	11/46	2950	,,	7/1935	2	,,	10/62
64882	11/48	4882	12/46	2951	,,	8/1935	2	,,	9/59
64883	7/49	4883	12/46	2952	,,	8/1935	2	,,	4/61
64884	10/48	4884	12/46	2953	,,	8/1935	2	,,	3/60
64885	11/48	4885	12/46	2981	,,	8/1935	2	,,	3/62
64886	4/51	4886	12/46	2982	,,	9/1935	2	,,	2/61
64887	7/48	4887	12/46	2983	,,	9/1935	2	,,	11/62
64888	4/48	4888	12/46	2984	,,	9/1935	2	,,	1/60
64889	4/49	4889	12/46	2985	,,	9/1935	2	,,	10/62
64890	2/50	4890	11/46	2986	,,	9/1935	2	,,	8/60
64891	6/48	4891	12/46	2987	,,	9/1935	2	,,	3/60
64892	4/48	4892	12/46	2988	,,	9/1935	2	,,	2/60
64893	4/48	4893	12/46	2989	,,	10/1935	2	,,	5/61
64894	4/50	4894	1/47	2990	,,	10/1935	2	,,	7/60
64895	9/48	4895	12/46	2991	,,	10/1935	2	,,	10/59
64896	5/49	4896	12/46	2992	,,	10/1935	2	,,	8/60
64897	3/49	4897	12/46	2993	,,	10/1935	2	,,	12/62
64898	5/49	4898	1/47	2994	,,	10/1935	2	,,	2/60

B.R. No.		1946 No.		Orig. No.	Maker	Works No.	Built	Class Part (Tender Type) (a)	Brake	Withdrawn
64899	4/48	4899	12/46	2995	Darlington		8/1936	2	V	10/62
64900	6/48	4900	12/46	2996	"		8/1936	2	"	7/59
64901	1/49	4901	10/46	2997	"		8/1936	2	"	10/61
64902	6/49	4902	12/46	2998	"		8/1936	2	"	3/60
64903	9/50	4903	11/46	2999	"		8/1936	2	"	4/62
64904	6/48	4904	5/46	3000	"		8/1936	2, 1(11/54), 2(2/60)	"	10/61

B.R. No.		1946 No.		Orig. No.	Maker	Works No.	Built	Class Part (Tender Type) (a)	Brake	Withdrawn
64905	6/48	4905	9/46	1803	Beyer, Peacock	6802	9/1936	2	V	9/59
64906	3/49	4906	4/46	1813	"	6803	9/1936	2	"	4/61
64907	3/51	4907	8/46	1824	"	6804	9/1936	2, 1(1/60)	"	11/62
64908	8/48	4908	8/46	1828	"	6805	9/1936	2	"	3/61
64909	10/48	4909	8/46	1854	"	6806	9/1936	2	"	4/61
64910	2/51	4910	8/46	1856	"	6807	9/1936	2	"	11/62
64911	7/48	4911	8/46	1857	"	6808	10/1936	2	"	11/62
64912	8/48	4912	3/46	1869	"	6809	10/1936	2	"	12/59
64913	1/50	4913	3/46	1870	"	6810	10/1936	2	"	10/59
64914	7/48	4914	6/46	1532	"	6811	10/1936	1	"	7/61
64915	7/48	4915	4/46	1533	"	6812	10/1936	1	"	3/62
64916	11/48	4916	3/46	1534	"	6813	10/1936	1, 2(4/61)	"	8/61
64917	5/50	4917	6/46	1536	"	6814	10/1936	1	"	12/62
64918	11/49	4918	5/46	1539	"	6815	10/1936	1	"	12/62
64919	2/50	4919	5/46	1540	"	6816	11/1936	1, 2(1/60), 1(2/60)	"	11/61
64920	5/49	4920	6/46	1543	"	6817	11/1936	1, 2(6/60)	"	12/62
64921	4/48	4921	6/46	1544	"	6818	11/1936	1	"	11/62
64922	2/50	4922	8/46	1545	"	6819	11/1936	1	"	10/62
64923	12/49	4923	6/46	1547	"	6820	11/1936	1	"	11/62
64924	8/51	4924	5/46	1563	"	6821	3/1937	1	"	12/62
64925	6/48	4925	8/46	1577	"	6822	4/1937	1, 3(1/50), 1(12/59)	"	10/62
64926	1/50	4926	9/46	1580	"	6823	4/1937	1	"	12/62
64927	11/49	4927	3/46	1585	"	6824	4/1937	1, 2(9/52)	"	7/61
64928	10/49	4928	6/46	1586	"	6825	4/1937	1	"	11/62
64929	8/51	4929	9/46	1587	"	6826	5/1937	1	"	7/61
64930	9/48	4930	7/46	1875	"	6827	5/1937	1	"	10/61
64931	4/49	4931	9/46	1880	"	6828	5/1937	1	"	7/61
64932	9/48	4932	7/46	1894	"	6829	5/1937	1	"	7/61

B.R. No.		1946 No.		Orig. No.	Maker	Works No.	Built	Class Part (Tender Type) (a)	Brake	Withdrawn
64933	8/50	4933	4/46	1508	Darlington		12/1937	1	V	12/62
64934	7/51	4934	6/46	1509	"		1/1938	1	"	12/62
64935	6/48	4935	6/46	1535	"		2/1938	1	"	12/62
64936	12/48	4936	3/46	1537	"		2/1938	1	"	12/62
64937	4/48	4937	5/46	1538	"		2/1938	1	"	2/60
64938	3/50	4938	3/46	1541	"		3/1938	1	"	11/62
64939	4/49	4939	4/46	1542	"		3/1938	1	"	4/62
64940	2/50	4940	6/46	1546	"		3/1938	1	"	12/62
64941	12/49	4941	6/46	1548	"		3/1938	1, 2(10/61)	"	12/62
64942	6/50	4942	8/46	1551	"		3/1938	1	"	12/62
64943	6/49	4943	7/46	1558	"		4/1938	1	"	12/62
64944	4/48	4944	8/46	1560	"		4/1938	2, 1(11/38)	"	12/62
64945	9/49	4945	8/46	1804	"		3/1938	2	"	10/62

Summary of J39 Class (continued)

B.R. No.	1946 No.	Orig. No.	Maker	Built	Class Part (Tender Type) (a)	Brake	Withdrawn
64946	1/49	4946 7/46	1808	Darlington	3/1938	2	V	12/62
64947	4/48	4947 5/46	1835	"	4/1938	2, 1(7/54)	"	5/62
64948	4/48	4948 3/46	1862	"	4/1938	2	"	4/60
64949	11/48	4949 7/46	1896	"	4/1938	2	"	8/62
64950	9/49	4950 3/46	1863	"	4/1938	2	"	12/62
64951	7/49	4951 9/46	1898	"	4/1938	2	"	3/60
64952	8/51	4952 1/46	1903	"	4/1938	2	"	3/60
64953	4/48	4953 3/46	1922	"	5/1938	2	"	3/60
64954	4/48	4954 7/46	1926	"	5/1938	2	"	3/60
64955	8/49	4955 8/46	1927	"	5/1938	2	"	7/62
64956	10/50	4956 9/46	1928	"	5/1938	2	"	3/60
64957	9/48	4957 3/46	1930	"	5/1938	2	"	3/60
64958	4/48	4958 9/46	1933	"	5/1938	2, 3(6/59)	"	3/60
64959	10/48	4959 4/46	1940	"	5/1938	2	"	1/60 (b)
64960	7/50	4960 6/46	1942	"	6/1938	2	"	2/60
64961	4/50	4961 6/46	1943	"	6/1938	2	"	10/59
64962	12/48	4962 6/46	1952	"	6/1938	2	"	3/60
64963	6/50	4963 1/46	1965	"	6/1938	2	"	1/62
64964	9/48	4964 6/46	1971	"	7/1938	2	"	4/61
64965	6/49	4965 9/46	1974	"	7/1938	2	"	3/60
64966	11/49	4966 6/46	1977	"	7/1938	2	"	7/60
64967	7/48	4967 6/46	1980	"	7/1938	2	"	2/60
64968	1/49	4968 4/46	1984	"	7/1938	2	"	3/60
64969	9/50	4969 11/46	1996	"	8/1938	2	"	11/62
64970	9/48	4970 11/46	1997	"	8/1938	2	"	5/61
64971	1/51	4971 6/46	3081	"	2/1941	3, 1(5/58)	"	6/62
64972	6/48	4972 4/46	3082	"	2/1941	3	"	12/59
64973	1/49	4973 6/46	3083	"	2/1941	3	"	11/59
64974	8/48	4974 4/46	3084	"	3/1941	3	"	8/60
64975	9/48	4975 6/46	3085	"	3/1941	3	"	12/62
64976	4/48	4976 6/46	3086	"	3/1941	3	"	11/59
64977	6/48	4977 6/46	3087	"	4/1941	3, 2(6/59)	"	2/60
64978	12/50	4978 3/46	3088	"	4/1941	3	"	12/62
64979	1/51	4979 8/46	3089	"	5/1941	3	"	1/62
64980	12/48	4980 7/46	3090	"	5/1941	3	"	12/59
64981	6/49	4981 9/46	3091	"	5/1941	3	"	2/60
64982	5/49	4982 7/46	3092	"	5/1941	3, 2(2/50), 1(4/50)	"	12/62
64983	10/48	4983 8/46	3093	"	6/1941	3	"	11/59
64984	3/48	4984 5/46	3094	"	6/1941	3	"	12/59
64985	10/48	4985 10/46	3095	"	7/1941	3	"	12/59
64986	9/49	4986 7/46	3096	"	7/1941	3	"	12/62
64987	5/48	4987 9/46	3097	"	7/1941	3	"	3/61
64988	6/50	4988 12/46	3098	"	8/1941	3	"	12/59

(a) Class parts dispensed with after December 1952. Subsequent tender changes included for completeness.

(b) No. 64959 was withdrawn 1/1/60 but was included in the 1959 Statistical Year withdrawals.

CLASSES J40 AND J41

M. & G.N. CLASSES D AND D REBUILT – S. W. JOHNSON
5ft. 3in. ENGINES

ENGINES TAKEN OVER 1ST OCTOBER 1936 (Built 1896-99):
CLASS J40 – 058/9, 060/1/3-7, 070/2/3.
TOTAL 12
CLASS J41 – 062/8/9, 071. TOTAL 4.

The early locomotive working arrangements of the M. & G.N. were briefly discussed in Part 4 of this series (page 117). Here it will suffice to say that, on the formation of the Joint Committee in 1893, the M. & G.N. did not possess any 0-6-0 tender engines, but relied on a most ill assorted collection of locomotives to work the goods traffic. However, following the introduction of 4-4-0's of Midland Railway design in 1894, the Joint Committee ordered from Neilson & Co. in January 1896, at £2,345 each, eight 0-6-0's of S. W. Johnson's standard Midland type which were delivered later that year. Then, in May 1898, the Joint Committee accepted the tender of Kitson & Co. for the supply of a further eight similar 0-6-0's at £2,830 each. These engines were built in 1899, the last one being delivered on 29th April, as stated in Johnson's report on the M. & G.N. engine stock read at the Joint Committee meeting on 9th January 1900. In the same report Johnson recommended the purchase of a further twelve six-coupled goods engines. To this the Committee agreed and tenders were invited to be received by the Secretary of the M. & G.N. Joint Committee at King's Cross by 6th March 1900, on which date the Committee met but postponed consideration of the tenders. Then, at the meeting on 1st May, the Committee was informed that the Great Northern had offered to transfer to the M. & G.N. "twelve new six wheels-coupled goods engines, delivery to be made on or before September next at

contractor's price of £2,985 each". The G.N.R. offer was accepted and the tenders which had been submitted for Johnson 0-6-0's were declined. Thus did Johnson's efforts to impose a pattern of uniformity on the M. & G.N. locomotive stock come to an abrupt halt. The Derby drawing office copy of the specification for the twelve Johnson 0-6-0's was duly endorsed "Not let on 6th March 1900, 12 goods engines bought of G.N. Ry. instead and known as class DA, Nos. 81-92". (For full details of the 0-6-0's acquired from the G.N.R. see Part 5, pages 12-32).

Variations in the sixteen Johnson 0-6-0's first appeared in 1906 with the rebuilding of No. 62 with a Midland Railway round-topped class H boiler, with a maximum outside diameter 6¼in. greater than that of the original boilers. A further engine was similarly rebuilt in 1909, and in 1921 two more were rebuilt with R. M. Deeley's Belpaire version of the H class boiler. Finally, in 1923 and 1928, the two H class rebuilds were also fitted with Belpaire boilers. The four engines rebuilt with Belpaire boilers were known as class "D Rebuilt". When first taken over by the L.N.E.R., the engines retained their M. & G.N. classifications, but in July 1942 the unrebuilt engines became class J40 and the rebuilds class J41. For convenience the 1942 classifications have been used as far as possible. even when referring to events of an earlier period.

As mentioned in Part 4 (page 114), some of the M. & G.N. engines in service when the L.N.E.R. took over the operation of the Joint Line on 1st October 1936 were not taken into L.N.E.R. locomotive stock as they were considered to be worn out. Five of the Johnson 0-6-0's came into this category, these being Nos. 63/6/7, 72 of class J40, and No. 68 of class J41, which were

M. & G.N. Nos.	Maker	Order No.	Works Nos.	No. Built	Date
58-65	Neilson & Co.	E761	5032-9	8	1896
66-73	Kitson & Co.	205W	3873-80	8	1899

withdrawn from service in 1936-37. During 1937 the remaining eight J40's and three J41's were officially added to L.N.E.R. stock. Withdrawals of both classes, took place at intervals, the J41's becoming extinct in 1943, followed by the J40's in 1944.

The J40's were built to a standard Midland Railway design, of which the Midland had several hundred examples, and the Somerset & Dorset Joint Railway also had a few. The last unrebuilt example of the Midland engines was not withdrawn from B.R. stock until 1951, seven years after the design had disappeared from the L.N.E.R.

Standard L.N.E.R. Dimensions, 1937

	J40	J41
Cylinders (2 inside)	$18'' \times 26''$	$18'' \times 26''$
Motion	Stephenson with slide valves	
Boilers:		
Max. diam. outside	4' 3"	4' $9\frac{1}{8}$"
Barrel length	10' 6"	10' $5\frac{11}{16}$"
Firebox length outside	5' 11"	7' 0"
Pitch	7' $1\frac{5}{16}$"	7' $7\frac{7}{8}$"
Diagram No.	46A	46C
Heating surface:		
Firebox	110 sq.ft.	127 sq.ft.
Tubes	968 sq.ft.*	1,257 sq.ft.
Total	1,078 sq.ft.	1,384 sq.ft.
No. of tubes ($1\frac{3}{4}$" diam.)	194	252
Grate area	17.5 sq.ft.	21 sq.ft.
Boiler pressure	160 lb./sq.in.	175 lb./sq.in.
Coupled wheels	5' 3"	5' 3"
Tender wheels	4' $2\frac{1}{2}$"	4' $2\frac{1}{2}$"
Tractive effort (85%)	18,184 lb.	19,890 lb.
Length over buffers	50' $2\frac{1}{16}$"	51' $8\frac{1}{2}$"
Wheelbase:		
Engine	8' 0"+8' 6"=16' 6"	
Tender	6' 6"+6' 6"=13' 0"	
Total	37' $8\frac{1}{4}$"	38' $9\frac{1}{4}$"
Weight (full):		
Engine	38T 16C	46T 11C
Tender	33T 11C	33T 11C
Total	72T 7C	80T 2C
Max. axle load	15T 1C	16T 10C
Water capacity	2,950 galls.	2,950 galls.
Coal capacity	3T 0C	3T 0C

* Engines with 194 tubes; the L.N.E.R. engine diagram showed No. 060 still with 196 tubes. (No. 063 had 196 tubes in 1936, but was one of the engines not taken into L.N.E.R. stock, and is thus not mentioned on the diagram).

L.N.E.R. Renumbering

With the exception of three J40's withdrawn in 1937, these engines had an "0" prefix added to their M. & G.N. numbers by the L.N.E.R. including Nos. 063/8 which were *not* taken into L.N.E.R. stock (see the Summary).

The five surviving J40's were allotted Nos. 4100-4 in the L.N.E.R. general renumbering scheme prepared in July 1943, but by the time that the printed version appeared in December 1943 No. 071 had been withdrawn and the number 4104 was left blank. The remaining four engines were withdrawn before the scheme was introduced in January 1946.

Rebuilding

CLASS J40

These 0-6-0's were built to the final 1896 version of Johnson's standard (small-boilered) Midland design. The original boilers on all sixteen engines were of M.R. class B, the same class of boiler being used also on the M. & G.N. class C 4-4-0's (L.N.E.R. class D52). The class B boiler had been introduced on the Midland Railway in 1874, but over the years there had been alterations in tube arrangements and details and, by the time that the J40's appeared in 1896, it had become Midland standard practice to make the boilers of mild steel in place of the wrought iron previously used, although the basic external dimensions remained unaltered from those of 1874.

The barrels were made in three lap-jointed rings with outside diameters, from front to back, of 4ft. 1in., 4ft. 2in. and 4ft. 3in. respectively. There were 244 $1\frac{3}{4}$in. outside diameter tubes, giving a heating surface of 1,142 sq.ft. which with the firebox figure of 110 sq.ft., gave a total of 1,252 sq.ft. Here it should be explained that at this time it was the practice at Derby to calculate the tube heating surface from a tube length which included not only the distance between tubeplates but also the thickness of the two tubeplates. Furthermore, the old Derby practice was to make no deduction for the firehole or for the tubeholes in the firebox tubeplate when calculating the firebox heating surface. (On page 119 of Part 4 it was stated incorrectly that the original tube heating surface figure included the area of the front tubeplate).

Derby had introduced an altered tube arrangement for the class B boilers built from 1909 onwards, with 196 $1\frac{3}{4}$in. tubes, giving a tube heating surface of 989 sq.ft. and a total of 1,099 sq.ft. Subsequent spare boilers supplied to Melton Constable by Derby appear to have had this arrangement, although in some cases Derby

Source of figures	Tubes	Tube H.S. (sq.ft.)	Firebox H.S. (sq.ft.)	Total H.S. (sq.ft.)
Derby 1909,				
M. & G.N. 1936	196 × 1¼″	989	110	1,099
Derby 1910	,,	977	103	1,080
Derby 1916	,,	977.5	102	1,079.5
M. & G.N. 1936	194 × 1¼″	979	110	1,089
Derby c.1923	,,	967.5	102	1,069.5
L.N.E.R. Diagram	,,	968	110	1,078

supplied boilers without tubes. Spare boilers to the Derby design were also built at Melton Constable, the dates of these boilers being indicated by small plates on the front end frames of the engine below the smokebox, lettered "BOILER M. & G.N. 19--". Photographic evidence suggests that most of the J40's had Melton-built boilers when taken over by the L.N.E.R.

Derby had evidently had some misgivings about their method of calculating heating surface figures, and in 1910 had produced new figures based on the methods in use elsewhere, but had not adopted these figures for existing designs. Then in 1916 Derby drawing office produced a revised table of "Standard Heating Surfaces" calculated as agreed on by the Association of Railway Locomotive Engineers in November1914. The 1916 figures were based on a tube length measured between tubeplates, with deductions made in the firebox figure to allow for the area of the firehole and of the tube holes in the firebox tubeplate, and in fact differed but little from the 1910 figures; but Melton Constable apparently continued to use the original Derby figures.

Early in the 1920's the standard number of tubes began to be reduced to 194, thus introducing yet another set of figures! By the time that the L.N.E.R. took over the working of the M. & G.N., ten of the twelve J40's had boilers with the final arrangement of 194 tubes (as shown in the table of standard L.N.E.R. dimensions), but Nos. 60 and 63 still had 196 tubes. The L.N.E.R. recalculated the tube heating surface figures but unfortunately retained the 1909 Derby figure of 110 sq.ft. for the firebox.

Whilst these variations may be considered to some extent academic, it is felt that the reasons should be explained in order to account for the varying figures which have been published in the past (see accompanying table).

No new boilers had been fitted to the J40's for some years prior to their being taken over by the L.N.E.R. The newest boiler was that on No. 64, dated December 1924.

CLASS J41

As built, the M. & G.N. Johnson 0-6-0's had boilers with a maximum outside diameter of 4ft. 3in., but on both new and rebuilt 0-6-0's the Midland Railway had introduced in 1903 the class H boiler with a barrel formed in two rings having outside diameters of 4ft. 8in. and 4ft. 9½in. Melton Constable ordered one of these boilers from Derby in 1904 and fitted it to No. 62 in 1906. To accommodate the new boiler, which had a firebox 13in. longer than the original boiler, extension plates were fitted to the frames at the back end. Larger cab side panels were provided but the upper part of the cab remained as before. Johnson's final pattern of smokebox door with hinge straps, and a centre locking handle and handwheel, was fitted and the chimney was of the flowerpot type introduced by the Midland in 1903. The new boiler had 258 1¾in. outside diameter tubes giving a heating surface of 1,303 sq.ft. (recalculated as 1,285.5 sq.ft. in 1916) and a firebox heating surface of 125 sq.ft. (118.5 sq.ft. by the 1916 calculations). The grate area was 21.1 sq.ft. and the working pressure 175 lb. per sq.in. In 1909 No. 69 was similarly rebuilt and given a cab like No. 62.

R. M. Deeley had introduced a Belpaire version (class G7) of the H boiler at Derby in 1909 and in the same year M. & G.N. 4-4-0 No. 45 was rebuilt with one of these boilers (see Part 4, page 120), followed by others of the class in subsequent years. On the Midland Railway the 0-6-0's began to be rebuilt with G7 boilers in 1916, but it was not until 1921 that any M. & G.N. 0-6-0's received this class of boiler. No. 68 and 71 were rebuilt in that year, and showed a number of variations from the standard Midland design.

Contrary to Derby practice *at that time* the M. & G.N. G7 rebuilds retained their original frames (as did a number of L.M.S. post-Grouping rebuilds), requiring extension plates to be provided at the back to accommodate the longer firebox. An extended smokebox was fitted, and the frames were also lengthened at the

the front end. The cab, whilst basically of the same design as the Midland rebuilds of 1916 onwards, had a lower roof without a ventilator. This lower roof, together with the front-end frame extension and longer smokebox, contrived to give the M. & G.N. rebuilds a curiously elongated appearance when compared with the orthodox Derby design. The two H rebuilds, Nos 62 and 69, were rebuilt with G7 boilers in 1923 and 1928 respectively. The G7 boilers are believed in all cases to have been supplied by Derby.

It is possible that some of the four G7 rebuilds may at first have had the original Derby tube arrangement with 254 1¾in. tubes, but in the early 1920's the standard number of tubes was reduced to 252, which figure appeared in M. & G.N. records dated 1936 and on the L.N.E.R. engine diagram. The M. & G.N. heating surface figures of 1936 were based on the original Derby method of calculation, giving a tube heating surface of 1,273 sq.ft. and a firebox figure of 127 sq.ft., making a total of 1,400 sq.ft. As with the J40's, the L.N.E.R. corrected the tube figure but retained the original figure (of 127 sq.ft.) for the firebox which, according to the Derby recalculation (using the A.R.L.E. method of 1914), should have been 122.75 sq.ft.

Before leaving the subject of boiler dimensions, it is perhaps appropriate to point out that the Derby boiler diagrams identified the diameter of a boiler by the outside diameter of the front ring, whereas the L.N.E.R. diagrams referred to the maximum outside diameter. In the case of the J40's the Derby figure was thus 2in. less than the L.N.E.R. figure, whilst for the J41's the Derby figure was 1½in. less.

TABLE OF REBUILDING DATES

No.	H boiler	G7 Boiler (J41)
62	1906	12/1923
68	–	8/1921
69	1909	1/1928
71	–	6/1921

Details

When new the D class had 5ft. 2½in. wheels with 2¾in. tyres, but the fitting of 3in. tyres in later years increased the wheel diameter to 5ft. 3in.

In later M. & G.N. days, Midland-style brass power classification numerals were fitted to the upper cab side sheets. As on the Midland Railway, the unrebuilt engines were class 2 and the large-boilered rebuilds class 3.

Carriage warming apparatus had been fitted to J40's Nos. 059/60/1/4/5/70/3, of which Nos. 061/5/73 are known to have had both front and rear end connections. Carriage warming, with both front and rear end hoses, was also fitted to J41's No. 062/9/71 of which No. 071 received the apparatus in the course of a heavy repair at Stratford completed in April 1938. It is not known whether any other M. & G.N. Johnson 0-6-0's ever had carriage warming. Although the front-end hoses were not unduly conspicuous, their presence was made very evident by the lagged steam pipe running along the left-hand platform angle-iron (fig. 49).

As built, all sixteen engines had steel-faced wooden buffer planks as was normal practice on contemporary Midland 0-6-0's. On the four Belpaire rebuilds these were replaced by solid steel bufferbeams, and in later M. & G.N. days the majority of the unrebuilt engines also received this pattern. A feature of the original bufferbeams had been the characteristic Johnson style curved ends, and this was retained on the new beams on the J41's, although on the J40's the new bufferbeams had straight ends (see figs. 48/9 and 52).

Rather unusually for 0-6-0's, the maker's plates were on the leading splashers. This was a relic of the early days of these engines when the more usual position on the driving splasher had been occupied by the armorial device of the M. & G.N. Joint Committee. The four J41's had lost their original plates on rebuilding, but the majority of the unrebuilt engines kept their maker's plates until withdrawn. The only plates on the J41's were the boiler date plates on the main frames ahead of the leading splashers. These boiler date plates could also be found on most of the J40's (fig. 48).

CLASS J40

As built, all sixteen engines had Johnson's standard Midland Railway cast-iron chimneys tapering inwards towards the top, but these were eventually replaced by chimneys tapering towards the base, with raised front lips. There was also a similar pattern of chimney without a raised lip which seems to have been fitted to most of the twelve unrebuilt D class engines by the 1930's (fig. 48), although Nos. 065 and 073 still had chimneys with raised lips as late as 1937 (fig. 49).

The original flush-fitting Johnson smokebox doors with plate hinges were replaced in the 1920's or early 1930's by the later dished variant of Deeley's smokebox door with hinge straps and secured by clips. At the same time the handrail over the top of the smokebox door was replaced by a straight rail across the door.

On the L.N.E.R. engine diagram a short wide chimney, tapering towards the base, is shown with a height from rail to top of chimney of only 11ft. 9½in. Whilst this chimney was fitted to class J41 No. 069 (see later) and a number of class D52 and D54 engines, no evidence has been found that any of the J40's ran with one.

The safety valves were arranged in the usual fashion for Johnson small-boilered engines with a pair of Salter spring balance valves on the dome and a single direct-acting safety valve on the firebox, the latter valve being encased in a brass "funnel", to quote the term used in contemporary Derby specifications (fig. 48). This arrangement remained unaltered throughout the lives of the J40's, although the L.N.E.R. diagram described the safety valve on the firebox as a lock-up valve.

At least one engine, No. 058, had received an extended cab roof by 1937 (fig. 54). The roof was extended almost to the rear of the footplate and was supported on pillars which rested on the top of the lower cab panel a few inches forward of the rear edge. Photographs of this engine taken in May 1937 show M. & G.N. livery with the extended cab roof, the number 058 in final M. & G.N. style on the front bufferbeam, and in quasi-L.N.E.R. style on the cab side, in combination with the letters "M. & G.N." on the tender (fig. 54).

The J40's had retained the old Midland arrangement of using the small ejector as a blower, but after 1936 Stratford fitted independent blowers to Nos. 061 and 073 and possibly others (fig. 51). The independent blower was operated by a rod running along the right-hand side of the boiler above the vacuum train pipe.

Class J41

When Nos. 62, 68 and 71 were rebuilt with G7 boilers in 1921-3, Melton Constable with typical individuality fitted Midland-pattern dished smokebox doors with hinge straps and centre locking wheels and handles as on Johnson's final Midland designs, in conjunction with continuous handrails curving over the top of the smokebox door. This was a style which had gone out of vogue at Derby in 1906, and which the Midland had never used in conjunction with an extended smokebox. Deeley 2ft. 5$\frac{7}{16}$in. chimneys were fitted, these being the same as on the Midland G7

rebuilt 0-6-0's. Details of No. 69 as first rebuilt cannot be confirmed, but by the early 1930's all four engines were running with Deeley-pattern dished smokebox doors with clip fastenings and straight handrails and had 2ft. 5$\frac{7}{16}$in. chimneys (fig. 55).

In 1935-36 Nos. 68, 69 and 71 had their smokeboxes lengthened and at the same time received new tapered stovepipe chimneys (fig. 53). No. 71 was also provided with a jumper-top blastpipe, but on this very free steaming class of engine, the blast had a tendency to lift the fire, requiring the fireman to keep the firehole door open continuously.

Later, No. 069 was fitted with a short, wide, downward tapered chimney with a raised front lip as fitted to some of the D52's and D54's (fig. 52). This was the pattern of chimney shown on the L.N.E.R. engine diagram of class J41.

No. 062 retained the original shorter version of the extended smokebox, but by 1939 had received a Deeley 2ft. 2$\frac{7}{16}$in. chimney, possibly acquired from one of the D54's (fig. 50).

All four engines had twin Ramsbottom safety valves on the firebox, but Nos. 68 and 71 which had boilers built in 1921, had in addition a single lock-up safety valve behind the Ramsbottom valves. This was a Midland Railway practice discontinued in the early 1920's. However, No. 071 had lost its lock-up valve by 1939. The L.N.E.R. diagram compromised by showing the lock-up valve behind the Ramsbottom valves on the drawing portion of the diagram but including only the Ramsbottom valves in the table of "Leading Dimensions & Ratios".

Although the J41's should have been painted in the L.N.E.R. standard goods livery of unlined black, the three engines taken into L.N.E.R. stock were repainted in black with red lining. No. 069 was turned out thus from Stratford Works in 1938, whilst Nos. 062 and 071 were photographed in lined black livery in May 1939 (fig. 52).

Brakes

Johnson's usual Midland Railway arrangement of steam brake on the engine and tender with vacuum ejector for the train brakes was provided. The small ejector was mounted on the back of the firebox with its exhaust pipe passing through the boiler to the blastpipe top, thus performing the function of a blower. The vacuum train pipe ran from the cab along the outside of the boiler on the right-hand side (where it served as a handrail) to the large ejector which was mounted on the side of the boiler just to the rear of the smokebox tubeplate. The front-end train pipe passed under the cylinders and curved up the side of the boiler to a tee-connection at the rear end of the large ejector casting (fig. 48). Steam for the large ejector was supplied through a valve which was mounted on the front ring of the boiler and operated from the cab by rodding which ran alongside the boiler behind the train pipe.

Tenders

The engines were built with Midland Railway pattern tenders of Johnson's design, holding 2,950 gallons of water and 3 tons of coal, although the contemporary Midland 0-6-0's had 3,250-gallon tenders. One modification carried out quite early by Melton Constable was to reduce the size of the shovelling hole in the tender front plate, although the beading following the profile of the original opening was retained. To increase the coal capacity the M. & G.N. provided the tenders of the four J41's with an additional coal rail on each side (cf. figs. 48 and 52), together with a vertical plate across the back of the coal space. However, the L.N.E.R. engine diagram for the J41's omitted the additional coal rail and still showed the coal capacity as 3 tons.

Since the M. & G.N. did not have any water troughs, none of the tenders was provided with a water scoop. Whittaker tablet catchers were mounted on the left-hand side of the tender (fig. 49).

Allocation and Work

The class J40 and J41 0-6-0's were always regarded on the M. & G.N. as goods locomotives and were not diagrammed like the 4-4-0's for mixed traffic duties, e.g. a passenger working out and a goods train back. Nevertheless, at times of heavy traffic in the summer when there was a shortage of power, both classes were used on ordinary and special passenger trains.

The J40's were principally used on goods traffic between Yarmouth Beach, Melton Constable and South Lynn. They worked to Norwich City and Peterborough rather less frequently and on odd occasions to Spalding. They steamed freely and could sustain a good speed, but had little water to spare. Water was always a cause of concern to M. & G.N. enginemen because consumption was high when handling heavily loaded trains, particularly if a strong headwind was blowing across the Fens.

For this reason the G.N. type 0-6-0's, which carried more water, were generally kept on duties at the western end of the M. & G.N. system. At times the J40's were used to assist heavy excursion trains from the Midlands to Yarmouth onwards from South Lynn. They were usually detached at Melton Constable, the stretch from South Lynn being the hardest part of the M. & G.N. route.

The four class J41 rebuilds were kept for the heaviest and fastest goods turns. At one time in Joint days Nos. 62/9, 71 were allocated to South Lynn where they formed a separate link involving three duties. These were: (1) a fast goods to Melton Constable, then back with a fish train through to Peterborough and returning to South Lynn on a fast goods, (2) a return trip to Peterborough with fast goods trains and (3) an empty coal train to Bourne, returning to Lynn with a fast goods. No. 68 was stationed at Melton Constable and was employed on a duty which began with the aforementioned coal empties to South Lynn (where engines were changed), returning to Melton with a through goods train. This was followed by a short trip to Holt and back. As the water capacity of the tenders attached to the rebuilds was not increased, the water problem was even more pressing than on the unrebuilt engines. The increased boiler pressure was a help, but the loads hauled by the J41's were generally higher.

Frequently M. & G.N. engines were grossly overloaded by standards ruling elsewhere: on one occasion in the summer of 1936 rebuilt 0-6-0 No. 68 was called upon to work seventeen Gresley bogie coaches to Weybourne. It stalled with this enormous load at Holt down distant signal, on a gradient of 1 in 90. The train had to be divided and then re-assembled at Holt station.

At the time of the takeover by the L.N.E.R. the allocation of these 0-6-0's was:- Melton Constable Nos. 58, 61/4/7, 70/2, Yarmouth Beach 66/9, South Lynn 59, 60/2/3/5/8,71/3. Withdrawals began almost immediately and within a year four J40's (Nos. 063, 66/7, 72) and J41 No. 068 had been condemned. In September 1938 No. 059 was sent from South Lynn to Melton Constable where it replaced No. 058 which was withdrawn the same month. In October 1939 class J41 No. 062 was scrapped. The depletion in the M. & G.N. stock of 0-6-0's was initially met by transferring ex-G.C.R. class J11's to the section. These were followed by J17's from the G.E. Section, which type eventually took over the majority of the goods workings on the M. & G.N. The outbreak of War

Fig. 51   Class J40 No. 061 at Melton Constable, May 1939.

Independent blower with operating rod above vacuum train pipe alongside boiler. Note M. & G.N. classification "D" in L.N.E.R. style on bufferbeam.

Fig. 52   Class J41 No. 069 at Stratford shed, March 1938.

Short wide tapered chimney, steel bufferbeam with curved ends, lined black livery, tender with three coal rails.

Fig. 53   Class J41 No. 071 at Peterborough North station, May 1939.

Lengthened smokebox with stovepipe chimney. Note Midland Railway style lamps as used on the M. & G.N.

Fig. 54   Class J40 No. 058 on a goods near Melton Constable, May 1937.

Extended cab roof, M. & G.N. livery with quasi-L.N.E.R. style numbers on cab side but M. & G.N. style on front bufferbeam.

Fig. 55   Class J41 M. &. G.N. No. 62 on a South Lynn-Melton Constable goods near Massingham, August 1936.

Deeley dished smokebox door and 2ft. $5\frac{7}{8}$ in. chimney.

in 1939 caused a slowing down in withdrawals and no more J40's were condemned until 1941. Thereafter they went steadily, No. 059 of Melton Constable being the last to go in June 1944. The remaining two J41's were also withdrawn in this period, the class becoming extinct in July 1943 when No. 071 of South Lynn was condemned.

Engine Diagrams

Section M. & G.N., 1937. Class D. Diagram shows engine with short wide chimney. Details given for 194 boiler tubes with a note that engine No. 60 had 196. Reclassified J40 in 1942

Section M. & G.N., 1937. Class D Rebuild. Short wide chimney depicted. Reclassified J41 in 1942.

Classification: J40 – Route availability 3 (the class did not, in fact, survive the publication of the scheme in 1947); J40 and J41 – Southern Area load class 2.

Summary of J40 and J41 Classes

1946 No.	1936 No.		Maker	Works No.	Built	L.N.E.R. Class	Withdrawn
–	058	10/36	Neilson & Co.	5032	8/1896	J40	9/38
(4100)	059	8/37	”	5033	8/1896	”	6/44
–	060	11/37	”	5034	8/1896	”	5/41
–	061	1/39	”	5035	8/1896	”	12/42
–	062	5/37	”	5036	8/1896	J41	10/39
–	063	10/36	”	5037	9/1896	J40	2/37*
(4101)	064 by	5/37	”	5038	9/1896	”	3/44
(4102)	065	9/37	”	5039	9/1896	”	3/44
–	(066)		Kitson & Co.	3873	3/1899	”	10/37*
–	(067)		”	3874	3/1899	”	1/37*
–	068	11/36	”	3875	4/1899	J41	11/36*
–	069	3/37	”	3876	4/1899	”	7/42
(4103)	070	1/38	”	3877	4/1899	J40	3/44
–	071	5/37	”	3878	4/1899	J41	7/43
–	(072)		”	3879	4/1899	J40	10/37*
–	073	9/37	”	3880	4/1899	”	5/41

* Not taken into L.N.E.R. book stock.

2-6-0 CLASSES
SUMMARY OF CLASS TOTALS

Class	Rly.	1-1-23	31st December															
			1923	1924	1925	1926	1927	1928	1929	1930	1931	1932	1933	1934	1935	1936	1937
K1	G.N.	8	8	8	8	8	8	8	8	8	7	6	5	5	4	1	
K2	G.N.	67	67	67	67	67	67	67	67	67	68	69	70	70	71	74	75
K3	G.N.	10	10	37	70	70	70	70	90	99	119	119	119	132	159	185	193
K4	L.N.E.																1
Total		85	85	112	145	145	145	145	165	174	194	194	194	207	234	260	269

Class	31st December															
	1938	1939	1940	1941	1942	1943	1944	1945	1946	1947	1948	1949	1950	1951	1952
K1								1	1	1	1	62	71	71	71
K2	75	75	75	75	75	75	75	75	75	75	75	75	75	75	75
K3	193	193	193	193	193	193	193	192	192	192	192	192	192	192	192
K4	6	6	6	6	6	6	6	5	5	5	5	5	5	5	5
K5								1	1	1	1	1	1	1	1
Total	274	274	274	274	274	274	274	274	274	274	274	335	344	344	344

Class	31st December															
	1953	1954	1955	1956	1957	1958	1959	1960	1961	1962	1963	1964	1965	1966	1967
K1	71	71	71	71	71	71	71	71	70	67	60	48	31	24	
K2	75	75	74	70	62	56	24	10	2						
K3	192	192	192	192	192	192	180	163	121						
K4	5	5	5	5	5	5	5	5							
K5	1	1	1	1	1	1	1								
Total	344	344	343	339	331	325	281	249	193	67	60	48	31	24	Nil

The 2-6-0 type originated in the U.S.A in 1842. At first intended for slow goods work, later designs were developed for mixed traffic duties but by the turn of the century this wheel arrangement was regarded as too small for such work on main lines in America. The first British 2-6-0's were fifteen built for the G.E.R. in 1878-79 for the Peterborough to London coal traffic. These engines, which had a number of American features, were not a success and all were withdrawn during 1885-87. By the end of the century the need for new construction of locomotives in Britain had outstripped the ability of the workshops of some railway companies to keep up with demand. Outside contractors in this country also had full order books and so a number of railways turned to suppliers in the U.S.A. The G.C.R., G.N.R. and M.R. all ordered 2-6-0 goods engines to meet their needs. These locomotives were very American in design and were constructed to that country's idea of a short working life to be followed by replacement by more modern designs, and all had gone to the scrap yard by the end of 1915.

Meanwhile, during the early 1900's there had been an increase in the number of fast goods services run in Britain, often powered by specially-designed 0-6-0's with wheels larger in diameter than hitherto customary. This period also coincided with the adoption of superheating as a means of increasing the efficiency of locomotives. Churchward on the G.W.R. and Gresley on the G.N.R. both appreciated at about the same time that the 2-6-0 wheel arrangement might prove suitable for development to operate this traffic. The engines concerned would also be useful for working special and holiday passenger trains at peak periods, a role that the 0-6-0 had in the past performed. The extra weight of the superheater could better be carried by a pair of leading wheels and the resultant wheel arrangement would also be a more satisfactory vehicle on the track at higher speeds. Churchward's 43XX class 2-6-0 appeared first in June 1911 and was followed just over a year later by Gresley's design. Both had 5ft. 8in. coupled wheels and outside cylinders. The mixed traffic 2-6-0 type was further developed in Britain and rose to its zenith during the thirties, but thereafter was displaced by the 4-6-0 and 2-6-2 types and then sank back to use mainly on slow goods work.

In Gresley's first design the boiler was 4ft. 9¼in. in diameter and a total of ten engines was built. For further construction, from 1914 onwards, the size of the boiler was increased to 5ft. 6in. and sixty-five engines of this type were turned out up to 1921. Before Grouping, two of the earlier engines were rebuilt with the bigger boiler. The L.N.E.R. classified the remaining eight original engines K1, the larger engines taking the classification K2. During 1931-37 the remaining engines of class K1 were rebuilt to K2, so that eventually there were seventy-five engines in the latter class. They were used extensively on the N.B. and G.E. Sections as well as on their native G.N. lines. Withdrawal took place in 1955-62.

In 1920-21 Gresley built for the G.N.R. ten three-cylinder 2-6-0's with a boiler of the very large diameter of 6ft. 0in. On these engines he made the first use of his simplified conjugated valve gear using two-to-one levers for the middle cylinder. This type of locomotive, classified K3 by the L.N.E.R., represented the maximum development of the 2-6-0 design in Britain. It was adopted as a Group Standard design and 183 more were built up to 1937 when construction ceased on account of the introduction of the class V2 2-6-2 for main line mixed traffic duties. In 1945 Thompson rebuilt class K3 No. 206 with only two cylinders. A boiler of similar design as before, but working at a higher pressure, was

used. The rebuild was classified K5 and remained a solitary example. It was scrapped in 1960, whilst the K3's were withdrawn in 1959-62.

Class K4 was a special design for the West Highland line and was introduced in 1937. Only six engines were built. The wheel diameter was reduced to 5ft. 2in. and the three cylinders were similar to the K3 type. A 5ft. 6in. boiler was fitted, basically of K2 size but with a B17 firebox. In 1945 Thompson rebuilt No. 3445 with two cylinders, forming class K1 (this classification having become vacant in 1937). After Thompson retired in 1946, Peppercorn adopted the K1 class as a standard design and placed an order for seventy new engines of this type. They were not however delivered until 1949-50, in B.R. days. The prototype K1 was withdrawn in 1961, whilst the new engines lasted until 1961-67. The remaining K4's were all withdrawn during 1961, one of them, *The Great Marquess,* being preserved, as also was No. 62005 of class K1.

CLASSES KI AND K2
G.N.R. CLASSES H2 AND H3 – GRESLEY
5ft. 8in. ENGINES

CLASS K1 – ENGINES AT GROUPING (Built 1912-13): 4630/2/3/4/6-9. TOTAL 8.
CLASS K2 – ENGINES AT GROUPING (Built 1913-21): 4631/5/40-99, 4700-4. TOTAL 67.

In January 1912 Gresley's attention was drawn to the number of goods trains which were being worked by passenger engines. A new class of engine was urgently required specially designed to haul the heavier goods trains, which the passenger engines could not manage, at speeds of 30 to 40 miles per hour. Drawings were quickly prepared for such an engine with a 2-6-0 wheel arrangement. The pony truck was intended to reduce wear on the leading coupled wheels and track, thereby providing steadier riding than with the 0-6-0 type and thus permitting higher speeds with safety. Gresley incorporated his patent double swing link suspension which he afterwards used in all his designs which had pony trucks.

The boiler was based on that fitted to the Ivatt

superheated 0-8-0's (L.N.E.R. classes Q1 and Q2), with however a shorter barrel. The Schmidt 18-element superheater was the largest practicable in the 4ft. 8in. diameter barrel. The cylinders were 20in. diameter by 26in. stroke, with 10in. piston valves above them, outside the frames and operated by Walschaerts valve gear. Similar cylinders were afterwards used in a number of other two-cylinder classes, culminating in the Peppercorn class K1 2-6-0's some thirty-six years later.

In March 1912 the construction order was issued for the first engine. The G.N.R. already possessed some 2-6-0 goods engines of American origin (class H1), so that when No. 1630 appeared in the following August it was classified H2. That same month a further nine engines (Nos. 1631-9) were ordered and these were turned out during the early part of 1913. These later engines had 3ft. 2in. diameter pony truck wheels instead of 3ft. 8in. as in the first engine.

Drawings appeared in July 1913 for a larger diameter boiler which it had been decided to fit to the next batch of 2-6-0's, ordered one month later. The barrel was 5ft. 6in. diameter instead of 4ft. 8in. though the distance between the tubeplates was almost identical. The firebox casing was 6in. longer overall but, as the throatplate sloped backwards, the effective length at the bottom was the same. The larger barrel provided room for a 24-element superheater, this time of the Robinson type. Longer frames were used and the distance between the leading coupled axle and the pony truck wheels was increased by 4 inches. Nos. 1640-9 appeared in 1914 to the new design and were classified H3.

Ten similar larger diameter boilers were ordered in October 1913 for fitting to Ivatt 0-8-0's. In the event only No. 420 was thus rebuilt, in February 1914 (L.N.E.R. class Q3), and the remaining nine boilers were held back for use on the next batch of new 2-6-0's, ten of which were ordered in July 1914 on the eve of the outbreak of War. There was some delay before Nos. 1650-9 appeared, spread over the whole of 1916, and there were sufficient detail differences for these later engines to receive a separate Part classification in early L.N.E.R. days. In particular the coupled wheel axle journals and connecting rod cranks had larger bearing surfaces.

In 1915 the G.N.R. called for quotations for the construction of thirty more 2-6-0's. Beyer Peacock quoted a price of £4,050 each, without tenders, and in June 1915 an order was placed with this firm for twenty, only, at a special price of £3,800 – Doncaster supplying rough axles, tyres, steel boiler plates and frame plates. In

January 1916 quotations were called for in connection with a further fifteen engines, but in this case no contract was awarded.

Beyer Peacock ran into production difficulties after making a start on the order. There was of course a war on and the Ministry of Munitions clamped down on further work. Eventually, after negotiations between the Ministry and the G.N.R., the Chairman of the company, Sir Frederick Banbury, arranged for the order to be transferred to the North British Locomotive Co. in November 1917 for completion. Beyer Peacock forwarded on the wheels, valve gear and firebox wrapper plates together with the part-finished material they had originally received from Doncaster. Nos. 1660-79, which had a new cylinder arrangement, were delivered in 1918. The original contract price agreed between the G.N.R. and Beyer Peacock in 1915 was paid, eventually, by the G.N.R. to the Ministry of Munitions who apparently settled the accounts of both manufacturers based on the true costs.

A final batch of twenty-five engines was ordered in February 1920 from Kitson's, at a price (without tenders) of £9,960, which was a considerable increase over the previous contract. The actual cost to the G.N.R. was £10,036 as it included £27 for extras not in the original contract and £49 G.N.R. expenses. Nos. 1680-1704 were delivered between June and September 1921, after delays caused by the coal strike that year which badly affected industry. These engines when new were distinguished from the earlier engines by having Ross pop safety valves and no cylinder piston tail rods.

The construction of the seventy-five engines is summarised in the accompanying table.

G.N.R. Nos.	Maker	Order No.	Works Nos.	No. Built	Date
Class H2					
1630	Doncaster	270	1354	1	1912
1631-9	,,	272	1372-80	9	1913
Class H3					
1640-9	,,	277	1425/6/8-35	10	1914
1650-9	,,	281	1466-75	10	1916
1660-9	N.B. Loco. Co. (a)	L698 (b)	21971-80	10	1918
1670-9	,,	L699 (c)	21981-90	10	1918
1680-1704	Kitson & Co.	492T (d)	5330-54	25	1921

(a) Transferred from Beyer Peacock; Order No. 01050, Works Nos. 5955-74.
(b) Completed at Hyde Park Works.
(c) Completed at Queen's Park Works.
(d) Doncaster E.O. 295 also allocated, 1/1921.

No spare boilers were constructed for the original H2's, but the position was eased in 1920 when No. 1635 was rebuilt to class H3. The engine entered works in December 1919 and was subject to a certain amount of cannibalisation. The coupled wheels were removed from their axles, altered and then fitted to No. 1000, the first three-cylinder 2-6-0. New wheel centres were then ordered for No. 1635, which eventually re-entered traffic in June 1920. No. 1631 was also rebuilt in March 1921.

By the end of 1921 the G.N.R. possessed a stud of seventy-five 2-6-0's with two cylinders, well suited to both express goods and ordinary passenger work. They were also employed on express passenger work in the West Riding where their extra adhesion gave them an advantage over the four-coupled engines on the gradients out of both Leeds and Bradford. The eight H2's became L.N.E.R. class K1 and the H3's became class K2.

Confusion can arise over the subdivision of class K2. From 1924 to 1929 distinction was made between the original engines (Nos. 4640-9)

in Part 1 and those with larger bearing surfaces (Nos. 4650-4704) in Part 2. No account was taken of Nos. 4631/5 which had been rebuilt from class K1, with their shorter frames and different wheel spacings. Class parts were reintroduced in 1938 by which time class K1 had become extinct by rebuilding. Part 1 was then used for these ten rebuilds (Nos. 4630-9) and Part 2 for the remaining engines.

It was not until 1955 that the first K2, No. 61722, was withdrawn. The class became extinct in June 1962 with the withdrawal of No. 61756, by which time inroads had already begun into class B1, which had been designed as a replacement for the K2's, amongst other classes.

L.N.E.R. Renumbering

In 1946 Nos. 4630-4704 were renumbered 1720-94 in number order. It should be noted that the two batches which were delivered from Hyde Park and Queen's Park Works of the N.B. Loco. Co. (Nos. 1660-9 and 1670-9 respectively) were delivered simultaneously during 1918.

Standard L.N.E.R. Dimensions at Grouping

	K1	K2
Cylinders (2 outside) ..	$20'' \times 26''$	
Motion	Walschaerts with 10" piston valves	
Boiler:		
Max. diam. outside ..	4' 8" (a)	5' 6"
Barrel length	11' 8"	11' 11$\frac{1}{8}$" (b)
Firebox length outside	8' 0"	8' 6"
Pitch	8' 7"	8' 8$\frac{1}{2}$"
Diagram No.	6	3
Heating surface:		
Firebox	136 sq.ft.	152.0 sq.ft.
Tubes	647 sq.ft.	1082.0 sq.ft.
Flues	296 sq.ft.	395.5 sq.ft.
Total evaporative ..	1079 sq.ft.	1629.5 sq.ft.
Superheater	230 sq.ft.	305.0 sq.ft.
Total	1309 sq.ft.	1934.5 sq.ft.
Tubes	$118 \times 1\frac{3}{4}$"	$197 \times 1\frac{3}{4}$"
Flues	$18 \times 5\frac{1}{4}$"	$24 \times 5\frac{1}{4}$"
Elements	$18 \times 1\frac{1}{4}$"	$24 \times 1\frac{1}{4}$"
Grate area	24.5 sq.ft.	24 sq.ft.
Boiler pressure ..	180 lb./sq.in.	
Leading wheels ..	3' 2" (c)	
Coupled wheels ..	5' 8"	
Tractive effort (85%) ..	23,400 lb.	

Wheelbase:	Nos. 4630-9	Nos. 4640-9	Nos. 4650-4704
Engine	8′ 7″ + 7′ 3″ + 9′ 0″ = 24′ 10″	8′ 11″ + 7′ 3″ + 9′ 0″ = 25′ 2″	8′ 11″ + 7′ 3″ + 9′ 0″ = 25′ 2″
Total (engine and tender)	46′ 10¼″	47′ 5¾″	47′ 7½″ (d)
Length over buffers ..	56′ 6″	56′ 11½″	57′ 1¼″ (d)
Weight (full):			
Engine	61T 14C (e)	63T 14C	64T 8C (f)
Total (engine and tender)	104T 16C (e)	106T 16C	107T 10C
Adhesive	51T 14C (e)	53T 8C	53T 18C (f)
Max. axle load ..	18T 0C (e)	18T 12C	18T 16C (f)

Leading particulars applicable to tenders fitted:

Wheelbase	7′ 0″ + 6′ 0″ = 13′ 0″
Weight (full)	43T 2C
Water capacity	3,500 gallons
Coal capacity	6T 10C

(a) The front ring of the barrel was 4′ 9⅛″ diameter – see p. 65.
(b) The engine diagram quoted 11′ 5½″, which was the length of the barrel less the amount by which the smokebox tubeplate was recessed into it.
(c) 3′ 8″ for No. 4630 only.
(d) The extra 1¼″ was correct for tenders fitted with the later cast steel dragboxes.
(e) K1 weights and therefore applicable only to Nos. 4630/2/3/4/6-9 at Grouping.
(f) Slightly higher figures were quoted by N.B. Loco. Co. for Nos. 1660-79 when new:-

Engine weight	64T 13C
Adhesive weight	54T 11C
Max. axle load	18T 18C

Development and Rebuilding

Other than the completion of the rebuilding of class K1 to K2, the principal alterations made by the L.N.E.R. to these engines were concerned with the overall height, style of cab and system of braking in order to permit their use on the G.E.R. and N.B.R. lines. Although full details of these changes are given in the pages that follow, it may be found helpful to summarise them here.

Shortly after Grouping, the K1's were fitted with short chimneys to enable them to work on the G.E. Section though their appearance here was brief as they were soon replaced by K2's.

In November 1923 drawings were prepared for modifications to the K2's to enable them to work over the G.E. and N.B. Sections. These alterations comprised: short chimney and dome cover, substitution of Ross pop safety valves, lowering of cab roof and repositioning of whistle. In 1924-25 K2's appeared on both these Sections, having been displaced from the G.N. by new K3's. Thereafter the K2's became part of the accepted scene on the hilly West Highland line and the flatter terrain of East Anglia. Twenty engines were fitted with Westinghouse pumps in 1927-28 for working passenger trains on the Liverpool Street-Colchester and Cambridge lines.

From 1931 the remaining eight K1's were rebuilt to class K2 as their boilers became life expired and class K1 became extinct in July 1937.

The spartan cabs of the K2's were not popular with enginemen on the West Highland line and between 1932 and 1935 those in Scotland acquired side window cabs. Later, when further K2's were transferred to Scotland these too were given new cabs.

In June 1944 coal consumption tests were held between No. 4660 and class B1 No. 8301 *Springbok*. The latter was the first of a class of mixed traffic 4-6-0's intended to replace older classes as part of the L.N.E.R.'s post-war five year modernisation plan. The engines were booked to work the 8-35 a.m. Annesley-Woodford coal train and back with the 2-20 p.m.

Woodford-Annesley empty wagon train. The interest in this particular trial lay in the connection between the two designs: the B1 had cylinders which were direct descendants of the K2 type but with improved steam passages. The B1 had the advantage of a high pressure boiler.

The results of the trials are summarised in the accompanying table. The surprising result was the apparent economy in working of the K2 over the B1 for which no explanation was suggested in the report of the trials.

Date	Engine No.	Outward load (wagons/tons)	Return load (wagons/tons)	Coal consumption (lb./train ton mile)
27/6/44	8301	36/606	67/450	0.140
28/6/44	4660	40/661*	68/460	0.121
29/6/44	8301	40/659	67/458	0.130
30/6/44	4660	40/639	67/448	0.120

* Worked 10-0 a.m. special Bulwell Common – Woodford in lieu of scheduled train.

Details

G.N.R. Class H2 – L.N.E.R. Class K1

The main frames were 32ft. 0in. long, parallel throughout and with two lightening holes between the driving coupled and trailing coupled wheels. The largest hole gave access on the left-hand side to a firebox hand hole and on the right-hand side to the manual blow-off cock. Above these holes Nos. 1631-9 had two smaller ones that gave access to additional firebox hand holes. By Grouping, No. 1630 had been brought into line in this respect.

The coupled wheels had laminated bearing springs with nine plates (later increased to eleven) $\frac{5}{8}$in. thick at 3ft. 6in. centres. The coupled wheel journals were 8$\frac{1}{2}$in. diameter and 9in. long. When new, siphon oilboxes were provided for the journals but Wakefield mechanical lubricators were fitted instead from 1915 onwards. The lubricator was located half way along the right-hand side running plate though there was no consistency over its actual position (cf. figs. 56 and 63). (In August 1947, long after the engines had been rebuilt to class K2, instructions were issued that these mechanical lubricators had to be located on these ten engines to conform with the standard arrangement). The dates when mechanical lubricators were provided for the axleboxes were as follows:-

No.	Fitted	No.	Fitted
1630	11/1919	1635	6/1920*
1631	10/1915	1636	4/1918
1632	9/1915	1637	11/1922
1633	10/1923	1638	by 10/1921
1634	11/1915	1639	9/1915

* When rebuilt to class K2.

Gresley's pony truck with double swing link suspension and centring arrangement saw its first use on this class. Its design was intended to equalise the weight on the pony truck wheels when passing round curves. The frames were $\frac{7}{8}$in. thick, spaced 2ft. 11$\frac{1}{2}$in. apart, and the radius bar arm was 6ft. 4$\frac{1}{2}$in. long. The wheels were 3ft. 8in. diameter on No. 1630 only and 3ft. 2in. on the later engines. The bearing springs were laminated type at first with one plate $\frac{9}{16}$in. thick and six plates $\frac{7}{16}$in. thick at 2ft. 6in. centres. Helical springs were substituted at an early date, commencing with No. 1636 in December 1914. Latterly dust shields were provided in front of the axleboxes, though this addition generally did not take place until after the engines had been rebuilt to class K2. However, Nos. 4634/7 acquired them before they were rebuilt (cf. figs. 60 and 62). The upper part of the pony truck crosshead was encased in a box-like structure between the frames in front of the smokebox. The top was hinged to provide access for lubricating purposes, the structure being 6in. deep on No. 1630 but only 3in. on the later engines which had smaller diameter wheels.

The cylinders were a departure from usual Doncaster practice, this being dictated by the employment of outside Walschaerts valve gear. The cylinders were located outside the frames, arranged horizontally and driving on to the middle coupled wheels. The 10in. diameter piston valves had a maximum travel of 5$\frac{3}{8}$in. at 75 per cent cut-off. They were the Doncaster "double admission" type valves, with additional large openings in their circumference that aided starting but had no effect when running. The exhaust clearance was $\frac{3}{8}$in. and the steam lap of the valve $1\frac{5}{16}$in., but these dimensions were changed after 1917 to $\frac{7}{16}$in. and $1\frac{1}{4}$in. respectively. This type of piston valve was retained until after Grouping when it was gradually superseded by the G.E. pattern (Knorr type), see p. 67 under class K2 for further details.

No. 1630 was the first British two-cylinder engine with Walschaerts valve gear, though the G.N.R. had experience with this gear on two rail motors and a few four-cylinder Atlantics. Gresley introduced improvements which were designed to reduce the amount of slip of the radius block in the link by providing a firmer support. Instead of supporting the rear end of the radius rod from a link arm attached to the reversing shaft, the rod was extended through and beyond the radius link. The end was slotted to take a die-block which was attached to the reversing shaft arm. With this arrangement there was very little slip of the die in full gear and the slip was reduced to nothing as the engine was notched up.

The end of the piston valve rod, where it was attached to the combination lever, was guided between parallel sliding surfaces on an extension to the back of the steam chest. This valve spindle guide became a standard feature in later applications of this valve gear to Doncaster designs. The eccentric rods on Nos. 1630-3 were plain but on later engines they were fluted (cf. figs. 59 and 61). The slide bars for the piston rod tapered outwards to clear the connecting rod and were supported by a heavy motion plate which was itself anchored to the running plate above and to the frames at the side, behind the leading coupled wheels. A different arrangement was used for the K2's but these first ten engines were never altered. Plain brass bearings were provided throughout the motion, but in November 1919 No. 1630 was fitted with Ransome & Marles roller bearings at the radius link trunnion, radius link foot, crosshead arm and all three pins in the combination lever.

The engines had ordinary lever reversing gear, which was consistent with their status as goods engines. The reversing rod on No. 1630 was in view alongside the firebox on the right-hand side. On Nos. 1631 onwards a cover was provided beside the firebox to protect the rod and a similar cover was provided on the left-hand side of the engine over the rodding for the cylinder cocks (cf. figs. 59 and 60). In July 1913 No. 1638 was fitted with horizontal screw reversing gear, of the type which was fitted to the small Atlantics (L.N.E.R. class C2). The benefit was presumably

doubtful because the gear was removed some time before Grouping and lever reverse reinstated.

A feature of No. 1630's reversing gear was the vacuum-operated locking gear which held the reversing shaft firmly in position once the driver had set the reversing lever in the desired cut-off setting. The catch which held the lever moved over the range of the quadrant so that it was necessary to connect it by means of a Bowden wire to the application valve on the firebox faceplate. The valve was connected by pipes to the vacuum chamber pipe and to the reversing shaft clutch locking cylinder. According to the position of the catch, air was either admitted to the cylinder to release the grip on the shaft or extracted from it to lock the shaft. Hitherto this locking gear had been fitted only to the Ivatt express passenger Atlantic engines (L.N.E.R. classes C1 and C2) and had not been considered necessary on other types.

The locking gear was not however fitted to Nos. 1631-9 when they were new and the drawing which had been prepared for this purpose was returned to the drawing office endorsed "not required". Nevertheless the next series of 2-6-0, which had larger boilers (see later under class K2), did have the clutch gear and in 1915 the drawing was reissued with instructions that Nos. 1631-9 were to be fitted during the course of repairs. No dates are recorded for the fitting and it is possible that only No. 1634 may have been altered (in November of that year) for the drawing was again withdrawn in June 1916. Three engines were then fitted in 1920: No. 1635 (when rebuilt with a larger boiler) and Nos. 1637/9.

The locking gear still appears to have been considered an unnecessary feature on the 2-6-0's for in August 1921 a start was made replacing the Bowden wire arrangement, which was automatic in action, by a three-way cock on the firebox faceplate which the driver had to operate if he wished to use the clutch gear. Thus the driver could choose not to use this feature if he was working slow moving goods trains or whilst shunting. At such times the locking gear was not only unnecessary but a hindrance. Nos. 1634/7 were altered in this manner during 1922, as well as a number of the later engines with larger boilers (see later).

The live steam pipes from the superheater header ran down inside the smokebox and through the saddle to enter the steam chests on a horizontal plane. A Wakefield mechanical lubricator was provided, mounted on the right-hand running plate just in front of the dip, to supply oil to the cylinders and valves whilst the engine was running. (These lubricators were repositioned above the leading coupled wheels after 1947 on these ten engines). The oil feeds for the steam chest passed through the top of the running plate, with separate feeds at front and back. In July 1915 No. 1636's oil feed was provided with a steam jet attachment which atomised the oil before it came into contact with the piston valves and piston heads. The supply of steam had to be controlled by the driver by means of a valve on the manifold and was not automatically linked to the regulator. The fitting was removed from this engine at a later date before it was rebuilt.

The boiler and outer firebox casing were constructed from $\frac{9}{16}$ in. plate throughout. The barrel was made of two telescopic rings with the front one, unusually for Doncaster, the larger diameter of the two (4ft.9¼in.). The distance between the tubeplates was originally 11ft. 11⅞in. but replacement copper fireboxes had 1in. thick tubeplates, instead of ⅞in., which reduced the distance to 11ft. 11¾in. There were four wash-out plugs on each side of the firebox above the boiler handrail exactly opposite one another, which was unusual (figs. 56 and 57). After Grouping at least five of these boilers were altered to a staggered arrangement of three wash-out plugs on each side (figs. 57 and 60). On the L.N.E.R. the K1 boilers took Diagram number 6 in the boiler classification system. They were not interchangeable with any other class.

Schmidt 18-element superheaters were originally provided, with long-loop elements similar to the type which was fitted for example to the Klondyke No. 988 (L.N.E.R. class C2), but 1ft. 5in. shorter in length. The heating surface was originally quoted as follows:-

Firebox	137.0 sq.ft.
Tubes (125 × 1¾″)	981.0 sq.ft.*
Flues (18 × 5¼″)	
Total evaporative	1118.0 sq.ft.
Superheater (18 × 1¼″)	302.8 sq.ft.
Total	1420.8 sq.ft.

* Combined figure only quoted for tubes and flues.

A damper box was at first fitted over the element ends in the smokebox on Nos. 1630-4 to prevent overheating. This arrangement had certain disadvantages and it was dispensed with on Nos. 1635 onwards, with the earlier engines quickly brought into line. Twin anti-vacuum valves were fitted to the saturated side of the

header on all engines at first, but these were replaced by the single mushroom shaped valve at a later date, before Grouping.

By 1916 an amended heating surface figure had appeared on the engine diagram. In particular, the superheating surface had been recalculated using the more conventional inside area of the elements instead of the outside. There was also a breakdown of the tube figure.

Firebox	136.0 sq.ft.
Tubes	686.0 sq.ft.
Flues	296.0 sq.ft.
Total evaporative	1118.0 sq.ft.
Superheater	229.5 sq.ft.
Total	1347.5 sq.ft.

The top row of small tubes was dispensed with from 1918. In addition the boiler pressure was raised from the original 170 lb. to 180 lb. per sq. in. from 1920. The amended heating surface figure is shown under "Standard L.N.E.R. Dimensions at Grouping".

The smokebox was attached to a separate saddle casting, which was of course necessary as there was neither a cylinder nor steam chest casting between the frames. The chimney was 1ft. 11¼in. high and the distance above rail level to the top was 13ft. 4in. No. 1630's smokebox was 4ft. 6¼in. long whilst those on Nos. 1631-9 were 1ft. 0in. longer (cf. figs. 59 and 60). No. 1630 retained its shorter smokebox until it was rebuilt to class K2.

Ramsbottom safety valves were fitted to the K1's and these were retained to the end, except on No. 4636 which acquired Ross pop safety valves in July 1930 (fig. 60). These latter were mounted on a special raised seating as they could not be fitted directly to a boiler which had been drilled to take the Ramsbottom type.

The underside of the running plate above the coupled wheels was 5ft. 9½in. above rail level, i.e. just sufficient to clear the radius link but not quite high enough to clear the flanges on the 5ft. 8in. diameter wheels. A separate horizontal splasher casing, 7in. wide and 2½in. deep was therefore provided over the wheels. The overall width of the running plate was 8ft. 6in. throughout, whilst the cabs were 7ft. 1in. wide inside and 4ft. 8¼in. long, with circular windows in the front plate. The cabs sides were straight, matching the tender width. The cabs had to be altered when the engines were rebuilt with larger diameter boilers as described later.

No. 1630 had steam-operated sanders in front of the leading coupled and driving coupled wheels (fig. 59), with gravity sanders for reverse running behind the trailing coupled wheels. Nos. 1631-9 differed in that the sanders in front of the leading coupled wheels were gravity fed (fig. 61), the operating rod for which being out of sight below the running plate on the left-hand side, coming into view just in front of the dip behind the cylinders.

In 1919 No. 1635's right-hand frame cracked badly at the front. The fracture was welded and a 1¼in. thick strengthening plate was bolted over the weld on the outside of the frame. It was at this repair that the opportunity was taken to rebuild the engine with a larger boiler and Robinson superheater. No. 1631 was also rebuilt before Grouping. The remaining eight engines continued to run for some time longer in their original condition and then in 1927-28 their Schmidt headers were replaced by the Robinson type, without rebuilding. This alteration only affected the method of attaching the element ends to the header and the superheating surface was unchanged. The dates when the superheaters were changed are set out below:-

No.	Robinson	No.	Robinson
4630	1/1927	1635	6/1920*
1631	3/1921*	4636	6/1928
4632	2/1928	4637	5/1927
4633	10/1928	4638	2/1927
4634	8/1928	4639	2/1928

* When rebuilt.

The original chimney was 1ft. 11¼in. tall (fig. 58) and the same pattern was also in use on the class J6 0-6-0's at Grouping, and afterwards for a variety of ex-G.N.R. classes, including C2, D1, D2, D3, J1, J3, J5 and Q2. In April 1923 Nos. 1630/6/7/9 received 1ft. 5¾in. high chimneys from class R1 0-8-2T's, which reduced the height above rail level to 12ft. 10in. to enable them to work on the G.E. Section of the L.N.E.R. (fig. 56). Nos. 1630/7, which had been called into Doncaster Works specially for this alteration only, continued to run in G.N.R. green livery with "G N R" on their tenders giving the misleading impression that the smaller chimney had been fitted before Grouping. A further three K1's were altered later in 1923 during the normal course of repairs, followed by the last one, No. 4638, as late as August 1924. However, the latter engine remained on the G.N. Section whereas all the others did work for a time on the G.E. Section. At a later date this particular engine was noted once more with a taller chimney. The dates when the K1's acquired R1 chimneys are set out as follows:-

No.	Fitted	No.	Fitted
1630	4/1923	1636	4/1923
1632	5/1923	1637	4/1923
1633N	10/1923	4638	8/1924
1634	6/1923	1639	4/1923

G.N.R. Class H3 – L.N.E.R. Class K2

Nos. 1640 onwards had larger boilers as a result of which certain alterations were necessary. The frames were 32ft. 5½in. long, i.e. 3½in. longer at the rear end, 4in. longer between the leading coupled wheels and pony truck wheels and with 2in. less overhang at the front, when compared with Nos. 1630-9. The frames of the latter engines however were not lengthened when they were afterwards rebuilt with larger boilers so that this distinction between the two sizes of frame remained to the end.

In 1932 a method was devised for replacing the rear half of a badly worn frame, either on both sides of the engine or on one side only according to the severity. A new rear end was butt-welded to the original front half, with the join made between the driving and trailing coupled wheels in line with the running plate support bracket. A strengthening plate was then riveted to the outside face of the frame, so that a frame thus renewed was recognisable by the absence of the large lightening holes (fig. 68). Seven engines were dealt with at Doncaster Works between 1932 and 1939 as follows:-

No.	Side	Date
4640	Left	7/1934
4641	Right	8/1934
4647	Both	5/1938
4657	Left	6/1936
4658	Both	6/1939
4659	Both	8/1932
4660	Left	12/1935

In addition, photographic evidence shows that latterly Nos. 61746/61/7, at least, also had a replacement rear end either on one side or both sides. As far as is known Cowlairs Works never adopted this method.

On Nos. 1640-9 the coupled wheel journals were 8½in. diameter and 9in. long. The laminated bearing springs had nine plates (later increased to eleven), ⅜in. thick at 3ft. 6in. centres. Nos 1650 onwards had larger journals, 9½in. diameter and 11in. long, and their springs had eleven plates. The engines had a Wakefield mechanical lubricator on the right-hand side running plate for axlebox lubrication (fig. 65). In December

1926 No. 4673 was fitted with special axleboxes and Franklin grease lubricators. Lubrication was achieved by means of a solid block of grease which was pressed up against a perforated zinc plate under the journal. Enginemen feared that a hot bearing could develop undetected and normal axleboxes with mechanical lubrication were restored in October 1928.

The pony truck was similar to those fitted to Nos. 1631-9 except that the radius bar arm was 6ft. 7in. long. Nos. 1640-7 originally had laminated bearing springs, with seven plates $\frac{9}{16}$in. thick, whilst Nos. 1648 onwards had helical springs when new. The first eight engines were brought into line before the end of 1914. Dust shields were provided in front of the axleboxes, possibly commencing with No. 1641 when new. No. 4640 was still devoid of them in the early thirties. The top of the pony truck crosshead was encased in a box-like structure between the frames in front of the smokebox. The structure was 3in. deep, as on Nos. 1631-9, and the top was hinged to provide access to the Menno grease cups for lubrication purposes. From October 1940 the lubrication was changed to oil feed. A small siphon oilbox was mounted on the inside face of the right-hand side frame just in front of the smokebox. One feed led to the swing link pins and the second led into the top of the crosshead centre. This entailed deepening the box-like structure above the centre by $3\frac{3}{4}$in., for clearance purposes, though it then fouled slightly the lifting holes in the frame of Nos. 4640 onwards (fig. 74). Guard irons were originally fitted to both the main frames and the pony truck, but the pair on the main frames was dispensed with during the fifties (cf. figs. 68 and 77).

The cylinders on Nos. 1640-9 were identical to those fitted to Nos. 1630-9, with their centres 6ft. 7in. apart and live steam pipes out of sight between the frames. Commencing with No. 1650, the length of the bearing surface of the connecting rod big-end was increased from 5in. to $5\frac{1}{2}$in. The larger bearing meant that the centres through the motion on the two sides of the engine were $\frac{1}{2}$in. further apart, i.e. 6ft. $7\frac{1}{2}$in. The cylinder castings therefore needed a $\frac{1}{4}$in. thicker flange where they were bolted to the frames in order to keep the cylinder centres in line with the motion. Consequently, cylinders were not directly interchangeable between the two distinct varieties (though see later). Apart from the thicker flange, the cylinders on Nos. 1650-9 were similar to those on the previous engines, all of which had a Wakefield mechanical lubricator

fitted on the right-hand side running plate to supply oil to the cylinders and valves whilst working.

The piston valves on Nos. 1640-79 were the Doncaster "double admission" type, as fitted to Nos. 1630-9 (see earlier). The entire valve surface was sprung in the steam chest valve liner to make a steamtight fit. As a result lubrication was difficult, wear was heavy and a good deal of energy was wasted during the actual valve travel. Nos. 1680-1704 had C.P.R. type piston valves. These consisted of a solid centre ring with a $\frac{1}{8}$in. wide split ring on each side of it. The energy lost through frictional resistance was reduced as only the two outer rings were sprung in the liner and not the entire valve as before. The earlier engines were not brought into line. The C.P.R. valve was eventually found to be unsatisfactory due to steam finding its way through the fine gaps between the individual rings.

A new type of piston valve was introduced in 1922 which replaced the C.P.R. type on Nos. 1680-1704. This had a broad split ring (like the earlier Doncaster type) but with the large openings in the lap portion of valve replaced by a number of tiny holes in the circumference, which admitted just sufficient lubricated steam to give a start but which had no effect when running. The chief difficulty remained the problem of getting any lubricating medium along the full length of the ring.

In October 1923 No. 1693N was fitted with G.E. pattern (Knorr type) piston valves. These had a solid (unsprung) head which was $\frac{1}{32}$in. diameter less than that of the valve liner to eliminate friction. Four narrow split rings were fitted in slots in each head to provide the necessary steamtight fit. Diagonal bridges were provided in the port openings of the valve liner to prevent the narrow rings breaking and pieces dropping down into the cylinder below. This arrangement eventually became standard on all engines of classes K1 and K2. The final refinement came in October 1932 when the ring control method was adopted, by which means the valve events were controlled by the outer edges of the two outer rings, positioned further apart, instead of by the heads themselves.

In the early days the chief problem with mechanical lubrication was carbonisation. The G.N.R. already had a few engines with Detroit sight feed lubricators, e.g. Nos. 573/6-80 (L.N.E.R. class J6), and they generally gave less trouble. It was therefore decided to fit this type of hydrostatic lubricator to the later 2-6-0 engines, feeding the oil into the live steam pipes rather than directly into the steam chest so that it was atomised or thoroughly mixed with the steam before it came into contact with the piston valves. As the steam pipes were somewhat inaccessible, this needed a new arrangement in which the steam pipes left the smokebox near to the top of the saddle and passed through the running plate to enter the cylinder casting from the top. Between the smokebox and steam chest the path of the steam was tortuous, with three almost right-angular bends including a short elbow bend casting which became a standard feature in a number of later classes. The lubricating oil was fed into the top of this particular elbow bend. The whole arrangement was hidden from view inside a box-shaped cover (cf. figs. 67 and 69).

Nos. 1660-1704 had Detroit sight-feed lubricators with this new pattern of cylinder. The lubricator was located inside the cab on the fireman's side and the feed pipes ran alongside the boiler to the smokebox. On Nos. 1660-79 these pipes were on both sides of the boiler, but on the last twenty-five engines they were on the left-hand side only (fig. 69). The Detroit lubricators eliminated most of the previous trouble from carbonisation. No. 1644 also acquired a sight-feed lubricator, from the S.E.C.R., in October 1921. On this engine the oil feeds ran along both sides of the boiler and then passed through the smokebox saddle to reach the inside steam pipes. This engine regained a Wakefield mechanical lubricator in the thirties; the date is not recorded but was probably May 1935 when it received a new right-hand cylinder.

When new, the engines up to No. 1679 had cast steel piston heads with tail rod extensions to guide the pistons and so reduce the wear of the cylinder walls. Wear instead took place in the tail rod extensions (fig. 65) and by Grouping these had a renewable brass sleeve, which was screwed into a cast-iron bush then held in place with a nut. Nos. 1680-1704, however, had cast-iron piston heads and the tail rods were dispensed with. In July 1921 No. 1658 was tried out with phosphor bronze rims cast on its steel piston heads and its tail rods were removed. In June 1924 it was reported that trouble was being experienced on those engines with tail rods due to the brass sleeves and their nuts breaking up and pieces dropping down into the cylinders. As a safety precaution it was decided to revert to the earlier arrangement of fitting solid brass bushes. In September 1924 consideration was given to dispensing altogether with these tail rods and they were removed from Nos. 4651/5/9 in

February-March 1925 as an experiment (fig. 67). Following satisfactory reports, tail rods were gradually removed from the remaining engines, possibly commencing with No. 4649 in December 1926.

In 1925 a start was made in replacing the cylinders on Nos. 4630-59 by the later type with outside steam pipes as renewals fell due. This allowed the lubricating oil to be fed into the steam pipe in a similar manner to that on the engines with Detroit lubricators. The change was made gradually, for the cylinders were usually replaced one at a time and occasionally obsolescent cylinders with inside steam pipes were fitted instead. The difference was not readily apparent because Doncaster Works frequently provided two outside steam pipe covers when a cylinder was changed, whether or not they were actually necessary. Some engines therefore ran for a while with two such dummy covers whilst others, which had a later pattern cylinder on one side only, had one genuine cover and one dummy (fig. 68). As far as class K1 was concerned, three engines received outside steam pipe covers as follows:-

No.	Fitted	Remarks
4632	10/32	Both sides dummies
4638	7/31	Left side dummy
4639	by 12/33	Left side dummy

Towards the end of 1937 alternative methods were sought to tackle the carbonisation problem of the piston valves on the engines which still had inside steam pipes. In November 1937 No. 4650 was provided with an additional Wakefield mechanical lubricator, mounted on the left-hand running plate, to enable the piston valves to be fed from separate lubricators. The intention was to fill these with different types of oil and compare the effect. Anti-carbonisers were also provided, which was an innovation on class K2. Nos. 4653/41 were similarly fitted in December 1937 and January 1938 respectively, and probably No. 4643 in May 1938. Nos. 61731/40/3 (ex-4641/50/3) retained the additional lubricator to withdrawal (fig. 75).

From October 1938 anti-carbonisers were fitted to all the K2's with Wakefield mechanical lubricators for their cylinders (Nos. 4630-59), regardless of whether the oil was fed into the steam chest at each end directly above the valve heads (fig. 74) or into the outside steam pipes (fig. 75). This device atomised the oil before it came into contact with the piston valves and thereby reduced the problem of carbonisation. The reason for the delay in the fitting of anti-carbonisers to the engines with the old pattern cylinders could be understood if there had been no significant improvement following the trial fitting in 1915 on No. 1636, mentioned earlier, but there was no such excuse on the engines with the new pattern cylinders, for this fitting had been standard for a number of years on other classes with outside steam pipes. In most cases the steam for the anti-carboniser fittings was taken in the normal manner from the dome, with a shut-off cock on the left-hand side of the smokebox (fig. 74), whilst in a few cases it was taken from the steam manifold in the cab with the steam pipes occasionally in view running along the left-hand side of the boiler but usually out of sight (fig. 75).

No. 4653 was the last K2 to receive outside steam pipe covers, in May 1947. However four months later there was a reversion when Cowlairs Works returned No. 1734 to traffic without its dummy cover on the left-hand side (fig. 74) where it still had the early pattern cylinder which was fitted in 1929. As it needed a cover on the right-hand side for its later pattern cylinder it presented an asymmetrical appearance when viewed head on. It was noted still in this condition as No. 61734 as late as October 1954.

Doncaster Works stocked one size of cylinder casting, with the thick flange as essential for fitting to Nos. 4650 onwards. If a new casting was required for one of the earlier engines in the 4630-49 series, whether K1 or K2, it was first of all necessary to machine off $\frac{1}{8}$in. from the face of the flange to suit the closer setting of the valve motion, as described earlier. This slight difference needed careful attention in the Works to ensure that the correct size casting was used. An error was made on one occasion, about 1945, when one of the earlier engines was given a new cylinder without first of all machining $\frac{1}{8}$in. off the flange. The mistake was realised afterwards but the Running Department was not officially informed. Discreet enquiries were regularly made at the shed by one of the works staff who was always surprised to find that the misalignment was giving no trouble. Not surprisingly there is no official record of the engine concerned and it is understood that the matter was put right at its next shopping.

The engines which were fitted with Detroit sight-feed lubricators do not seem to have presented any problems, though in August 1935 the Scottish Area made enquiries about altering these engines to mechanical feed. Doncaster informed them that there were no conversion drawings available which seems to have put an end to the matter, though there is a suggestion that some of the Detroit lubricators may have been replaced by the similarly acting Eureka type. Latterly, however, No. 61755 was noted with a Wakefield mechanical lubricator for its cylinders and valves though the date of change is not recorded. Latterly too several engines numbered in the 61750-69 series had their sight-feed pipes on the left-hand side of the boiler only, conforming to the arrangement standard for the 61770-94 series. Engines so altered included Nos. 61763/4/7/9 (fig. 76).

The arrangement of the Walschaerts valve gear differed in minor details from its application on Nos. 1630-9. The motion plate was further forward alongside the wheels so that it could only be secured at the top, to the underside of the running plate. The slide bars were shorter and parallel throughout (cf. figs. 64 and 65). Plain brass bearings were provided throughout the motion, except that on Nos. 1655 and 1680-1704 the eccentric return crank pins had Skefko ball bearings. As a wartime measure Hoffmann ball bearings were substituted from July 1940 when renewals were needed.

The engines had ordinary lever reverse, with the reversing rod encased alongside the firebox. All the engines when new had the same arrangement of vacuum-operated locking gear for the reversing shaft as fitted to No. 1630, with a Bowden wire connection between the reversing lever catch and the adjacent application valve on the firebox faceplate. Commencing in August 1921 the Bowden wire arrangement was removed and replaced by a three-way cock on the faceplate, which the driver operated if he wished to take advantage of the locking gear, for example when working an express goods or passenger train. About a third of the class were altered in this manner between August 1921 and March 1923 but it is not clear if the scheme was abandoned or simply that the records are incomplete.

The modification to the design of the big-end made on Nos. 1650 onwards also required an adjustment to the wheel balance, though this does not seem to have been decided upon until after Nos. 1650/1 were both in traffic. Pending production of new wheel centres, those on hand for Nos. 1652/3/4 were adapted by adding extra weights to the spokes and drilling a hole in the main balance weight on the right-hand side. Nos. 1655 onwards had the correct new wheel centres and Nos. 1650/1 were presumably brought into line at a later date. Nos. 4652/3/4 retained their odd wheels into L.N.E.R. days until they eventually needed to be renewed (fig. 66). The official photograph of No. 1680 when new, the first of the Kitson engines, shows an extra balance weight on the driving wheel centres, but in this case no explanation has been found.

The valve settings were modified after Grouping on those engines which worked in Scotland to provide more even thrust on both sides of the piston when working at long cut-offs (instead of at the usual 30 per cent) to suit conditions on the West Highland line where overheated bearings were an early problem when working at 45 to 50 per cent cut-off.

A 9 in.-wide box-like cover in the reverse curve of the running plate provided access to the oil container on the top of the combination lever (fig. 72). This box was removed in the forties from the engines in the Southern Area and replaced by a simple flap in the running plate and a separate siphon oilbox just in front (fig. 75). This modification was not extended to the Scottish engines, except those subsequently transferred from England.

The 5ft. 6in. diameter boiler (L.N.E.R. Diagram 3) was a smaller version of the type introduced in 1913 for the two-cylinder 2-8-0 mineral engines (class O1). The tubes were 4ft. 0in. shorter and the firebox 1ft. 0in. shorter. The firebox throatplate sloped back on the 2-8-0's to clear the horn blocks for the third pair of coupled wheels and this slope was retained for the 2-6-0's so that the same flanging blocks could be used in the manufacture, though there was no similar clearance problem with the K2's. The larger diameter barrel than on the K1 class enabled more tubes to be fitted, though they were the same length as before, and a larger superheater was accommodated. However, although the firebox casing was 6in. longer overall, the horizontal length at the bottom was still 8ft. 0in. because of the sloping throat plate. As thicker plates were used and a wider water space was provided above the foundation ring at the front and rear ($3\frac{1}{2}$in. instead of 3in.), the actual grate area was in fact slightly less. Allowing for the difference in the overall length of the respective boilers and the different method of attaching to the smokebox, the firebox faceplate in the cab was 8in. further back on the K2's than on the K1's.

The boiler barrel was constructed of $\frac{5}{8}$in. plate, with two telescopic rings, 5ft. 6in. (back) and 5ft. $4\frac{3}{4}$in. (front) diameter respectively. The dome casing was located on the back ring. The smokebox tubeplate was recessed $5\frac{5}{8}$in. into the front ring and, prior to 1916, the distance

between the tubeplates was 12ft. 0in. Later copper fireboxes had 1in. thickness tubeplates instead of $\frac{7}{8}$in., which reduced this distance to 11ft. $11\frac{7}{8}$in. Boilers constructed after 1931 had one-piece barrels, tapering slightly from 5ft. 6in. to 5ft. $4\frac{3}{4}$in. so that they could be attached without modification to the original smokeboxes.

The inner firebox was supported by nineteen rows of vertical roof stays with two girder bar stays at the front end. There were six wash-out plugs on the firebox sides, above the boiler handrails, three on each side in a staggered arrangement. The ashpan below the firebox had a front damper door. On the earlier engines the damper rodding ran back below the firebox to the cab. On Nos. 1650 onwards this rodding was located above the running plate, in the shallow casing on the left-hand side of the firebox in company with the rodding for the cylinder cocks and leading sand gear. Nos. 4630-49 were not brought into line.

The unstayed area between the top row of side stays and the end stay of each row of roof stays gave some concern to Gresley. He considered that when the boiler was working, the expansion of the copper firebox tended to pull down the top of the wrapper plate, consequently forcing out the sides. A test was made which proved his theory to be right – the shoulders of the outer firebox casing were forced out under working conditions. Commencing with No. 1642 in October 1919, transverse stays were gradually fitted to these fireboxes as renewals became necessary, and they became standard for new boiler construction commencing with Nos. 1680-1704. There were six transverse stays, positioned after every fourth row of roof stays. The wash-out plugs on the left-hand side of the firebox were repositioned about 4in. further forward than in the earlier boilers to clear the new stays.

The girder bar stays were replaced by one row of expansion and sling stays on new boilers constructed after 1931, but there was no external evidence of this change. However, boilers ordered after March 1934 had inspection doors (hand holes) provided in place of wash-out plugs: three on the left side and two on the right (cf. figs. 67 and 68).

It had originally been intended to fit a Doncaster type 24-element superheater to the first batch of K2's and ten sets were ordered in August 1913. This order was cancelled three months later when it was decided to fit Robinson 24-element superheaters instead. A mushroom-shaped anti-vacuum valve was provided in the usual place behind the chimney and there was no smokebox damper gear.

Over the years a number of different versions of superheating surface figures have been published for the K2's. Originally the outside area of the elements was used in the calculations, instead of the inside, and the area of the elements inside the smokebox was also included. The outside diameter of the elements remained 1¼in. throughout their lives. At first the inside diameter was quoted as 1¼in., then $1\frac{7}{32}$in. as a closer approximation was obtained. From December 1932 10 S.W.G. tubes became standard (1.244in. inside diameter) and this latter figure appeared on engine diagrams from 1938. There was a final reversion to 9 S.W.G. from (officially) November 1944 (1.212in. inside diameter), though this last change was not recorded on the engine diagrams. The various published heating surface figures are quoted in the accompanying table.

Date ..			1914	1916 (a)	1918 (b)
Firebox	..	..	144 sq.ft.	152.0 sq.ft.	152.0 sq.ft.
Tubes ..	..	..	1523 sq.ft. (c)	1131.5 sq.ft.	1082.0 sq.ft.
Flues ..	..	..		395.5 sq.ft.	395.5 sq.ft.
Total evaporative	..		1667 sq.ft.	1679.0 sq.ft.	1629.5 sq.ft.
Superheater	..	..	403 sq.ft.	305.0 sq.ft.	305.0 sq.ft.
Total ..	..	..	2070 sq.ft.	1984.0 sq.ft.	1934.5 sq.ft.
No. of tubes (1¼″ diam.) ..			206	206	197
Boiler pressure (lb./sq.in.)			170	170	170 (d)

(a) These figures first appeared on the 1916 engine diagram.
(b) Top row of tubes deleted 1918.
(c) One combined figure quoted for tubes and flues.
(d) Increased to 180 lb./sq.in. from 1920.

The smokebox was 5ft. 4⅞in. long. The chimney was 1ft. 7½in. high and the distance above rail level to the top was 13ft. 4in. (fig. 65). The same pattern was also fitted to several other classes, including C1, O1, O2 and Q3. Ramsbottom safety valves were originally fitted, except on Nos. 1680-1704 when new which had the Ross pop type. The cabs on Nos. 1640 onwards were remodelled to take into account the larger diameter boilers and longer frames. The width was 8ft. 0in. and the side sheets curved inwards at the rear to match the narrower width of the tender, whilst the length was 1⅛in. less than on class K1 because the firebox faceplate was further back. The horizontal handrail on the cab side was 4in. higher up to match the higher pitching of the boiler handrails. The roof was extended 9in. beyond the rear edge of the cab to provide extra cover for the enginemen and the windows on the front plate were shaped to follow the contours of the firebox and cab roof instead of being circular. The running plate alongside the cab was widened to 8ft. 9in. overall, though in front of the cab the width remained 8ft. 6in. as on the K1's.

As a consequence of the coal strike already referred to, Nos. 1641/74 were converted to oil burning in April 1921 on the Scarab system, as were Nos. 1667/8/9/71 two months later. In August 1921 No. 1666 was converted on the Fowler system, which was employed on the Midland Railway as a modification of the "Best" burner, widely used in America. This particular engine gave some trouble and the head of the experimental section of the locomotive drawing office at Derby, H. Chambers, was sent to King's Cross to investigate the problem. He found that the burner in the firebox had been set too high, causing the oil jet to strike the front portion of the brick arch; this was adjusted correctly. In addition the broken brickwork in the grate was too big, creating large air gaps in several places; this was broken up and spread properly. A trial run was held on 30th September on the 8-10 a.m. slow passenger train from King's Cross to Hitchin and return. The engine steamed freely and the only coal needed, from the reserve tub on the tender, was a few shovelfuls at the start of the outward journey and when running into Hitchin to allow engine duties to be performed with the burner off. The next day No. 1666 worked the 10-32 a.m. slow to Peterborough and returned with the 3-15 p.m. express, loaded to eleven vehicles, around 350 tons. The return trip was carefully monitored. A good start was made and no difficulty was encountered on the bank to Abbots Ripton, passed 3 minutes ahead of schedule, with the boiler full and pressure 160 lb. per sq.in. Up the bank the oil burner had been supplemented with about twelve shovelfuls of coal. The exhaust steam injector was then shut off for a few minutes whilst full boiler pressure was recovered, which was then maintained for the remainder of the journey. The engine steamed well on the bank between Hitchin and Stevenage without any supplementary coal and the latter station was passed 5 minutes ahead of time. Passing Potters Bar a few shovelfuls of coal were spread under the firehole door and the oil burner was completely shut off. The engine coasted for practically the remainder of the journey into King's Cross, where the arrival was 3 minutes early. Nos. 1667/8 were converted back to coal firing in October 1921 followed by the remaining engines a month later.

Drawings were prepared in November 1923 for alterations to be made to the K2's to enable them to work over the G.E. and N.B. Sections, whose respective load gauges were less generous than that of the G.N.R. Nos. 1653/74N were altered first, in December 1923. A new 1ft. 2in.-tall chimney was fitted (of the type fitted shortly before this to class C1 No. 1447N) which reduced the height above rail level at this point to 12ft. 10½in. (fig. 66). The regulator valve was modified and a 2¾in. shorter dome casing fitted. The new dome cover had a flattened appearance and the overall height was reduced to 12ft. 10$\frac{15}{16}$in. (cf. figs. 65 and 66). The Ramsbottom safety valves were replaced by the Ross pop type, which needed a special seating so that they were noticeably higher on these two engines than on Nos. 1680-1704 which already had these valves (cf. figs. 66 and 69). The cab was reduced in height by 3in. and the whistle, whose stem originally passed through the roof, was repositioned immediately behind the safety valves (cf. figs. 65 and 66).

Five new boilers were constructed in 1924 and these too had Ross pop safety valves. Three of these boilers had been drilled to take the Ramsbottom type and therefore needed the special seating. The other two boilers of this particular batch, and all subsequent boilers built from 1926 onwards, were correctly drilled to take

the Ross type and consequently did not need special seatings.

A further nine engines Nos. 4631/44/7/52/6/95/8, 4700/4, were altered to clear the G.E. and N.B. load gauges during 1924. Of these, only Nos. 4695/8, 4700/4 had low-pitched Ross pop safety valves. Some of these engines went to the G.E. Section, whilst others apparently stayed on the G.N., at least for the time being. In December 1924 four of these engines, Nos. 4695/8, 4700/4, were loaned to the N.B. Section, as a result of which a further ten engines, Nos. 4691-4/6/7/9, 4701/2/3, were similarly altered during 1925 and these also went to Scotland.

The remaining engines were gradually altered, mainly during 1927-28 when further K2's were drafted to the G.E. Section. Oddly No. 4671, recorded ex-works in April 1928 as "altered to G.E. Section gauge", was noted shortly afterwards operating on this Section still with Ramsbottom safety valves, which were 13ft. 0$\frac{7}{8}$in. overall height. Dates are not recorded for the alterations in all cases, particularly for the K2's that remained on the G.N. Section, some of which received shorter chimneys before the other alterations (fig. 68). As Doncaster shopped K2's for both the G.N. and G.E. Sections, boiler exchanges led to further engines appearing on the G.E. with Ramsbottom safety valves, including Nos. 4644/7/69. In addition Nos. 4682/9, which had changed to the Ramsbottom type in 1928 for the first time, were transferred to Scotland in 1931-32, where they were strictly out of gauge. Their boilers afterwards rotated amongst other K2's shopped at Cowlairs, Nos. 4694/5, 4704 (fig. 72). By January 1937 there were only four K2 boilers still fitted with Ramsbottom safety valves and their latter history is as follows:-

No. 4647 (5/33-7/37).
Nos. 4672 (10/35-10/37, 4650 (11/37-2/44).
No. 4694 (5/36-11/41).
No. 4704 (2/36-3/40).

The last of these particular boilers, which had been removed from No. 4650 in February 1944, was one which had been fitted with Ross pop safety valves without a special seating when new in 1926, on photographic evidence. If correct, this is the only known example of a Doncaster boiler making such a change from Ross to Ramsbottom.

There were further oddities in the boiler mountings of some engines. For instance, in the early thirties No. 4703 still had its whistle in the original position above the cab roof. No. 4702

Fig. 56   Class K1 No. 1639 at Stratford shed, June 1923.

Reduced chimney and dome, cylinders with inside steam pipes, Ramsbottom safety valves, four wash-out plugs on firebox, mechanical lubricators above driving coupled wheels for axleboxes and in front of reverse curve of running plate for cylinders, L.N.E.R. green livery.

Fig. 57   Class K1 No. 4633 at Colwick shed, August 1926.

Three wash-out plugs on firebox, tail rods to cylinders, black livery.

Fig. 58   Class K1 No. 4638 at Grantham shed, c. 1928.

Original tall chimney and dome, cylinder tail rods removed.

Fig. 59   Class K1 No. 4630 at Colwick shed, September 1926.
3ft. 8in. pony truck wheels, short smokebox, four wash-out plugs on firebox, no cover above running plate alongside firebox, plain eccentric rod, steam operated forward running sanders.

Fig. 60   Class K1 No. 4636 at Mexborough shed, September 1932.
Ross pop safety valves, three wash-out plugs on firebox, cover over rodding for cylinder cocks above running plate alongside firebox, normal length smokebox (cf. fig. 59).

Fig. 61   Class K1 No. 4638 at Doncaster shed, April 1934.
3ft. 2in. pony truck wheels, old style cylinder with dummy steam pipe cover, fluted eccentric rod, gravity sanders in front of leading coupled wheels and steam operated sanders in front of driving coupled wheels.

Fig. 62   Class K1 No. 4634 on a class A goods at New Basford, c. 1928.
Dust shields in front of pony truck axleboxes.

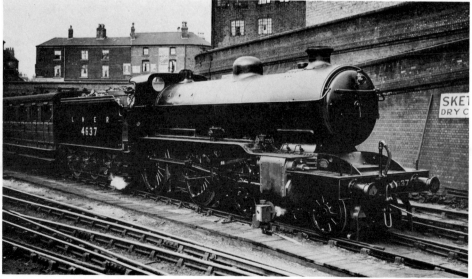

Fig. 63   Class K1 No. 4637 on a stopping train at Nottingham Victoria, c. 1927.
Mechanical lubricator for axleboxes located above motion bracket.

Fig. 64   Class K2 No. 4635 near Burton-on-Trent, May 1925.

Rebuilt before Grouping, retaining K1-style motion bracket, short length cab with deeper cut-out, with lower horizontal handrail and with shaped front windows, mechanical lubricators for axleboxes and cylinders, smokebox door handrail above top hinge strap.

Fig. 65   Class K2/1 No. 1645 at King's Cross shed, c. 1924.

Original 1ft. 7½ in. chimney and tall dome, Ramsbottom safety valves, full length cab with whistle above roof, motion bracket further forward than on K1 class, tail rods to cylinders, mechanical lubricator for axleboxes located above motion bracket and for cylinders above leading coupled wheels, smokebox door handrail below top hinge strap, L.N.E.R. green livery.

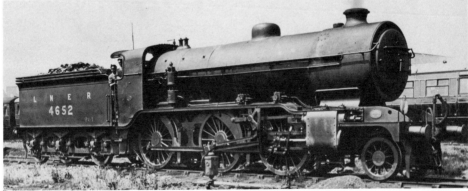

Fig. 66   Class K2/2 No. 4652 at Stratford, c. 1928.

Replacement 1ft. 2in. chimney and low dome, Ross pop safety valves on a raised seating, cab roof lowered 3in. and whistle behind safety valves, Westinghouse pump on side of firebox, old style cylinder with valve lubrication passing through smokebox saddle into steam pipe, hole in balance weight of driving coupled wheel.

(later 61792) was noted in September 1939 with a flat-topped dome cover which it carried through to withdrawal (fig. 78). No. 61792 was noted after its July 1948 repair with a plain chimney which was the normal height though it regained a standard K2 chimney later. No. 61764 was observed in July 1956 with a plain chimney (fig. 76), perhaps the one which had been previously fitted to No. 61792, which it then carried through to withdrawal.

When the K1 engines were rebuilt with larger boilers to class K2 their cabs were widened and shaped front windows replaced the circular ones (cf. figs. 57 and 64). Apart from this essential alteration, there was no consistency in other details, complicated by the fact that the original frames were not lengthened though the firebox was set further back. In the case of Nos. 1631/5 (altered before Grouping) and Nos. 4630/3/4 (altered in 1931-33), the cabs were shortened by about 5½in. and set back so that their rear edges lined up with the back of the frames. In the case of Nos. 4632/6-9 (altered in 1935-37) the cabs were not shortened, so that their whistles had to be positioned off centre to the left in front of the cab to clear the safety valves. A further point of difference was that on the first three rebuilds only (Nos. 1631/5, 4634), the horizontal cab handrails were not raised to match the higher pitching of the boiler handrails (fig. 64). Nos. 61721/2/9 (ex-4631/2/9) eventually acquired side window cabs, see later.

In September 1932 Cowlairs fitted No. 4691 with a cab having a single side window on each side (fig. 70). The remaining engines in the Scottish Area were similarly dealt with in 1933-35 except that the roof was extended 9in. further back to give added protection (fig. 73). No. 4691 was brought into line in March 1935. In December 1945 No. 4639 was transferred to Scotland in exchange for Thompson class K1 No. 3445. No. 4639 was one of the original ten engines with odd cabs, but Cowlairs managed to fit a side window cab in 1949. Because the frames were shorter at the rear, the whistle remained off centre to clear the safety valves. One month after receiving its new cab this engine returned south to remain the sole K2 in England with a side window cab. A further ten K2's were transferred to Scotland during 1951, including Nos. 61721/2 with odd cabs, and they all received side window cabs in 1951-53. No. 61722 was dealt with like No. 61729 (ex-4639) so that its whistle remained off centre. However, No. 61721 had its cab lengthened at the same time and although its whistle remained in line with the safety valves, its

stem then passed through the roof. Altogether thirty-one K2's acquired side window cabs and the dates when they were fitted are set out in the Summary.

In February 1933 sight screens were fitted to No. 4692's original cab (fig. 71) but they were removed in July 1934 when the side window cab was fitted. From August 1938 glass sight screens were fitted to the side window cabs, mainly at first on the engines operating over the West Highland line, but gradually on all the engines in Scotland (fig. 76). From time to time they were noted missing on individual engines, on one side or the other, but they were usually replaced later. A fixed padded seat was provided for the fireman, which in later years was replaced by the tip-up variety. In 1945-46 the engines with side window cabs acquired a seat for the fireman, with a padded back similar to those fitted to the new class B1 4-6-0's.

In 1934-36 the engines which were shedded at Eastfield were fitted with drop grates. The operating rod was on the left-hand side of the engine and ran down at an angle from the cab to the bottom of the firebox (fig. 73). Two more K2's were similarly fitted after nationalisation. The fitting dates were as follows:-

No.	Fitted
4674 (61764)	5/1934
4682 (61772)	7/1934
4684 (61774)	11/1934
4685 (61775)	12/1933
4691 (61781)	3/1935
4692 (61782)	7/1934
4693 (61783)	12/1934
61784	10/1948
61786	12/1949
4697 (61787)	2/1936
4698 (61788)	6/1934
4699 (61789)	6/1934
4700 (61790)	4/1934
4701 (61791)	9/1934
4704 (61794)	2/1936

In August 1930 No. 4647, on the G.E. Section, was fitted with a Stone's smokebox ash ejector. Ash was blown out of the left-hand side of the smokebox through a 2in. diameter pipe which led down between the frames to waste on to the track. This apparatus was still in use at nationalisation. The Scottish Area K2's were fitted with spark arresters inside the smokebox, the earliest fitment dates recorded being April 1947 for Nos. 1784/7/8/9.

The boiler handrails curved round the front of the smokebox and there was a separate handrail on the smokebox door above the top hinge strap (fig. 64). An exception was noted shortly after Grouping in the case of No. 1645 whose door handrail was below the top hinge strap (fig. 65), and No. 4632 was noted likewise about 1933. Six of the Scottish Area engines, Nos. 4694/6/8/9, 4701/4, were also noted about 1934 with their door handrails similarly placed when a new style lampiron was substituted in order to take a destination board (fig. 72). In later days there were numerous exceptions to the general rule, particularly after the introduction of B.R. numberplates in 1948. Handrails then sometimes appeared below the top hinge strap or even above the numberplate, whilst in March 1958 No. 61762 (Eastern Region) was noted with the handrail missing altogether. In addition there were many examples of the knobs being missing from the doors after a visit to Cowlairs Works. Another oddity noted at different times was that the boiler handrails on Nos. 4681/98/9 (pre-war) and 61736/7/48/79, at least, stopped short on the smokebox sides (fig. 73).

The buffers were originally the standard G.N.R. pattern, 1ft. 6in. long, with parallel cases and round bases. The K2's in the Scottish Area usually had packing blocks inserted between the bufferbeam and buffer bases in accordance with Cowlairs practice (fig. 77). Several K2's in England (e.g. Nos. 61727/36) also latterly had these blocks following visits to Cowlairs Works for overhaul. No. 4702 acquired Group Standard

buffers pre-war and they were noted still fitted to this engine (by then numbered 61792) after nationalisation (fig. 68). Buffers with larger diameter heads than usual were noted on, for example, No. 4659/64 (pre-war) (fig. 78) and No. 61781 (after nationalisation). The engines normally had screw couplings at the front end in L.N.E.R. days, but after being transferred to the Scottish Area No. 4693 was noted with an ordinary three-link coupling instead whilst No. 4697 had both screw and three-link couplings for a time. Many of the Scottish K2's were adapted at the front end to take small snow ploughs which could be fitted at the sheds at short notice (fig. 86). The modification consisted of a row of holes in the bufferbeam along the bottom and an extra attachment plate above the bufferbeam in the centre.

Amongst the fittings provided for K2's from time to time are occasional references to speed indicators, though no photographic evidence has been found to show how they were arranged. No. 1646 acquired the Flaman type, fitted at a shed about October 1919. In April 1934 Cowlairs recorded the transfer of a speed indicator from No. 4674 to No. 4700. This indicator, which was reported as being the Smith type, was noted as still being on No. 4700 following a repair visit to Cowlairs in October 1938.

The broad subdivisions of class K2 in L.N.E.R. days are summarised in the accompanying table.

CLASS K2 DIFFERENCES

Nos.	Pony Wheels (diam.)	Engine wheelbase	Cpld. wheel journals	Big-end bearing (length)	Lubricators (b)		Cylinders with outside steam pipes
					Axlebox	Cyls.	
4630	3' 8"	24' 10"	8½" × 9"	5"	Mech.	Mech.	No (a)
4631-9	3' 2"	,,	,,	,,	,,	,,	,,
4640-9	,,	25' 2"	,,	,,	,,	,,	,,
4650-9	,,	,,	9½" × 11"	5½"	,,	,,	,,
4660-79	,,	,,	,,	,,	,,	Detroit	Yes
4680-4704	,,	,,	,,	,,	,,	,,	,,

(a) Outside steam pipes gradually fitted from 1925.
(b) Exceptions and subsequent changes are referred to in the text.

Brakes

Vacuum brakes were provided for engine, tender and train. The K1's had twin 18in. diameter brake cylinders, whilst the K2's had a single 21in. diameter cylinder, in both cases below the cab. The earlier engines were not brought into line when they were rebuilt to class K2 as the shape of the dragbox precluded the fitting of a centrally placed brake cylinder. However Nos. 4632/7/8 acquired *twin* 21in. diameter cylinders when rebuilt in 1936. On the K1's the vacuum ejector exhaust pipe passed through the boiler from the cab to the smokebox, whilst on the K2's the pipe passed along the outside of the boiler on the right-hand side between the handrail and the clothing plate.

In the latter part of 1927 twelve K2's operating on the G.E. Section were provided with an 8in./8½in. Westinghouse air pump for alternative train braking (i.e. the engine and tender brake was still vacuum). A further eight engines were similarly equipped during the early part of 1928, making a total of twenty fitted for working Westinghouse-braked passenger trains. (In 1931 No. 4674 was transferred to Scotland and its equipment was removed and put on to No. 4677). The Westinghouse pump was fitted on the right-hand side of the firebox (fig. 66). The vacuum brake stand-pipe at the front was moved to the opposite side of the draw-hook and its position on the left side (facing) was taken by the Westinghouse brake stand-pipe (fig. 74). During the fifties the Westinghouse equipment was removed from some of the K2's. The vacuum brake stand-pipe was sometimes returned to its original position (where the Westinghouse pipe had been) but in other cases it remained on the wrong side. Full details are not available for the removal of the equipment, but the dates which are known are given in the Summary.

The vacuum brake stand-pipe at the front end of four Scottish Area engines, Nos. 4698/9, 4701/4, was repositioned pre-war behind the bufferbeam, conforming to Cowlairs practice. This was probably done to facilitate the fitting of snow ploughs. These four engines retained this distinctive feature to the end (fig. 86) and in addition No. 61790 was similarly altered after nationalisation.

A number of Scottish Area K2's were equipped with Raven's cab signalling apparatus to enable them to work over the N.E. Area main line. Fitting and removal dates are recorded for four St. Margaret's engines, as follows:-

No.	Fitted	Removed
4694	5/1927	2/1935
4695	8/1927	1/1935
4696	9/1927	12/1933
4702	6/1927	4/1934

In addition Cowlairs recorded its removal from No. 4685, an Eastfield engine, in December 1933 which could have been a clerical error. It would appear likely that the other K2 shedded at St.

Margaret's in the late twenties, No. 4703, was similarly equipped for a while.

As a result of the disastrous collision on 10th December 1937 at Castlecary, it was decided to equip the line between Edinburgh (Waverley) and Glasgow (Queen Street) with automatic train control. The Hudd system, which worked on the electro-magnetic inductive principle, was selected (for a full description see pp. 60/1 of Part 2A of this series). In November 1938 Doncaster was instructed to send fifteen sets of automatic train control equipment to Cowlairs Works, to Derby's drawings, for fitting to K2's. Nos. 4691, 4702/3 were fitted initially in mid-1939, followed by 4684 towards the end of 1940 and finally Nos. 4685/9/92/3/6/7 were fitted in mid-1941. Development work was curtailed by the War and the equipment was soon removed from these engines, though not all dates are recorded. These engines retained the bracket on the pony truck stretcher bar where the receiver had been placed. Fitment dates were as follows:-

No.	Fitted	Removed
4684	11/1940	7/1942
4685	8/1941	12/1941
4689	5/1941	10/1942
4691	8/1939	5/1942
4692	6/1941	
4693	8/1941	
4696	8/1941	12/1942
4697	8/1941	
4702	6/1939	
4703	7/1939	1/1943

Tenders

There were two distinct varieties of the final G.N.R. class B tender, which held 3,500 gallons of water and 6¼ tons of coal. On the earlier examples (numbered 5021-5110) the side sheets curved down at the front end and a hand grip was provided in the curve which it formed (fig. 71). On the post-1912 tenders (numbered 5111-5210/3-22/33-52) the side sheets were extended forward to eliminate this hand grip (fig. 70). All these tenders were built at Doncaster. The various batches of engines which contractors supplied during this period were ordered without tenders, these being provided by the G.N.R.

Tenders built from about 1911 had cast steel dragboxes at the front end which projected forward slightly and there was an extra 1½in. spacing between engine and tender. Older 3,500-gallon tenders were gradually brought into line when it was necessary to replace the original dragbox. This small difference was noted on the engine diagrams issued in 1924 for Nos. 4640-9 and 4650-4704 respectively (see under "Standard L.N.E.R. Dimensions at Grouping"). Because of frequent exchange of tenders the position was more complicated than this simple division suggested. In any case, the actual distance between the rear coupled wheels and leading tender wheels seldom agreed with the nominal figure and no two engines were necessarily alike. As far as class K1 was concerned, the figure shown on the L.N.E.R. engine diagram was for the old style of dragbox.

During the 1921 coal strike seven engines were temporarily fitted for oil burning. The oil was stored in a cylindrical tank of 1,000 gallons capacity on the top of the tender. The engines were converted back to coal firing after a few months and the oil tanks were removed.

In 1923 an extra coping rail was added to several tenders which were at that time attached to large Atlantics (see Part 3A, class C1). One such tender was subsequently paired with No. 4679, by June 1928, but was transferred to a class O2 in June 1934. Another of these tenders was attached to No. 4693 by April 1925, was transferred to No. 4689 in 1938, then temporarily attached to No. 4701 in 1946 and finally finished its time paired with No. 1781 from April 1947 (fig. 77).

From March 1940 two footsteps were provided at the rear of the tender and a vertical handrail was fitted on the left-hand side at the back (fig. 75). In company with certain other classes, the use of the water pick-up apparatus was dispensed with from March 1946. The external fittings were removed after April 1950 in the case of the engines working in England and from towards the end of 1955 in the case of those in Scotland. For working over the former M. & G.N. lines a number of K2's had Whittaker tablet catchers fitted to their tenders. Engines so noted included Nos. 61738/40/2/3/8. In addition engines working latterly on the G.N.S. Section were occasionally noted fitted with tablet catchers, including No. 61766.

Maintenance

The engines were of course shopped at Doncaster Works in G.N. days, but mention must be made of six engines which were sent to Vickers Ltd., Barrow, in 1921 as part of a Government scheme to assist factories hard pressed for work after the War had ended. During the course of the repairs the Doncaster

works plates were mixed up; the possibility even that the frames themselves were mixed up cannot be ruled out, though this is only a conjecture. The works plates displayed before and after the repairs at Vickers were as follows:-

Engine No.	Works No. and Date before	after
1643	1429/14	1429/14
1646	1432/14	1466/16
1649	1435/14	1432/14
1650	1466/16	1435/14
1652	1468/16	1469/16
1653	1469/16	1468/16

The engines which were transferred to the N.B. Section after Grouping were normally shopped at Cowlairs, with four recorded exceptions. No. 4702 spent two weeks in Gateshead Works for light repairs in October 1931 after a collision with class C7 No. 2203 at Blaydon and the same engine, as No. 61792, visited Inverurie twice during 1955. No. 61790 also visited Inverurie in 1956. Those allocated to the G.E. Section were occasionally shopped at Stratford instead of Doncaster, particularly if the repairs were of a light nature. In August 1943 two March engines, Nos. 4648/90, were sent to Cowlairs. Gradually the number of Southern Area engines visiting Cowlairs increased until by 1946 almost all repairs to K2's were being carried out there. On rare occasions K2's visited Gorton Works for casual light repairs, e.g. Nos. 4634 (July 1931), 61747 (January 1954) and 61773 (June 1954).

Liveries

When new, Nos. 1630-51 were painted in the green livery of the period, whilst Nos. 1652-79 appeared in dark grey with the engine only lined out in white. Some of the earlier engines also received this austere livery. The final batch of K2's, Nos. 1680-1704 from Kitson's, were painted green.

Early in 1923 Nos. 1639/45, 1703 were turned out in the new L.N.E.R. green livery (figs. 56 and 65). This was before it had been decided to paint the K1's and K2's black, lined out in red, in which condition the remaining engines gradually appeared, joined by Nos. 4639/45, 4703 in due course. As already mentioned on page 66, Nos. 1630/7 visited Doncaster Works in April 1923 for short chimneys to be fitted which would enable them to work over the G.E. Section. They emerged with paintwork untouched, including the letters "G N R" on their tenders.

For reasons of economy the red lining was omitted from the black livery from November 1941 whilst from July 1942 the lettering on the tender was changed from "L N E R" to "N E". In this respect the K2's were treated no differently from other classes, but as described below its effect was still in evidence until long after nationalisation, which was unusual.

In August 1947 Cowlairs Works began painting K2's in green livery as they passed through shops for general repairs. No. 1782 was the first, followed by Nos. 1732/4 from the Southern Area (fig. 74); otherwise only Scottish engines were thus dealt with. By February 1948 Nos. 1732/4/64/72/6/82/7/8/9/91 were green with the letters "L N E R" in full on the tender.

From March 1948 "BRITISH RAILWAYS" appeared in full on the tenders at general repairs, coincident with the introduction of the new B.R. numbers though No. E1773 ex-Doncaster Works that month provided an example of a K2 with the Regional prefix "E". Cowlairs continued to paint Scottish members of the class in L.N.E.R. green livery and by July 1948 Nos. 61775/81/3/6/90/2/4 had been so dealt with when the practice ceased.

Meanwhile Eastern Region K2's continued to be turned out from both Doncaster and Cowlairs Works in unlined black, including No. 1734 which reverted from green in June 1948 as the result of an accident. Towards the end of April 1948 it was standing in the yard at Stratford shed when it was moved by an untrained employee. Steam pressure was low and on opening the regulator wide the engine "caught the water". No. 1734 proceeded at speed down the yard, across the turntable and ended up in the Channelsea. After some difficulty (a wire broke at the first attempt) it was hauled out and subsequently returned to Cowlairs Works for a light repair.

A full repaint was normally only undertaken at a general repair, whilst at other works visits the paintwork was often simply touched up. Cowlairs in particular had a habit of ignoring the tender and some interesting variations were observed in 1948-49 when engines were renumbered at these other repairs. Nos. 61774/83/93 for example remained plain black and continued to display the wartime letters "N E" on the tender (though No. 61783 acquired green livery two months afterwards at a general repair), whilst Nos. 61764/72/87/8/9/91 retained their green livery and letters "L N E R".

In September 1948 lined-out black livery became standard and the change was normally made at the next visit to works for a general repair. The first style of B.R. emblem appeared on tenders in August 1949 (fig. 77). The later style made its appearance in August 1957 after withdrawals had commenced and was applied to no fewer than twenty-five K2's (fig. 78). Exceptionally, certain green K2's reverted to black at other than general repairs instead of having their paintwork patched up, e.g. Nos. 61782 (lined-out, January 1949), 61790 (unlined, April 1949). Cowlairs' practice of painting tenders at general repairs only, together with some indiscriminate exchanging of tenders, led to further anomalies. No. 61783 (whilst green) acquired a black tender, almost certainly at Cowlairs Works in May 1952, whilst No. 61786 (lined-out black) at the same time acquired a green tender lettered "BRITISH RAILWAYS". No. 61784 (also lined-out black) acquired a tender with the wartime lettering "N E", in December 1950 possibly from No. 61793, and was still attached to it in May 1953.

The dates the K2's were painted green are as follows, together with subsequent dates of reversion to black based on available evidence.

No.	Green	Black
1732	10/1947	8/1949
1734	9/1947	6/1948
1764 (a)	11/1947	6/1950
1772 (a)	2/1948	12/1953
61775	7/1948	10/1951
1776	11/1947	12/1949
61781	5/1948	10/1949
1782	8/1947	1/1949
61783	6/1948	1/1955 (b)
61786	4/1948	12/1949 (c)
1787 (a)	1/1948	6/1951
1788 (a)	12/1947	12/1949
1789 (a)	1/1948	12/1950
61790	4/1948	4/1949
1791 (a)	10/1947	10/1949
61792	7/1948	12/1953
61794	7/1948	5/1949

(a) Retained green livery after receiving B.R. number.
(b) Acquired a black tender, possibly 5/1952.
(c) Afterwards acquired a green tender, possibly 5/1952

Names

In 1933-34 the thirteen K2's which worked regularly over the West Highland line received the names of Lochs near to that line. Loch Shiel was rendered *Loch Sheil* and this was never corrected. Curved nameplates were fitted. These were attached to curved segment-shaped backing plates on the running plate above the middle coupled wheels. The dates the names were applied are given in the Summary.

British Railways

All seventy-five engines entered British Railways stock in 1948 and duly received an addition of 60,000 to their numbers.

Allocation and Work

Gresley's maiden design for the G.N.R. filled an urgent need for more powerful mixed traffic engines enabling expansion of the braked goods services to go ahead. Notwithstanding Ivatt's provision of twenty-five mixed traffic 0-6-0's (L.N.E.R. classes J1 and J2), many instances of fast goods trains being worked by passenger engines were seen. The first allocation of the ten K1's was:- King's Cross 3, Colwick 6, Doncaster 1. The large number at Colwick were used to operate the G.N. braked goods trains running to Liverpool (Huskisson) and Manchester (Deansgate). From London No. 1630 made its inaugural run with the 5-10 p.m. King's Cross-Baldock passenger train on 3rd October 1912. Such workings were destined to fall to the Gresley 2-6-0's for more than twenty years thereafter, since the short distance slow passenger duties could be fitted in between braked goods workings which mainly were at night. In an exacting trial run with a dynamometer car No. 1630 successfully hauled fifty-seven loaded vans from London to Peterborough. Three further tests were made during the last week of February 1914 with the G.W.R. dynamometer car using Nos. 1634 (Peterborough-Hitchin on the 25th), 1635 (Peterborough-Hornsey the following day) and 1631 (Clarence Yard-Doncaster on the 28th). No other details of these tests are available.

When the first ten K2's were delivered in 1914 they were allocated:- King's Cross 4, Colwick 1, Doncaster 3, West Riding 2. This enabled King's Cross to dispose of its three K1's to Peterborough, Colwick and Doncaster. Many changes in the nature of traffic occurred during the War of 1914-18 providing much work for the "Ragtime" engines as the Gresley 2-6-0's were called by the enginemen. It was said this nickname originated on account of the outside Walschaerts motion, until then not a common feature of G.N.R. locomotives, and the fact that the engines could be lively at speed. In later years, particularly in L.N.E.R. days, "Ragtimer" became the accepted nickname. As

successive batches came into service during 1916-18, Peterborough and Doncaster received a large proportion, thus enabling most of the main line fast goods workings to be covered by 2-6-0's and releasing the two Ivatt 0-6-0 classes for less important duties.

Severe disruption was caused to all railways during a prolonged miners' strike lasting from 1st April to 30th June 1921. As the strike progressed successive reductions had to be made in the number of trains run each day. In May drastic cuts were made in the principal express services to and from King's Cross. For instance the normal 10-0 and 10-10 a.m. departures for Scotland and the West Riding were combined in one train leaving at 9-50 a.m. on an easier schedule to compensate for increased loading. Similar combinations involved the 1-30 and 1-40 p.m. departures for Leeds and Harrogate/Hull, and the 5-30 p.m. to Newcastle was combined with the 5-40 p.m. to West Riding towns. Double-heading of these heavy trains was ruled out by the coal shortage thus precluding Ivatt Atlantics from working their rostered turns. To overcome these problems, use was made of Gresley 2-6-0's on all the heavy passenger trains. There has been much publicity concerning the part played by the large three-cylinder engines which eventually became L.N.E.R. class K3, but the smaller Ragtimers were also used. Examples recorded on 23rd May 1921 were: 1-40 p.m. down No. 1664 with sixteen coaches, 5-40 p.m. Newcastle/Leeds No. 1654 on thirteen coaches and 10-30 p.m. down Scottish sleeping car train No. 1656 on fourteen heavy vehicles. The up combined Leeds and Scottish express due King's Cross at 6-48 p.m. was hauled by No. 1668. Another unusual working at the time was No. 1663 on a down eighty-wagon goods train. Such a load was normally only taken by the more powerful 2-8-0's.

As has been recorded in the Details section earlier, several K2's were equipped for oil burning at this time. The first of these to arrive at King's Cross was No. 1674 on 28th May 1921, followed by Nos. 1641/71 on 1st and 4th June respectively. For the most part these oil burners were confined to daytime stopping passenger trains and night goods. Two particular passenger duties noted were on the 1-45 p.m. to Peterborough, arriving back with the 10-0 p.m. slow at King's Cross also the 10-0 p.m. to Hitchin, returning with a goods. No. 1674 was seen on a more arduous duty on 29th June working the 4-15 p.m. semi-fast ex-King's Cross to Peterborough whence it returned with the heavy West Riding express due in London at 9-50 p.m., loaded to fourteen bogies, two six-wheelers plus two vans.

By Grouping, two of the K1's had been rebuilt to K2 and a further twenty-five K2's had been built by Kitson & Co., bringing the total stock of Ragtimers up to seventy-five allocated as follows:- K1- King's Cross 1, Peterborough 1, Colwick 3, Doncaster 2, West Riding 1; K2-King's Cross 14, Peterborough 24, Colwick 2, Doncaster 22, West Riding 5. At this time the G.N. Section was very well provided with mixed traffic engines, having a total of eighty-five including the ten three-cylinder K3's. In the London District during the early months of 1923 the Ragtimers were very much to the fore, regularly working eleven braked goods and four slow passenger trains each day, as well as many special coal trains.

When the first standard K3's entered service in 1924-25 they took over the heaviest braked goods jobs, many of which were subsequently divided into two categories viz: No. 1 express timed at an average of 45 m.p.h. with sixty wagons fully vacuum-fitted and No. 2 express timed at 35 m.p.h. with fifty wagons partially-fitted. It was usual then for the No. 1 braked goods turns to be K3 hauled and the No. 2 by K2's. Receipt of the new K3's, together with a number of class B4 4-6-0's from the G.C. Section, enabled six K1 and six K2 engines to be transferred to the G.E. Section in 1924 and fourteen K2's to the Scottish Area during 1924-25. Both of these events will be described later. Another notable transfer took place in August 1925 when Nos. 4678/88 moved from Doncaster to York in the N.E. Area. They were on trial for a period of eight months whilst two class B15 4-6-0's were at Doncaster.

For the first few years following Grouping those K2's remaining on the G.N. Section continued with the duties they had previously undertaken, except for the fastest and heaviest braked goods trains which had been taken over by the more powerful K3's. In the London District K2's had regular diagrams on two stopping passenger trains to Hitchin or Baldock at 6-2 and 9-10 p.m., the first returning on a local goods at night and the other working an early morning passenger train from Hitchin to King's Cross arriving shortly before 9-0 a.m. For many years K2's appeared on the 4-5 p.m. No. 2 goods for York and the 10-0 p.m. to Nottingham, both of which they took only to Peterborough. As a fill-in duty one sometimes took the 9-25 a.m. High Barnet goods from Highbury Vale, arriving back at 2-45 p.m. The return had to be made

tender-first, but as the grades were mostly downhill this was not a serious drawback. On rare occasions they also worked a similar duty to Edgware. On Sundays one was booked for the 7-15 a.m. empty coaches Hitchin-Huntingdon to form the 8-25 a.m. stopping train to King's Cross.

For the Peterborough engines there was unlimited scope on many of New England's numerous duties, sharing the braked goods with K3's working to London, Colwick, Grimsby and Doncaster. Other regular duties up to 1930 were on the 7-15 a.m. passenger to King's Cross, calling at all stations to Hatfield then Potters Bar and Finsbury Park only. The return was made at 12-35 p.m. with braked fish empties. A well known passenger diagram often worked by New England K2's commenced with the 1-14 p.m. Parliamentary ex-Peterborough, due King's Cross at 4-35 p.m. This train commenced at Leeds Central at 7-8 a.m. and stopped at all stations to New Southgate before making a non-stop dash to Finsbury Park! The return working was the 6-15 p.m. semi-fast to Peterborough. An unusual working for a K2 shewn in the Working Time Tables for 1929-30 was the No. 2 braked goods empties leaving New England at 7-10 p.m. and running to Hertford East via Langley Junction and Hertford North. After reaching Hertford East at 10-8 p.m. the engine was detached and returned light to Hitchin.

Amongst other duties, Colwick engines worked over the G.N. line via Derby (Friargate) to Burton-on-Trent and Stafford, often in the hands of Derby men. One such duty commenced with the 6-22 a.m. Nottingham Victoria to Leicester Central slow passenger train and 8-10 a.m. return, then on to Burton at 10-10 a.m. all stations. Several local trips were then undertaken in the Burton-Derby area before one to Grantham and back to Derby to finish the day at 10-50 p.m. Next day the engine left Derby at 12-50 p.m. on a goods to Stafford Common, afterwards taking the 5-45 p.m. milk train to Egginton Junction, where it came off and the train was taken forward to Grantham by a Colwick J1 or J2 class engine. The K2 remained at Egginton Junction until 10-50 p.m. when it took a second milk train (formed there) to Netherfield, where a Grantham C1 took over. The G.C. main line also saw periodic use of Colwick K2's on excursion and relief passenger trains southwards to Banbury and Marylebone.

Over longer distances there were Colwick workings to York at 12-45 p.m. via Newark and Doncaster and at 10-50 p.m. to Hull by the same route. Both trains were worked on a lodging basis alternating with N.E. Area engines and men. Other notable turns were with beer trains from Burton-on-Trent via Egginton Junction, Derby, Colwick and Newark. The first ran Mondays to Fridays, leaving Burton at 7-45 p.m. for Hull with a return service from Hull at 7-55 p.m. This was taken on a lodging basis by Colwick engines and Derby (Friargate) men alternating with N.E. Area engines and men who lodged at Derby. On Tuesdays and Thursdays there was a 4-15 p.m. Burton-Newcastle beer train, worked by Colwick as far as York. In some cases these turns were shared with G.C. 4-6-0's of class B8 which were allocated to Colwick after Grouping. For many years there were three daily braked goods trains from King's Cross to Colwick. From there one of these ran to Liverpool (Huskisson) via Annesley, Shirebrook, Sheffield and the G.C. route to Guide Bridge and Stockport and one to Manchester (Deansgate) via Guide Bridge. The third train used G.N. running powers over the former Midland line to Manchester travelling via Codnor Park Junction, Chesterfield, Dore and Chinley. All three trains were at times worked by the Colwick Ragtimers but from 1925 onwards class B8 4-6-0's also took a share. On Cup Final days it was usual for two or three K2's to work excursions to King's Cross via Grantham. For instance on 26th April 1930 three well-groomed K2's arrived in quick succession – No. 4643 at 9-47 a.m. from Pinxton, No. 4646 at 10-1 a.m. from Burton-on-Trent and finally No. 4640 at 10-22 a.m. from Derby. All duly returned the same night with their booked trains. In 1931 there were only two through workings, by Nos. 4643 and 4659 from Pinxton and Burton respectively.

Over a period of some five years between 1930 and 1935, Grantham housed a solitary K1: No. 4630 was there from December 1930 until it was rebuilt to K2 in October 1932 and was replaced by No. 4639 which remained until December 1935, when it too was rebuilt. During this time these engines were employed on both slow passenger and goods duties to Nottingham and Lincoln. One regular turn took the 8-10 p.m. passenger to Lincoln returning to Grantham with the 11-30 p.m. goods.

Doncaster used their K2's on a wide variety of duties in all directions. Slow passenger trains were worked to Penistone, Sheffield, Hull, York, Cleethorpes, and Leeds, some having return or outward workings on goods trains. Southwards to Peterborough there were several No. 2 express goods turns and the 12-40 a.m.

parcels on Saturday/Sunday nights. Along with several other types, a K2 often worked the 8-9 a.m. slow passenger from Doncaster to Peterborough via the loop through Lincoln and Boston. As early as 1925 No. 4660 was reported as working between Woodford and Banbury and No. 4661 over the C.L.C. lines beyond Manchester. Doncaster K2's often appeared on the two weekday triangular diagrams operating to York and Hull; the first at 7-18 a.m. from Doncaster to York and 10-5 a.m. York-Hull slow passenger trains, returning direct to Doncaster with the 1-20 p.m. fish from Hull, and the second on slow passenger trains at 1-26 p.m. from Doncaster to Hull, 4-0 p.m. Hull-York and 7-45 p.m. York-Doncaster. The day was completed on the 9-25 p.m. Doncaster-Retford, returning light to Doncaster.

For the first five years after Grouping West Riding K2's were still active on their customary duties. Copley Hill worked mainly stopping passenger trains to Doncaster but Ardsley had a more varied set of diagrams including lodge turns to Liverpool, Manchester, Grimsby and Colwick. After 1928 these duties were taken over by K3's and ex-G.C.R. 4-6-0's of class B6. Apart from an isolated loan to cover the Bowling Tide holidays in 1931 and a few months in 1932-33, no K2's were allocated to the West Riding between 1928 and 1936 when they re-appeared at Bradford and Copley Hill. From Bradford they were regularly used on the through portions of expresses to King's Cross, taken to and from Wakefield (Westgate) normally, but in peak times they worked complete trains to Doncaster and return. Extensive use of them was also made on excursion and relief trains to a variety of destinations, as on 4th September 1937 when No. 4661 of Copley Hill worked the 10-15 a.m. from Leeds Central through to Skegness. The Bradford enginemen were said to have liked the K2's which they retained until 1940.

In 1936 Boston acquired its first permanent allocation (having had K2's for only brief periods from 1933 onwards) keeping them until the end of the summer in 1938. There was a nightly goods working to Doncaster leaving at 8-15 p.m., with a return from Doncaster at 8-0 p.m. the following night. This was shared on a lodging basis with Doncaster engines and men. Much excursion work was also undertaken at the time.

Apart from the permanent transfers to the G.E. Section and Scottish Area there were some moves to G.C. Section sheds. In May 1925 Nos. 4664/5 were sent to Annesley. During their stay, which lasted until January 1927, they were frequently seen on goods or coal trains to Woodford. During 1925-27 Nos. 4654/70 were at Liverpool (Brunswick) and are believed to have worked their braked goods lodging turn to Ardsley. The greatest number of Ragtimers allocated to a former G.C. shed was at Mexborough. The first to arrive were Nos. 4634/7 in May 1929, followed by Nos. 4632/6 in 1930 and 4633/8 in January 1931 and April 1935 respectively. Apart from No. 4633 which left for Doncaster in December 1935, they all remained at Mexborough until February 1940. Initially they replaced old ex-G.C.R. 4-4-0's and later ex-G.N. Klondykes on all of Mexborough's local passenger duties. These extended from Penistone and Sheffield in the west to Hull and Cleethorpes in the east. On Saturday 4th September 1937 three were seen at Doncaster on these diagrams. No. 4636 arrived at 9-47 a.m. and went on to Cleethorpes, returning at 4-41 p.m. with the 2-6 p.m. (SO) Skegness (via Grimsby) to Barnsley. No. 4638 left Doncaster on the 9-43 a.m. to Sheffield and arrived back at 1-37 p.m. with the 11-22 a.m. Manchester-Cleethorpes, which it worked through. The third, No. 4632, arrived at 10-46 a.m. on the 9-18 a.m. ex-Penistone and returned westwards with the 11-44 a.m. Barnetby-Sheffield at 1-22 p.m.

Introduction of more K3 engines during the period 1930-35 meant less work in the London District for the K2's. Nevertheless both King's Cross and New England retained small numbers which were in regular use on secondary duties right up to the outbreak of war in 1939. There were five allocated to King's Cross in 1935, working on mixed traffic duties such as the 1-40 a.m. goods to Hitchin, returning with the 7-50 a.m. Baldock-King's Cross passenger train, 12-5 a.m. goods to Peterborough via Hertford North, 3-0 a.m. pick-up to New England, 4-35 a.m. Hatfield goods and the long established passenger turn at 6-2 p.m. to Baldock. Two of these K2 diagrams provided for the engines to remain at Hitchin overnight on Saturday and Sunday. One, off the 5-54 p.m. (SO) ex-King's Cross slow passenger, on Sunday worked the 9-35 a.m. Baldock-King's Cross and returned with the 10-45 a.m. stopping train. The second engine having taken the 4-35 a.m. Hatfield goods on Saturday, then went forward to Hitchin and on Sunday took the 8-21 p.m. Royston-King's Cross, returning with the 11-0 p.m. to Letchworth. In 1936 the King's Cross K2's were reduced to four. These, Nos. 4645/9/68/79, had all been there since before Grouping and

remained until February 1940 when all were transferred to New England. Afterwards no more K2's were ever allocated to King's Cross as running stock.

Those few Ragtimers still at New England were also used regularly into London. For instance on Monday 24th June 1935 No. 4672 took the 8-30 a.m. King's Cross-Doncaster No. 2 braked goods, No. 4635 brought up the 4-58 p.m. slow passenger and returned on the 6-15 p.m. semi-fast for Cambridge and Peterborough and No. 4654 went down on the 11-0 p.m. No. 2 braked goods to Peterborough, having arrived during the night on a similar working.

During 1942 there was a measure of concentration applied to the K2 stock on the G.N. Section whereby only four sheds housed the thirty-two engines. New England and Boston had six apiece, Colwick five and Doncaster no less than fifteen—the highest number at that shed since 1923. An unusual movement in July 1943 sent Nos. 4634/7 from Doncaster to Frodingham for three weeks. Probably these were used on special traffic for the airfield at Elsham. During the war years Colwick K2's were noted on goods trains to Sheffield but a most remarkable sight was of No. 4656 from March working a ten-coach passenger train of L.N.E.R. stock northwards through Cricklewood L.M.S. on 9th April 1944.

During 1945-46 there was a brief re-appearance of K2's at Ardsley and Bradford, with the transfer of Nos. 4633/7/42/51/78/9. During this time No. 4651 of Ardsley was seen on 12th October 1945 working the 9-20 a.m. Newcastle-Liverpool express loaded to ten bogies and piloted from Ripon to Leeds by class A6 4-6-2T No. 688, bunker first. The Bradford engines were once again regularly used on through portions of King's Cross trains, to either Wakefield or Doncaster. The 9-25 p.m. Bradford-Doncaster, for example, had Nos. 4679 (14th October) and 4642 (4th November). Meanwhile on 31st October No. 4633 (with Bradford driver W. H. Hockon) was assisting class B4 No. 6098 (of Ardsley) on the 9-55 a.m. Bradford-King's Cross, loaded to twelve bogies, when the left-hand connecting rod big-end collapsed. This dug itself into a trailing connection at Carcroft station, resulting in the derailment of almost the entire train. Although travelling at between 50 and 60 m.p.h. the train came to a rapid halt within its own length and the only wheels which had not left the rails were the pony truck, leading coupled and driving coupled of No. 4633, which were ahead of the obstruction, and the rear bogie of the last coach, which stopped just short of it. The K2 sustained only superficial damage whilst the B4 finished up on its side. The train was well loaded but the only injuries were bruises to the engine crews. The K2's were eventually transferred from Ardsley and Bradford to Colwick in August 1946, in exchange for class J39 0-6-0's.

The whole class of seventy-five engines passed into British Railways ownership at the end of 1947 at which time thirty-one were based on the Western Section of the Southern Area, twenty-three on the Eastern Section and twenty-one in Scotland. At this time Colwick housed an increased number in order to cater for traffic diverted from the direct route to Manchester via Sheffield due to the rebuilding of Thurgoland tunnel. Several goods trains were routed via Egginton Junction, Uttoxeter and thence the Churnet Valley line to Macclesfield. A new venue was Immingham where eight had been transferred just before Vesting day.

In 1947 the M. & G.N. Section was in urgent need of more powerful engines than those it then possessed. In an attempt to solve the problem, four K2's from Stratford went to South Lynn during the latter part of 1947, followed by two more early in 1948. The South Lynn shedmaster at the time was Mr. R. H. N. Hardy, who had ample experience of handling the Gresley 2-6-0's. He devised some special diagrams enabling regular men to have each K2 on the Lynn to Yarmouth trains. Because most of the engines were somewhat rough there was some initial difficulty with the M. & G.N. crews but in time they came to get good work out of their unaccustomed mounts. All the K2's had left South Lynn by October 1952 for sheds on the G.N. Section.

On 14th April 1948 No. 1741 from Colwick was noted on the 5-43 p.m. Manchester Central-Guide Bridge passenger train, the rostered duty of the engine (usually a J39) off the previous night's 11-20 p.m. Colwick-Deansgate goods which travelled to Trafford Park shed before taking the passenger train from Manchester to Guide Bridge. It then ran light to Dewsnap for the 7-10 p.m. No. 3 braked goods to Colwick.

Due to the fact that no K2's were then allocated to King's Cross or Peterborough, it became less common to see them south of Peterborough after 1950 but on 2nd May 1951 No. 61731 of Boston was observed on a down empty wagon train from Hornsey. It was in good condition, still with "L N E R" in shaded lettering on its tender. At Easter 1954 another

Boston K2 was at King's Cross, on an R.A.F. leave special ex-Henlow. During 1953 when Colwick had a regular fast goods working to King's Cross, K2's 61751/3/77 were all used at various times instead of rostered K3's and on 5th November 1954 this duty was taken by No. 61767 of Boston. It is believed the last Ragtimer to work over the southern end of the G.N. main line was No. 61756 on the afternoon parcels from Boston in 1956.

Lincoln was given five K2's in 1952, increased to seven in the following year. During their stay there these engines were used on passenger trains over the former L.M.S. line to Newark (Castle), Nottingham and Derby (Midland). In the reverse direction Colwick K2's were also seen on both passenger and goods trains. In the North Eastern Region, No. 61773 from Colwick was seen working the 3-5 p.m. Stockton-Neville Hill goods on 3rd May 1955. This was normally a B16 duty.

To refer now to major transfers of the class, production of the first standard K3's in 1924-25, of which forty-four were allocated to the Southern Area, heralded great changes for the original Gresley 2-6-0's. Throughout the G.N. main line the K3's gradually assumed the heaviest and fastest goods duties, thus making many Ragtimers redundant. Shortly after Grouping there had been some experimental working by two K2's (Nos. 1676N and 1682N) on the vacuum-braked fast goods trains between March and Doncaster via the G.N & G.E. Joint line. This was followed by further trials of ex-G.C.R. class B8 4-6-0's. Recently it has become clear that in 1924-25 three ex-G.E.R. class B12 4-6-0's were stationed at March (Nos. 8507/20/68) and were seen at Lincoln regularly working at least one of the vacuum-braked express goods turns. Later when a number of Gresley K1 and K2 2-6-0's were allocated to the G.E. Section they took over these duties until replaced at March by K3's in 1926.

The first major move by Ragtimers came in 1924 when six K1 and six K2 engines were transferred to G.E. Section sheds. The K1's went to March (No. 4630) and Stratford (Nos. 1632/4/6/9, 1633N) whilst the K2's were at March (Nos. 1676N, 4652), Cambridge (Nos. 4631/44) and Stratford (Nos. 1674N, 4647). At first much of their work was on vacuum-braked express goods trains down the Cambridge line from Spitalfields to Whitemoor and on to Doncaster or Pyewipe Junction, Lincoln. One train involved was the 8-35 p.m. Spitalfields-Doncaster which had been running since the early part of the century. By 1908 there was an additional train at 10-5 p.m. from Spitalfields to Doncaster and in 1924 the 8-35 p.m. was supplemented by the 9-5 p.m. Spitalfields to Pyepipe and the 10-5 p.m. Tottenham to Doncaster. For many years the 8-35 p.m. had been worked by Claud Hamilton 4-4-0's of classes D14 and D15 with loads limited to twenty-five wagons, whilst the Gresley 2-6-0's took forty. The locomotives worked in two stages; London to March and March to Doncaster. For the Joint Line section a March Claud (or sometimes a D13) took the train through to Doncaster, returning home on the 6-0 a.m. stopping passenger. A second duty was on the 6-50 p.m. March-Doncaster express returning on the 9-30 p.m. Ardsley-Bishopsgate braked goods, known in the Doncaster area as the "Swedie Vacuum" as late as 1937-38. On certain workings the Stratford engines returned to Temple Mills yard on coal trains. In L.N.E.R. days certain of these trains ran from Cambridge to March via St. Ives instead of via Ely.

In June 1925 No. 4652 was transferred to Colwick, though it returned to the G.E. Section within three weeks. The return was possibly the result of a change in policy as five out of the six K1's were transferred back to the G.N. Section, instead, between June and August leaving only No. 1632 at Stratford. In August 1925 No. 1676N was transferred to King's Cross in exchange for No. 4656, as the former engine had not been cut down to clear the G.E. Section load gauge. In April 1926 the last K1 was returned to the G.N. Section in exchange for No. 4653. In June 1927 No. 4670, still conforming to the G.N. Section load gauge, was transferred from Liverpool (Brunswick) to Cambridge but was re-allocated to Doncaster a month later. At this time there were then seven K2's on the G.E. Section, Nos. 4631/44/7/52/3/6/74.

Between July 1927 and May 1928, as part of the locomotive construction and withdrawal plan, thirteen more K2's were sent to the G.E. Section to balance withdrawal of class E4 2-4-0's, making the total allocation up to twenty engines, all of which were then equipped with Westinghouse apparatus for train braking. These additional engines were numbered 4650/5/62/3/4/7/9/71/5/6/87/8/90.

Apart from one or two short spells back on the G.N. Section during the period 1929-32 by Nos. 4644/63/76, all twenty engines remained on the G.E. Section until after nationalisation, except that when No. 4674 was included in a further

batch of the class sent to the Scottish Area, No. 4677 was fitted with its Westinghouse equipment and sent to the G.E. Section in December 1931 in replacement. In addition during the thirties Nos. 4633/40/6/61/6/70/8/83 made brief appearances on the G.E. Section though No. 4683 managed to stay for two years. In 1937 Nos. 4640/8/58 were transferred to March and remained on the G.E. Section until after nationalisation. None of these had Westinghouse equipment.

At the time of the first transfers to the G.E. Section there was a very serious shortage of motive power for main line passenger working in East Anglia. Until the delivery of the further ten B12 class engines and the initial engines of class B17, the K2's did a considerable amount of work on top link passenger workings from Stratford shed in addition to the express goods workings. Thereafter they worked a variety of duties often deputising for 4-6-0's on secondary passenger trains. The use of No. 4664 on 29th July 1927 to work the 10-23 a.m. Liverpool Street-Clacton relief express is said to have been the first occasion on which a K2 worked an express passenger train out of the G.E. London terminus. During the fishing season the K2's at Lowestoft and Yarmouth were primarily intended for fast fish trains to London but in summer were found working some of the heavy passenger trains to and from Norwich. Frequent transfers between Lowestoft, Yarmouth and Norwich sheds occurred over the years to suit traffic requirements. The Cambridge engine (throughout the thirties until March 1939 it was No. 4656, but two others were there in 1936-38) occasionally appeared on passenger duties at times of shortage of other suitable power and the March engines were normally on goods work, but also appeared on passenger trains from time to time, often being pressed into service at week-ends from sheds where their goods duties had terminated. The workings of all the class frequently included excursion trains in the summer period.

In 1930 March had two mixed passenger and goods diagrams taking K2's to Lincoln daily. The first worked to Lincoln on the 8-10 p.m. stopping passenger and returned with the 2-15 a.m. Pyewipe-Whitemoor vacuum goods. The second was operated on a lodging basis commencing with the 8-20 p.m. Whitemoor-Pyewipe goods and returning next afternoon on the 2-32 p.m. express from Lincoln to March, except Saturdays when the 4-20 p.m. goods ex-Pyewipe was taken. At Cambridge a similar mixed passenger and goods diagram existed, starting at 7-40 a.m. with empty coaches to Royston to form the 8-22 a.m. passenger to Cambridge and then all stations to Hitchin, returning with the 12-55 p.m. pick-up goods to Cambridge.

A rostered express duty was introduced into the Stratford Express Goods link in November 1935. Hitherto the 7-45 a.m. Cambridge-Liverpool Street passenger and 6-30 p.m. return had been a Cambridge Claud duty, the engine of which like other Cambridge and Colchester line peak hour duties after arrival at Liverpool Street took coaches to Stratford before the engine went to Stratford shed. The men returned home "on the cushions" with a fresh crew travelling up in the afternoon to bring the engine out for the return working. There were exceptions on Newmarket Race days and on Summer Saturdays when the Cambridge engine returned on a morning special (on Saturdays a 4-6-0 was usually provided). These workings were wasteful and following representations made to L. P. Parker, the District Locomotive Superintendent, by the late Frank E. Wilson it was arranged, after Cambridge had agreed to have a standby engine ready for emergencies, to revise the diagrams. Under the revised arrangements a K2 took the 6-30 p.m. down and returned on a goods from Cambridge; a second K2 worked through to March on a goods and back to Cambridge on another, there taking over the 7-45 a.m. express to Liverpool Street, except on Newmarket Race days when Cambridge were required to get an engine up to London. When fog delayed the down leg of this diagram, as it sometimes could, Cambridge had to produce their standby engine, often another shed's Claud. In later years when K3 engines appeared at Stratford that class took over the working which included the 7-45 a.m. from Cambridge; the 6-30 p.m. down continued to be a K2 but with J39 class engines appearing on both workings at times. An above average performer on the 6-30 p.m. down was non-Westinghouse fitted No. 4683, at Stratford at the time the revised workings were introduced. By then the trains concerned were composed of vacuum-braked stock.

One of the authors travelled regularly on the 6-30 p.m. from Liverpool Street, mentioned above. It loaded from 325 to 335 tons gross as far as the first stop at Broxbourne. One experienced on this train many different classes of engine; superheated Clauds of all variants, B12/1, B12/3, B17, J39, K2 and latterly K3, but the best

performers were the K2 class engines. On 6th July 1936 No. 4677 set up a record that lasted two years. Passing Tottenham three minutes late it then ran the 11.1 miles to Broxbourne on the rising gradient with a maintained maximum of 65 m.p.h. Then on 27th July 1938 No. 4652 beat all previous records for best section times from Ponders End onwards, hitherto held also by classes B17 and J39 on the 6-30 p.m. and other trains of comparable loading. No. 4652 made a slightly faster run with a sustained maximum of 66 m.p.h. Next evening No. 4677 with the same driver did even better, running the 11.1 miles from passing Tottenham to the Broxbourne stop in 11 mins. 10 secs. with an average speed of 68 m.p.h. over 5.3 miles from Brimsdown to Wormley Box. These two K2's thereafter held the record as against all other classes for section times between Ponders End and Broxbourne, performances which showed that when rostered to regular drivers the soundness of the basic design was fully exploited by the expert Stratford men. Properly driven, the K2's were free running engines with their long travel valve gear and large well-proportioned boiler able to provide ample steam at all times.

An unusual route for rostered K2 workings was operating regularly in 1938-39 on a No. 1 vacuum-fitted goods leaving Marks Tey at 8-20 p.m. and travelling over the single line through Sudbury and Haverhill to Shelford and Cambridge, thence via St. Ives to March and Whitemoor Yard. It was often worked by either No. 4640 or 4648 which had been transferred from the G.N. Section to March in May-June 1937.

Other workings undertaken by K2's over the period 1925-39 were the special banana trains originating at Victoria Docks, London, to Manchester and other northern destinations. The unripe bananas were loaded into special steam-heated vacuum-fitted vans and taken from the docks to Temple Mills by a class J69 0-6-0T having steam heat equipment. At Temple Mills the vans were made up into longer trains and run forward to March as specials, perhaps as many as four per day. When the supply of K2's ran out, B12's or even Clauds were employed. No problems arose from the workings of the engines being unbalanced since they could be employed on return coal trains to Temple Mills from Whitemoor. The engines allocated to the Norwich District did useful work in summer months between Norwich and Cromer, Yarmouth and Lowestoft on heavy passenger trains that had reversed at Norwich. Almost annually the engines were transferred from Norwich shed to Lowestoft or Yarmouth in the autumn for fish traffic, remaining there throughout the winter.

After the War the K2's on the G.E. Section were mostly confined to secondary goods duties and by the end of 1947 two were at Colchester, four had left for South Lynn on the M. & G.N. line and the remaining seventeen were concentrated at Stratford shed. Two more moved to South Lynn in April 1948. Quantity production of class B1 4-6-0's in 1946-47 transformed much of the G.E. Lines operating methods and work for the older classes declined rapidly. In 1949 one more K2 left for the G.N. Section, then in 1951 a wholesale clearance began. Most transfers were to G.N. sheds and by the end of 1952 no Ragtimer remained on the G.E. Section. Towards the end of their stay Nos. 1737/80 were seen working excursions to Southend from Chingford in the summer of 1950 and on 13th November 1951 No. 61767 took the down "Day Continental" out of Liverpool Street.

In August 1924 Doncaster recorded the transfer of No. 4695, newly altered to clear the G.E. and N.B. Section load gauges, to the N.B. Section. However, this movement is not confirmed in the Daily Stock Registers for the period, nor was its presence in Scotland noted by contemporary observers. Towards the end of December 1924 six K2's were sent to Scotland, Nos. 1703, 4695/6/8, 4700/4, all except No. 4698 being noted on Eastfield shed on New Year's Day 1925. Nos. 1703 and 4696 still conformed to the G.N. Section load gauge and had presumably been sent north in error, for they returned to England on 5th January. Between February and August ten further engines were sent to Scotland, including Nos. 4696 and 4703 for the second time, after receiving the necessary alterations to permit them to clear the N.B. load gauge. The fourteen engines concerned were transferred permanently to N.B. Section book stock on 1st October 1925. Six further engines were transferred in 1931-32, making the Scottish K2 total twenty. This number remained constant until 1945-49, during which period one additional K2 was temporarily allocated to the Scottish Area. In 1951 a further ten K2's went permanently to Scotland. Two more were also sent north in January 1951, Nos. 61739/66, but they returned to England three months later.

The original fourteen Scottish K2's, Nos. 4691-4704, were initially allocated to Eastfield shed, though Nos. 4694/5/6, 4702/3 went to St.

Margaret's in 1926-27. The six additional engines in 1931-32 were shared between Eastfield (Nos. 4674/82/4/5) and St. Margaret's (Nos. 4686/9). Between 1938 and 1943, Nos. 4674/82/4 were moved to St. Margaret's and Nos. 4686/9 to Eastfield. The 1945 transfer to Scotland was No. 4639 (in place of Thompson class K1 No. 3445, then working in the Southern Area) which worked from Eastfield until 1947 and then Parkhead until 1949. The engines transferred to Scotland in 1951 were also based initially at Eastfield, but soon moved on to Parkhead (Nos. 61722/33/5/69), Dunfermline (Nos. 61721/34/58) and Thornton (Nos. 61741/55/70). No. 61734 subsequently moved to Thornton and later Ferryhill, and No. 61780 went to Dunfermline. In 1952 nine K2's were sent to the G.N.S. Section (Kittybrewster and Keith sheds), Nos. 61734/41/55/79/82/3/90/2/3. After Cowlairs Works became responsible for the maintenance of Southern Area K2's from 1943 onwards, English K2's were often borrowed (chiefly by Eastfield and St. Margaret's) for train working while on their way to and from Cowlairs.

The Eastfield engines were principally employed on the passenger service between Glasgow, Fort William and Mallaig, and it was the usual practice to have about six of the class out-stationed at Fort William and two at Mallaig. These were nominally regarded as sub-sheds of Eastfield, although separate allocations were listed from time to time. The Eastfield and Fort William men worked between Glasgow and Fort William, completing a single trip and lodging, until the 1939-45 war when it became customary to changeover en route. On the Mallaig extension, Fort William and Mallaig men worked a double trip (i.e. out and home). Between Glasgow and Fort William the load for a K2 was 220 tons, as compared with 190 tons for a D34, but even so double-heading with a Glen or another K2 was frequent. The K2's also worked goods traffic and fish trains on the West Highland. Eastfield K2's were also to be found on express goods trains to Edinburgh, and also in the early days through to Carlisle (the latter duties being more usually covered by K3's). At the outset Eastfield used the K2's on goods work only (former J37 turns), and the story goes that on a busy day the foreman at Fort William was unable to provide a pilot when it was found that a passenger train for Glasgow was over the load for the rostered Glen. So he decided to substitute a K2 which was available, and when the driver arrived at Eastfield he gave a good account of the

2-6-0. Be that as it may, the official authorisation for the use of K2's on passenger trains between Glasgow and Fort Wiliam was dated 17th July 1925, and in the usual cautious manner of the Civil Engineer's department, "the right was reserved to withdraw".

The St. Margaret's K2's were chiefly used on express goods trains, previously worked by J37's, mainly to Newcastle and Glasgow. The most important turn was the 11-55 p.m. Duddingston to Forth (Newcastle) beer train, which ran via the Border Counties, the return working being the 9-25 p.m. ex-Blaydon, via Berwick. This was a lodging turn not shared with another depot, and so St. Margaret's always had two engines rostered for this duty each week. Most of the express goods trains ran through the night and consequently were not often seen by observers, but a notable exception was the 11-55 a.m. South Leith and High Street, known to the Edinburgh enthusiast fraternity as the "Dinnertime Goods". To railwaymen, however, it was always known as the "Pigs' Feet", from the nature of the traffic conveyed, and an interesting feature of its operation was that it ran via Waverley (normally banned to through goods traffic during the daytime). To obviate "running round" at Portobello it completed the first part of its journey – the two miles to South Leith Junction – with one of the yard pilots (usually an N15) pulling and the train engine pushing. The K2's also worked goods trains from Edinburgh to Perth and Dundee, and during the 1939-45 War they were employed on the through workings to Heaton, with change of crews at Tweedmouth. The St. Margaret's K2's often worked Saturdays Only passenger trains to Hawick, Glasgow and Dundee. They also ran excursions, sometimes to unusual destinations (e.g. No. 4689 from Niddrie to Blantyre, L.M.S., on a special from Hawick, 17th June 1933), and an interesting development was the working of excursions from Edinburgh to Blair Atholl, L.M.S., with a St. Margaret's K2 going through. The first time one of these trains ran was on 10th April 1933, when No. 4703 was piloted from Perth by L.M.S. 4-6-0 No. 14678 *Gordon Castle*. The St. Margaret's men went to Blair Atholl, but an L.N.E.R. driver from Perth acted as conductor, and the engine usually carried a "Blair Atholl" N.B.-style headboard.

The Parkhead K2's were employed on express goods work to Edinburgh via Bathgate and as these were night shift duties (e.g. 8-55 p.m. High Street and Portobello), it was the usual practice to utilise the engines for local duties during the

day, such as the 8-40 a.m. Camlachie, Sighthill, Cadder and Gunnie.

At Dunfermline the K2's were employed on passenger and goods trains to Edinburgh, and those at Thornton were utilised for similar duties, often working to Glasgow as well.

The first batch of K2's to come to Scotland did so when the Model T Ford motor car was at the height of its popularity, and it is not surprising that the nickname applied to these cars was also bestowed on the Scottish K2's – "Tin Lizzies". The K2's were regarded as good engines in Scotland, but the discomforts of the cab, their rough riding, and such alien features as right-hand drive and horizontal pull-out regulator handle militated against their popularity with the enginemen.

On the G.N.S. Section they normally worked branch and pick-up goods trains. On 6th October 1952 No. 61792, still in green livery took the 12-35 p.m. Keith-Kittybrewster goods whilst in April 1954 No. 61779 was regularly on the daily goods from Kittybrewster to Macduff. Later in that year No. 61782 *Loch Eil* was on Keith-Boat of Garten goods turns and in September 1956 No. 61792 was the Boat of Garten passenger engine. During 1957 there were two daily passenger workings into Inverness on which K2's regularly appeared: (1) 7-17 a.m. Elgin-Inverness, 9-45 a.m. Inverness-Forres and 10-52 a.m. Forres-Elgin; (2) 10-45 a.m. Elgin-Inverness, 6-0 p.m. Inverness-Elgin, empty coaches Elgin-Keith. In May 1958 No. 61783 was noted on the 8-25 a.m. Aviemore-Elgin (via Craigellachie) goods.

The former L.M.S. main line from Glasgow to Aberdeen saw occasional use of K2's, as in August 1953 when No. 61786 worked the 8-5 p.m. Glasgow (Buchanan Street)-Aberdeen goods. In July 1954 the same engine took the 4-0 p.m. Aberdeen-Perth, normally a C1.5 4-6-0 turn. Another working over former L.M.S. metals was on 14th April 1952 when No. 61722 of Parkhead took the 4-25 p.m. St. Enoch-Ardrossan, whilst on 6th September of that year No. 61735 worked an evening excursion from Hamilton to Ayr. On 2nd July 1955 Nos. 61722/30 both appeared at Ayr.

Notwithstanding an influx of more modern engines on the West Highland, the K2's remained in use there until 1961. The last to be stationed at Mallaig was No. 61784 which on 3rd August 1960 managed two return trips to Fort William and the very last one to work a passenger train over the line was No. 61764 *Loch Arkaig* on 17th June 1961 when it took a charter special at 2-50 p.m. from Glasgow to Crianlarich and return. It was withdrawn in September 1961, having spent thirty years in Scotland, all but four of them at Eastfield shed.

Withdrawal of class K2 had begun in September 1955 with No. 61722, a Scottish Region engine. In the next three years eighteen were taken out of stock, followed in 1959 by no fewer than thirty-three.

From 1955 onwards there was insufficient work available throughout the year to keep all forty-five K2's on the Eastern Region at work. Sheffield (Darnall) received nine in 1955 for storage. Five were noted still in store on 11th March 1956, but the others had been returned to traffic for use on trains diverted via Barnsley and Mexborough to points in the east due to the closure of the normal route via Worksop and Retford whilst the Retford underpass was being constructed. Four remained stored at Sheffield by early 1960 but all were in traffic for the summer season. Except for one sent to King's Cross for use as a stationary boiler, they were withdrawn in December 1960. Also in 1960, six remained in service at Colwick employed on light goods and summer specials from both Nottingham and Leicester Belgrave Road to Mablethorpe and Skegness taking loads of ten or eleven bogies. Three were stored at Colwick in October 1960.

Four K2's were put into use as stationary boilers whilst remaining in running stock. New England received No. 61759 from Boston in June 1959, but it soon moved on to Colwick and was replaced by No. 61763 which lasted until February 1961. No. 61761 went from Colwick to King's Cross as a stationary boiler in January 1961, but was withdrawn almost at once and replaced by No. 61756 which remained in use until June 1962 when it was withdrawn as the last

of its class. So ended the first true Gresley engines after a full and varied life spanning almost fifty years.

Allocation at 31st December	1922	1938	1947	1954
CLASS K1				
King's Cross	1	–	–	–
New England	2	–	–	–
Colwick	4	–	–	–
Ardsley	1	–	–	–
CLASS K2				
King's Cross	14	4	–	–
New England	27	8	2	–
Boston	–	1	6	12
Colwick	2	7	15	19
Lincoln	–	–	–	7
Doncaster	19	5	–	–
Immingham	–	–	8	7
Mexborough	–	4	–	–
Ardsley	5	–	–	–
Bradford	–	3	–	–
Copley Hill	–	1	–	–
March	–	4	–	–
Cambridge	–	1	–	–
Norwich	–	8	–	–
Colchester	–	–	2	–
Stratford	–	9	17	–
South Lynn	–	–	4	–
St. Margaret's	–	7	–	–
Eastfield	–	3	13	10
Fort William	–	9	7	5
Parkhead	–	–	1	5
Mallaig	–	1	–	–
Kittybrewster	–	–	–	4
Ferryhill	–	–	–	1
Thornton	–	–	–	2
Dunfermline	–	–	–	3

Engine Diagrams

Section N, 1/1924.	K1	Nos. 4630/2/3/4/6-9. Pony truck wheel diameter 3ft. 8in. added 12/1924, which was correct only for No. 4630. Engines rebuilt to class K2 and diagram deleted 12/1937.
Not issued, 1/1924.	K2	Nos. 4631/5 rebuilt from class K1. Omission rectified 12/1938. Meanwhile the Diagram Book Index issued in 1924 referred to these engines as "K1 5' 6" boiler."
Section N, 1/1924.	K2/1	Nos. 4640-9. Replaced by composite diagram 12/1929.
Section N, 1/1924.	K2/2	Nos. 4650-4704. Replaced by composite diagram 12/1929.
Section N, 12/1924.	K2	No class part; engines "altered for G.E. loading gauge"; journal particulars correct for Nos. 4650-4704. Note "for N.B. loading gauge" added later. Replaced by composite diagram 12/1929.
Section N, 1929.	K2	Composite diagram for Nos. 4640-9 and 4650-4704 (shown as 4705 in error), with engines reduced in height. Diagram replaced 12/1938.
Section N, 1936.	K2	Engines in Scottish Area, side window cab depicted; journal particulars correct for Nos. 4650-4704. Superheater element diameter altered from 1¼in. to 1.244in. and class Part 2 added, 12/1938.
Section N, 1938.	K2/1	Engines rebuilt from class K1, Nos. 4630-9. Alternative pony truck wheel diameters 3ft. 8in. (No. 4630 only) and 3ft. 2in. (remainder) shown.
Section N, 1938.	K2/2	Composite diagram for Nos. 4640-9 and later engines, with alternative journal particulars. Alternative widths over centres of cylinders 6ft. 7in. (Nos. 4640-9) and 6ft. 7½in. (later engines) added, 12/1940.

Classification: K1 Southern Area load class 3. K2 Southern Area load class 5; Southern Scottish Area load class S; Route availability 5; B.R. power class 4MT.

Fig. 67   Class K2/I No. 4655 at York station, c. 1926.

Old style cylinders with inside steam pipes and lubrication for steam chest entering valve chests at both ends, cylinder tail rods removed, three wash-out plugs on firebox.

Fig. 68   Class K2 No. 4659 at Nottingham Victoria station, August 1937.

Short chimney and tall dome, old style cylinder with dummy steam pipe cover, two hand holes in place of wash-out plugs on firebox, large buffer heads, two sets of front guard irons, new rear-end frame with strengthening plate.

Fig. 69   Class K2/I No. 1685N at Doncaster shed, c. 1924.

Ross pop safety valves without raised seating, new pattern cylinder with outside steam pipe cover, sight feed lubricator pipes passing alongside boiler from cab to cylinders.

Fig. 70   Class K2 No. 4691 at Eastfield shed, October 1932.

Side-window cab with short roof extension, mechanical lubricator for axleboxes only, post-1912 3,500-gallon tender without handgrip, small lettering "L N E R".

Fig. 71   Class K2 No. 4692 *Loch Eil* at Eastfield shed, c. August 1933.

G.N. cab with glass sight screens, sight-feed lubricator pipes to both cylinders passing along left-hand side of boiler, smokebox door stop mid-way between hinges, pre-1912 3,500-gallon tender with handgrip.

Fig. 72   Class K2 No. 4694 at Blair Atholl (L.M.S.), August 1939.

Scottish Area engine but still with Ramsbottom safety valves, box-shaped cover in reverse curve of running plate above combination lever, smokebox door stops as extensions to hinge straps, handrail below hinge straps, destination board.

Fig. 73   Class K2 No. 4699 *Loch Laidon* at Eastfield shed, September 1934.
Side-window cab with longer roof extension, drop grate with rodding in front of cab, boiler handrails cut back at front.

Fig. 74   Class K2/2 No. 1734 at Haymarket shed, September 1947.
Old style cylinder on left-hand side (only) with inside steam pipe, anti-carboniser fitting behind smokebox saddle for cylinder lubrication with shut-off cock on smokebox side, vacuum brake stand-pipe on right (facing) of screw coupling and Westinghouse connection on left, deep casing between frames above pony truck, 1946 green livery.

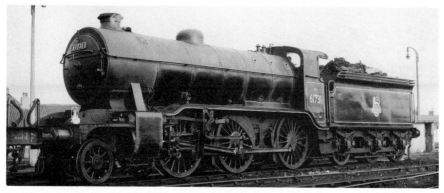

Fig. 75   Class K2/2 No. 61731 at Boston shed, April 1956.
Altered lubrication for combination lever without box-shaped cover in reverse curve of running plate above, additional mechanical lubricator for left-hand cylinder, anti-carboniser fitting behind smokebox saddle with steam taken from manifold in cab, G.N.R. tender with extra handrail at rear.

Fig. 76　　Class K2/2 No. 61764 *Loch Arkaig* at Eastfield shed, July 1956.

Side-window cab with glass sight screens, plain chimney, no sight-feed lubricator pipes along right-hand side of boiler.

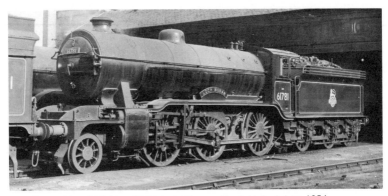

Fig. 77　　Class K2/2 No. 61781 *Loch Morar* at Eastfield shed, June 1954.

G.N.-type buffers with packing blocks behind bases, guard irons removed from main frames, G.N.R. tender with extra coal rail, first style B.R. emblem.

Fig. 78　　Class K2/2 No. 61792 at Inverness shed, May 1959.

Flat-topped dome cover, Group Standard buffers without packing blocks, tender with later style B.R. emblem.

Fig. 79   Class K2 No. 4659 on a down goods near Sandy, May 1937.

Fig. 80   Class K2/2 No. 4679 passing Wood Green with the 5-50 p.m. King's Cross-Baldock
stopping train, c. 1928.
Still with original tall chimney.

Fig. 81   Class K2/2 No. 4652 passing Crowlands with the 9-55 a.m. Liverpool Street-Clacton
Pullman train, July 1928.

Fig. 82   Class K2/2 No. 4656 passing Romford with an up goods, June 1926.

Fig. 83   Class K2/2 No. 4670 leaving Nottingham Victoria with an up fish train, c. 1927.

Sight-feed lubricator pipes passing alongside boiler from cab to cylinder.

Fig. 84   Class K2 No. 4684 *Loch Garry* leaving Shandon with a Fort William-Glasgow train, 1936.

Fig. 85   Class K2/2 No. 1764 *Loch Arkaig* and No. 4701 *Loch Laggan* with a
Fort William-Glasgow train at Mallaig Junction, June 1946.

Fig. 86   Class K2/2 No. 61788 *Loch Rannoch* and class 5 4-6-0 No. 44970 on the morning
Fort William-Glasgow train at Tulloch, March 1959.

Vacuum brake stand-pipe behind bufferbeam to facilitate fitting of snow plough.

Summary of K1 and K2 Classes

K1

B.R. No.	1946 No.	1924 No.	Maker	Works No.	Built	Rbt. to K2 by G.N.R.	1923 Class	Rbt. to K2 by L.N.E.R.	West. pump fitted	West. pump removed	Side window cab fitted	Withdrawn
61720 5/50	1720 5/46	4630 3/24	Doncaster	1354	8/1912	—	K1	10/32	—	—	—	6/56
61721 9/48	1721 2/46	4631 9/24	,,	1372	2/1913	3/21	K2	—	12/27	1/54	11/51	12/59
61722 4/49	1722 1/46	4632 12/25	,,	1373	2/1913	—	K1	10/36	—	—	7/51	9/55
61723 3/49	1723 9/46	4633 7/24	,,	1374	2/1913	—	—	1/33	—	—	—	11/59
61724 2/50	1724 7/46	4634 7/24	,,	1375	2/1913	—	—	6/31	—	—	—	1/58
61725 9/50	1725 9/46	4635 1/25	,,	1376	3/1913	6/20	,,	—	—	—	—	1/58
61726 6/49	1726 10/46	4636 1/25	,,	1377	3/1913	—	K2	7/37	—	—	—	5/57
61727 4/48	1727 7/46	4637 2/25	,,	1378	3/1913	—	K1	6/36	9/27	—	—	6/56
61728 9/50	1728 1/46	4638 8/24	,,	1379	4/1913	—	,,	2/36	—	—	—	12/60
61729 10/49	1729 4/46	4639 10/25	,,	1380	4/1913	—	,,	12/35	—	—	10/49	6/57

K2

B.R. No.	1946 No.	1924 No.	Maker	Works No.	Built	1923 Class	Rbt. to K2 by L.N.E.R.	West. pump fitted	West. pump removed	Side window cab fitted	Withdrawn
61730 12/48	1730 11/46	4640 12/24	Doncaster	1425	4/1914	K2		—	—	—	8/57
61731 8/50	1731 12/46	4641 5/25	,,	1426	4/1914	,,		—	—	—	6/59
61732 4/49	1732 8/46	4642 10/24	,,	1428	4/1914	,,		—	—	—	4/57
61733 9/48	1733 6/46	4643 11/24	,,	1429	4/1914	,,		—	—	—	10/57
61734 4/48	1734 5/46	4644 7/24	,,	1430	4/1914	,,		2/28	1/52	10/52	7/56
61735 4/48	1735 2/46	4645 1/25	,,	1431	5/1914	,,		—	—	1/52	1/57
61736 2/49	1736 2/46	4646 3/25	,,	1432	5/1914	,,		—	—	4/51	5/57
61737 9/49	1737 4/46	4647 10/24	,,	1433	5/1914	,,		9/27	—	—	11/56
61738 5/48	1738 3/46	4648 8/25	,,	1434	6/1914	,,		—	—	—	7/59
61739 11/50	1739 10/46	4649 10/24	,,	1435	6/1914	,,		—	—	—	2/59
61740 1/49	1740 3/46	4650 10/25	,,	1466	1/1916	,,		4/28	3/55(a)	—	1/61
61741 9/49	1741 3/46	4651 3/25	,,	1467	2/1916	,,		—	—	—	3/60
61742 5/48	1742 5/46	4652 8/24	,,	1468	5/1916	,,		7/27	7/55(a)	6/53	5/62
61743 1/50	1743 5/46	4653 2/25	,,	1469	6/1916	,,	—	10/27	12/55(a)	—	6/59
61744 7/48	1744 12/46	4654 3/25	,,	1470	7/1916	,,		—	—	—	1/57
61745 11/49	1745 7/46	4655 3/25	,,	1471	10/1916	,,		—	—	—	11/60
61746 1/49	1746 8/46	4656 8/24	,,	1472	11/1916	,,		10/27	10/54(a)	—	2/59
61747 4/48	1747 1/46	4657 5/24	,,	1473	11/1916	,,		9/27	5/55(a)	—	12/60
61748 3/49	1748 11/46	4658 5/24	,,	1474	12/1916	,,		—	—	—	2/59
61749	1749 10/46	4659 2/25	,,	1475	12/1916	,,		—	—	—	1/59
61750 12/48	1750 10/46	4660 1/25	N.B. Loco. Co.	21971	6/1918	,,		10/27	6/53	—	6/59
61751 3/50	1751 9/46	4661 12/24	,,	21972	6/1918	,,		10/27	3/54(a)	—	6/59
61752 9/50	1752 3/46	4662 2/25	,,	21973	6/1918	,,		7/27	6/54(a)	—	12/59
61753 8/49	1753 10/46	4663 12/24	,,	21974	7/1918	,,		—	—	—	9/59
61754 4/48	1754 11/46	4664 5/25	,,	21975	7/1918	,,		—	—	—	12/59
61755 5/48	1755 11/46	4665 12/24	,,	21976	7/1918	,,		—	—	8/53	11/59
61756 12/48	1756 10/46	4666 2/25	,,	21977	7/1918	,,		4/28	4/55(a)	—	6/62
61757 10/48	1757 11/46	4667 2/25	,,	21978	8/1918	,,		—	—	—	2/59
61758 5/48	1758 8/46	4668 3/25	,,	21979	8/1918	,,		2/28	—	10/52	6/59
61759 7/49	1759 8/46	4669 3/25	,,	21980	8/1918	,,		—	—	—	1/60(b)

Summary of K1 and K2 Classes (continued)

B.R. No.	1946 No.	1924 No.	Maker	Works No.	Built	1923 Class	Name	Date named	West. pump fitted	West. pump removed	Side window cab fitted	Withdrawn
61760 4/50	1760 12/46	4670 1/25	N.B. Loco. Co.	21981	6/1918	K2	—	—	—	—	—	12/60
61761 3/49	1761 6/46	4671 10/25	„	21982	6/1918	„	—	—	4/28	4/54(a)	—	1/61
61762 7/48	1762 3/46	4672 2/26	„	21983	6/1918	„	—	—	—	—	—	6/59
61763 1/49	1763 4/46	4673 12/24	„	21984	6/1918	„	Loch Arkaig	3/33	—	—	4/34	2/61
61764 1/49	1764 6/46	4674 3/26	„	21985	7/1918	„	—	—	11/27	11/31	—	9/61
61765 2/49	1765 5/46	4675 11/24	„	21986	7/1918	„	—	—	9/27	9/55(a)	—	5/58
61766 8/49	1766 11/46	4676 10/25	„	21987	8/1918	„	—	—	10/27	11/54	—	1/61
61767 6/48	1767 10/46	4677 10/24	„	21988	8/1918	„	—	—	11/31	10/55(a)	—	1/61
61768 8/48	1768 11/46	4678 6/25	„	21989	8/1918	„	—	—	—	—	—	1/59
61769 10/48	1769 11/46	4679 3/25	„	21990	8/1918	„	—	—	—	—	5/51	9/60
61770 11/48	1770 7/46	4680 3/24	Kitson & Co.	5330	6/1921	„	Loch Lochy	5/33	—	—	7/52	7/59
61771 4/48	1771 10/46	4681 4/24	„	5331	6/1921	„	—	—	—	—	—	12/60
61772 4/48	1772 8/46	4682 3/24	„	5332	6/1921	„	Loch Garry	7/33	—	—	7/34	11/59
61773 4/50	1773 11/46	4683 3/24	„	5333	6/1921	„	Loch Treig	12/33	—	—	—	12/60
61774 6/48	1774 1/46	4684 4/24	„	5334	6/1921	„	—	—	—	—	10/34	4/58
61775 7/48	1775 2/46	4685 by 5/25	„	5335	6/1921	„	—	—	—	—	12/33	5/58
61776 12/49	1776 1/46	4686 3/25	„	5336	6/1921	„	—	—	2/28	8/55(a)	11/34	3/59
61777 6/48	1777 2/46	4687 6/25	„	5337	6/1921	„	—	—	3/28	10/56(a)	—	5/59
61778 12/50	1778 2/46	4688 6/24	„	5338	7/1921	„	—	—	—	—	—	10/59
61779 4/48	1779 1/46	4689 6/24	„	5339	7/1921	„	—	—	—	—	10/34	5/60
61780 2/50	1780 2/46	4690 9/25	„	5340	7/1921	„	Loch Morar	8/33	3/28	8/55(a)	—	10/59
61781 5/48	1781 5/46	4691 4/24	„	5341	7/1921	„	Loch Eil	2/33	—	—	9/32	12/58
61782 1/49	1782 4/46	4692 3/25	„	5342	7/1921	„	Loch Sheil	3/33	—	—	7/34	6/60
61783 4/48	1783 1/46	4693 5/25	„	5343	7/1921	„	—	—	—	—	12/34	6/59
61784 10/48	1784 2/46	4694 5/25	„	5344	7/1921	„	—	—	—	—	2/35	3/61
61785 12/48	1785 1/46	4695 7/24	„	5345	7/1921	„	—	—	—	—	1/35	4/59
61786 4/48	1786 1/46	4696 5/24	„	5346	8/1921	„	Loch Quoich	6/33	—	—	12/33	12/59
61787 6/48	1787 5/46	4697 5/24	„	5347	8/1921	„	Loch Rannoch	7/33	—	—	11/34	10/59
61788 9/48	1788 4/46	4698 7/24	„	5348	8/1921	„	Loch Laidon	6/34	—	—	6/34	6/61
61789 10/48	1789 4/46	4699 5/24	„	5349	8/1921	„	Loch Lomond	12/33	—	—	6/34	9/59
61790 4/48	1790 9/46	4700 8/24	„	5350	8/1921	„	Loch Laggan	5/33	—	—	9/34	11/59
61791 11/48	1791 7/46	4701 11/24	„	5351	8/1921	„	—	—	—	—	4/34	3/60
61792 7/48	1792 11/46	4702 6/25	„	5352	8/1921	„	—	—	—	—	4/34	9/60
61793 6/49	1793 2/46	4703 6/25	„	5353	9/1921	„	Loch Oich	6/33	—	—	10/33	2/59
61794 7/48	1794 1/46	4704 9/24	„	5354	9/1921	„	—	—	—	—	10/34	7/60

(a) These dates are not officially confirmed.
(b) No. 61759 was withdrawn on 1/1/60, but included in the B.R. 1959 statistical year withdrawals.

CLASS K3

G.N.R. CLASS H4 – GRESLEY
5ft. 8in. ENGINES
AND

CLASS K5

ENGINE REBUILT BY THOMPSON

ENGINES AT GROUPING (Built 1920-21): 4000-9. TOTAL 10.

ENGINES BUILT AFTER GROUPING (1924-37): 17, 28, 32/3/6/8/9, 46, 52/3/8, 69, 73/5, 80, 91/2, 109/11-4/6/8/20/1/5/6/7/34/5/40/1/3/ 6/53/6/8/9/63/7/70/8/80/4/6/8/91/5, 200/2/ 3/4/6/7/8/27/8/9/31, 1100/1/2/6/8/17/8/9/ 21/5/33/5/7/41/54/6/8/62/4/6, 1300/2/4/6/ 7/8/10/2/8/22/4/5/31/2/3/9/45/64/5/7/8/ 86-9/91/2/4-9, 2417/25-9/38/9/40/2/3/5-51/3/ 5/8/9/61/3/5-8/70-3/98/9, 2761-9, 2934-40, 3813-32. TOTAL 183.

In August 1917 Gresley considered a scheme for a new G.N.R. express goods engine, based on the H3 (L.N.E.R. class K2), but having alternatively 20in. or 20½in. diameter cylinders with 28in. stroke. The existing H3 boiler would have been retained, with however its boiler pressure raised to 180lb. per sq. in., so that with the 20½in. cylinders the tractive effort would have been 20 per cent greater than that of the H3's. Particular attention was given to the bearing surfaces of the coupling rod pins and connecting rod crank pins which would have had to be increased commensurate with the greater piston loads. This was possibly one reason why the scheme was not pursued.

At this time Gresley's first three-cylinder 2-8-0 mineral engine, No. 461, was under construction (L.N.E.R. class O2). It appeared in May 1918 and incorporated his patent valve gear for operating the piston valve for the middle cylinder from the motion for the two outside valves. Gresley was so pleased with this engine that he announced soon afterwards that he intended in future to concentrate his efforts on three-cylinder designs.

He then turned his attention to a three-cylinder 2-6-0 express goods engine and the first outline drawing appeared in December 1918. The cylinders were 18½in. diameter by 26in. stroke and the boiler pressure was 180 lb. per sq. in., giving a 36 per cent increase in tractive effort over the two-cylinder H3 engines, which at that time still had 170 lb. boilers. The inside cylinder was inclined steeply to clear the leading coupled axle whilst the two outside cylinders were almost horizontal. Such a layout was possible by adjusting the valve gear in the manner suggested to Gresley by Holcroft. Gresley also decided to use 2 to 1 levers ahead of the cylinders instead of a rocking shaft behind them. The boiler was enlarged to provide an adequate supply of steam. The diameter was an unprecedented 6ft. 0in. and a 32-element superheater was fitted. The firebox had a grate area of 28 sq. ft. The first ten engines, numbered 1000-9, appeared in 1920-21 Although intended for fast goods work, during the coal strike of 1921 they made a name for themselves on express passenger trains out of King's Cross with loads of up to twenty bogie vehicles.

When this class was introduced in 1920, jazz music was just becoming popular in this country. The engines soon earned the nickname "Jazzers" which happened to be singularly appropriate because of their syncopated exhaust beat and gyratory movement at the trailing end.

Early trials with No. 1000 showed that there was over-travel of the middle valve when coasting at high speeds, in part due to the arrangement of the conjugate gear as any slackness in the pins and joints was multiplied, and partly due to the extra whip action of the motion levers at speed. Gresley took prompt action to reduce the travel by limiting the maximum cut-off to 65 per cent.

This 2-6-0 class, which became K3 on the L.N.E.R., was adopted as a Group Standard design and was added to after Grouping until it eventually stood at 193 engines. All the post-Grouping additions to the class were lower in height than the G.N.R. series in order to comply with the new Composite Load Gauge and so permit widespread use on the L.N.E.R. system. The K3 design was subject to continuous refinement and improvement (including the fitting of long lap valves) and by 1935 the class was subdivided into six Parts, as follows:-

Part
1	Nos. 4000-9 to G.N.R. load gauge.
2	17 series, built Darlington 1924-25.
3	1300 series, built Doncaster 1929.
4	2761 series, built Darlington 1930.
5	1100 series, built by contractors 1931.
6	1302 series, built by contractors 1934-35.

The differences between Parts 2 to 6 were relatively minor so that at the end of 1935 it was decided to incorporate Parts 4, 5 and 6 into Part 2. The new K3's built in 1936-37 were also included in Part 2. Part 1 became extinct during 1940, when all of Nos. 4000-9 had been altered to clear the L.N.E.R. Composite Load Gauge and were included in Part 2. The remaining class Parts 2 and 3 were finally discontinued from December 1947.

In June 1945 Thompson rebuilt No. 206 with two cylinders and a high-pressure boiler, allocating to it class K5 four months later. Although trials suggested No. 206 to be superior to the K3's, it was decided not to rebuild any more and the engine remained the solitary example of its class until its withdrawal in June 1960. Between 1945 and 1959 large numbers of these new boilers were built and although they were freely used in class K3, the pressure was always reduced to 180 lb. per sq.in. Only three of them ever worked at their designed pressure of 225 lb. per sq.in., in each case when fitted to the K5.

No. 61898 was the first K3 to be withdrawn in February 1959, due to the condition of its middle cylinder. Although Doncaster was still fitting new boilers to K3's after this date, considerable withdrawals soon took place and the last ones to be withdrawn were condemned in December 1962. However, three engines condemned in September 1962 survived for a while longer as stationary engines at various former G.N.R. sheds (see under Service Stock).

Standard L.N.E.R. Dimensions

	K3	K5
Cylinders	(3) $18\frac{1}{2}'' \times 26''$	(2) $20'' \times 26''$ (outside)
Motion	Walschaerts/Gresley with 8″ piston valves	Walschaerts with 10″ piston valves
Boiler:		
Max. diam. outside	6′ 0″	6′ 0″
Barrel length	12′ $1\frac{5}{8}''$(a)	12′ $1\frac{5}{8}''$(b)
Firebox length outside ..	9′ 6″	9′ 6″
Pitch	9′ 0″	9′ 0″
Diagram No.	96(c)	96A
Heating surface:		
Firebox	182 sq.ft.	182 sq.ft.
Tubes ($217 \times 1\frac{3}{4}''$)	1192 sq.ft.	1192 sq.ft.
Flues ($32 \times 5\frac{1}{4}''$)	527 sq.ft.	527 sq.ft.
Total evaporative	1901 sq.ft.	1901 sq.ft.
Superheater	407 sq.ft.	407 sq.ft.
Total	2308 sq.ft.	2308 sq.ft.
Elements	$32 \times 1\frac{1}{4}''$ (d)	$32 \times 1.244''$
Grate area	28 sq.ft.	28 sq.ft.
Boiler pressure	180 lb./sq.in.	225 lb./sq.in.

Leading wheels	..	..	..	3' 2"	3' 2"
Coupled wheels	..	..	..	5' 8"	5' 8"
Tractive effort (85%)	..	..	..	30,031 lb.	29,250 lb.
Wheelbase (engine)	..	..		8' 11" + 7' 6" + 8' 9" = 25' 2"	
Weight (full):					
Engine	..	..	..	71T 14C (e)	71T 5C
Adhesive	..	..	..	60T 0C (e)	61T 5C
Max. axle load	..	..	..	20T 0C (e)	20T 13C

Leading particulars applicable to tenders fitted:

			K3 ex-G.N.R.	*K3* 1924-25	*K3* 1929-37	*K5*
Wheel diam.	..	..	4' 2"	3' 9"	3' 9"	3' 9"
Wheelbase	..	..	7' 0" + 6' 0"	7' 3" + 6' 3"	7' 3" + 6' 3"	7' 3" + 6' 3"
			= 13' 0"	= 13' 6"	= 13' 6"	= 13' 6"
Total wheelbase						
(engine and tender)	..	..	48' 0¼"	49' 1"	49' 1"	48' 11¾"
Length over buffers						
(engine and tender)	..	..	57' 5¾"	59' 4"	59' 6"	59' 4¾"
Weight (full)	..	..	43T 2C	51T 10C (f)	52T 0C (g)	52T 0C
Water capacity	..	..	3,500 gallons	4,200 gallons	4,200 gallons	4,200 gallons
Coal capacity	..	..	6T 10C	7T 10C	7T 10C	7T 10C

(a) The engine diagram quoted 11' 5½", which was the length of the barrel less the amount by which the smokebox tubeplate was recessed into it.
(b) The engine diagram quoted the distance between tubeplates (11' 11⅞"). See under Details.
(c) Diagram 96A boilers, working at 180 lb./sq.in. pressure, were also latterly fitted to certain K3's.
(d) Later amended to 1.244".
(e) Weights applicable to Parts 1, 2, 4 only. The weights for other Parts were as follows:-

Part		3	5*	6
Weight (full)		72T 10C	72T 12C	73T 8C
Adhesive	..	61T 0C	60T 17C	62T 3C
Max. axle load	..	20T 10C	20T 7C	21T 5C

* Part 5 weights later became accepted for all K3's.
(f) Amended to 52T 0C from 1937.
(g) These weights originally applied to Part 3 engines only. Alternative weights shown were: 50T 10C (K3/4), 51T 9C (K3/5), 51T 0C (K3/6). 52T 0C became the accepted weight for this type of tender from 1937.

L.N.E.R. Renumbering

Under the scheme implemented in 1946, the engines were renumbered 1800-1992, generally in order of building. This included the solitary K5, which had been allocated the number 1863 when the scheme was formulated in 1943 before it was known that the engine would be rebuilt in 1945. It will be noted that the numbers 1803-6 were allocated to 4003/6/4/5, in that order, being the order of the Doncaster works numbers and the dates into traffic. No. 1108 became 1903 in the sequence of the Armstrong Whitworth works numbers although it was delivered out of this order. The two contractors, Armstrong Whitworth and R. Stephenson, each delivered a batch of K3's at the same period in 1934 and these followed one another in the renumbering scheme.

Development and Rebuilding

G.N.R. Class H4 – L.N.E.R. Class K3

The order for these engines was placed in June 1919 and the first one appeared in March 1920. No. 1000 was a direct descendant of Gresley's first 2-6-0 of only eight years before (L.N.E.R. class K1), but the contrast was most marked. The new engine had a 6ft. 0in. diameter boiler which was at that time the largest employed on a British railway. The boiler mountings were squat by comparison with Doncaster tradition. The chimney was 1ft. 1½in. high and 13ft. 4in. above rail level to the top. The liner and cowl were separate castings, with the liner riveted to the chimney. The bell mouth of the cowl was 2ft. 0in. diameter, located 1ft. 1⅜in. above the top of the blastpipe, which latter had a 5in. diameter orifice, see chimney dwg. (A), page 105.

The cab had the usual austere appearance which Gresley had inherited from Ivatt and had so far done nothing to improve, see p. 101 cab dwg. (A). There were no side windows and the cut-out in the sides for the driver to look out was 1ft. 6in. deep, with the roof extending back 9in. over the cab entrance. The inside length of the cab was 5ft. 1¼in. and width 8ft. 0in. The height above rail level to the beading on the top of the roof was 13ft. 1⅜in. The cab sides curved inwards at the rear to match the narrower sides of the standard coal rail tender which was provided.

The regulator valve followed usual Doncaster practice. This was a vertical sliding type comprising a cast-iron slide which covered the pilot valve slots in a bronze slide, which in turn covered the main valve apertures in the cast-iron regulator head at the end of the main steam pipe. The initial ¼in. lift (⅜in. from June 1927) opened the pilot valve first, admitting a small amount of steam into the main steam pipe thereby putting the main valve into equilibrium. A further ⅜in. lift then opened the main valve with the least effort, thus avoiding a sudden rush of steam through the valve apertures and the risk of priming. The regulator valve was operated in the cab by means of a pull-out handle at each side of the firebox faceplate in place of the traditional G.N.R. horizontal handle.

Soon after No. 1000 entered service it was fitted with cylinder horsepower indicating gear. The arrangement was unsatisfactory at first and Gresley wrote to Vincent Raven for assistance. The N.E.R. had had experience indicating three-cylinder engines some years before and Raven sent drawings and photographs which enabled Doncaster to modify their indicating gear. In ensuing tests the centre steam chest cover was damaged by contact with the valve spindle crosshead. This resulted from coasting in full gear with the regulator closed, which was the custom with conventional valve gears at that time to avoid creating a vacuum in the cylinders. Evidently there had been a certain amount of over-travel of the centre valve due to imperfections in the 2 to 1 arrangement.

On 26th May 1920 Gresley ordered the maximum cut-off to be reduced from 75 to 65 per cent, with stops put in the radius links to achieve this. The nominal valve travel in full forward gear was thereby reduced from 6⅛in. to 5⅜in. so that when over-travel occurred no damage would result. Drivers were also cautioned to set the gear at 25 per cent cut-off when coasting at speeds above 25 miles per hour. This setting was a compromise between two opposing needs: mid-gear position to eliminate over-travel completely and full-gear to reduce cylinder vacuum.

The regulator valve was not easy to operate, though this may have been partly due to unfamiliarity with the new style handle. Following the above-mentioned tests, enquiries were made of A.B.C. Coupler Ltd. with a view to fitting the Lockyer type. This was a modern variation of the Ramsbottom double-beat type, with two seatings, which sealed in the closed position by the top valve offering a slightly larger area to the pressure of steam than the bottom one. Little effort was needed to overcome this difference in pressure after which the two valves lifted together, with the top one opening first. After ⅜in. lift, the bottom valve then opened to give a further ⅜in. lift. The valve was in two halves to facilitate removal. The upper part rested on the top seating of the regulator head and was easily lifted clear. The lower part was too wide to pass through this opening and a large cover was therefore provided on the front of the head for it to pass through instead. The drawing for its application to the new 2-6-0's was signed by its designer, N. J. Lockyer, on 29th May 1920. However, for the time being no further action was taken and the later engines of this series appeared with the usual slide regulator valves.

The delivery of Nos. 1001-9 was spread over fifteen months from June 1920 to August 1921. These engines incorporated some of the lessons learned from the early trials with No. 1000 and there were no further experiments until after all ten engines were in traffic. The construction is summarised in the table below.

In October 1921 No. 1002 was fitted with a Lockyer regulator for trial, as a result of which similar valves were afterwards fitted to the Gresley Pacifics (see Part 2A, p. 53). Unfortunately there were difficulties maintaining a steamtight fit at both seatings due to gradual

G.N.R. Nos.	Maker	Works Nos.	Order No.	No. Built	Date
1000-9	Doncaster	1509/13/4/5/7/20/16/22/6/9	290	10	1920-21

wear and also to unequal heat expansion. The valve was afterwards removed from No. 1002 and no further engines of this class were fitted.

No. 1009's cylinders were horsepower indicated during the first week of October 1921. On the first two days of the tests the engine worked goods trains without difficulty, as the loads were well within its capabilities. On 6th October it was tested on the 3-18 p.m. passenger train from Peterborough to Doncaster with thirteen coaches (fifty-four axles). A good start was made and the average speed up the bank to Stoke was 55 miles per hour, whilst the highest speed reached on the journey was 70 miles per hour. There should have been a further test the next day, but No. 1009 ran its left driving coupling rod pin hot whilst working outward from Doncaster and class C1 No. 1451 had to be substituted for the return journey. The load was slightly greater, fifty-six axles, and the Atlantic had much greater difficulty maintaining steam. Speed up the bank to Stoke was about 30 miles per hour.

The tests with No. 1009 showed that there was insufficient lead steam in the middle cylinder at the front port. The valves on this engine only were altered experimentally to give $\frac{3}{16}$in. lead by taking $\frac{1}{16}$in. off the steam edge of the rings. This alteration was applied equally to all three cylinders, front and back. (When the Pacifics appeared in 1922 they had $\frac{3}{16}$in. steam lead). In September 1922 the exhaust clearance in No. 1002's valves was increased from $\frac{1}{8}$in. to $\frac{1}{4}$in. by chamfering the outer edge of the valve rings and the resulting valve events then became standard for the class until long lap valves were eventually introduced after 1928.

Other post-Grouping developments were all aimed at bringing these engines into line with current practice and as such it is appropriate to describe these changes under the Group Standard series. The dates when the more important alterations took place, i.e. fitting of long lap valves (1929-33) and side window cabs with reduced boiler mountings (1939-40), are given in the Summary. When the last mentioned event took place, the engines concerned were reclassified from Part 1 to Part 2.

L.N.E.R. GROUP STANDARD CLASS K3

After Grouping, Gresley adopted this class for development and construction only ceased after the new V2's had proved themselves to be more than adequate replacements. Altogether 183 K3's were built between 1924 and 1937 to the L.N.E.R. Composite Load Gauge and it is convenient to divide these engines into five series.

17 SERIES – One early effect of Grouping was the placing of an order in October 1923 for twenty-five K3's from Darlington Works, to which a further twenty-five were added one month later. These engines appeared between August 1924 and April 1925, taking over blank running numbers in the N.E.R. series between 17 and 200. Whilst basically a continuation of the original G.N.R. design, Darlington took the opportunity to incorporate some of its own features whilst modifying the design to fit the new Composite Load Gauge.

The chimneys were plain waisted with curved lips, giving them a distinct N.E.R. appearance. They were 9½in. high and 13ft. 0in. above rail level to the top. The liners were correspondingly 4 inches shorter than those fitted to Nos. 4000-9 so that the distance between the cowl and the blastpipe was unchanged. Otherwise the proportions of liner and blastpipe conformed to Doncaster practice, see chimney dwg. (B). The domes were lower than on the G.N.R. series. The whistles were shorter and positioned lower down off centre with the control lever no longer above the roof (cf. figs. 88 and 91).

The cab had a typical N.E.R. appearance with side windows, see cab dwg. (B). The length inside remained the same as in the G.N.R. series, but the height above rail level to the top was reduced to 12ft. 10¾in. The side sheets were straight throughout their length, matching the wider Group Standard tenders which were also specially designed at Darlington (fig. 90). These new tenders held more coal and water than the G.N.R. type. In November 1924 a complaint was made that the cab side windows were too low. Commencing with No. 135, part way through the order, the later engines had their window apertures raised 3½in. (fig. 92). The handrails above and below the windows were similarly

Engine Nos.	Maker	Order No.	Date ordered	Works Nos.	No. Built	Date	Part
17 Series							
17,28,32/3/6/8/9,46,							
52/3/8,69,73/5,80,91/							
2,109/11-4/6/8/20	Darlington	–	10/1923	–	25	1924	2
121/5/6/7/34/5/40/1/							
3/6/53/6/8/9/63/7/							
70/8/80/4/6/8/91/5,							
200	,,	–	11/1923	–	25	1925	2
202/3/4/6/7/8/27/8/							
9/31	,,	–	11/1924	–	10	1925	2
1300 Series							
1300/12/8/31/45/64/5/							
7/8/86	Doncaster	315	8/1927	1711-20	10	1929	3
1387/8/9/91/2/4-8	,,	316	,,	1721-30	10	1929	3
2761 Series							
2761-9	Darlington(a)	–	12/1928	–	9	1930	4
1100 Series							
1100/1/2/6/8/17/8/9/							
21/5/33/5/7/41/54/6/	Armstrong						
8/62/4/6	Whitworth	L86	5/1930	1111-30	20	1931	5
1302 Series							
1302/4/8/10/24/06,							
2934-7	,,	(b)L88	2/1934	1156-65	10	1934-35(c)	6
1325/32/3/9/99/22/07,							
2938/9/40	R.Stephenson	E152	,,	4075-84	10	1934-35(c)	6
2425-8/38/9/40/2/3/	N.B.						
7-51/9/61/3/6/7/8	Loco. Co.(d)	L890	1/1935	24225-44	20	1935	6
2470/3/98/9	Darlington	–	3/1935	–	4	1936	2
3813-32	,,	–	9/1935	–	20	1936-37	2
2417/29/45/6/53/5/8/	Armstrong						
65/71/2	Whitworth	L92	12/1935	1270-9	10	1936	2
					Total 183		

(a) Boilers supplied by N.B. Locomotive Co.
(b) These engines were originally ordered in November 1933 from Darlington Works. Order transferred in February 1934 to Armstrong Whitworth.
(c) The last two Armstrong Whitworth engines and the last five R. Stephenson engines were put into store on delivery to the L.N.E.R. in 1934, as their construction had been authorised on the 1935 programme. They were sent into traffic in January 1935.
(d) Hyde Park Works.

raised and the vertical handrail near the cab entrance was lengthened from 2ft. 4in. to 2ft. 7½in. between pillar centres, see cab dwg. (C).

Other alterations made to the design included the use of double-case buffers instead of the G.N.R. straight shank type, larger footsteps on the running plate alongside the cab, a revised cab floor and a different joint ring on the smokebox for the door. These are more fully described under Details. Despite all these changes, the maximum weight of these Part 2 engines, and the axle load, was stated to be the same as the G.N.R. series.

No. 141 differed from the earlier engines by having steam reversing gear, following N.E.R. practice (fig. 92). There were two handles in the cab for operating the gear. One handle rotated the rod which ran alongside the boiler on the driver's side and served two purposes. First of all it opened a valve which admitted steam from the boiler to the reversing cylinder between the frames. At the same time rodding from an arm just behind this valve led down to a valve on the oil cataract cylinder, which opened to allow the cataract fluid to flow between the opposite ends of the cylinder. The reversing handle controlled the admission of steam to one or other side of the reversing cylinder piston, thus lifting or lowering the radius rod as required. When the desired setting was reached, the driver restored the first handle to its original position. This cut off steam to the reversing cylinder and simultaneously closed the oil valve on the cataract cylinder, thereby locking its piston in whichever position it was in and also the reversing gear. The forward gear had five notches on the indicator which approximated to the 15, 25, 35, 45 and 65 per cent cut-off positions in the conventional screw reversing gear.

In November 1924 a further ten engines of this series had been ordered and these appeared from Darlington Works between August and December 1925 numbered between 202 and 231, again filling in existing blanks. These engines had steam reversing gear like No. 141, but two new features were the provision of steam brake for engine and tender, and left-hand drive operation (fig. 93). No further K3's were built until 1929 and the intervening period was one of continuing development and improvement. Before passing on to the next series of K3 it is convenient to complete the narrative of the development of this first Darlington series (which however did not stop in 1929).

Between November 1927 and April 1928 Nos. 28, 33/6/8, 46, 52/3, all allocated to the N.E.

Area, were fitted with steam-operated reversing gear with the usual two-handle arrangement (fig. 94). Then in July 1928 Doncaster altered No. 141 to conform to the arrangement used on the first twenty class D49 4-4-0's (see Part 4 of this series, p. 98). This retained the N.E.R. system of employing an oil cataract cylinder to hold the gear in the desired position, but had one handle only. The handle which was dispensed with was the one which previously controlled both the steam valve on the side of the boiler and the oil valve on the cataract cylinder. The steam valve was still needed but was normally left open and was now controlled by turning a small wheel in the cab. The driver therefore had only the reversing handle to manipulate. This controlled the admission of steam into the reversing cylinder as before, but it also now opened the oil valve on the cataract cylinder and closed it automatically when the reversing gear was in its new position.

In April 1929 the Southern Area Running Department reported that they had made a few minor alterations; otherwise the new arrangement on No. 141 was satisfactory. In particular the new type of control was no doubt superior to the old two-handle system. There had been a little creep at first but this had been cured by adjusting the reversing shaft spring. Between November 1929 and June 1930 the remaining engines with steam reversing gear were brought into line with No. 141, with the exception of Nos. 202/6.

Meanwhile, following successful results from applying long lap valves to the Pacifics, Doncaster was instructed on 28th February 1928 to fit one K3 in a similar manner. No. 134 was modified in October 1928 and quickly showed a considerable economy in coal consumption. It is convenient at this point to summarise in the table on page 98 the sequence of developments in the valve gear details, from the time the G.N. series appeared until the introduction of long lap valves in 1928.

Commencing with the 1300 Series, to be described later, new K3's had the improved valve gear arrangement whilst in June 1929 Doncaster was instructed to alter five more of the existing engines. Nos. 109/43, 203, and also 4004/6 of the earlier G.N.R. series, were dealt with between October 1929 and March 1930. Of these, No. 203 had steam-operated reversing gear and this had to be altered slightly as the full travel of the cataract spindle, which was 8¼in., could not be increased to give the required additional drop of the radius arm. The cataract spindle and

	New	5/1920	11/1921*	9/1922	10/1928
Maximum cut-off (%)	75	65	65	65	65
Maximum valve travel (in.)	$6\frac{1}{8}$	$5\frac{3}{4}$	$5\frac{5}{8}$	$5\frac{3}{4}$	$5\frac{5}{8}$
Steam lap (in.)	$1\frac{1}{2}$	$1\frac{1}{2}$	$1\frac{7}{16}$	$1\frac{1}{2}$	$1\frac{5}{8}$
Steam lead (in.)	$\frac{1}{8}$	$\frac{1}{8}$	$\frac{3}{16}$	$\frac{1}{8}$	$\frac{1}{8}$
Exhaust clearance (in.)	$\frac{1}{8}$	$\frac{1}{8}$	$\frac{1}{4}$	$\frac{1}{4}$	0

* No. 1009 experimentally

reversing shaft arm were both shortened and the connecting arm between them was lengthened, to provide the necessary leverage combination. No. 203 was altered to the new one-handle control system at the same time.

In August 1930 the Running Department reported that in comparative tests No. 109 (with long lap valves) was about 7½lb. per mile lighter on coal than No. 111. It was also found to be better for starting, pulling and running. In view of these excellent results Doncaster was instructed on 25th August 1930 to fit the remaining K3's under its maintenance with long lap valves. Maintenance of the Scottish Area K3's was transferred to Doncaster from February 1931 so that these engines were then altered too. Due to an oversight, instructions were not sent to Darlington until November 1933 so that for the time being the short lap valve engines in the N.E. Area were not altered (see later).

On 4th September 1929 one of the Southern Area K3's with steam-operated reversing gear, No. 208, was working an express goods train at high speed when its middle valve spindle guide was struck and broken by the end of the equal motion lever, due to whip action. The engine had been coasting with the regulator shut and the reversing gear full forward, which was contrary to Gresley's directive of May 1920 to which reference has already been made. There had been similar cases before this and the usual remedy had been to chip away about ¼in. from the front of the guide and to provide a further ⅛in. clearance on the engines with long travel valve gear.

In September 1930 Doncaster started removing steam-operated reversing gear from the K3 engines as they passed through shops and screw reversing gear was substituted. For the time being no similar action was contemplated by the N.E. Area, whose engines were shopped at

Darlington and Gateshead. In January 1931 Doncaster Works was instructed to send the surplus equipment to Darlington where it was required for fitting to the class T1 4-8-0T's (see part 9B, pp. 31/2). By this time, however, the steam-operated reversing gear taken from Nos. 202/6/29 had been scrapped and Doncaster was only able to send eight sets during 1931.

In October 1933 Gresley called for details of all K3's which had long lap valves, either fitted when new or altered subsequently. The replies drew attention to the fact that instructions had never been issued to Darlington to alter the nine engines operating in the N.E. Area which still had short lap valves. The necessary order was issued on 7th November 1933 for Darlington to alter these engines as they passed through works. No. 17 was dealt with first, in March 1934, though curiously it was sent to Doncaster Works which was most unusual at that time for an engine operating in the N.E. Area (see under Maintenance). This left eight engines to be dealt with, including seven which still had steam-operated reversing gear. No. 53 was taken in hand first by Darlington but after its valve gear had been altered it was realised that the spindle in the cataract cylinder gave insufficient movement to obtain 65 per cent cut-off. Doncaster had of course dealt with this situation in December 1929 when they fitted No. 203 with long lap valves. Darlington did not seek Doncaster's assistance but simply replaced the steam reversing gear by screw reverse.

The Works Manager at Darlington then suggested that in addition to removing the steam reversing gear, where still fitted, the opportunity should be taken to convert these last six engines to left-hand drive when they were given long lap valves. This was agreed and the engines concerned were altered accordingly between October 1934 and April 1936, together with the screw reverse engine No. 39. For completeness

98

Nos. 17 and 53, which already had the modified valve gear, were also altered to left-hand drive in September 1935 and May 1937 respectively (fig. 95). This eliminated right-hand drive K3's from the N.E. Area. The dates when the engines received all these modifications are set out in the Summary.

The engines of this series all had the G.N.R. slide regulator when new, about which there were constant complaints that it was difficult to operate. In 1929 the trial fitting was ordered of the Joco combined regulator and drifting valve, marketed by A.B.C. Coupler. This comprised three single-beat valves mounted concentrically on a spindle. The small drifting valve opened first, admitting sufficient steam to the steam chest and cylinders for coasting purposes whilst at the same time placing the second valve in equilibrium. Further movement of the regulator handle then opened this second valve, which in turn placed the third valve in equilibrium, and finally opened the latter. One advantage of the Joco regulator was that having three separate valves eliminated the effects of heat expansion between their seats. The chief disadvantage was the number of working parts and pins. This valve was fitted to No. 17 in March 1929, at about the same time as its trial appearance on classes A1 No. 2568 (see part 2A, p. 54), D49 No. 2754 (see Part 4, p. 89) and J39 No. 1459 (see p. 20). The valve was removed from No. 17 in December 1932 and transferred to No. 38 in March 1933. It was removed from this latter engine in August 1934 and possibly scrapped.

Three K3's were fitted in 1930 with the North British Locomotive Co. patent double-beat regulator, actually of French design, as previously fitted to class B17 Nos. 2805-9 (see Part 2B, p. 104). The valve itself was similar in action to that of the Lockyer type described on p. 94. The two valves lifted together, with the top one opening first. After $\frac{5}{16}$in. lift, the bottom valve opened to give a further $\frac{11}{16}$in. lift. The principal difference lay in the regulator head, which had a loose top seating that was easily removed to enable the entire valve to be lifted out for inspection. This eliminated the need for a loose front cover which was difficult to keep steamtight on the Lockyer type. These valves were fitted in 1930 to Nos. 52 (March), 39 (April) and 53 (May). The only removal date recorded was for No. 52 (July 1932). Similar valves were fitted at about the same time to three J39's (see p. 20) and they were afterwards fitted to the Gresley Pacifics from August 1933 (see Part 2A, p. 54).

Following success with the improved slide regulator on the 2761 series engines (see p. 104), Darlington Works started fitting similar valves after December 1930 to the engines of the 17 series for which they were responsible. Doncaster was not advised of this development until March 1931, but after checking the drawings it was immediately agreed that Doncaster Works should alter the remaining K3's as they passed through works for repair. The process of replacement was slow and in July 1934 the Southern Area Running Department complained that drivers were having difficulty on the earlier engines of the class, with regulators working stiffly and causing problems in controlling the right amount of steam required when shunting. In particular a comparison was drawn between No. 69, which had still to be altered, and No. 2761. Eventually all the K3's had the improved type of slide regulator valve after which no further complaints were received. When No. 206 was rebuilt in 1945 it received a B1-type regulator handle in common with a number of other Thompson classes, though as a result of subsequent boiler changes it may have reverted afterwards to the Gresley pull-out type. With regard to the K3's which afterwards acquired Diagram 96A boilers, a number of these also had B1-type regulator handles.

The K3's had a reputation for rough riding, which was so bad at times that the bolts fastening the cab to the footplate were shaken loose – a problem which was never cured. As early as February 1926 No. 118 was found to have broken both its engine and tender dragboxes. As the engine was not much more than a year old, the authorities at Doncaster asked Darlington for their comments. Darlington suggested that the engines must be receiving some very rough treatment in the south! Broken dragboxes on tenders attached to K3's then became relatively common, despite steps taken to strengthen them.

The gap between each coupled wheel axlebox and its hornblock was packed by a tapered steel wedge which could be adjusted vertically to compensate for longitudinal wear. The wedge was secured by a horizontal bolt which passed through a vertical slot in the hornblock. The trouble with this arrangement was that the bolts slipped in the slots and the wedges then worked loose. This caused the axleboxes to "knock". In March 1930 Gresley decided to dispense with wedges altogether and the K3's which were built in 1931 had solid hornblocks. The existing K3's had their wedges secured permanently after they had been adjusted.

Permanently securing the wedges introduced complications, as it was difficult to compensate for the inevitable wear. The wheels for example had to be dropped to get at the wedges to release them. The matter came to a head in April 1932 when No. 4002, of the G.N. series, was booked for bad riding and knocking in the boxes. The slack in each of the coupled wheel horns was found to be greater than the maximum permitted clearance, though the engine had only been out of shops a month. The wedges were readjusted and the securing bolts were firmly held by putting blocks of iron under them in the slots. The bolts, and thus the wedges, could no longer slip, but the facility was there to raise them later as wear took place. This simple remedy was effective and from November 1932 it became standard practice for the K3's which had wedges.

By 1931 the frames were showing signs of severe fractures, particularly in the upper corners of the trailing horn gaps. In April 1931 it was discovered that whereas Nos. 4000-9, the G.N. series engines, had auxiliary oilboxes for lubricating the horn cheeks, for some reason they had been omitted from the post-Grouping engines, but this deficiency was quickly put right.

About this time, Doncaster started shopping the Scottish Area K3's, whose frames were found to be in a particularly bad condition. The repair of No. 186 was held up whilst a decision was taken to replace the left-hand frame behind a point midway between the middle and trailing horn gaps, and fit a patch over the join. The engine was eventually returned to traffic in September 1931. Thereafter, other K3's were similarly dealt with if the condition of their frames warranted it (fig. 112). Usually one side only of the engine needed a new rear end, in which case the original hornblocks with wedges were put back. Occasionally both sides were renewed, when it was the practice to fit new solid trailing hornblocks, even after 1934. Apart from No. 186, other K3's dealt with at Doncaster during the thirties included Nos. 32/9, 52, 75, 113/4/6/8/25/6/7/34/5/43/56/8/9/70/84/91/5, together with Nos. 4002/4/7/8 of the G.N. series. Several engines of the later 1300 and 1100 series were also provided with new rear end frames (see later).

The coupled wheel bearing springs were originally 3ft. 6in. across their centres (eleven ⅜in. thick plates). In February 1933 Nos. 112/95 were fitted instead with D49 type springs (fifteen ¼in. thick plates), and Nos. 140 and 229 were similarly fitted a month later. These springs appeared to be an improvement on the original

type and following good reports from the Running Department it was agreed in May 1933 to fit D49 type springs to the remaining engines. Within two months however, reports were being received of rough riding on engines which had been so altered.

In October 1933 Gresley drew attention to the springs fitted to the S.R. Schools class 4-4-0. These were 4ft. 0in. across their centres (sixteen ¼in. thick plates) and their greater flexibility came from the larger span. It was agreed to fit one K3 for trial with similar springs and No. 134 was altered in February 1934. The Running Department reported in April 1934 that whilst the new springs were a considerable improvement over the original K3 springs, there was hardly any difference between them and the D49 type. It was decided to continue fitting the D49 type to existing K3's to avoid having to reposition spring hanger brackets 6in. further apart, but new engines built from 1934 onwards had the Schools type. The comparative deflections per ton of the three types of springs were as follows:-

Type		Deflection (per ton)
Original	..	0.1425in.
D49 ..	..	0.204 in.
Schools ..	..	0.26 in.

Reference has already been made to early complaints that the cab side windows were too low on the engines numbered from 17 to 134 and that the height had been raised by 3½in. on the later engines of this series, but nothing was immediately done about the earlier engines. Then in October 1929 the Southern Area Running Department made a further complaint that the side windows on the later engines were also too low so that "even a man of average height is liable to strike his head on the top of the window frame". Commencing with No. 227 in January 1930, the engines in the Southern Area had their cabs altered and the last engine, No. 203, was dealt with in August 1931. The windows on the engines up to No. 134 were raised by 6½in. and those on the later engines of this series by 3in. The handrail above the windows was of necessity dispensed with, though in the early forties this was compensated for by providing a short vertical handrail on the cab front plate (fig. 95). The Scottish Area engines of this series were dealt with between March 1931 and July 1932 after Doncaster took over their maintenance. Two N.E. Area engines, Nos. 17 and 28, were

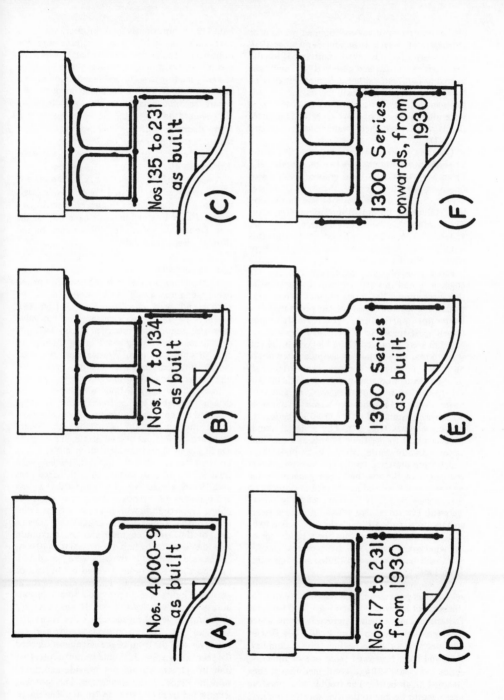

(A) Nos. 4000-9 as built

(B) Nos. 17 to 134 as built

(C) Nos 135 to 231 as built

(D) Nos. 17 to 231 from 1930

(E) 1300 Series as built

(F) 1300 Series onwards, from 1930

101

also altered when they were shopped specially at Doncaster in March 1934 and September 1938 respectively. No. 39 was transferred to the Southern Area in September 1940 and was altered at Doncaster either in September 1941 or November 1943. The remaining engines of this series in the N.E. Area, Nos. 33/6/8, 46, 52/3, were altered by about 1944-46 after Doncaster finally took over their maintenance. See cab dwg. (D).

The front spectacle windows in the cabs of the 17 series were originally in two pieces (fig. 91). From May 1938 they were gradually altered to one-piece as they passed through Doncaster Works, both in the interests of standardisation and to improve the forward look-out (fig. 130). The engines in the Scottish Area, Nos. 32, 184/6/8/91/5, 200, missed out on this modification, which was not carried out at Cowlairs Works.

Fixed padded seats were provided for the enginemen and this arrangement also applied to the succeeding 1300 series engines. They were fastened to the cab sides with the result that they were not particularly comfortable when travelling at speed. In March 1930 the seats on No. 143 were arranged to be hinged on the cab sides so that they could be collapsed when not in use. The remaining engines were afterwards brought into line and this arrangement was provided when new for the later 2761 and 1100 series. From 1934 what were termed piano stool seats became standard on the new 1302 series and existing engines (fig. 97). The pedestal stands were fastened to the floor boards and the seats were generally more comfortable than those which were attached to the cab sides. However the height of the seat had been gauged for the high side windows and they were not popular on the engines in the N.E. Area whose windows were still low down. No official protest appears to have been made although the drivers had to be almost contortionists to put their heads out of the windows. Finally, it is believed that padded seats with backs were substituted in a few cases from 1946.

The engines of the 17 series were generally regarded as poor steamers, though the reason for this was not known. The Southern Area Running Department made their own investigations which they reported upon in April 1929. They first of all fitted one of these engines with a chimney, liner and cowl borrowed from one of the G.N. series (Nos. 4000-9) and confirmed that it then steamed much better. The trouble was therefore presumed to be due to the 4in. shorter chimney.

No. 112, a notoriously bad steamer, was then fitted with a 4in. shorter blastpipe and the improvement was so marked that it was even possible to open out the orifice of the blastpipe to 5½in., leading to a noticeable reduction in coal consumption. The Running Department in their report recommended that the post-Grouping K3's should have 4in. shorter blastpipes with a 5⅛in. diameter orifice. This was agreed and instructions were issued on 28th May 1929 to alter the engines of this series as they passed through shops.

A new arrangement of chimney, liner and cowl was introduced in March 1939 following trials with one of the engines of the 1100 series (see later). The N.E.-style chimney gave way to the new Doncaster pattern as the engines passed through shops for repair.

1300 SERIES – The second post-Grouping series appeared from Doncaster in 1929 and comprised twenty engines which were numbered in the 1300's and were classified Part 3 (fig. 98). Features of this series were the long lap valve gear, side window cab modelled on the D49 type, new draughting arrangement in an attempt to cure steaming troubles, Westinghouse brake on engine and tender with vacuum ejector for alternative train braking and screw reversing gear with left-hand drive. Minor alterations to the design (described under Details and Tenders) included the cutting away of the lower corners of the front bufferbeam, a change to Group Standard buffers, an altered arrangement of sanding gear, provision of a drop grate, larger bearings for the middle big-end, tenders with flush sides and ends instead of with flared tops and, from engine No. 1387 onwards, a new arrangement of firebox staying and wash-out plugs. The weight in working order of this series was given as 72 tons 10 cwt. (as against 71 tons 14 cwt. of the earlier engines) and the maximum axle load went up by half a ton to 20 tons 10 cwt.

The side windows in the cabs were placed high up with their top frames levelled off instead of curved as in the 17 series. The cab sides were cut away at window level to provide a 10in. long cut-out, as in the Gresley Pacifics. It was necessary therefore to lengthen the cab sides from 5ft. 1⅛in. to 5ft. 7in. to provide room for the windows, and the front of the cab almost touched the rear safety valve. It should be noted therefore that the larger cab did not provide additional working space for the enginemen. The roof was lengthened from 6ft. 10in. to 7ft. 4in. The top of the cab sides where they met the roof at the back had a 5in. radius curve instead of 12in. as in the previous series. The front spectacle windows were in one piece instead of two (though the majority of the 17 series acquired one-piece windows later). See cab dwg. (E).

In February 1930 the N.E. Area Running Department complained that the profile of the rear edge of the cabs on these latest Doncaster engines afforded no protection for the enginemen's backs, which were unnecessarily exposed to wind and rain. Doncaster could not understand this complaint as the latest cab "had been designed at Darlington, on the lines of the D49 type, to suit working conditions on their own Section"! However, the latest K3 cabs were 6in. shorter than the D49 type and the seats had therefore been placed further back to clear the vertical screw reverse column. Gresley asked if the seats could be placed further forward but this was not possible. He then agreed to the side sheets being filled in at the back and the side windows repositioned so that they were again centrally placed. The cabs on these twenty engines were altered at the first opportunity, No. 1318 being dealt with at Doncaster Works in July 1930 and the remainder at Darlington Works in 1930-32 (fig. 99).

The N.E. Area also complained about the loss of the horizontal handrail, no longer provided above the windows. Gresley agreed to the provision of a short vertical handrail on the cab front plate, and the necessary instructions were issued in March 1930. As mentioned already this modification was subsequently extended to the 17 series engines.

The new cab profile was adopted without change for the later series and was also used for the G.N. series engines, Nos. 4000-9, when they were altered in 1939-40 to bring them within the Composite Load Gauge (fig. 89). See cab dwg. (F).

The draughting arrangement was remodelled, the liner and cowl being replaced by a parabolic cone following N.E.R. practice. The profile of this cone resembled the cooling towers of some present day power stations. The base of the cone was 1ft. 8in. diameter and 1ft. $1\frac{7}{16}$in. above the blastpipe, which still had a 5in. diameter orifice. The cone was attached to the inside of the smokebox by struts using the same bolts which held the chimney in place. Because of the difference in the methods of attaching the N.E.-style cone and the G.N.-style liner and cowl, they were not interchangeable. The pattern of the chimney was also altered and it had the more usual Doncaster appearance. See chimney dwg. (C).

Following the report from the Running Department in April 1929 on the steaming trials with No. 112 (see earlier) it was decided to fit new engines with the improved arrangement of 4in. shorter blastpipe with a $5\frac{3}{8}$in. diameter orifice, as recommended for the 17 series. Commencing with No. 1318 when new, the shorter blastpipe became standard and Nos. 1300/12 were afterwards brought into line. The same arrangement was employed for the later series when they were built. Finally, a new arrangement of chimney, liner and cowl was introduced in March 1939 following trials with one of the engines of the 1100 series (see later). Externally, the difference was barely detectable though the chimney casting was 1in. larger in diameter at the base.

The engines had the usual slide regulator valve. Soon after delivery to the N.E. Area commenced, drivers were registering complaints about stiffness in operation. Darlington modified the design for the later 2761 series (see p. 104) and after December 1930 brought the engines of the 1300 series into line.

All these twenty engines were based in the N.E. Area and were at first shopped at Darlington Works, which was not always kept informed of developments at Doncaster. In February 1935 Darlington reported that the frames were particularly troublesome on engines of this series, with fractures having been dealt with so far on Nos. 1300/45/68/86/7. No. 1345 was currently receiving attention to a crack which had gone through the rear upper corner of the left trailing horn, where similar cracks had been welded twice already on this engine, in February 1932 and September 1934. Darlington considered that a contributory factor was slackness in the horn stays, the rear ones being particularly difficult to adjust at the sheds because of the proximity of the ashpan. Darlington also asked if it was true that Doncaster occasionally fitted new rear end frames, as they had not been officially informed. The repairs to No. 1345 were held up awaiting drawings from Doncaster and it was in works from 16th January to 31st October 1935. A new rear end frame may have been fitted, but this has not been confirmed. Of the engines which had already given trouble, Nos. 1300/87 at least afterwards acquired a new rear end frame at one side, whilst No. 1364, another engine from this series, received new rear end frames at Darlington in July 1939.

2761 Series – This series comprised nine engines built at Darlington in 1930 (fig. 100). They had the new style of cab, without the cut-out, which was being currently fitted to engines of the 1300 series as they passed through shops. The draughting arrangement conformed to current practice, as introduced with No. 1318. The engines and tender had steam brake with a vacuum ejector provided for train braking.

An improved regulator was introduced on this series. There had been many complaints, particularly from drivers in the N.E. Area, concerning the stiffness in working of the slide regulators on the earlier engines of the class. Darlington modified the design by reducing the area of the sliding surfaces which were in actual contact with one another. This eased the problem of excessive wear on the surfaces and made the valves easier to operate. The arrangement was adopted for all the later engines of the class and the earlier engines were eventually brought into line.

There was a slight improvement in the drop grate gear (see p. 114); otherwise no major new developments were associated with this series. Nevertheless they were for a time separately classified as Part 4. The weight in working order and maximum axle load were the same as for the K3/1 and K3/2 engines.

1100 Series – This series comprised twenty engines built by Armstrong Whitworth in 1931 and classified K3/5 (fig. 101). They generally resembled the preceding 2761 series, with steam brake also for engine and tender. One new feature, found on this series only, was the absence of axlebox wedges. Instead they had solid hornblocks following Gresley's decision in March 1930 to dispense with wedges in an attempt to eliminate axlebox "knock" (see under 17 series). Once again a change of weight was recorded, an increase to 72 tons 12 cwt. The maximum axle load was 20 tons 7 cwt., slightly less than K3/3.

One new development was first tried out on an engine of this series which afterwards became standard for the class. The position in 1937, by which time the last K3 had been built, was that there were three different draughting arrangements. The G.N. series still had their original chimneys, liners, cowls and 5in. diameter blastpipe tops. The engines of the 17 series had short Darlington-style chimneys, Doncaster-style liners and cowls and short 5⅛in. diameter blastpipes. The engines of the later series had short Doncaster-style chimneys,

Darlington-style cones and short 5⅛in. diameter blastpipes.

The post-Grouping engines now steamed equally well, whether they had the liner and cowl combination or the cone. The improvement in steaming had stemmed from the blastpipe modification, so the time had come to standardise the other fittings. In October 1937 No. 1125 received a new pattern of liner and cowl whose dimensions were based on the cone; in particular the diameter of the bell mouth was only 1ft. 8in. The liner was supported by the chimney which therefore had to be redesigned. Externally it looked no different from the Doncaster-style chimneys which were fitted to the K3's built from 1929 onwards, but the base was 1in. larger in diameter. The new arrangement was satisfactory and it was agreed in March 1939 to fit the new chimney, liner and cowl combination to the remaining K3's as they passed through shops for repair. This also coincided with alterations made to Nos. 4000-9 to bring them within the L.N.E.R. Composite Load Gauge so that by about mid-1941 all the K3's for the first time had the same draughting arrangement. See chimney dwg. (D).

One engine of this series, No. 61906 (ex-1119), was observed latterly with a new rear end frame on the right side (fig. 114).

1302 Series – This series comprised the last seventy-four engines which were built during 1934-37, with construction shared between Armstrong Whitworth (two separate orders), R. Stephenson, N.B. Locomotive Co. and Darlington (figs. 102 to 106). Features of this series were the reintroduction of axlebox wedges with however the wedge securing bolts fitted at an angle instead of horizontally, 4ft. 0in. span coupled wheel bearing springs of the type fitted experimentally in April 1934 to No. 134 (see earlier under 17 series), piano stool seats for the enginemen (also referred to under 17 series) and vacuum brakes throughout.

Other detail changes were a further modification to the sanding gear, the addition of stops to prevent the smokebox door opening too far, and the provision of roller bearings to certain parts of the valve gear. No. 2425 onwards had larger diameter steam pipes to the cylinders, whilst the engines built in 1936-37 were provided with footsteps at the front end (fig. 105). The final batch, Nos. 3813-32, had hand holes in the upper firebox casing in place of wash-out plugs (fig. 106).

Fig. 87   Class K3 No. 1007N at Hornsey shed, November 1923.

G.N. series. Tall chimney and dome, whistle lever above cab roof, right-hand drive, 8 in. deep cover for reversing rod alongside firebox, mechanical lubricators for cylinders (front) and axleboxes (rear), post-1912 G.N. tender with 3ft. 7in. handrails.

Fig. 88   Class K3/1 No. 4000 at Doncaster shed, c. 1926.

Gravity fed sanding gear to middle coupled wheels and behind trailing coupled wheels, steam sanding in front of leading coupled wheels, Group Standard 4,200-gallon tender with stepped-out coping plate.

Fig. 89   Class K3/2 No. 4000 at Doncaster Works, June 1939.

Reduced boiler mountings and side-window cab fitted.

Fig. 90   Class K3/2 No. 32 at Eastfield shed, c. June 1927.

17 series. Side-window cab with low windows and handrail above, 9½ in. deep cover for reversing rod alongside firebox, G.N.-style double-case buffers, first engine with a Group Standard 4,200-gallon tender.

Fig. 91   Class K3/2 No. 33 at Darlington Works, September 1924.

Vertical handrails on cab matching those on tender, front spectacle window in two pieces, whistle off-centre and lower down, four sight-feed lubricator pipes passing alongside boiler from cab to cylinders and valves, oil feed to valves entering steam pipe cover, painted shop-grey.

Fig. 92   Class K3/2 No. 141 at Doncaster shed, c. 1925.

Cab side windows 3½ in. higher with handrail above, vertical handrails on cab 3½ in. longer than those on tender, steam reversing gear, modified sight-feed arrangement with lubricator pipe for right-hand valves passing along right-hand side of boiler, divided oil feed to valves entering steam chest from above, no lagging for exhaust steam pipes on either side of live steam pipe. Note classification "2.6.0." on bufferbeam.

Fig. 93   Class K3/2 No. 227 at Doncaster shed, September 1929.
Left-hand drive, steam reversing gear.

Fig. 94   Class K3/2 No. 28 at Sheffield Victoria, September 1929.
Altered from screw to steam reversing gear, altered to mechanical lubrication for cylinders and valves. Note striker for Raven fog signalling
apparatus behind middle coupled wheels.

Fig. 95   Class K3/2 No. 17 at Doncaster shed, May 1937.
Altered to left-hand drive, altered cab sides with high windows and no handrails above, handrail in front of cab, raised sandbox filler
with flat top for leading gravity sanders (changed from steam operation), middle sanders now steam operated.

Fig. 97   Class K3/2. 2761 series cab layout, 1938.
Left-hand drive, steam brake with vacuum ejector, now fitted with piano stool seats.

Fig. 96   Class K3/1. G.N. series smokebox layout.

Fig. 98   Class K3/3 No. 1300 at Doncaster Works, April 1929.

1300 series. Westinghouse brake with pump on smokebox side, D49-style cab profile, side windows high up with top frames levelled off, three wash-out plugs on firebox above handrail, 4,200-gallon tender with separate coping plate and short handrails, air reservoir under rear dragbox.

Fig. 99   Class K3/3 No. 1391 at Heaton shed, c. 1932.

Left-hand drive, cab profile altered with windows repositioned centrally and handrail in front, Group Standard buffers.

g. 100   Class K3/4 No. 2769 at Eastfield shed, August 1932.

2761 series. Four wash-out plugs on firebox above handrail.

Fig. 101   Class K3/5 No. 1125 at Doncaster Works, April 1931.

1100 series. Raised sandbox filler with flat top for leading gravity sanders, 4,200-gallon tender with separate coping plate, short handrails and usual angle-iron below running plate.

Fig. 102   Class K3/6 No. 2937 at Scotswood Works, 1934.

1302 series, built Armstrong Whitworth 1934. Raised sandbox filler with slanting top for leading sanders, 4,200-gallon tender with coping plate integral with side sheet, long handrails, usual angle-iron absent below running plate.

Fig. 103   Class K3/6 No. 1333 at Darlington shed, September 1934.

Built R. Stephenson 1934. Simplified drop grate rodding alongside frames below running plate, steam heating pipe from manifold in cab to front mechanical lubricator sloping down alongside boiler, smokebox door stops as extensions to hinge straps, vacuum reservoir behind coping plate at rear of tender on right-hand side.

ig. 104   Class K3/2 No. 2448 at Doncaster shed, c. September 1935.

Built N.B. Loco. Co. 1935. Two hand holes on firebox above handrail, two vacuum reservoirs behind coping plate at rear of tender.

g. 105   Class K3/2 No. 2417 at Heaton shed, May 1936.

Built Armstrong Whitworth 1936. Footsteps at front behind bufferbeam.

g. 106   Class K3/2 No. 3832 at Perth (N.B.R.) shed, May 1938.

uilt Darlington 1937. No reverse running sanders, lagging for exhaust steam pipes on either side of live steam pipe, hand holes in upper firebox casing, usual riveted tender.

Fig. 107   Class K3/5 No. 1158 at Doncaster shed, September 1932.

Fitted with cylinder horsepower indicator shelter, two sets of front guard irons.

Fig. 108   Class K3/2 No. 227 at Colwick shed, c. 1937.

Gresham & Craven feed water heater with Gunderson foam detector, smokebox door stop mid-way between hinges, glass sight-screens betwee
cab side windows, longer handrails on tender.

Fig. 109   Class K3/2 No. 1935 at Doncaster shed, May 1947.

1946 green livery – the only K3 so painted.

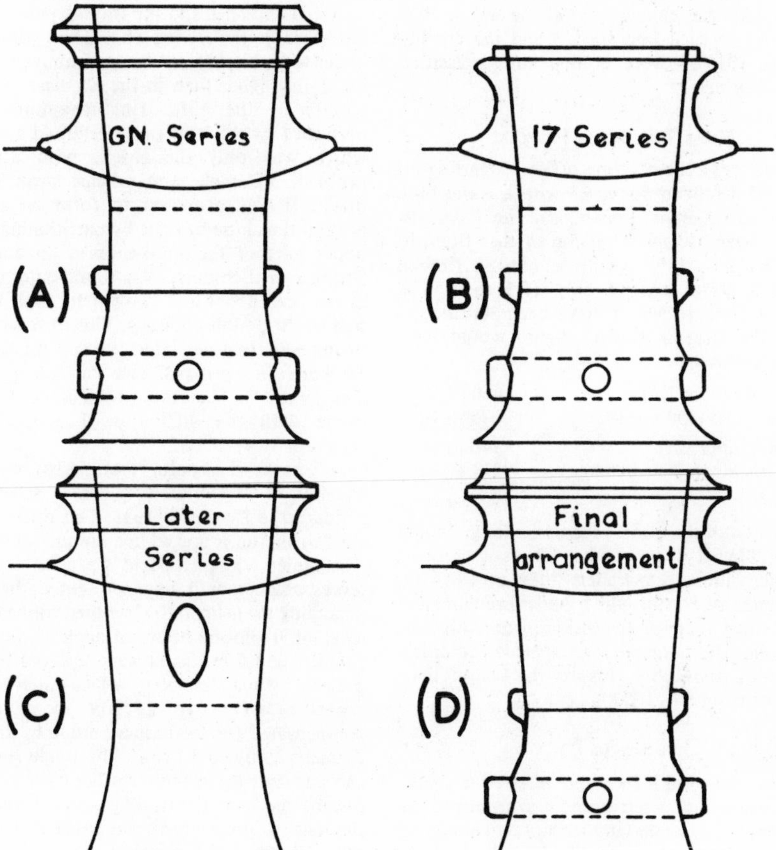
GN. Series
(A)
17 Series
(B)
Later Series
(C)
Final arrangement
(D)

COMPARATIVE CHIMNEY DIMENSIONS

Style	(A)	(B)	(C)	(D)
Height	1′ 1½″	9½″	9½″	9½″
Diameter:				
Top	1′ 10″	1′ 8⅛″	1′ 9⅝″	1′ 9⅝″
Lip	2′ 2″	2′ 0″	2′ 1⅝″	2′ 1⅝″
Waist ..	1′ 8⅜″	1′ 7½″	1′ 8⅜″	1′ 8⅝″
Base	2′ 4¾″	2′ 3″	2′ 3″	2′ 4″

This series was the heaviest of all and weighed 73 tons 8 cwt. in working order. The maximum axle load was 21 tons 5 cwt., 15 cwt more than the K3/3 engines. Part 6 was at first allotted to these 1302 series engines, but at the end of 1935 they were merged into Part 2 and the engines built in 1936-37 were consequently classified K3/2 when new.

WATER TUBE BOILER PROPOSAL

In July 1931 the drawing office at Darlington produced a scheme for a K3 with a water tube boiler (see Appendix, drawing 2). The boiler was to have been a smaller version of that fitted to class W1 No. 10000, with a narrow firebox having a grate area of only 21.5 sq.ft. The working pressure was to have been 300 lb. per sq.in. The heating surface figure would have been as follows:-

Firebox (234 × 2½")	460 sq.ft.
Small tubes (450 × 2")	686 sq.ft.
Total evaporative	1146 sq.ft.
Superheater (12 elements)	311 sq.ft.
Total	1457 sq.ft.

Apart from the boiler, the basic design would have followed that of the K3 as closely as possible, with three cylinders (lined up to 14¼in. to compensate for the higher boiler pressure) and 2 to 1 valve gear for the inside piston valve. In the event the scheme was shelved doubtless because satisfactory results had not been obtained from No. 10000.

IMPROVED K3

Two "improved K3's" were referred to on the 1932 building programme, announced in January 1932. The design incorporated a number of K3 features, including boiler, pony truck, axles, axleboxes, connecting rods and motion, but the improvements proposed were sufficient for the design to be referred to as class K4 on one of the outline drawings.

There were two innovations. The diameter of the coupled wheels was 6ft. 2in. which took the design out of the category of express goods engine and into one of mixed traffic duties. There was an articulated bogie under the cab, joining engine and tender in the manner of the two class C9 rebuilds which appeared late in 1931 (see Part 3A). Unlike these latter engines, however, the bogie would not have incorporated a booster and its sole purpose was to provide a steadier ride at high speed than was associated with the K3 class.

Preliminary design work was carried out at Darlington in 1931. The drawing (not illustrated) showed that the main difficulty was one of overhead clearance. As the coupled wheels were larger in diameter and the trailing pair were 1ft. 3in. closer to the driving wheels, this required the boiler to be pitched at 9ft. 4½in. above rail level, i.e. 4½in. higher than in the K3 class. Working strictly to the 13ft. 1in. maximum height permitted by the load gauge required a chimney which was only 6in. high, with attendant problems of smoke and exhaust steam drifting down. It was proposed to form an air duct around the chimney cone by partitioning off the upper part of the smokebox at an angle and fitting a dual-chimney. Air would enter the duct at the open front and leave it through the rear half of the double chimney. This form of smoke-lifting was tried out later on class A3 No. 2751 *Humorist* in April 1932 (see Part 2A, p. 24 and figs. 59 & 61). The other problem was the squat dome with the difficulty of arranging the regulator valves.

It was at this point that design work was transferred to Doncaster where a scheme was produced in December 1931. This differed from the Darlington proposal in a number of respects. The boiler was pitched at 9ft. 3in. above rail level, which would have presented difficulties arranging the ashpan to clear the trailing coupled axle, but it allowed a normal single chimney to be fitted. The K3 cylinders were replaced by a new pattern, 19in. diameter, which increased the tractive effort to 29,109 lb. and thus compensated for the reduction due to the larger diameter coupled wheels. The bogie under the cab was repositioned 6in. further back so that the distance between the trailing coupled wheels and the leading bogie wheels was 5ft. 6in. instead of only 5ft. 0in. – the problem here was probably clearance on curves between the bogie frame and the coupled wheel rim. The cab was set 9½in. further back which gave more room than was provided in a K3, but it meant that the distance from the firehole door to the shovelling plate on the tender front was 6ft. 0in. which might have produced complaints. Clearance for the regulator valves was solved by abandoning the dome altogether and fitting a smokebox regulator (see later).

Some further minor adjustments to the design were afterwards made, also in December 1931 (see Appendix, drawing 3). The wheelbase of the bogie under the cab was increased from 6ft. 3in. to 6ft. 6in. with a corresponding reduction in the distance between this bogie and the rear tender bogie. The engine frame was shortened by about 4in. at the cab end where it had been too close to the tender frame.

Gresley considered two ways of fitting a smokebox regulator. First of all, on 9th December 1931 Swindon sent him a drawing of their own arrangement, so that Doncaster could see if it was possible to fit something similar. A scheme was prepared but this particular idea was dropped in March 1932. Meanwhile Gresley investigated the possibility of fitting a multiple valve regulator header in the smokebox, as fitted to class D49/3 No. 335 *Bedfordshire* when new in August 1928 (see Part 4, p. 101). In this proposed application however it was intended to take the steam supply from a perforated pipe inside the boiler barrel instead of from the dome. The Superheater Co. suggested a design which had four 3½in. diameter main valves in the header and one pilot valve, controlled by rodding which passed along the left-hand side of the boiler. Gresley intended fitting Trofinoff Automatic By-pass (T.A.B.) piston valves which he hoped would obviate the need for fitting anti-vacuum valves. Alternatively, The Superheater Co. suggested fitting a steam drifting valve so that a small quantity of steam always entered the cylinders when the engine was running. This firm then prepared a scheme for fitting a steam drier to the main steam pipe in the boiler, but it was thought that its proposed 1in. diameter orifice would be too restrictive for a K3 boiler, assuming an estimated maximum evaporation rate of 30,000 lb. steam per hour. Gresley asked for accurate details of the amount of steam used per hour by a K3 running at 25 per cent cut-off at 60 miles per hour. The cylinders of No. 1158 were accordingly horsepower indicated on 21st September 1932 when it worked the 1-10 p.m. Leeds-King's Cross express between Doncaster and Grantham (fig. 107). The load was 263 tons and the calculations showed that the steam evaporation had been 21,930 lb. per hour.

The scheme to fit the multiple-valve regulator header was suspended in March 1933 due to difficulty in arranging suitable rodding to the header. The authority to construct the two "improved K3's" was then cancelled in October 1933. This was only eight months before the appearance of the first V2 scheme, which was the next logical step forward from the 2-6-4-4 proposal.

REBUILDING TO CLASS K5

The only reference to the K3 class in Thompson's 1941 standard engine proposals was

its eventual replacement by Pacifics, rebuilt B7's and new B1's. However in 1943 details appeared for the rebuilding of the K3's with B1-type cylinders. The total cylinder volume was less so that it was necessary to increase the boiler pressure to provide a comparable tractive effort. It would have been a retrograde step to have fitted a Diagram 100A boiler as the K3's already had larger boilers. What was needed was to raise the working pressure of the Diagram 96 boiler to 225 lb. per sq.in. New boiler drawings were therefore prepared with the thickness of the barrel plate increased from ⅝in. to ¾in. to withstand the higher pressure. It was also proposed to fit a steel firebox, as a wartime measure, which would have necessitated a rearrangement of the small tubes and a reduction in their number to 213. Thompson signed the new drawings on 28th September 1943 and the first ten Diagram 96A boilers, as they were described, were ordered on 8th November 1943.

Thompson then had second thoughts about the steel firebox and fresh drawings were prepared in February 1944 for a conventional copper firebox, with a reversion to 217 small tubes. The boiler order was amended accordingly. Certain other detail drawings necessary for the rebuilding, e.g. for the frames, had still to appear and there appeared to be little urgency with the matter.

No. 206 was eventually selected for rebuilding and entered Doncaster Works on 20th February 1945. Very little of the original engine was retained (apart from its short length cab) and the frames, driving wheels, buffers, cylinders and boiler were all new. Larger coupled wheel springs were fitted, of the type used on the K3's which had been built from 1934 onwards, with a 4ft. 0in. span (see earlier on page 100 for details). The engine retained its previous style chimney, liner and cowl layout but a shorter blastpipe was fitted, which had a 5½in. diameter orifice instead of 5⅜in. The distance from the bell mouth of the cowl to the top of the blastpipe was increased to 1ft. 9½in.

The B1 pattern cylinders were inclined at 1 in 30 and drove the middle pair of coupled wheels. The cylinders were 1in. further apart than in the B1 class. This was necessary so that certain K3 motion parts could be retained and ½in. thickness plates had therefore to be placed between the frames and the cylinder castings to make up the difference. Reversing was by vertical screw as before but the maximum cut-off position was 75 per cent in both fore and back gears. The maximum valve travel was 6⅜in.

The pony truck was provided with helical side control springs in place of swing links. These springs were of L.M.S. design, copied from the Stanier 8F class O6 2-8-0's which the L.N.E.R. was currently building. The bearing springs were the laminated type, as fitted to the pony trucks of classes L1 (No. 9000 only), K1 (No. 3445) and V2 (first seven with modified pony trucks). These springs were 2ft. 6in. across their centres (seven ½in. thick plates). The vertical deflection under load of each bearing spring was 0.1674in. per ton, which equalled the deflection of a pair of helical springs as used in the K3 pony truck.

Eliminating the third cylinder brought about a total weight saving, but the adhesive weight and maximum axle load were both greater. The tractive effort had been reduced, but No. 206 now had the advantage of being able to start at 75 per cent cut-off whereas the K3's were limited to 65 per cent.

No. 206 left works rebuilt on 16th June 1945 and was reclassified K5 in October 1945 (fig. 134). Trials were held between it and class K3 No. 2425 in the early part of 1946, but the results were spoiled by bad steaming on the part of the latter engine.

Until instructions were received regarding further rebuildings, it was decided to fit these new Diagram 96A boilers to K3's, with the pressure simply lowered to 180 lb. per sq.in. (fig. 111).

The Chief General Manager called for further tests to be held between Nos. 206 and 2425 when they had reached a mileage of around 45,000 to 50,000. Trials were accordingly arranged for September 1946 when No. 206 (then 1863) had reached 50,000 miles. As No. 2425 (then 1939) had only run 42,000 miles since its last heavy repair, a third engine was introduced into the tests – No. 1951 (ex-2450) with 50,000 miles. The engines took turns working outward with the 7-40 a.m. Ferme Park – New England class A empty wagon train, returning with the 12-43 p.m. New England – Ferme Park class A coal train. No. 1863 worked these trains on the 17th, 18th and 27th; No. 1939 on the 20th and 23rd; No. 1951 on the 25th and 26th September 1946. Coal and water consumption figures are quoted in the accompanying table for the best day's performance of each engine, from which it will be seen that the K5 produced the best results.

In the report, issued on 23rd January 1947, the Running Department stated that the K5 had three definite advantages: improved riding, accessibility of two outside cylinders and motion, and easier shed maintenance. The report concluded that although the rebuilt engine was a success, further rebuildings should be left in abeyance due to the time taken in works to rebuild a K3, compared with the time taken to give it an ordinary repair. The C.M.E. (now Peppercorn) agreed with the recommendation and in May 1947 further rebuildings were suspended. The original order, which had been for ten rebuilds, was finally endorsed "no further action" in February 1949. The engine remained a solitary example of its class and was eventually condemned in June 1960.

Date	Engine No.	Outward load (wagons/tons)	Return load (wagons/tons)	Coal consumption (lb./mile)(lb./ton mile)		Water consumption (gall./mile)
17/9/46	1863	63/419	45/709	58.08	0.103	43.54
23/9/46	1939	61/414	45/721	62.93	0.111	47.28
26/9/46	1951	61/399	40/752	65.99	0.115	42.38

Details

FRAMES AND RUNNING GEAR

The main frames were 1⅛in. thick with two circular lightening holes between the leading coupled and driving coupled horn gaps and two larger holes alongside the firebox. The coupled wheel journal surfaces were 9½in. diameter and 11in. long.

The bufferbeam at the front was 8ft. 5in. wide, 1ft. 4in. deep and 1in. thick. The engines built from 1929 onwards had their lower corners cut away so that the overall width here was only 6ft. 11in., as in the Gresley Pacifics. The earlier engines were brought into line after 1935 when front footsteps were fitted (cf. figs. 116 and 117).

The buffers on Nos. 4000-9 were of G.N.R. pattern, 1ft. 6in. long with parallel cases (fig. 87). The engines built at Darlington in 1924-25 had 1ft. 6in. long double-case buffers (fig. 90) as fitted before Grouping to the three-cylinder

2-8-0's built by N.B. Locomotive Co. for the G.N.R. (class O2). The engines built from 1929 onwards had 1ft. 8in. long Group Standard buffers (fig. 99). The earlier engines were not generally brought into line though No. 206 received these longer buffers when it was rebuilt in 1945 (fig. 134). In addition, Group Standard buffers were also noted latterly on No. 61808 (fig. 110). The height above rail level to the centre of the buffers was 3ft. 6¼in. prior to June 1929, when it was reduced to 3ft. 5½in. (the standard R.C.H. goods wagon buffer height) for new construction commencing with No. 1331. Earlier engines were not usually brought into line though No. 206 had the new height after it was rebuilt in 1945, as did No. 61808 mentioned above.

Footsteps were added at the front from 1935 and they appeared when new on the engines which were built in 1936-37 (fig. 105). This involved cutting away a small portion of the angle iron below the running plate in the case of the pre-1929 engines, with the lower corners of the bufferbeam cut away to match. The engines built in 1924-25, which had double-case buffers, were distinguishable from the remaining engines in two respects: the support plate for the footsteps was set ¾in. further forward and the top step was 2in. wider than the lower one. A small handgrip was also fitted to the running plate above the footsteps.

Guard irons were originally fitted to both the main frames and the pony truck frames. In common with a number of other classes, the guard irons were later removed from the front end of the main frames as the pair on the pony truck were better placed and gave adequate protection (cf. figs. 107 and 110). The K5 was altered during the course of rebuilding in 1945 and the K3's were dealt with during the fifties.

The pony truck on the K3's incorporated Gresley's patent double swing link suspension. The truck itself had ⅞in. thick frames, spaced 2ft. 11¼in. apart, with helical bearing springs on the outside of them. The radius arm was 5ft. 11½in. long and the wheels, which were 3ft. 2in. diameter, had a maximum translation of 4½in. to each side, in an arc. The journals were 6¼in. diameter and 9in. long. The minimum radius curvature which the engines could negotiate was 4 chains.

The swing links were so arranged that the effect of side translation was to raise the front of the engine, so that its weight then tended to restore the truck to its original central position. The maximum lift with full translation was 1⅛in.

Alternatively, the bearing springs could be depressed instead or, what was more likely, there would be a combination of both factors. No-one knew what really took place on a curve but it was calculated what might happen. First of all the front of the engine would lift, with a corresponding fall at the cab end. The engine as a whole would then lift throughout its length until the various spring deflections gave the correct total weight and the same centre of gravity. Under this assumption, the respective axle weights for one of the Part 2 engines would be: pony truck 16 tons 14 cwt., leading coupled 13 tons 18 cwt., driving coupled 18 tons 2 cwt. and trailing coupled 23 tons 1 cwt. It was admitted that this calculation ignored the effects of centrifugal forces, super-elevation of the outer rail and the twisting effect on the swing links caused by the radial movement of the truck.

To verify this assumption, an experiment was carried out in the weigh house at Doncaster Works in August 1934. A greased plate was placed under the pony truck of No. 120 and readings were taken with the wheels pushed hard over. The results confirmed that there was an appreciable weight shift from the leading coupled wheels to the pony truck wheels and trailing wheels. Furthermore, the new weight distribution was not equally shared between the left and right sides of the engine. For example, on the pony truck wheels there was 6 tons 18 cwt. more weight on the wheel which had been pushed inwards than on the other one. Gresley had already abandoned swing links on his Pacific bogies and it is surprising that he did not take similar action with pony trucks, but presumably there was never any real evidence that the expense was justified.

The swing link pins were also difficult to lubricate. Wear was considerable and renewals frequent. They were originally fitted with Menno grease cups but these were not entirely satisfactory. From about 1933 the Tecalemit system of grease lubrication was made standard. There was also a proposal in May 1935 to fit the pony truck swing link pins on a K3 with Ransome & Marles needle roller bearings, but no record has been found of any actually fitted.

The outside cylinders of the K3's were inclined at 1 in 30 with their centres 6ft. 8½in. apart. The inside cylinder was inclined at 1 in 7.96 (confirmed by calculation, though official sources variously quoted 7.96, "8 approximately" and 8.5) to enable the inside connecting rod to clear the leading coupled axle. The inside connecting rod was forged from nickel-chromium steel of light section to save weight. In the thirties Gresley pioneered the use of nickel-chromium-molybdenum steel for inside connecting rods, which combined the qualities of high tensile strength (nickel) and hardness (chromium) with resistance to brittleness during the tempering process (molybdenum), giving very good fatigue and shock resisting properties. All three connecting rods were 8ft. 1in. long between centres and drove on to the second coupled axle.

The three steam chests were positioned in the same horizontal plane, with the one for the inside cylinder close to the left-hand frame. The piston valves were 8in. diameter. The inside valve was operated by means of two horizontal motion levers. The large lever had two unequal length arms in the ratio of 2 to 1. The pin at the end of the long arm was coupled to the right-hand side valve tail rod, through a short link. The pin at the short end was the floating fulcrum of the "equal motion" lever, whose outer pins were in turn coupled to the middle and left-hand side valve tail rods respectively, again through short links. (See drawing on p. 36 of Part 2A which shows a similar arrangement for the Gresley Pacifics). A cover plate in front of the smokebox gave access to the motion levers, e.g. for lubricating the joints which were out of sight between the frames.

With this conjugated valve gear it was essential that the fixed fulcrum of the large (2 to 1) motion lever and the floating fulcrum of the small (equal) motion lever had their pins fitted to close limits. The weight of the large motion lever was taken at its fulcrum by Hoffmann ball (thrust) bearings, which were located between the two sets of Hoffmann roller bearings. The latter allowed the lever to rock freely without play or undesirable friction. The equal motion lever however had two sets of roller bearings at its fulcrum at first and no thrust bearing. Plain mild steel case-hardened bushes were used for the outer pins of the levers.

In September 1921 No. 1006's equal motion lever was fitted with a ball thrust bearing between the two sets of roller bearings, which brought it into line with the large motion lever. Conversely, in October 1921 the ball and roller

bearings for the fulcrum joint of No. 1000's large motion lever were replaced by plain brass bushes. As a result of experience with these variations it was quickly decided to standardise on the method used in No. 1006, i.e. both ball and roller bearings at the fulcrums of both levers. This then became the standard arrangement for all Gresley classes which had the 2 to 1 gear, until wartime exigencies dictated otherwise (see later). A further modification appeared in 1921. The curved plate between the frames was replaced by a vertical plate and a horizontal plate. The vertical one had a hole provided to facilitate lubrication of the pins in the middle valve's connecting link. This removed the need for drivers to open the cover plate in front of the smokebox, thus keeping out unwelcome smokebox ash, though from April 1933 hinged covers had to be fitted over the hole in the vertical plate as ash was found to be getting in through the hole instead (cf. figs. 116 and 117).

One cause of over-travel of the middle valve was the whip action of the motion levers, and the engines which appeared from 1924 to 1930 inclusive had their large motion levers forged from nickel-chromium alloy steel of a lighter section to reduce weight. The equal motion levers were still made from mild steel. In December 1929 No. 203 received a set of lightweight levers made from Hiduminium aluminium alloy. (Its piston valve heads were made of this alloy too, see later). Tests were carried out in April 1930 to measure the amount of over-travel of the middle valve at high speed, compared with No. 143 which had the conventional arrangement of nickel-chromium steel 2 to 1 lever, mild steel equal motion lever and cast-iron piston heads. Results showed that there was even greater over-travel on No. 203 and so its special levers were quickly replaced. In December 1930 No. 120 received a mild steel 2 to 1 lever and in similar tests which were carried out in January 1931, the over-travel in this engine was found to be least of all. In consequence mild steel motion levers became standard from April 1931. Specimen results are given in the accompanying table of the over-run at each end of the middle steam chest, when coasting in full forward gear. In June 1931 No. 112 was tried out with a cast steel 2 to 1

Engine No.	Speed (m.p.h.)	Over-run	Remarks
143	60	1⅙in.	Nickel-chromium alloy steel for 2 to 1 lever
203	60	1$\frac{5}{32}$in.	Aluminium alloy motion levers and valve heads
120	64	½in.	Mild steel motion levers

lever. When this engine next visited shops, in January 1933, the lever was found to be fractured and it had to be scrapped and replaced by a conventional forged mild steel lever.

Nos. 1000-9 when new had C.P.R. type piston valves. The piston ring consisted of a $1\frac{7}{8}$in. wide centre ring with a $\frac{5}{8}$in. wide split ring on each side of it. The diameter over the three rings was the same as the inside diameter of the steam chest liner, so that together they presented a steamtight fit, whilst at the same time frictional resistance was kept to a minimum as only the outer rings were sprung. However, steam did find its way through the fine gaps between the three rings and so the C.P.R. type gradually fell into disfavour.

From February 1922 the piston valve heads were fitted instead with a single broad split-ring which was $3\frac{1}{8}$in. wide, or effectively 3in. wide from September 1922 when the outer edge was chamfered. A number of tiny holes were bored in the circumference of the ring through to the hollow centre of the head, which admitted sufficient lubricated steam to the surface of the ring to help overcome friction when starting. Unfortunately the design was not far removed from that of the type Doncaster had employed prior to 1918 on other classes (see class K2, p. 67). As the rings were once more sprung throughout their length to make a steamtight fit, surface lubrication was again a problem, wear was heavy and a good deal of energy was wasted during the travel of the valve. Similar valves, though actually based on Gateshead practice, were fitted to twenty-five of the engines built at Darlington in 1924-25.

Thirty-five engines built in 1924-25, numbered between 75 and 158 inclusive and between 202 and 231, had Knorr type piston valves, based on Stratford practice. The valve heads were machined with a $\frac{1}{64}$in. clearance all round within the steam chest valve liner and rendered steamtight by fitting each head with four $\frac{1}{16}$in. wide packing rings. Because the area of the valve in direct contact with the liner was thus greatly reduced, surface lubrication was less of a problem, wear was reduced and only a small amount of energy was lost through frictional resistance. From February 1926 Knorr type piston valves were fitted to the remaining engines of the class which still had the broad ring type. Meanwhile long lap valves had been introduced in 1928, in which the valve heads were $3\frac{1}{4}$in. long.

Knorr piston valves were afterwards criticised on the grounds that the valve events were controlled by the outer edges of the valve heads, which had $\frac{1}{64}$in. clearance all the way round inside the liner, whereas hitherto the events had been controlled by the outer edges of the steamtight split-rings. From October 1932 the ends of the valve heads were reduced in diameter from $7\frac{11}{32}$in. to $7\frac{1}{8}$in., so that the events could be more positively controlled by the edges of the two outer valve rings instead, positioned accordingly further apart. A senior draughtsman at Doncaster, E. Windle, was at the time unconvinced. In December 1932 he wrote that the effect of the $\frac{1}{64}$in. clearance of the Knorr type valve was "imperceptible on the indicator card and any deviation from simple design made with the object of transferring the control of the event from the valve head to the ring is a questionable refinement". However the new method of "ring control" remained standard to the end of steam.

The Hiduminium piston valve heads which had been fitted to No. 203 in December 1929, were removed from this engine in July 1931 and fitted to No. 4007 in the following month. In August 1934 it was reported that heavy wear had taken place and they were replaced by ordinary cast-iron heads during its next visit to shops, in December 1934. The Hiduminium alloy was returned as scrap to High Duty Alloys Ltd. In October 1937 No. 1125 was fitted with T.A.B. piston valves but no further details are available.

The K3's had Skefko ball bearings in their eccentric cranks, though, as a wartime expedient, from July 1940 Hoffmann ball bearings were substituted when renewals were required. No. 206 lost its ball bearings altogether when it was rebuilt in 1945, but they were fitted again in August 1954.

The engines built from 1934 onwards had Ransome & Marles roller bearings applied at the following joints in the valve gear: radius link trunnion (fitting detected by the presence of the cover plate), radius link foot and all three joints in the combination lever. In addition, No. 127 was fitted with Ransome & Marles needle roller bearings in December 1934 at the following joints: radius link foot, crosshead arm and all three joints in the combination lever. Needle roller bearings were considered to be more suitable than ordinary size ones where there was a rocking rather than a rotating movement.

As a wartime expedient, the roller bearings in the combination lever were replaced by plain bronze bushes when renewals were required. Finally, from May 1953 bronze (YM-1 alloy) bushes gradually replaced roller bearings in the radius link foot, crosshead arm (where applicable) and combination lever. This last modification applied to all the Gresley three-cylinder classes.

From January 1944 it became the practice to fit plain brass bushes at the fulcrum joints of the motion levers owing to the non-availability of ball and roller bearings, when renewals were required. The extent to which this became necessary is not known. In June-July 1949 six K3's (Nos. 61803/80/8,61905/18/26) were fitted with Silentbloc bearings in the fixed fulcrums of their large motion levers. No further details are available of this experiment.

Nos. 4000-9 had a vacuum-operated clutch gear on the reversing shaft operated by a catch on the reversing screw column. This mechanism prevented creep from taking place in the reversing gear when it had been set in position. In September 1921 Ferodo linings were fitted to the clutch gear in No. 1006, which thereafter became standard. The first fifty engines built at Darlington in 1924-25 were intended to have steam brake on the engine and tender, with a vacuum ejector for train braking. Darlington pointed out that this meant that there was no vacuum chamber to which to connect the clutch gear. On 24th November 1923 Gresley gave instructions that these engines were to be fitted with vacuum brake throughout so that the clutch gear could be provided. The last ten engines built in 1925 had steam brakes and consequently no vacuum chamber. One of these engines, possibly No. 202, had a vacuum-operated clutch, which was probably connected to the train pipe. This was tried out in the Southern Area before it was decided that the clutch was not needed on these particular engines.

The engines built in 1929 had Westinghouse brakes. It is believed that they had vacuum-operated clutch gear connected to the small vacuum chamber in the cab. The question of fitting the reversing shaft clutch was again raised by Darlington in connection with Nos. 2761-9 which had steam brake. The first decision was that the clutch gear was not necessary, on the grounds that it was not fitted anyway to the class D49 4-4-0's. Then a steam-operated arrangement was considered in August 1929 before it was finally decided to fit the standard vacuum-operated locking clutch connected to a small vacuum chamber in the cab. The earlier engines with steam brake were afterwards brought into line.

The engines always had mechanical lubrication for their axleboxes. Wakefield No. 7 lubricators were usually fitted, on the right-hand side running plate above the middle coupled wheel

(fig. 87). No. 159 acquired a Silvertown six-feed mechanical lubricator instead in October 1931, which was still fitted in B.R. days. The engines built from 1931 onwards had a steam heating pipe running from the steam manifold in the cab, at a downward slope along the right-hand side of the boiler to the lubricator (fig. 103).

Michell axlebox bearings were fitted to No. 109 in July 1926. The main feature of this design was the interposing of a number of bearing blocks between the journals and the body of the axlebox. The blocks were arranged to rock or tilt so that they tipped slightly under load, thus facilitating the entrance of lubricating oil between the journal and blocks on the basic principle that no lubricated bearing can possibly be efficient where the rubbing surfaces are perfectly parallel and it is essential for the two surfaces to take up a tapered formation when under pressure. Michell bearings had been applied successfully in marine work and wear over a period of time was practically negligible. Because of the room taken up by the bearing blocks, it was not possible to fit them in a normal bronze axlebox and cast steel ones were used instead. Details of the engine's performance are not recorded but it is known that a modification had to be made to these axleboxes in October 1926 at the recommendation of the makers, and that they were finally removed altogether from this engine in March 1927. In March 1939 No. 2934 was fitted with new driving coupled axleboxes with Friedman bearings. No further details are available except that they were removed in July 1942.

Nos. 4000-7/9 and the engines built from 1929 onwards had a Wakefield No. 7 mechanical lubricator for the cylinders and valves. This was fitted on the right-hand side running plate, above the leading coupled wheel (fig. 87). Anti-carbonisers were provided, with the steam shut-off valve on the right-hand side of the smokebox. The oil feed to the piston valves was introduced into the steam pipes.

No. 4008 was fitted instead with a six-feed Detroit sight-feed lubricator in the cab on the fireman's side, with feeds passing along both sides of the boiler to the smokebox and thence to the cylinders and valves. The engines built at Darlington in 1924-25 had a Detroit No. 32A sight-feed lubricator with however only four feeds. On the early engines the pipes passed along the outside of the boiler on the left-hand side at a slight downward slope to the smokebox. Three feeds each took oil to one steam pipe whilst the fourth feed divided into three branches at the front end, with one split feed to each cylinder (fig. 91). Supplying oil into the steam pipes without the benefit of the anti-carboniser was not entirely satisfactory. Later engines, probably commencing with No. 58, had an improved method in which the valve feed entered directly into the steam chest immediately above each valve head. This involved dividing the valve feed in the vicinity of the steam pipes, with separate branches disappearing from sight through the running plate (fig. 92). A further difference was that the feed for the right-hand steam chest now passed along the right-hand side of the boiler instead of the left. On the last ten engines built in 1925 the feed pipe for the middle steam chest also passed along the right-hand side of the boiler instead of the left, so that there were then two feeds running along each side of the boiler.

The sight-feed principle was not foolproof when used in conjunction with split-feeds, because if one branch was blocked, the others would still pass oil and there would be no indication in the sight-glasses that anything was amiss. Between July 1927 and April 1928 there was almost an epidemic (twelve cases) of broken piston heads among the K3's with Detroit lubricators shedded at New England. There was no obvious cause for this though it was perhaps significant that in the same period this shed only had one case of a broken piston head involving a K3 with mechanical lubrication for the cylinders (No. 4003). In August 1928 Gresley ordered the removal of the Detroit lubricators and the fitting of Wakefield mechanical lubricators instead, like Nos. 4000-7/9. The change was mainly carried out in 1929-30, with No. 114 altered as late as January 1931, (fig. 94).

In October 1931 No. 159 acquired a Silvertown six-feed mechanical lubricator for cylinder lubrication, at the same time as the one it received for its axleboxes. This was still fitted in B.R. days.

After rebuilding to class K5, No. 206's mechanical lubricators were both transferred to the left-hand side running plate (fig. 134).

The original sanding arrangement on Nos. 4000-9 was steam-operated gear in front of the leading coupled wheels, gravity feed in front of the middle coupled wheels and gravity feed behind the trailing coupled wheels (fig. 88). The front sandboxes were between the frames above the pony truck, with lengthy delivery pipes at a shallow angle. The steam sand valve was high up on the driver's side of the cab. The gravity feed lever for forward running was also on the

driver's side. There was a separate lever for reverse running at each side of the cab on top of the rear sandboxes.

The engines built at Darlington in 1924-25 were similarly arranged except that the reverse running sanders were now operated by one lever only, at the fireman's side of the cab. On these engines the steam sand valve was located just above the rear side window and in such a position that the driver was liable to strike his head on it when the engine lurched. On the engines built from 1929 onwards, and the Darlington engines when their cabs were afterwards altered, this valve was repositioned below the side window where it could cause no harm.

From about October 1926 the arrangement of the forward running sanders was altered. The leading coupled wheel sanders on the existing engines were changed to gravity feed, with the sandboxes relocated behind the middle cylinder to give a more vertical sand flow, with a raised flat-topped filler, and the driving sanders were altered to steam operation (fig. 95). The engines built from 1929 onwards had this new arrangement (fig. 101). In addition those built from 1934 had their front sandbox lids set at an angle to reduce spillage between the frames (fig. 102); some of the earlier engines, e.g. Nos. 61800/57/8/76, 61911/7/8, were similarly altered later.

The reverse running sanders were dispensed with on the engines which were built in 1936-37 (fig. 106). Latterly these reverse sanders were in the way of the A.W.S. battery box, when fitted to some of the earlier engines. They were either completely removed or positioned behind the middle pair of coupled wheels in the manner of the Peppercorn K1's (fig. 114).

The diagram 96 boiler was constructed of $\frac{5}{8}$in. plate in one parallel ring having an outside diameter of 6ft. 0in. The front tubeplate was $\frac{3}{4}$in. thick, recessed into the barrel, and the radius of its flange was $\frac{1}{2}$in. The distance between the tubeplates was 11ft. 11$\frac{7}{8}$in. The outer firebox plates were also $\frac{5}{8}$in. thick. The inner copper firebox was made of $\frac{9}{16}$in. plate throughout, except for the tubeplate which was 1in. The water space above the foundation ring was 3$\frac{1}{2}$in. wide at the front and rear and 3in. at the sides.

On the early boilers there were six wash-out plugs on the sides of the firebox, three on each side above the handrail (fig. 98). Commencing with No. 1387, new in 1929, the fireboxes had expansion and sling stays at the front in place of girder bar stays. These fireboxes were identified by having four wash-out plugs on each side instead of three (fig. 100). From 1935 these wash-out plugs were replaced by hand holes on new boilers, with three on the right and two on the left (fig. 104).

On the engines built in 1929 the front part of the firebox grate sloped down and had a drop section. This was operated by a vertical screw mechanism in the cab with rodding out of sight underneath. The engines built from 1930 onwards had drop grates with simplified operating gear. The rodding was taken directly from the drop grate shaft, alongside the frames on the right-hand side at a steep angle to the screw mechanism in the cab (fig. 103). A large counterbalance coil spring was located on the opposite end of the drop grate shaft, on the left-hand side of the engine. This was a better arrangement and the 1929 engines were subsequently brought into line, e.g. No. 1318 in April 1933. Some of the earlier engines also acquired drop grates later, including the following, which is not a complete list.

Engine No.	Fitted	Engine No.	Fitted
17	1/33	52	/
28	1/32	140	6/31
32	8/37	159	10/31
36	4/33	188	8/37
38	3/33	200	2/37
39	?8/32		

In addition the K5, No. 206, had drop grate gear.

The ashpan had two doors originally – one at the front end and one nearer the back just ahead of the rear axle. It was reported that the rear damper allowed ashes to get into the trailing axleboxes causing overheating, and also into the cab where it was most objectionable. Experiments were carried out which showed that the engines steamed just as well with the back damper shut and in fact burned less coal. Commencing with No. 1158 in August 1932, new ashpans were fitted which had a front door only. Early reports showed that the alteration was an improvement: the engines steamed well, were working round trips without the need to clean the fire and there was an absence of dirt in the cab.

Hopper ashpans and rocking grates were fitted to twelve K3's in 1954-55, as fitted for example to most of the class B1 4-6-0's. The rocking grate was operated by a lever in the cab, whilst the hopper door was opened by turning a handle at the side. The engines were fitted as follows:-

1954: Nos. 61923/81 (January),
61969 (February), 61942 (March),
61930/86 (April).
1955: Nos. 61971/5 (April), 61980 (May),
61977 (July), 61950 (August),
61938 (September).

In all but three cases, Nos. 61938/75/80, the boilers were in fact the later Diagram 96A (see later). The experiment was concluded in December 1955 with the comment that the grates were easy to clean and there had only been slight distortion of the ashpan plates and gear. Other K3's may have been fitted afterwards.

Diamond soot blowers were fitted to some of the K3's including Nos. 1300/12/8/31/45, 2761-6 when they were new. These were mounted on the back of the firebox and directed a jet of steam on to the tubeplate by manual operation of a control valve. The high velocity steam combined with the firebox gases were to sweep through the tubes and into the smokebox accumulation of soot and ashes. Eventually, in March 1936 it was stated that there was no real advantage in retaining them and they were to be removed as the engines passed through shops for repair. No. 1158 was then fitted with a steam-operated sand gun in May 1937. Its action was similar to that of the Diamond soot blower, except that a blast of sand was directed at the tubeplate instead of steam only. A small sandbox was fitted on the firebox backplate on the fireman's side. The removal date is not recorded.

In August 1935 No. 227 acquired a Gresham & Craven feed water heater, combined with a Hulburd boiler cleaner (or blow-down apparatus). Feed water from the injectors passed along both sides of the boiler to a top feed in front of the dome. The pipes passed through casings which were lagged with asbestos blocks to prevent heat loss. Inside the boiler the jets were directed against a vertical plate just above the highest water level. The plate was an extension of a submerged "skimmer trough" whose purpose was to collect sludge. This was periodically blown off through a perforated pipe in the bottom of the trough, which led out through a valve on the right-hand side of the boiler and down to waste on to the track. The valve was controlled by the fireman turning a small wheel in the cab. The rodding passed alongside the boiler and a section of the handrail had to be removed on the right-hand side just beyond the dome, where the rodding sloped upwards to the valve. When the engine had been in traffic ten weeks it was reported that so far there had been no loose scale found in the boiler and only a small amount of sediment. The condition of the boiler was better than usual but there had still been seven reported cases of priming. It was claimed that because of its softened water, the engine could run for two months between boiler wash-outs, or about ten times the usual period. It was later claimed that the apparatus prevented priming to some extent, but in June 1936 a Gunderson foam meter was fitted, which was an electrically operated foam detector. No exact details are known, but photographs show two connections entering the boiler just behind the dome with leads running back to the cab on the fireman's side (fig. 108). The entire equipment was removed from No. 227 in October 1940.

No. 1158 was fitted with continuous blow-down apparatus in December 1938. Its purpose was to blow off scum from the surface of the water in the boiler whilst the regulator was open. Its removal date is not recorded.

In May-June 1960 thirteen K3 tenders were fitted with Alfloc briquette tube feeders in an experiment to soften the feed water chemically after the tank had been filled. These tenders were attached to Nos. 61813/4/46/57/92/3/7/9, 61902/3/4/32/41. Three more tenders were similarly fitted in 1961, attached to Nos. 61819, 61901/85. All of these engines were at the time allocated to Dairycoates shed. No details are available of the success or otherwise of this experiment, which came very late in the life of the class.

A 32-element Robinson superheater was fitted to the K3's. The elements were the standard long-loop type, 1⅛in. outside diameter and 9 S.W.G. thick (inside diameter approximately 1$\frac{7}{32}$in.). From December 1932 the thickness was reduced to 10 S.W.G. (inside diameter 1.244in.). The thickness reverted to 9 S.W.G. from (officially) November 1944, though this final change was not recognised on the engine diagrams, nor were any changes made to the quoted heating surface figures.

The steam pipes in the smokebox which carried the steam from the superheated side of the header to the steam chests, were originally 4½in. diameter inside. Commencing with the engines built by N.B. Locomotive Co. in 1935 they were 5in. diameter, on new engines only.

Between 1920 and 1944 a total of 240 Diagram 96 boilers was built. Future construction was then concentrated on the improved Diagram 96A, of which 153 were constructed between 1945 and 1959. The barrel plate was ¾in. thick instead of

⅞in., although the firebox wrapper and back plates were reduced to $\frac{9}{16}$in. from ⅝in. The throat plate remained ⅝in. The flange of the tubeplate at the front of the boiler had a ½in. radius instead of ⅓in. These new boilers had eleven rows of transverse stays, which was three more than in the Diagram 96, and they were pitched closer together, with the usual two rows of expansion and sling stays supporting the front end of the inner copper firebox. There were nine hand holes (instead of five) on the firebox sides above the handrail, four on the right and five on the left, which was the main distinguishing feature of these particular boilers. The safety valves were positioned 1ft. 3in. further forward on the top of the firebox, so that they were no longer in close proximity to the whistle and the cab front (fig. 111).

The first Diagram 96A boiler was fitted to No. 206 when it was rebuilt in June 1945. The boiler had a "Through" bolt type superheater header, requiring elements with ball-jointed (Melesco type) ends instead of the usual Robinson type. In addition, Vulcan Foundry supplied ten Diagram 96A boilers in 1950 which also had this type of header. These were initially fitted at Doncaster to Nos. 61822/4/61/7/77/89, 61947/56/7/84. These eleven boilers subsequently rotated amongst other engines of the class. Diagram 96A boilers worked at 225 lb. per sq.in. when fitted to the K5, but at 180 lb. per sq.in. when fitted to K3's.

GENERAL

The overall width over the running plate was 8ft. 6in., except alongside the cab where it was 8ft. 9in. There was a footstep half way up the reverse curve in the running plate beside the cab. On the engines which were built after Grouping this step was 5⅓in. wide and 1ft. 0in. long. Nos. 4000-9 had shorter steps which they retained to the end. The K5 had its running plate stepped above the reversing shaft and was 3½in. higher ahead of this point to provide clearance for the longer radius link with a deeper drop in front of the cylinder necessitating the provision of a step in the curve. The cover in the running plate alongside the firebox, which protected the reversing rod on the driver's side for example, was 8in. deep on Nos. 4000-9. On later engines it was 9½in. deep and it is believed that the first ten engines were never brought into line (cf. figs. 87 and 90).

The boiler handrails curved round the front of the smokebox. After nationalisation they were cut short and terminated on the sides of the smokebox (fig. 114), though not all the engines may have been altered in that way.

On the G.N. series when new the smokebox door was 5ft. 6in. diameter and it fitted flat against a steel sealing ring, 5ft. 8½in. outside diameter, which was the only aid towards preserving an airtight fit. On the 17 series engines a new style of joint ring was introduced, 5ft. 9in. outer diameter, with a ¾in. wide recess all the way round, packed with asbestos following standard N.E. practice. The flat edge of the door rim provided a more satisfactory fit when pressed against this packing. The 1300 series engines onwards also had this asbestos sealing ring, but in their case the edge of the door was rounded to provide an even better fit. As a wartime expedient rivets were dispensed with on replacement smokebox doors after December 1940. The outer diameter of the joint was reduced to 5ft. 7¼in. and it was welded to the smokebox front. The door hinge straps, however, continued to be secured by rivets.

Stops were fitted to the smokebox door hinges on No. 4000 in November 1930 to prevent the door from being opened too far back. Stops were also provided on the engines which were built in 1934-37, whilst existing engines meanwhile received a simpler arrangement in which one stop was fitted to the smokebox front plate, half way between the hinges (cf. figs. 103 and 108). As smokeboxes were changed around the two varieties became intermingled later.

The handrail on the smokebox door was fitted above the top hinge strap to match the height of the boiler handrails. The official length of the handrail was 4ft. 0in. between pillar centres, but shorter ones were fitted at various times to some smokeboxes (fig. 110). Odd length hinge straps were also noted in one or two cases latterly, in particular on No. 61992 which had very short straps at one period about 1948 (fig. 115). B.R. smokebox numberplates were usually fitted above the door handrail and the top lampiron had to be raised out of its way, so that the lamp support was located at 11ft. 6¼in. above rail level. This was higher than in any other class operating on the G.E. Section and from December 1949 it was generally lowered to 11ft. 3⅜in. for safety in connection with electrification on this line (cf. figs. 110 and 114). There were at least two exceptions, Nos. 61867 and 61924, which at one time were noted with their numberplates below the handrail.

The vacuum ejector exhaust pipe ran horizontally alongside the boiler and entered the smokebox on the driver's side of the engine (either right or left, as the case may be). On Nos. 4000-9 a drain was provided immediately in front of the cab. Inside the smokebox the pipe curved down and then up again to join the chimney cowl or cone (fig. 96). It was found that water collected in this curved portion of the pipe and was then ejected through the chimney when vacuum was created. This could be objectionable to anyone unfortunate enough to be standing close to the front of the engine, so that from about 1929 a ⅜in. bore copper pipe was fitted to this bend to drain away any water which collected. At first this drain pipe led down to discharge inside the smokebox at the bottom. This was not satisfactory and from about 1935 the pipe passed through the base of the smokebox, then dropped down between the frames behind the cylinders to discharge under the engine.

From November 1952 the vacuum ejector exhaust pipe was arranged to slope down gradually so that at the smokebox end it was 1⅝in. lower than at the cab end. This helped to prevent water from accumulating in the pipe. The curved portion in the smokebox was eliminated and the drain pipe was taken instead from the exhaust pipe just before it entered the smokebox. The drain pipe ran down the outside of the smokebox, passed through a hole cut in the running plate ahead of the cylinder and disappeared from view (fig. 110).

The engines built from 1929 onwards had longer big-end bearings in their inside connecting rods. These were 8¼in. diameter, as before, but 6in. long instead of 5½in. The earlier engines were not brought into line. Commencing with No. 1308 in May 1938, the engines were fitted with fluid containers in their inside connecting rod big-ends to give an early warning of overheating before damage could result.

In September 1934 Gresley noticed that the exhaust steam passages on either side of the steam pipe, outside the smokebox and above the running plate, were not lagged on the K3's (fig. 92). He asked for them to be lagged forthwith, in the manner applied to the class O2 2-8-0's (fig. 106). The existing engines were dealt with as they passed through shops and it would seem probable that the first new engines fitted were the last two from Armstrong Whitworth (Nos. 2936/7) and the last five from R. Stephenson (Nos. 1307/22, 2938/9/40), which were in store waiting to go into traffic in January 1935. A photograph of No. 2938, taken in the works yard at Doncaster, shows this lagging in position.

No. 140 was fitted with Ashcroft cut-off control gauge equipment from March 1928 to June 1931 in place of its steam chest pressure gauge. This showed the mean effective pressure in the cylinders which was thought to be of more assistance to the driver.

The cab platform was 10in. high, except under the enginemen's seats where it was 1ft. 8in. high so forming a central well in front of the firebox. On Nos. 4000-9 there was an 8in. high wood platform on the tender footplate, with the gap between the engine and tender bridged by a steel fall plate, 7ft. 2½in. wide and hinged on the cab platform. On the engines built after Grouping the cab platform extended 1ft. 0in. further back so that it almost filled the gap in the entrance doorway. The tender did not need a wood platform and the fall plate was hinged on the tender front plate.

The first two engines built after Grouping, Nos. 17 and 28, were paired with G.N. tenders. The cab platform was extended 1ft. 0in. further back so as to almost fill the gap in the entrance doorway. The tender platform was shortened by 8¾in. and raised 2in. to be on the same level as the cab platform. The short intervening gap was bridged by a steel fall plate hinged on the tender platform. A dangerous situation could arise if the tender was low on its springs as the leading edge of the fall plate would ride up.

The first engine to receive a Group Standard tender was No. 32. The tender platform was dispensed with and the fall plate was hinged instead on the tender front, sufficiently high to slope downwards even when the tender was low on its springs. A supplementary steel fall plate was provided at running plate level, about 6in. shorter than the cab platform extension above it.

Four more engines were paired with G.N. tenders in 1925, Nos. 184/6/91/5. The cab platform was not extended back in their case, and the entrance was bridged by a fall plate that was hinged on the cab platform and rested on the tender platform in the manner of Nos. 4000-9. The supplementary fall plate was not fitted.

There were thus three methods of arranging the cab platform and alterations were necessary before a tender type change could take place. Nos. 4000-6/8/9 acquired Group Standard tenders between 1925 and 1929. Wood platforms were fitted to the tenders to support the engine fall plate. The tender fall plate in turn rested on the engine fall plate. There were difficulties climbing into the cab, bearing in mind that the respective fall plates were of different widths (engine 7ft. 2½in., tender 7ft. 8in.), whilst the

overall lengths over the running plates were 8ft. 9in. and 8ft. 6in. respectively. On 8th March 1928 a passed cleaner injured himself at Doncaster when his foot slipped when climbing on the footplate of No. 4004. The engine fall plates on these particular engines were afterwards widened to 7ft. 7in. When Nos. 32, 80, 140, 188 and 200 acquired G.N. tenders in the same period, they were altered to conform to Nos. 184/6/91/5. Finally Nos. 17 and 28 were provided with Group Standard tenders, which brought them into line with Nos. 32 onwards. On the engines built in 1934-37 the length of the supplementary fall plate was increased to 7ft. 9¼in.

In June 1934 the Southern Area Running Department recommended abandoning the Group Standard method of fitting the fall plate to the tender front and returning to the G.N. practice of fitting it to the cab platform. Three reasons were given. The Group Standard arrangement restricted the area of the fixed footboards in the cab; if the fireman was negligent in not clearing the coal from under the fall plate, its leading edge formed a raised obstruction which could trip someone up; and there was a possibility of a man's boot being trapped between the fall plate and the cab side when the engine was moving round a sharp curve. The reasons given were not sufficiently convincing to justify the alteration being made at that time. However, the decision was reversed later and from about 1941 alterations were made, which only affected Group Standard tenders paired with post-Grouping engines. The tender fall plate was removed and replaced by a 10in. deep wood platform which projected forward and almost filled the gap in the cab entrance; the cab footboards were shortened, stopping short on a level with the rear edge of the cab sides; and the main fall plate was hinged to the cab footboards. The supplementary fall plate at running plate level was dispensed with. After February 1955 the fall plate was given a "chequered" surface to provide a better foot-grip.

It has been mentioned that the engines often rode so roughly that the bolts which fastened the cab to the footplate could be shaken loose. In May 1955 the bolts securing No. 61891's cab to the platform were fitted with Nyloc type P nuts, from Simmonds Aerocessories Ltd., in an endeavour to prevent them from working loose. The results were satisfactory but the experiment came rather late in the day for the K3's and their use was not extended to other members of class.

Glass sight screens were fitted to the side window cabs from November 1931 (fig. 108). They were also fitted to Nos. 4000-9 which had G.N. cabs without side windows. In their case the screens were fitted just in front of the cab cut out, too high up at first but lowered later to clear the load gauge, commencing with No. 4009 in December 1936.

The whistle on Nos. 4000-9 was the usual G.N. type with the operating lever above the cab roof (fig. 87) and the height above rail level to the top was 13ft. 5in. The K3's which appeared after Grouping had the N.E. style of whistle with the operating lever alongside the base, so that the top of the whistle was inside the L.N.E.R. Composite Load Gauge. On these engines too the whistle was located 1ft. 0in. to the left of the centre line, so that the lever could clear the steam manifold, instead of being in line with the safety valves (fig. 91). The first ten engines were brought into line by about 1930, though, when the Part 1 engine diagram was amended in December 1938 to recognise the lowering of the whistle, it was altered in error to show 13ft. 3$\frac{7}{8}$in. which was approximately 6in. too high.

Steam heat fittings were provided at the tender end, and at the front end also on a number of engines (fig. 122).

Brakes

Nos. 4000-9 had vacuum brakes following G.N.R. practice. There were two 21in. diameter brake cylinders under the cab. The fifty engines which were ordered in 1923 from Darlington Works were intended to have steam brakes on the engine and tender with a vacuum ejector for train braking. Darlington drew Gresley's attention to the requirement for the reversing shaft to be locked by vacuum-operated clutch gear. Whilst this would be alright when working passenger trains it would present a problem when working non-braked coal trains. Either the driver would have to operate the vacuum ejector continuously, or a vacuum reservoir would have to be provided solely for the clutch gear, which would mean the driver keeping a careful watch on the vacuum gauge and periodically operating the ejector. On 24th November 1923 Gresley instructed Darlington to fit these new engines with vacuum brakes instead, so that the normal reversing shaft locking gear could be fitted.

A batch of K3's appeared in the second half of 1925 and comprised ten engines built at Darlington for the Southern Area. They had steam reversing gear, which meant that the reversing shaft clutch gear could be dispensed with. Steam brakes were provided for engine and tender with a vacuum ejector for train braking. The 11in. diameter brake cylinder was located under the cab.

The next batch of K3's appeared in 1929 and were built at Doncaster for the N.E. Area. They had Westinghouse brakes for engine, tender and train with a vacuum ejector for alternative train braking. The 18in. diameter brake cylinder was located under the cab, with a large auxiliary reservoir in front of it. The 8in./8$\frac{1}{2}$in. air compressor was located on the right-hand side of the smokebox (fig. 98), where it was less susceptible to trouble caused by vibration, whereas on the Westinghouse-braked D49's, for example, it had been fitted on the side of the firebox. A small vacuum chamber was provided inside the cab on the driver's side with the air equalising reservoir above it. Following N.E.R. practice, the front-end connection was from a union just below the bufferbeam, no Westinghouse stand-pipe being provided.

Darlington built nine engines in 1930 and Armstrong Whitworth built twenty more in 1931. These engines had steam brakes on engine and tender with a vacuum ejector for train braking. However the tenders that were attached to engines built for the Scottish Area, Nos. 2767/8/9, differed in having larger brake blocks.

By the time the twenty engines had appeared in 1929 with Westinghouse brakes, the Unification of Brakes Programme had already begun, as a result of which these engines were converted to steam brake between October 1931 and July 1933. Before the conversion programme was completed, Gresley issued instructions in March 1933 that in future new K3's should be fitted with vacuum brakes throughout instead of steam on the engine and tender. He also suggested that when the Westinghouse-braked K3's were converted, they should receive vacuum brakes in preference to steam. However by this time only Nos. 1318/65/7 remained to be dealt with, and two of these were actually in works being altered. The recommendation was therefore received too late to be effective and was disregarded. The dates that the engines were altered are set out in the Summary. The K3's built from 1934 onwards had vacuum brakes throughout in accordance with Gresley's new policy.

The engines allocated to the N.E. Area, and also No. 32 which was in the Scottish Area, were originally provided with Raven's cab signalling apparatus for use when working over the East Coast main line in the N.E. Area. The system ceased to be used from October 1933 and the equipment was afterwards removed, though the dates were not recorded.

A.W.S. equipment was fitted to many engines of the class in B.R. days. Those which had steam brakes had an additional vacuum reservoir provided on the right-hand side running plate just in front of the cab (fig. 114).

When No. 206 was rebuilt in 1945 it retained its steam brake and vacuum ejector. Because of the increased boiler pressure, the 11in. diameter steam brake cylinder was replaced by a 9in. diameter one and the leverage of the brake rigging was also altered.

Tenders

For most of the L.N.E.R. period ten G.N.R. tenders (seven from 1942) were allocated to class K3, though individual allocations changed. The remaining engines all had 4,200-gallon Group Standard tenders. In the following narrative the tenders are identified by reference to the engines to which they were originally attached.

G.N.R. CLASS B

Nos. 4000-9. – At Grouping, Nos. 4000-9 had G.N.R. class B tenders which held 3,500 gallons of water and 6¼ tons of coal. There were two distinct varieties, both of which were represented in class K3. On the earlier examples the side sheets curved down at the front end and a hand grip was provided in the curve which it formed. On the post-1912 tenders the side sheets were extended forward to eliminate the hand grip (fig. 87). There was a small point of difference within these later tenders. On some the vertical handrail at the front was 2ft. 7in. long between pillar centres whilst on others it was 3ft. 7in. During the period 1925-29 Nos. 4000-6/8/9 acquired Group Standard tenders and finally No. 4007 was brought into line in January 1942.

Nos. 17, 28. – When the first fifty post-Grouping engines were ordered from Darlington Works in October 1923 there was some doubt as to the type of tender to be attached. As a result of this, construction of the Group Standard tenders lagged behind that of the new engines. Doncaster had to send two G.N.R. class B tenders to Darlington to enable Nos. 17 and 28 to go into traffic in the N.E. Area. Doncaster eventually provided two second-hand Group Standard tenders, from Southern Area K3's, which were probably attached to Nos. 17 and 28 at Darlington Works in March and August 1929

respectively, though the dates are not officially confirmed.

Nos. 184/6/8/91/5, 200 – These six engines were allocated to the Scottish Area, for which purpose they were to have been provided with G.N. tenders to facilitate turning where shorter turntables were a limiting factor. Having already sent two such tenders Doncaster only provided four more (which were attached to Nos. 184/6/91/5, see fig. 119), presumably at that time expecting Darlington to make the necessary change with Nos. 17 and 28, though this was not done. In consequence Nos. 188 and 200 were initially paired with the Group Standard type. No. 188 went to Scotland in March 1925 whilst No. 200 was sent straight to the Empire Exhibition at Wembley and did not effectively enter traffic until the following November. Meanwhile, in May 1925 Doncaster had supplied a spare G.N. tender which was attached to No. 188 at Cowlairs Works on 3rd June, whilst No. 200 received its G.N. tender in March 1929.

LATER CHANGES. – The changes in tender type so far related were concerned with adhering to the original intention of providing the six Scottish engines with G.N. tenders and at the same time providing six of the original G.N. series engines with the Group Standard type. As early as June 1925 this intention was upset when the Scottish Area acquired No. 32 at Carlisle (see page 124). This engine also required a G.N. tender, which was duly provided at Cowlairs Works, probably in June 1927 though the date is not officially confirmed. There were no spare Group Standard tenders, so to facilitate the change which affected Nos. 17 and 28, Doncaster Works provided two Southern Area engines, Nos. 80 and 140, with G.N. tenders (probably both in March 1928, see fig. 118), which then released two tenders for the N.E. Area. At the beginning of 1930 therefore, the ten G.N. tenders were attached to Nos. 32, 184/6/8/91/5, 200 in the Scottish Area and Nos. 80, 140, 4007 in the Southern Area.

Further changes took place in the Southern Area. In August 1933 No. 140's G.N. tender went to No. 134 in a straight exchange, but another change four months later put this G.N. tender with No. 91 instead. Whilst retaining the G.N. class B type, No. 80 had one of the 3,670-gallon variety from June 1935 until January 1942, when it regained one of the 3,500-gallon type.

There was a proposal in June 1941 to provide 4,200-gallon tenders for the ten K3's which had the G.N. type as part of a complicated deal involving classes D49, J39, O2 and V2. Three such tenders were transferred in 1942 to Nos. 80, 91 and 4007 (from class D49 Nos. 281, 309 and 306 respectively), but the transfer of J39 tenders to the seven K3's in the Scottish Area was abandoned. These latter engines, Nos. 1812/54-9 at nationalisation, continued to run with G.N. tenders until they were withdrawn, except that No. 61859 (ex-200) acquired a Group Standard tender in September 1962, only two months before its withdrawal.

The only alteration of note that took place on the G.N. tenders was the provision of footsteps at the rear of the tank and the fitting of an extra vertical handrail on the left-hand side of the tank at the back end, from March 1940.

GROUP STANDARD (1924-25)

NOS. 32 ONWARDS. – Design work commenced at Darlington in November 1923 on the Group Standard tender which held 4,200 gallons of water and 7½ tons of coal. This was developed from the N.E.R. 4,125-gallon self-trimming type and it is therefore appropriate to compare some of their respective features. In both cases their outside frames were ⅞in. thick, spaced 6ft. 1⅛in. apart, and their inside frames were ½in. thick, spaced 4ft. 1in. apart. However, the new design had 10in. longer outside frames and wheelbase, with the axles unequally spaced apart. A supplementary well tank, 11ft. 2⅜in. long inside, was located between the inside frames above the middle and rear axles. The feed water supply to the injectors was taken from the front of this well. The tender sides were 1ft. 0in. longer than those of the N.E.R. counterpart but the height and width were the same. This last feature afterwards influenced the cab widths of a number of Group Standard classes. The extra length of the tender increased the capacity to 7½ tons of coal and 4,200 gallons of water (but see later). The coping plate also flared outwards and up above the tank, though without coal rails and in this respect was similar to latest Gorton practice. The front plate was set well back from the tank front so that two tool boxes could be accommodated in front of it, high up on top of the tank. The top of the front plate was curved and 3in. higher at the centre than at the sides. The water scoop was located in front of the rear axle and the up-take pipe, which passed through the well tank, finally terminated in a dome at the top of the tank. The rear division plate for the coal space was located astride the dome. This plate also curved slightly to match the front plate. The vertical handrails on the tank sides were 2ft. 4in. long between pillar centres. There were two 18in. diameter vacuum brake cylinders located behind the front axle and a vacuum reservoir cylinder, 1ft. 4½in. diameter by 3ft. 8in. long, under the rear dragbox.

Fifty tenders were built in 1924-25 to this new design. Forty-four were intended for Nos. 17 onwards up to 180, leaving six spares to be sent to Doncaster for the earlier G.N. series engines. Doncaster used one of these spare tenders from April to November 1925 coupled to class A1 No. 4472 *Flying Scotsman*, on display at Wembley, because that year's Exhibition stand was slightly smaller and did not permit the use of an eight-wheel tender as used in the 1924 Exhibition. This Group Standard tender then went to No. 4003.

As related above, Nos. 17 and 28 first appeared with G.N. tenders and No. 32 was the first engine to run with the new Group Standard type (fig. 90). The next engine of the series, No. 33, was chosen to pose for the official works photograph, for which purpose it was given the traditional Darlington shop-grey painting with white lining (fig. 91). The two extra Group Standard tenders were temporarily attached to Nos. 188 and 200 (see p. 119).

NOS. 202 ONWARDS. – The tenders for the last ten engines built in 1925 differed from the preceding batch of fifty in having steam brake, with the 9 in. diameter brake cylinder ahead of the front axle. There was also one interesting innovation: with the exception of the tender that was attached to No. 228, they had disc wheels instead of the usual spoked variety.

Similar tenders were provided for the thirty-five J38's which appeared in 1926 and the first twenty-eight D49's which appeared in 1927-29. Altogether 123 of this particular variety were built, identifiable by their stepped-out coping plate. Due to subsequent changes they were afterwards attached to engines of other Gresley classes, including O2 and V2. Three of the D49 tenders were transferred to class K3 in 1942 (see earlier) whilst after nationalisation two more former D49 tenders were transferred from class O2. Post-1929 K3's, not normally associated with this variety, which were at one time or another attached to Group Standard tenders having stepped-out coping plates were No. 3815 (later 1975) from August 1941 to March 1949 and Nos. 61922/9/43/9/51/61/9/85 after national-isation.

Fig. 110   Class K3 No. 61808 at Blackpool Central shed, June 1957.

Guard irons removed from main frames, Group Standard buffers, short smokebox door handrail, top lampiron high up on door, drain pipe from
sloping vacuum ejector exhaust pipe at smokebox end.

Fig. 111   Class K3 No. 61811 at March shed, c. 1958.

Altered to left-hand drive, Diagram 96A boiler with altered arrangement of firebox hand holes and safety valves 1ft. 3in. further forward, tender
with high front (from class V2).

Fig. 112   Class K3 No. 61832 at Neasden shed, May 1960.

Diagram 96 boiler, new rear end frame.

Fig. 113 Class K3 No. 61853 on an engineer's train near Doncaster, c. 1958.
Tender with high front rebuilt from stepped-out type and with snaphead riveting.

Fig. 114   Class K3 No. 61906 at Doncaster Works, July 1961.
Boiler handrails stopped short on smokebox side, top lampiron immediately above B.R. numberplate, new rear end frame, fitted with A.W.S., reverse running sanders repositioned behind middle coupled wheels, B.R. lined-out black livery, coal division plate on tender further forward and made higher.

Fig. 115   Class K3 No. 61992 at St. Margaret's shed, 1948.
Short smokebox door hinge straps, B.R. number with "L N E R" lettering on tender.

Fig. 116   Class K3/1 No. 4002 on a down No. 2 express goods at Wood Green, 1925.
Bufferbeam with square corners, hole in fall plate below smokebox for access to 2 to 1 gear motion levers.

Fig. 117   Class K3/2 No. 4004 on an up parcels train at Doncaster, June 1938.
Bufferbeam with lower corners cut out, cover over access hole to motion levers.

Fig. 118   Class K3/2 No. 80 on an up express goods at Barkston, c. 1933.

17 series engine with G.N. tender.

Fig. 119   Class K3/2 No. 186 approaching Grantham with a down cattle train, July 1933.

Scottish Area engine with G.N. tender.

Fig. 120   Class K3/2 No. 1164 leaving Peascliffe tunnel with an up stopping passenger train,
October 1937.

Fig. 121   Class K3/2 No. 73 on the 12-5 p.m. Manchester-Cleethorpes passing Torside,
September 1946.

Fig. 126   Class K3/3 No. 1391 on a down No. 2 express goods near Darlington, March 1933.

Fig. 127   Class K3/3 No. 1395 leaving Scarborough, August 1939.

Gresley disliked the stepped-out appearance of the early Group Standard tenders, which he said reminded him of a funeral hearse, and post-1929 tenders had straight sides instead. The flare at the back of the tender was also omitted at the same time. The tenders built in 1929 (1300 series) had Westinghouse brakes, with the 16 in. diameter brake cylinder ahead of the front axle and the 12 in. diameter by 3 ft. 7 in. long auxiliary air reservoir cylinder under the rear dragbox in place of the vacuum reservoir (fig. 98). The tenders built in 1930-31 (2761 and 1100 series) had steam brakes, being otherwise generally similar to the 1300 series, which latter were altered to steam brake in the early thirties.

There were two other points of difference which distinguished them from the K3 tenders of 1924-25. At the front end, the lower footstep was located 3½ in. further forward and the profile of the outside frame was altered to accommodate this. The brake pull-rods were located out of sight between the wheels instead of being in view outside of them: this particular difference had been introduced in 1926 with the J38 tenders.

These tenders had vacuum brakes, being otherwise generally similar to the other post-1929 tenders. Their brake cylinders were 21 in. diameter, instead of 18 in., and the vacuum reservoir capacity was increased too. At first there were two cylinders, 1 ft. 10 in. diameter by 4 ft. 6 in. long, on top of the tender on either side of the filler hole behind the rear division plate, but from February 1936 the one on the left-hand side was dispensed with (cf. figs. 104 and 132).

ARMSTRONG WHITWORTH AND N.B. LOCO. CO. ENGINES. – Their tenders had tanks that were welded instead of riveted and, consequently, presented a smooth finish. In addition there was no angle-iron below the level of the running plate (figs. 102, 104 and 105).

R. STEPHENSON ENGINES. – Their tenders also had welded tanks and presented a smooth appearance, but the usual angle-iron was present (fig. 103).

DARLINGTON ENGINES. – Their tenders were riveted in the usual manner (fig. 106). A new feature was that their spring hangers were shorter than in the earlier 4,200-gallon tenders.

The vertical handrails on the sides of the tender were 2 ft. 4 in. between pillar centres on the original stepped-out tenders (fig. 91) and 2 ft. 10½ in. on the straight-sided ones built for the K3's in 1929-31 (fig. 98). From December 1932 the length was changed to 3 ft. 9½ in. for new construction and the earlier tenders were quickly brought into line in this respect (figs. 102 and 108). Water pick-up gear was not provided on eleven tenders for Scottish Area engines Nos. 2471/2, 2767/8/9, 2938/9/40, 3830/1/2. Some tenders had life guards on the frames at the rear whilst others had none. From June 1938 they were officially dispensed with on tenders in the N.E. Area, where they sometimes fouled the stops at the end of roads in sheds.

In 1937 the front end was redesigned and later tenders had a new style of front plate which was higher at the centre. As no further K3's were constructed, the only subsequent appearances of this high-front type were the result of either exchanges with other classes or rebuilding. In May 1947 No. 1811 (ex-28) acquired one of these tenders (fig. 111) from class V2 No. 847 whilst in October 1949 No. 61873 (ex-1331) acquired a similar one from class A2/1 No. 60510. The high-front tenders then remained with these K3's until they were withdrawn.

Two of the tenders which originally had stepped-out coping plates were rebuilt late in life with new straight-sided bodies on their original frames. The rebuilding dates are not recorded but were possibly December 1949 (No. 61853) and April 1950 (No. 61861). These tanks had high front plates like the tenders attached to Nos. 61811/73, but with snap-headed rivets on their side sheets (fig. 113). Similar tank bodies appeared on the four new tenders completed in 1949 for class B1 Nos. 61352/3/4/7 (see Part 2B, p. 136).

At one time or another, 4,200-gallon tenders were attached to a variety of Gresley classes, i.e. B17, D49, J38, J39, K3, O2 and V2. From 1938, figures on all new engine diagrams consistently showed the 1929 axle weights, regardless of detail differences, though there were in fact at least nine different versions of axle weight distributions for these tenders. There were no doubt other versions not recognised, mainly arising from differences in detail such as brake type, water scoop gear fitted or not, welded or riveted construction. In addition, the differences between the quoted empty and full weights ranged from 25½ tons to 26¾ tons, whereas the theoretical difference should have been 26¼ tons. Such a wide range was bound to throw doubt on the official figures and in August 1942 a high-front tender, currently attached to class V2 No. 4880, was specially weighed, first of all empty, then filled with water and finally fully coaled. The results are summarised below:-

Empty	26T	11C	
Water	17T	9C	(i.e. 3,910 gallons)
Coal	10T	9C	
Full	54T	9C	

The surprisingly high coal capacity was probably due in part to the deterioration in the quality of coal which was being supplied at that time, giving a small lump-size. The lower water capacity was to some extent confirmed by Swindon when they specially checked the high-front tender attached to class V2 No. 60845, whilst it was on test there in 1952-53. This was found to have a capacity of only 3,800 gallons.

In the mid-fifties a new division plate was fitted at the top of the tank on the Group Standard tenders, behind the coal space, which was 1 ft. 10½ in. further forward and 11 $\frac{3}{16}$ in. higher than before to reduce coal spillage (fig. 114).

Maintenance

The engines in the Southern Area were shopped at Doncaster apart from occasional visits to Gorton or Stratford Works of engines shedded on the G.C. and G.E. Sections respectively. K3's in the N.E. Area were shopped at Darlington, assisted by Gateshead (until its closure in January 1933), with only rare visits to Doncaster, e.g. No. 1318 in July 1930 for a new middle cylinder, No. 53 in August 1933 for a new crank axle and No. 1345 in March 1939 for attention to its frames. In addition, Nos. 17, 1397/92/89 were sent to Doncaster for heavy repairs on 22nd, 23rd, 24th and 25th January 1934 respectively, though the significance of these visits is not known. However, it was whilst No. 17 was undergoing repair at Doncaster that it received its new long lap valve gear. From mid-1944 Doncaster gradually took over maintenance of the K3's in the N.E. Area, though Darlington continued shopping some of them until August 1945. No. 17 also visited Swindon Works in November 1945 for attention to a hot axlebox on the trailing coupled wheels after working in from Sheffield. The engines in the Scottish Area were shopped at Cowlairs Works, except between February 1931 and June 1938 when they were dealt with at Doncaster.

The official minimum mileage between general repairs pre-war depended on the Area in which the engines operated, as follows: Southern (65,000), N.E. (70,000) and Scottish (55,000). These figures could of course be exceeded, given favourable circumstances. No. 1308 of Tweedmouth for example ran about 84,000 miles between February 1936 and February 1938, whilst No. 2467 of Gorton ran an exceptional 92,180 miles from new in November 1935 until its first shopping in March 1938. Under wartime conditions, mileages in excess of 80,000 became common, whilst in early B.R. days two engines in East Anglia each ran over 90,000 miles: No. 61948 of March with 90,825 miles from May 1948 to October 1950 and No. 61958 of Lowestoft with 95,569 miles from August 1948 to February 1951. Total mileage figures are recorded for a number of engines, from which it can be estimated that about half the members of the class ran just over a million miles in their career. The highest recorded figure is that of No. 61872 with 1,254,549 miles.

Liveries

The K3's were express goods engines and therefore only qualified for L.N.E.R. black livery, with red lining until November 1941. However No. 1007 was turned out in February 1923 in the new green livery following a general repair. This proved to be short lived as it was back in works four months later with a broken cylinder and emerged in October 1923 as No. 1007N, painted black (fig. 87). No. 1935 was repainted apple green in November 1946 (fig. 109) as part of the post-war intention to treat in this manner all L.N.E.R. engines (except the A4's and the W1 which were again to be blue). The scheme was not pursued and this engine remained the solitary green K3, until it was repainted black in May 1949. During B.R. days the engines were normally lined out in red, cream and grey (fig. 114).

British Railways

The 192 K3's and class K5 No. 1863 were handed over to B.R. on Vesting day, and all duly received numbers in the 60,000 series.

Later Trials

Between March and May 1950 dynamometer car trials were held with the 8-0 p.m. Leeds (Wellington Street) – London (East Goods) and the 6-55 p.m. King's Cross-York express goods trains, with their loads made up to former L.M.S. F.F.1 conditions, i.e. 50 wagons, vacuum fitted throughout, maximum speed 60 miles per hour. No. 61810 was deputed to work the test trains but proved to be such a poor choice that No. 61921 had to be substituted later in the trials.

The first test run was on 27th March 1950, with No. 61810 and a load of 541 tons on the up run. Steam pressure was insufficient between Peterborough and King's Cross, falling to 120 lb. per sq. in. at Brookman's Park where a special stop had to be made to regain pressure. The coal was of poor quality on this run and had to be replaced by a better grade for the return journey the next day, when however this engine still had difficulty steaming. Power tests were held on the next two days running, but it was obvious that the performance of No. 61810 was below standard and not representative of its class. No. 61921 was substituted and tests recommenced on 24th April. The engine steamed better but ran hot near King's Cross, necessitating repeat trials being held on the 1st and 2nd May. On the 1st, working the up train with a load of 489 tons, the maximum draw-bar horsepower recorded was 960 at 35½ m.p.h. between Retford and Newark, and the maximum speed was 55½ m.p.h. near Huntingdon. On the return journey next day the load was 550 tons, and the maximum draw-bar horsepower was 990 at 38½ m.p.h. between Crow Park and Tuxford on the 1 in 200 up grade (equivalent to a draw-bar horsepower of 1,120 on the level), and the maximum speed was 62.8 m.p.h. south of Abbots Ripton.

No. 61887 took part in dynamometer car tests in October 1958 between Doncaster and New England and back to determine a system of wagon equivalents based on the power required to pull the various classes of train, and to obtain the load classification of locomotives used for hauling express freight trains. Class B1 No. 61087 and B.R. Standard class 9F No. 92196 were also tested. The K3's part in these tests was to work a special train on 8th October formed of 42 wagons (12 Hyfits and 30 Vanfits) mostly loaded with scrap metal, and the dynamometer car, total weight 484 tons. Its performance was then compared with No. 61087 which had worked the same load the day before. The K3 had run 23,000 miles since its last heavy repair and was considered to be representative of its class. Despite being in a higher power class than the B1, it could not achieve the speeds which were required for an accurate comparison to be

made with the B1 performance, nor could it keep to the booked schedule. On the return journey, the K3 was worked at 40 per cent cut-off up the bank to Stoke and at one point boiler pressure fell to 155 lb. per sq.in. Based purely on one day's performance of this one K3, it was suggested that the load category of this class should be reduced to that of the B1.

Allocation and Work

At Grouping the ten original engines were shared between King's Cross, Peterborough (New England) and Doncaster. It was not until 1931 that their association with these sheds was first broken, when one of them had a short spell at Leeds (Copley Hill). By February 1940 seven of these engines were at former G.C. sheds, whilst after nationalisation six engines were at one time or another allocated to former G.E. sheds. Two ended their careers on the London Midland Region following the transfer of Woodford shed from Eastern Region control in 1958.

The sixty engines built at Darlington in 1924-25 to L.N.E.R. standard dimensions were distributed as follows:-

Built	1924	1925
Southern Area	15	29
North Eastern Area	10	–
Scottish Area	–	6

Ten of the engines in the Southern Area had steam brakes and were allocated to the G.C. Section at Gorton, though six were transferred shortly afterwards to the G.E. Section at March.

After a short break in construction Doncaster built twenty engines in 1929 which were dual-fitted for working Westinghouse or vacuum braked trains in the North Eastern Area. These were followed in 1930-31 by twenty-nine engines with steam brake on the engine and tender, with vacuum for train braking. The initial allocation of these forty-nine engines, which appeared from Doncaster (20), Darlington (9) and Armstrong Whitworth (20), was as follows:-

Built	1929	1930	1931
Southern Area	–	6	12
North Eastern Area	20	–	8
Scottish Area	–	3	–

Construction recommenced in 1934 with the final seventy-four engines which had vacuum brakes only. They were built by Armstrong Whitworth (20), R. Stephenson (10), N.B. Loco. (20) and Doncaster (24) and their initial allocation is summarised as follows:-

Built	1934	1935	1936	1937
Southern Area	2	22	19	–
North Eastern Area	11	2	5	5
Scottish Area	–	3	2	3

There was only one Area change during the period that the engines were under construction: In June 1925 Carlisle (London Road) shed was transferred from the N.E. to the Scottish Area and No. 32 then moved to the neighbouring Canal shed. Much later, in June 1938, four K3's were loaned to the Southern Area for the summer traffic, two each from Carlisle to March and from York to Retford. These moves were balanced by the transfer of four J39's. The eight engines concerned were exchanged back in August-September 1938. In March 1939 the closure of Berwick marshalling yard resulted in the transfer of seven N.E. Area K3's to St. Margaret's in the Scottish Area.

During the 1939-45 War changes were necessitated by varying demands and engine shortages. In particular the loss of ninety-two class O4 2-8-0's to the War Department brought about a reshuffle of motive power in 1942, including the transfer of ten K3's from the Southern Area to Scotland, whilst new construction of class V2 engines resulted in seven K3's being transferred from the North Eastern to the Southern Area about this time. Other transfers also took place so that the position at nationalisation on 1st January 1948 was as follows:-

Eastern Region	126*
North Eastern Region	40
Scottish Region	27

* This total included the K5.

Subsequent changes in these totals were brought about by inter-Regional transfers, in particular the changes to the Regional boundaries that took place from time to time. In September 1951 there was a large-scale transfer of eight-coupled engines (classes O1, O4 and W.D. 2-8-0) from the North Eastern to the Eastern Region, in exchange for six-coupled engines (classes B1, J39 and K3). As part of these changes five K3's were sent to Hull (Dairycoates). In 1956 the West Riding District (involving Ardsley, Bradford and Copley Hill) was transferred to the North Eastern Region though at that time there were no K3's at these sheds. In 1958 the G.C. system in the Manchester area and the main lines south of Heath (near Chesterfield) were taken over by the London Midland Region which gained the K3 allocations

of Gorton (4), Annesley (3) and Woodford (8). At the same time Carlisle (Canal), with seven K3's, returned to L.M. Region control from the Scottish Region. (This former N.B.R. shed had previously been under L.M. Region control from June 1948 until July 1951).

The end of the K3's was not protracted. The first to go were in the London Midland and Scottish Regions, when No. 61898 from Carlisle was withdrawn in February 1959, followed three months later by No. 61991 from St. Margaret's. Eastern Region withdrawals commenced in February 1960 with No. 61836 from Doncaster. At the beginning of 1961 the North Eastern Region had forty-eight K3's on its strength and the first withdrawal took place in May of that year, with No. 61874 of Hull (Dairycoates).

The last Scottish Region K3, No. 61968, was withdrawn in October 1961, whilst the last Carlisle K3 to be withdrawn was No. 61936, one month later. This latter engine had spent its entire life at Canal shed and was the only K3 to remain at one shed during its working life. There were others which only knew two home sheds, for example Nos. 61968/92 (St. Margaret's and Carlisle) and No. 61988 (Tweedmouth and St. Margaret's), whilst No. 61937 was at Carlisle continuously from January 1935 until withdrawn in March 1960 except for a short spell at March between June 1959 and February 1960. The London Midland Region completed their withdrawals in March 1962 with Nos. 61804/9/41 of Woodford. The Eastern Region withdrew the K5 in June 1960 and completed the withdrawal of their K3's in November 1962, when fifteen were taken out of stock. One month later the North Eastern Region withdrew no fewer than twenty-two – three from Ardsley and nineteen from Hull (Dairycoates). These were the last of the class to remain in stock.

The accompanying table shows the number of K3's at each shed at: (i) 31st December 1925, when the first sixty G.S. engines were in traffic, (ii) 31st December 1937, when the full number of engines had been delivered, (iii) 31st December 1947 on the eve of nationalisation and (iv) the end of 1954. Details of the duties of the class follow.

Allocation at 31st

December	1925	1937	1947	1954
King's Cross	10	12	–	–
New England	20	34	37*	–
Lincoln	–	–	10	15
Colwick	–	3	10	8
Doncaster	13	38	6	–

Ardsley	–	2	–	–
Copley Hill	1	3	–	–
Neasden	2	–	–	–
Woodford	–	–	7	–
Annesley	–	–	7	3
Gorton	8	18	–	6
Immingham	–	–	11	13
Mexborough	–	1	–	–
Trafford Park	–	1	–	–
Liverpool (Brunswick)	–	1	–	–
Stratford	–	–	–	19*
Norwich	–	–	11	10
Lowestoft	–	–	4	5
March	–	2	23	42
York	3	14	–	–
Hull (Dairycoates)	–	–	21	24
Gateshead	–	12	9	–
Blaydon	2	3	–	–
Heaton	4	14	10	9
Tweedmouth	–	17	–	8
St. Margaret's	–	5	20	23
Polmont	1	1	–	–
Eastfield	1	1	–	–
Carlisle (Canal)	5	11	7	8

* Includes the class K5 engine.

SOUTHERN AREA

The first Gresley three-cylinder 2-6-0 was allocated new to Peterborough (New England) shed. There it was given a regular two shift diagram each weekday commencing with empty fish vans departing from New England at 12-45 p.m. to New Clee and returning on the 6-0 p.m. express fish from New Clee to London, arriving at 10-40 p.m. Finally, the 12-27 a.m. King's Cross Goods to Grimsby was taken as far as Peterborough. The crews changed at New England on the up run. (This diagram persisted at New England at least until 1939). Nos. 1001/2/3 were also allocated to Peterborough though for a while they were loaned to King's Cross. Here No. 1001 was booked to one driver regularly in the Express Goods Link for a long spell of trial running, whilst Nos. 1002/3 were used on the nightly express braked goods trains to Peterborough and the corresponding up workings. All three engines were back working from New England shed by Grouping. Nos. 1004/5/6 all went new to Doncaster, Nos. 1007 to New England and Nos. 1008/9 to King's Cross. In G.N.R. days there was a regular working from New England to King's Cross during the early hours of the morning on a fast goods returning home on the 7-45 a.m. stopping passenger.

Great importance was attached to punctual running of the nightly express braked goods trains between King's Cross and Manchester (Deansgate), for which traffic the G.N.R. was in keen competition with both the L.N.W. and Midland lines. The down train left King's Cross Goods at 8-30 p.m. (9-0 p.m. on Saturdays), running via Peterborough, Grantham, Colwick thence on to the Midland line at Codnor Park to travel via Clay Cross, Dore South Junction and Chinley to arrive at Manchester shortly after 5-0 a.m. The corresponding up train left Deansgate at 5-0 p.m. but travelled via the G.C.R. route to Sheffield and Annesley, thence Colwick. (In L.N.E.R. days the working was changed to operate over the L.M.S. route in both directions). In 1921 reduced timings were specified for these trains between London and Colwick with the proviso that three-cylinder 2-6-0's be used on the Colwick-London section in each direction. Overall average speeds of 41.3 m.p.h. were scheduled with New England engines taking both down and up trains between New England and Colwick, and King's Cross engines working south of Peterborough.

Just as these new 2-6-0's were getting into their stride on the G.N.R. fast goods trains a prolonged miners' strike occurred, lasting for three months in 1921. One result of this stoppage was a severe reduction in train services. Certain express passenger trains were combined between King's Cross and Doncaster each way. At Doncaster these trains divided into West Riding and Newcastle or Scottish portions. Loads rose to 600 tons, far beyond the capacity of the Ivatt large Atlantics which were then the normal express engines. To avoid double-heading, the combined expresses were worked by 2-6-0's from each of the main sheds (King's Cross, Peterborough and Doncaster). Although the big 2-6-0's had little difficulty in working the huge loads to time between stops, time was lost through having to draw up at intermediate stations where train lengths exceeded the platform length. On 14th June 1921 three failures occurred. No. 1000 suffered fractures in the valve gear whilst working the West Riding express due into King's Cross at 11-42 a.m., No. 1002 had a warm middle big-end at Peterborough whilst working the 4-0 p.m. from London and when No. 1003 came off the 5-40 p.m. ex-King's Cross (Newcastle and West Riding combined express) it was found to have a hot middle big-end. No. 1002 was working goods trains the following day and No. 1003 six days later, but No. 1000 was off duty a long time.

These incidents have been referred to over the years and mostly cited as evidence of grave defects in the design. It should, however, be pointed out that these engines were put on to express passenger duties in the hands of drivers used only to Atlantics and with little or no experience of working the three-cylinder engines with their Gresley valve gear. When the miners' strike ended, passenger trains returned to normal loadings and the 2-6-0's to their express goods duties. On these, the London engines did not work beyond Peterborough, but Peterborough engines had turns to York, Doncaster, Grimsby and Colwick. The latter included one duty taking the 8-30 p.m. Manchester goods ex-King's Cross from Peterborough (Westwood) to Colwick, then the combined 5-0 p.m. ex-Liverpool (Huskisson) and 6-22 p.m. ex-Manchester (Deansgate) through from Colwick to London whence the engine returned to Peterborough on a milk empties. Doncaster engines worked to Peterborough and Leeds with some duties on the West Riding passenger trains.

At Grouping the G.N.R. was well equipped with mixed traffic 2-6-0's, handing over seventy-five two-cylinder (L.N.E.R. classes K1 and K2) and ten three-cylinder (L.N.E.R. class K3) engines. Between them they were well able to cover all the duties then scheduled. Of the first sixty K3's built to L.N.E.R. standard dimensions in 1924-25, thirty-four were allocated to the G.N. Section. This enabled six each of classes K1 and K2 to be transferred to the G.E. Section and fourteen K2's to the Scottish Area. It also enabled some of the braked goods services to convey increased loads at higher speeds. Generally the No. 1 express goods trains were taken by K3 engines leaving the lighter slower No. 2 timings to be worked by K2's. Seventeen of the first L.N.E.R. K3's went to Ardsley shed to be run-in before permanent allocations were made. The ten engines equipped with combination steam/vacuum brake all went new to Gorton (Nos. 202/3/4/6/7/8/27/8/9/31) but after a few months all had left. Four passed to Neasden and six to March where they remained until the first half of 1927 when all were transferred to G.N. Section sheds. Receipt of these engines on the G.N. Section released eight more K2's to the G.E. Section later in the year. No more K3's were allocated to the G.N. Section until 1930 (six) and 1931 (twelve) whereupon six more K2's went to Scotland. Between 1934 and 1937 the Southern Area took a further twenty-eight new K3's, all of which were at first allocated to Doncaster. After an initial running-in period, thirteen subsequently passed on to King's Cross, New England and Colwick, displacing several older members of the class which went away to G.C. and G.E. Section sheds.

By 1929 there were twelve K3's at King's Cross shed, increased to fifteen by the end of 1930. Their main duties covered all the weekday No. 1 express goods trains originating at King's Cross Goods yard and certain other duties. From 1929 onwards it was customary to roster them on Sundays to some of the regular half-day excursion trains as far as Peterborough to which point also one K3 took the 6-50 p.m. slow passenger returning on the milk train originating at Egginton Junction. In the period 1931-35 the King's Cross No. 3 (Express Goods) Link consisted of ten sets of men each allocated a regular K3 and working eight express goods trains (five of which were at night), one parcels train and one slow passenger to Hitchin only. All the express goods duties went no farther than Peterborough with return workings on similar trains, except that the engine off the 9-0 p.m. Huskisson goods from London returned from Peterborough on the Newcastle Mail due into King's Cross at 3-45 a.m. Regular observers in the Northern Heights never failed to be impressed by the evening parade of Jazzers seen between 8-30 and 9-45 p.m. Four or sometimes five could be seen, commencing with the up Hull Fish worked by the engine that had taken down the famous "Three-Forty Scotsman" earlier in the day, then in succession came three heavy down braked goods which started from King's Cross at 8-30 p.m. for Manchester, 9-0 p.m. for Liverpool and 9-30 p.m. for Leeds. On a clear night their well-tuned exhausts could be heard over long distances as they lifted their massive loads up the grade towards Potters Bar. Sometimes the evening parade commenced with a K3 on the 8-25 p.m. mail and on one well-remembered occasion this train was very late passing Oakleigh Park. Upon its emergence from Barnet Tunnel clearly something was amiss, speed was low and a heavy grinding noise was distinctly audible. Later it transpired that the normal Pacific had been requisitioned to work the 7-30 p.m. "Aberdonian" sleeping car train and a spare K3 equipped with the combination steam/vacuum brake put on the 8-25. The driver from No. 2 link was not renowned for his technical ability and was unfamiliar with the combination brake. He had great difficulty in keeping the steam brake off and much time was lost in consequence. At Peterborough he was able to do a deal with one of his colleagues in the Express Goods link and exchange his K3 for one with vacuum brake only for the return trip to London.

When in 1935-36 the 24XX series of K3's came out, five of them were put into the King's Cross link in place of older engines which moved away. From 1936 onwards as new V2 2-6-2's entered service they gradually replaced K3's in the link. By February 1939 there were no K3's left in this link and only seven remained on the King's Cross allocation at the outbreak of war in September. By the end of 1939 all had been transferred away and never again were any Jazzers allocated to Top Shed, although engines from other depots continued working into London for another twenty years or so.

In keeping with the greater amount of work allotted there, New England shed normally housed about thirty K3's. Their duties took them to Grimsby, Colwick, Doncaster, York and King's Cross. Their best turn was on the "Three-Forty Scotsman" which they took over at Westwood from a London engine for a non-stop run over the ensuing 111 miles to York, allowed 149 minutes with a maximum load of fifty wagons amounting to about 620 tons. The return from York was on the Newcastle Mail (8-0 p.m. from Newcastle), leaving York at 10-18 p.m. The Grimsby Fish working continued and had been joined by a second duty on which the engine went to Grimsby in the early morning on the night goods and remained there until required for the second fish train at night. The previous through working from Colwick to London on the Manchester goods ceased when a change of engines was introduced at New England.

Reductions in most express passenger train schedules in 1932 had focused attention upon the extremely slow-running coal trains operating in large numbers between Peterborough and Ferme Park Yard (Hornsey), often taking eight hours to cover the 73 miles. With a view to reducing line occupation as well as economising in train crew costs, two weekday fast coal trains were introduced to be hauled by K3 engines with loads limited to fifty-six 10-ton wagons, together with a loaded 50-ton vacuum-braked brick wagon next to the engine (to give additional brake power) and a 20-ton brake van. These trains started from New England at 6-30 and 8-25 a.m. and after running as much as possible on the fast lines, called at Hitchin for water and reached Ferme Park in about 3¾ hours. The crews were relieved on arrival by Hornsey men who turned and prepared the engines for quick return

workings by the New England men, after an hour, with sixty empty wagons non-stop to Peterborough in just over three hours. Similar trains ran from Doncaster to Peterborough as will be described later.

One turn frequently worked by a New England K3 was the famous 7-8 a.m. Leeds to King's Cross Parliamentary train which called at every station to New Southgate. (In latter years New Barnet was the last stop before King's Cross). This engine returned home on the 6-15 p.m. semi-fast from King's Cross which called at Finsbury Park and often raced with the 6-5 p.m. Broad Street to New Barnet local train which left Finsbury Park on the slow line at the same time for a non-stop run to New Southgate. Two very contrasting locomotives were involved; a 6ft. boilered K3 and a diminutive L.M.S. "Jinty" 0-6-0T. Usually the Jinty had the best of it until Hornsey was reached, helped by the down grade from the slow line platform at Finsbury Park, but afterwards the Jazzer would rapidly draw away. From 1930 onwards, on Sundays the New England K3's took their full share of passenger train duties. One worked up to London on an overnight sleeping car express to return with the 11-40 a.m. Newcastle and a second brought up an express goods, returning on the 12 noon King's Cross-Leeds. Both of these expresses were taken over by other New England K3's at Peterborough for the onward journeys to Doncaster. One returned on the heavy evening Leeds express at 6-38 p.m. from Doncaster and the other on a braked goods from Decoy yard. Others on appropriate occasions took the half-day excursions over from London engines at Peterborough, working to Doncaster, Grimsby and Skegness in season.

At Doncaster there was less emphasis on regular manning of their K3's, which had duties to York, Hull, Immingham, Sheffield, Whitemoor, Woodford, Colwick and Peterborough by both main and loop line routes. In many cases there were mixed slow passenger and fast goods diagrams. One notable Doncaster diagram current in the 1930's commenced with the 8-9 a.m. stopping passenger to Lincoln, then 10-38 a.m. on to Peterborough via Boston. The men lodged until just after midnight and then took over the 10-50 p.m. ex-King's Cross parcels which they worked to Leeds, reached at 5-6 a.m. Doncaster was regained by working the 7-50 a.m. express "Breakfast Train" from Leeds. On Sunday mornings this engine went to York on the parcels train, instead of Leeds, returning on the 6-0 a.m. goods. There were other diagrams on the Leeds line with slow passenger trains and braked goods. The Woodford duty commenced with the 10-0 p.m. Doncaster-York passenger train. Leaving York at 12-35 a.m. with a fast braked goods destined for Marylebone, Woodford was reached at 5-17 a.m. After lodging, the return was made on the 6-55 p.m. Woodford-Leicester and 8-42 p.m. Leicester-Sheffield (the Penzance-Newcastle) passenger trains. The final leg was by the 10-55 p.m. Sheffield-Doncaster, on which the K3 assisted a Sheffield 0-6-0 except on Saturday nights when a Mexborough based class C2 4-4-2 was booked only from Sheffield to Mexborough. There must have been many interesting combinations of engine power on this diagram over the years; the Working Timetable stipulated that if the load of the 12-35 a.m. ex-York exceeded fifty wagons the K3 must be assisted from Doncaster to Woodford, but by which class of engine was not stated. This train was in fact the 3-55 p.m. Glasgow High Street to Marylebone.

From 1932 onwards two class A unbraked trains with balancing return empties were put on from Doncaster to New England and hauled by Doncaster K3's. The loaded trains were limited to fifty-two 10-ton wagons plus 20-ton brake and the empties to sixty wagons plus 20-ton brake. The loaded trains started from Doncaster at 6-45 and 7-56 a.m., stopped at Newark for water and reached New England in 3 hrs. 25 mins. and 3 hrs. 56 mins. respectively. After an hour's break the engines and crews returned to Doncaster at 11-10 a.m. and 12-50 p.m.

As numbers increased, the Doncaster K3's saw frequent use on main line passenger trains, express and slow, particularly on reliefs at busy periods but were usually confined to the York-Peterborough section. Although it was not normal for Doncaster K3's to work to King's Cross, they often went through to Marylebone on excursions. Cup Final Saturdays were always occasions for such workings, but there were other instances. On Thursday 9th April 1936 four Doncaster K3's were seen at Neasden shed while on Friday 30th July 1937 no less than five were there. Summer relief and Saturdays Only trains to Scarborough from various points, including Leicester, were taken from Doncaster to destination and return by Doncaster K3's.

In the West Riding K3's were located at both Copley Hill and Ardsley sheds. As already mentioned, seventeen of the Darlington-built engines were run-in at Ardsley during 1924-25 prior to allocation to sheds in the Southern Area. One of this batch, No. 146, went new to Copley

Hill for use on its night goods to Doncaster and on stopping passenger trains. This was followed in 1927 by Nos. 202/3 to cover a new lodging turn to Whitemoor (SX), which commenced on the 7-25 p.m. slow passenger train from Leeds (Central) to Doncaster, continuing thence at 11-5 p.m. from Decoy yard to Whitemoor with a No. 1 express goods (9-33 p.m. ex-Ardsley). After lodging, the return was on the 6-50 p.m. March-Doncaster express passenger, thence to Leeds on the 10-10 p.m. slow, altered from 1936 to the 10-22 p.m. express (the Leeds portion of the 7-15 p.m. ex-King's Cross). In summer the Copley Hill K3's took Saturday expresses through to Lincoln or March, particularly the morning Leeds-Ipswich train which they worked both ways between Leeds and March. No. 135 went to Copley Hill in the autumn of 1935 for use on two daily return trips to Doncaster. There is only one known instance of a K3 working through from Leeds to King's Cross. This occurred on 6th May 1933, when No. 202 hauled an excursion to London and back. The usual power for such duties at that time was a class B4 4-6-0. Not until 1937-38 did Ardsley have a permanent allocation although some of the Copley Hill K3's had spent short spells at Ardsley over the years. One of the principal duties from Ardsley was a night goods to Immingham. In the early war years 1940-42 the K3's then at Copley Hill (Nos. 91, 135, 202/3/31) were all maintained in good order and frequently used on heavy passenger trains to Doncaster. There were some small fluctuations in the allocation at Copley Hill in 1943-45, in which latter year the last K3 left for New England (No. 2445 in July). In May 1959 Ardsley shed, then part of the North Eastern Region, once more received an allocation of K3's, when Nos. 61853/6, 61975/80 were transferred from the L.M. Region in exchange for four L.M.S.-type class 4MT 2-6-0's. Three were observed working from Low Moor shed in the 1960 summer season, taking excursions from Bradford to Blackpool, whilst on 10th August No. 61975 took a Clayton West to Morecambe special through and was serviced at Carnforth. In June 1961 Nos. 61853, 61975 were transferred to Low Moor for similar duties in the summer months. Afterwards No. 61853 returned to Ardsley but No. 61975 was withdrawn. Nos. 61917/34/84 were also transferred to Ardsley in September 1961, from Tweedmouth, and the six surviving K3's at Ardsley lasted until November-December 1962.

Retford was not normally a shed to house K3's, but in the summer months of 1938 Nos. 17 and 1300 were loaned from York, whilst in 1939 No. 4009 from Doncaster and No. 208 from King's Cross spent a few weeks at Retford, presumably for some special untraced duties. Throughout the 1930's many R.C.T.S. members participated in Sunday visits to various G.N. Section sheds, mostly travelling from King's Cross by a half-day excursion hauled by a K3. Such occasions were not noted for epic feats of speed but one on 15th May 1938 provided an excellent illustration of the work done by these engines. No. 2427 of King's Cross shed, loaded to fifteen coaches of 478 tons tare, departed from Peterborough three minutes late at 9-4 p.m. By Connington, 9 miles, speed had reached 64 m.p.h. and Ripton Bank was surmounted at a minimum of 50 m.p.h. By Huntingdon a little time had been regained and a maximum of 72 m.p.h. attained. A check to 40 m.p.h. came at St. Neots, making the train 3¼ mins. late through Hitchin. Thereafter sustained hard running, with Stevenage summit breasted at 45 m.p.h. and subsequent speeds in the high sixties, brought the train through Hatfield 58.7 miles in 64 mins. 3 secs. against the 65 mins. schedule. Adverse signals hampered progress between Wood Green and Finsbury Park but ultimate arrival there was one minute early, the 73.9 miles from Peterborough having taken 81 minutes against the 85 mins scheduled.

As elsewhere on the system, wartime events saw K3's on all manner of duties throughout the G.N. main lines but by nationalisation numbers at former G.N. sheds had fallen to sixty-three, of which just over half were at New England. As regular fast goods services were resumed the greater number were taken by V2's, although through workings from both Colwick and Immingham to King's Cross continued to have K3 haulage for some years. In the summer of 1953, for example, the 8-55 p.m. Colwick-East Goods and 9-50 p.m. King's Cross-Colwick return was regularly worked by Nos. 61821/2/4/6/33. The return working on Saturdays was later altered to run light to Welwyn Garden City for the 4-20 p.m. class D goods from there to Colwick. Immingham had two duties to London on the 5-30 and 5-58 p.m. class C fish trains, arriving at East Goods at 10-35 and 10-45 p.m. respectively. The first turn was worked by a Boston crew who returned on the 12-45 a.m. class D goods from King's Cross. The second Immingham engine went on to King's Cross shed to await the 9-40 a.m. fish empties next day, except on Sundays when the 3-0 a.m. newspaper train to Boston was taken.

For use on a parcels train leaving Boston in the late afternoon, No. 61943 was allocated there in July 1955, remaining regularly on this duty until the train ceased running in late 1957. This was the sole instance of a K3 at Boston shed although many from other depots passed through.

Colwick relied on class K2 2-6-0 and B8 4-6-0 engines for their extensive goods workings until 1937 when K3's first began to appear there. During the War the allocation increased from two to eleven by the end of 1944. Greatly increased activity by Colwick-based K3's was evident throughout the War and up to 1961. In addition to their more mundane goods duties, they were frequently used on wartime specials. Some of note were: on 16th December 1940 No. 2761 replaced class B7 No. 5470 at Nottingham on the 8-45 a.m. Ashford (Kent)-Newcastle Forces leave train and was then diverted via Retford to York because of enemy action; on 3rd July 1941 a Skegness-Portsmouth Naval special had No. 2440 from Nottingham to Banbury; on 7th January 1945 No. 1367 worked a Birkenhead-Yarmouth Troop train from Egginton Junction to Peterborough. After the War had ended, on 27th May 1947 No. 1816 worked empty stock from Basford to Sudbury (Staffs.), where repatriated German prisoners of war were entrained for Hull. The K3 worked the loaded train as far as Doncaster. Resumption of more normal passenger services saw No. 1826 on the 3-20 p.m. Skegness-Birmingham as far as Nottingham (Midland). In 1957 No. 61833 passed Etwall on an excursion to Llandudno on 21st July and on 18th August No. 61944 was seen there en route to Skegness, but the most remarkable sight was No. 61894 at Port Talbot on 5th April 1961 on a special goods for Milford Haven. This was not the first occasion that a K3 had penetrated westwards: on 13th August 1958 No. 61925 of Doncaster was noted on a Birmingham-Bristol express at Churchdown and later at the W.R. shed at Bristol (Barrow Road). Two weeks later this engine piloted an L.M.S. Jubilee 4-6-0 on the 8-30 a.m. Cardiff-Newcastle.

Ten K3's built at Darlington in 1925 and fitted with steam reverse and steam brake/vacuum ejector went new to Gorton shed where they were put to work on the night braked goods trains from Manchester to Sheffield, Lincoln and Marylebone in turn with the indigenous class B7 4-6-0's. The stay of the K3's at Gorton was brief, for in October 1925 Nos. 202/3 were transferred to Neasden, followed in February 1926 by Nos. 204/6. The remainder, Nos. 207/8/27/8/9/31, moved to March during May-June 1926.

Neasden put their four engines to work on duties normally undertaken by B7's including the 9-50 p.m. Marylebone-Manchester braked goods, which could load to thirty-eight wagons. This was a lodging turn, worked alternately by Neasden and Gorton engines and men, and was routed via High Wycombe to keep clear of the 10-0 p.m. mail from Marylebone to Manchester, which travelled via Aylesbury. Another Neasden duty was to Woodford on the 6-27 p.m. stopping passenger train, returning to London at 5-27 a.m. next day with a different crew. Except for the Manchester goods duty, none of the Neasden work was particularly heavy and it has been stated by Mr. E. D. Trask, the Assistant District Locomotive Superintendent of the period, that when Gresley found out that K3's were at Neasden he was very annoyed and insisted that they be removed to G.N. Section sheds where more important work was available. So between January and June 1927 all the Neasden K3's moved to the G.N. Section and never again did Neasden have the class on its allocation although they were frequently seen there on workings from provincial depots.

Annesley was the next G.C. shed to receive an allocation of K3's. In 1931 Nos. 58, 109 and 159 moved there from Doncaster in July, August and October respectively. Their arrival coincided with the introduction of the Annesley-Woodford out and home service of fast coal trains, soon nicknamed the "Windcutters" by those involved in their operation. Initially two trains each way, loaded southbound and empty wagons northbound, were operated on a generally similar basis to those running on the G.N. Section as mentioned above. Eventually the service was increased to four trains daily with a maximum of fifty wagons loaded and fifty-five empty. As far as possible the K3's made two return trips daily. When necessary B7's took part in the workings, which were manned by senior Annesley drivers. By October 1935 all three K3's had moved away from Annesley, leaving the B7's in command of the "Windcutters". There were occasions when Annesley sent their K3's to London on excursions, as on Cup Final day 23rd April 1932 when No. 159 was seen at Neasden (in company with three K3's from Doncaster shed) and on 28th April 1934, again the Cup Final, when No. 159 worked through on a Pinxton-King's Cross excursion, a duty which had hitherto been undertaken by Colwick K2's.

In September 1939 two K3's, Nos. 140 and 208, arrived at Annesley from King's Cross, where they had been displaced by V2's. They stayed only a few months but in October and November 1940 Colwick transferred six of the class to Annesley. From then until the end of hostilities there was a shifting but regular allocation of K3's there rising to a maximum of sixteen by November 1943 after a major re-allocation of power resulted in B7's being concentrated at Gorton and K3's sent from there to other G.C. sheds. Throughout the war period Annesley shared in the heavy troop, munitions and other traffic moving across the country via the connection with the G.W.R. at Banbury. In February 1958 the London Midland Region took over responsibility for Annesley shed, whose allocation then included three K3's (Nos. 61856, 61975/80). These engines were afterwards transferred to Ardsley in 1959.

No K3's were allocated to Gorton after the departure of the ten 2XX series mentioned earlier until 1934 when, for a short period between March and September, Nos. 1121/5 moved there from Doncaster in exchange for two B7's (Nos. 5461/75), presumably to test the suitability of K3's for current Gorton duties. All these engines returned to their original sheds in September 1934, but when deliveries of new K3's in the 24XX series took place in 1935 a number went to G.N. Section sheds, displacing engines built in 1924-25 to Gorton where seven of the new series also arrived. The Gorton stud replaced B7's on the cream of their fast goods turns embracing London, York, Lincoln and on Grimsby fish trains. In the Gorton No. 2 link K3's displaced class B2 4-6-0's and occasionally appeared on the 10-0 a.m. Manchester – Cleethorpes passenger train to Sheffield, continuing thence on the 11-37 a.m. (York – Bournemouth) express to Leicester and back to Manchester on the 2-36 p.m. (12-15 p.m. ex-Marylebone). By 1937 Gorton K3's were appearing regularly at Liverpool (Central) on the C.L.C. line trains, including the 7-25 a.m. Harwich – Liverpool boat train. The Gorton allocation of K3's reached its peak of thirty-one in July 1943, but all departed during the following October and November. There were brief allocations of Gorton K3's to Trafford Park where No. 3817 arrived in January 1937, to be exchanged for No. 80 in September 1937, then No. 134 in May 1939; the latter engine returned to Gorton in October 1940. For a month in early 1938 No. 153 was at Liverpool (Brunswick) and from August 1938 until June 1939 Walton housed No. 2429.

In 1949-50 Gorton once more began to receive K3's until a total of twenty was reached, reducing by four in 1951, increasing by one in 1952 and declining by eleven in 1954 when the Manchester to Sheffield and Wath electrification was inaugurated. Two more were transferred away in 1957. In February 1958 the L.M. Region took over responsibility for Gorton shed, whose allocation then included four K3's (Nos. 61832/65, 61910/3). These were transferred to Woodford shed during 1959-60. During their last years at Gorton some K3's were used on unusual duties as on 20th July 1957 when No. 61966 took a Huddersfield-Llandudno relief right through and returned light to Gorton and on 20th July 1959 No. 61910 also went to Llandudno with a relief from Stretford.

Elsewhere on the G.C. Section, Sheffield acquired nine K3's in 1940 when Nos. 1331/87 arrived from York, followed shortly afterwards by Nos. 195, 2471, 2767/9, 2940 from Carlisle and Eastfield and Nos. 2442/50 from March. In 1943 Nos. 120/1/59, 228 were received from Annesley. All had left Sheffield by June 1945 and it was not until June 1954 that the class again appeared there. For the summer excursion traffic of 1954 Nos. 61819/48, 61950 moved from Gorton and afterwards left for Lincoln. In September 1956 when the G.E. Section had surplus power three K3's moved to Sheffield from March (Nos. 61907/54/67) followed by Nos. 61825 and 61943 from Immingham and Boston in November 1957. No. 61816 was received from March in March 1959 (in exchange for No. 61954) and finally No. 61976 from Langwith in September 1961. The majority of these engines remained at Sheffield until withdrawn in 1961. A notable working by a Sheffield K3 on 20th June 1959 was on a Poole-Bradford express routed over the Calder Valley line behind No. 61825. Another, No. 61938, took the 8-0 p.m. Manchester Victoria-Normanton passenger train on 17th December 1961, just twelve days prior to its withdrawal.

Lincoln had one engine (No. 2762) for a day only in November 1940 afterwards taking Nos. 125/6, 1141, 4000/3/5 for a while in 1943-45. After the War Lincoln began to receive more permanent allocations, several lasting over ten years there, working mostly over G.C. routes but also on the G.N. & G.E. Joint line. Shortly before withdrawal, No. 61845 of Lincoln worked through from King's Cross to Leeds with a relief express on 25th August 1962.

Immingham first received K3's in 1940 when four (Nos. 153, 1141, 2453, 2762) arrived there,

followed by seven more (Nos. 125/6/7/41, 4000/3/5) in 1943. By the end of 1945 the stud had risen to eleven, which figure was maintained until after nationalisation, though by May 1951 the figure had reached a peak of eighteen. The bulk of their duties were over the G.N. East Lincolnshire line to Peterborough and King's Cross, as described earlier.

On the southern end of the G.C. main line, K3's were allocated to Woodford in January-February 1940 when Nos. 4000/3/5 arrived from Doncaster. These were joined by Nos. 125/6/7/41 in March 1943, but all six left two months later. In the following Autumn when concentration of B7's at Gorton took place, Woodford was given sixteen K3's in exchange which remained until 1946-49. With the greatly increased wartime traffic over the cross country lines between Banbury and the East and North of England there was ample work for the class at Woodford. That these engines travelled widely is indicated by reports of No. 112 seen at Tyseley (G.W.R.) on 28th July 1944, whilst on 4th November 1945 No. 17 failed at Swindon with a hot box after taking the Sheffield-Swindon through train. It was taken into the works for repair and replaced by G.W.R. Castle class No. 4083 for the return working. In June 1949 all the six remaining K3's at Woodford moved away, their duties being taken over by class O7 2-8-0's. Later, in September 1956, five engines made redundant at March moved to Woodford and these were joined by others from Colwick and Gorton between June 1957 and January 1958. In February 1958 the L.M. Region took over responsibility for Woodford shed, whose allocation then included eight K3's (Nos. 61804/9/24/38/41/2/3/53). They were subsequently joined by six further K3's from two other L.M. Region sheds, Gorton and Carlisle (Canal). It was during this period that they performed a lot of work on Woodford-Marylebone stopping passenger trains. An amusing incident involving No. 61809 in 1958 is related by a retired Locomotive Inspector who had been detailed to ride on the 3-10 a.m. York-Woodford class C goods, a York V2 diagram which turned out to have a Woodford K3 instead. A very strong wind was blowing when suddenly near Staverton Road the dome cover came adrift and was lifted by the wind to end up at the foot of the embankment! An interesting duty initiated on 16th June 1948 for Woodford K3's was a special train conveying Guinness Stout from Park Royal to Newcastle on Tuesdays and Fridays. The engine ran light from

Woodford to Greenford where it turned on the triangle before going north on the train. Other incursions on to Western Region territory sometimes occurred; No. 61913 was seen taking the 11-0 p.m. Woodford-Old Oak as late as 16th January 1962.

When the G.E. Section was being cleared of all steam engines during the early part of 1960, thirteen K3's were sent for storage at Staveley; two of these (Nos. 61877 and 61926) went back into traffic at Lincoln after a few weeks and three more (Nos. 61820/2, 61959) moved to Mexborough in June 1960. Nos. 61908/81/9 remained in store until June 1961 when they were put back into traffic at Mexborough, together with Nos. 61811, 61958/76 sent to Langwith whence they were used on coal trains to Immingham and regular Saturday football excursions to Nottingham. The latter two left after only three months, to Mexborough and Darnall respectively, leaving No. 61811 at Langwith for almost a year before it departed for Colwick. The remaining engines put into store at Staveley in 1960, Nos. 61826 and 61973, left for Colwick in June 1962. In September 1961 Nos. 61959/89 returned to Staveley for storage and were subsequently withdrawn.

Mexborough had one K3 (No. 3818) from January 1937 until August 1946. At first it was used on a nightly class A goods ex-Dringhouses to Woodford arriving at 6-0 a.m. After lodging, the engine and men returned to Mexborough with the 6-40 p.m. goods to York, running class A from Woodford to Leicester and No. 2 express forward. No. 3818 was kept in fine condition for this duty. Whilst at Mexborough No. 3818 also saw use on excursions to Marylebone – it was on Neasden shed on 12th May 1937 and on 9th April 1938 in company with others from Gorton, York and Doncaster. Apart from No. 3813 loaned by Doncaster for a couple of months in 1939 the only other K3 to be stationed at Mexborough in L.N.E.R. days was No. 1166 from March 1941 until August 1946, when it was sent to Doncaster with No. 1978 (ex-3818). Three more (Nos. 61850/7/8) arrived from March in 1956, joined by two (Nos. 61836/9) from Immingham early in 1959. All five departed to Doncaster in June 1959. Then the seven engines mentioned above arrived from Staveley in 1960-61. In July 1961, rather surprisingly, Nos. 61820/2, 61959/89 moved from Mexborough to the former Midland passenger shed at Millhouses (Sheffield) where they were immediately put to work on passenger trains. All four were seen at Derby (Midland) on 25th August 1961, Nos. 61820/2 on local trains,

No. 61959 on the 9-0 a.m. Nottingham-Manchester and No. 61989 on an up relief ex-Birmingham. During the following month Nos. 61820 and 61989 were noted on the 6-25 p.m. Derby-Chesterfield slow. Nos. 61959/89 returned to Staveley for store in September 1961 but Nos. 61820/2 moved to Canklow in December, where they remained for six months before going to Colwick for a couple of weeks and then on to Lincoln for the final few months of their existence.

It was not until 1938 that authority was given for K3 engines to work on the G.E. Section south of March but they had been used extensively on the G.N. & G.E. Joint line between Doncaster and March from 1925 onwards. The earliest allocations to a G.E. shed were in May 1926 when six engines with steam reverse and steam/vacuum brake moved from Gorton to March (Nos. 207/8/27/8/9/31). Each carried a plate in the cab indicating "This engine must not work south of March". Precise recording of their use has not survived but it is thought they were used on the nightly braked goods turns to Lincoln and Doncaster, with balancing duties on stopping passenger trains. Their stay at March was brief for in January 1927 all moved away to G.N. Section sheds where more suitable work was available. For one week only in May 1930 No. 228 was loaned by Doncaster to March but the first long-term allocations did not take place until the autumn of 1935 when March received Nos. 1125 and 2461 from Doncaster which were exchanged in March 1936 for Nos. 2762/5 from New England. Further engines were gradually drafted to March from 1938 onwards.

When route restrictions were lifted in 1938, Nos. 112, 2765/6 moved to Stratford for use on the night braked goods trains to and from Whitemoor, including the diagram involving the 7-45 a.m. from Cambridge to Liverpool Street and later the 6-30 p.m. Liverpool Street to Cambridge express passenger trains, referred to under class K2 (page 83). At week-ends in the summer Stratford used their K3's on relief expresses over both Colchester and Cambridge main lines. The three Stratford engines were exchanged in September 1938 with Nos. 153, 2417/67 of Gorton; whilst in December 1938 No. 2448 was acquired from New England. The Stratford stud was increased in the first half of 1939 by the arrival of Nos. 2426/8 from King's Cross where they had been displaced by new V2 2-6-2's. Through workings were introduced on the Spitalfields fast goods to and from Doncaster alternating with Doncaster K3's, which latter could on occasions turn up on other workings on the G.E. Section. G.E. drivers accustomed to K2's could handle the K3's well and naturally preferred their more modern lay-out and faster acceleration. By the end of 1941 Stratford had lost its K3's but the class continued working over the G.E. Section lines from March shed, which by June 1942 housed a total of thirty-one.

Norwich received Nos. 2453, 2762/4 from March in October 1938 for use on fast goods duties and sometimes on stopping passenger trains to Cambridge. Nos. 2443/73, 2935 were afterwards acquired from Doncaster but by the end of 1941 the K3's had all departed from Norwich.

From the end of the War there was a gradual return of K3's to the G.E. sheds other than March. At nationalisation thirty-eight were based in East Anglia: March 23, Norwich 11, Lowestoft 4. Norwich, being the District Headquarters, supplied both Lowestoft and Yarmouth with additional engines during the peak herring fishing season to cover additional fish train workings, using their own basic allocation on both goods and local passenger turns to March, Cambridge, Ipswich and London. Their K3's also worked to Cromer with special dispensation as this branch was R.A. 7. The Lowestoft engines were very active until the last examples moved away early in 1960. Lowestoft had daily through turns to London on fish and fast goods trains, also some slow passenger jobs to Ipswich. During the enginemen's strike in 1955, one Lowestoft crew maintained a daily train to London and back using No. 61955. Nos. 61926/49 were continuously at Lowestoft from 1947 until 1959 and Nos. 61958/9 stayed from November 1947 until March 1960 and from January 1949 until February 1960 respectively. They were the last to leave Lowestoft when diesel traction took over completely. No. 61949 in particular was kept in immaculate condition by its driver throughout its stay at Lowestoft and was a regular performer on an up fish train and back with the empties. Signalmen en route knew that if given the road the K3 could keep well ahead of any following express.

From 1949-52 Stratford gradually acquired an allocation once more until in 1953 sixteen K3's were there, together with the K5 rebuild. This engine apparently was used indiscriminately with the K3's and remained allocated to Stratford until it was withdrawn from service in June 1960. Like the K2's before them, Stratford's K3's found much work on all manner of goods duties

over both G.E. main lines together with relief and excursion passenger turns at busy periods. Notable occasions recorded were in June 1950 when No. 61831 took a Chingford-Portsmouth Harbour special as far as Kensington (Olympia) whilst a Parkeston-Liverpool Street boat train was seen on 14th June 1953 behind No. 61817 complete with "Day Continental" headboard, but even more unusual was No. 61912 of Immingham on the up "Scandinavian" on 3rd September 1959.

From March 1958 a new venue for K3's was Parkeston where six were transferred from Stratford, followed by six more in December, for use on heavy Continental goods duties to and from London. Five remained at Parkeston until 1960, the last two departing in December of that year, leaving only the March and Cambridge K3's on the G.E. Section. For use on oil trains over the former L.N.W.R. line to Sandy Heath and forward to Bletchley, Cambridge shed had acquired Nos. 61801/17/34/49/80 in 1958-59, retaining them until 1961.

When Norwich City met Sheffield United in the F.A. Cup in March 1959, six K3's worked through from Norwich to Sheffield. One of these trains travelled via Peterborough East, Stamford, Melton Mowbray and then down the Midland main line through the Erewash Valley. Special permission was given for the engine (No. 61827 of March) to use this route. The other trains used the more normal route via March, Lincoln and Retford to Sheffield Victoria behind Norwich engines Nos. 61908/49/71/3 and 61811 from March shed. In 1960 Norwich had a regular K3 working to Ely, then assisting a Britannia class 4-6-2 to Ipswich on the "North Country Continental", and thence back to Norwich.

Some unusual features were apparent on the occasion of the R.C.T.S. "Fensman No. 2" Rail Tour on Sunday 9th September 1956. For the first time a rail tour was operated starting with through portions from two centres. A six-coach portion from London including Cafeteria car and weighing 210 tons was worked from King's Cross to Peterborough North by K3 No. 61942, beautifully turned out by Stratford shed. The second portion started from Nottingham behind Hughes 2-6-0 No. 42784. After the two trains had been joined at Peterborough North, the tour proceeded on its journey through the Fens behind B1 No. 61391 and for the final stage from Sleaford to Bourne and Spalding behind K2 No. 61743. At Spalding the two portions were separated and No. 61942 took the London train back to King's Cross.

During 1960 the last K3's were cleared from Lowestoft (March), Stratford (July) and Parkeston (December), whilst during 1961 they were cleared from Norwich (January) and Cambridge (November), leaving March shed with sixteen engines. Nine of these lasted until 16th September 1962.

NORTH EASTERN AREA

The initial allocation of ten standard K3's to the North Eastern Area in 1924 was:- Blaydon (Nos. 17, 28, 32/3/6/8, 46, 52), York (Nos. 39, 53). In October 1924 Blaydon lost Nos. 32 to Carlisle (London Road) and 52 to York, followed shortly by Nos. 33/6/8, 46 to Heaton. No. 32 was transferred to Carlisle (Canal), in the Scottish Area, in June 1925. These ten engines made little impact on the locomotive position in the area. The seven engines at the main line sheds were chiefly employed in B16 links, working goods trains between York, Newcastle and Tweedmouth, while the Blaydon and Carlisle (London Road) engines worked similar trains over the Newcastle-Carlisle line. It was said that the 49ft. 1in. wheelbase posed problems on Blaydon's 50ft. turntables, so in 1927 the K3's were sent to York and replaced on the Carlisle line by class J39 0-6-0's. All twenty of the 13XX series of K3's built in 1929 were allocated to N.E. area sheds (York 7, Heaton 5, Tweedmouth 8) replacing B16's at the latter places and extending their duties to Edinburgh. The displaced B16's moved away to York and Hull. The next arrivals were eight of the 11XX series in 1931, four (Nos. 1100/1/2/6) to Gateshead, two (Nos. 1117/8) to Heaton and two (Nos. 1108/19) to Hull. At first the latter were at Dairycoates shed but soon moved on to Botanic Gardens for trial working on the Sheffield passenger trains which were becoming too heavy for the 4-4-0 engines then in use. However, after only a couple of months they moved to Tyneside and were replaced at Hull by class B16 Nos. 848/9 from York. A distinctly novel event occurred on Cup Final Day 25th April 1931 when brand new K3's Nos. 1100/1/2 all worked through excursions from Tyneside to King's Cross, hauling loads varying from 240 to 350 tons. Again on the following Saturday, 2nd May, both Nos. 1100/1 brought heavily loaded specials of 430 and 465 tons from York to London. Then on 18th May and 3rd June No. 1100 appeared once again on day excursions originating in Scotland. Such lengthy workings by the class were most unusual and, so far as is known, were never repeated.

For the first five years K3's rarely appeared on N.E. Area passenger trains and it was not until they were built in quantity from 1929 onwards that their mixed traffic capabilities were used more fully. At busy times main line relief and stopping passenger trains were worked, as in 1933 when on different days Nos. 1106 and 1367 were noted on the 6-35 p.m. arrival at Newcastle from Berwick and on Saturday 5th August No. 1312 took the five-coach 11-10 a.m. Newcastle-Leamside to South Shields. Two days later No. 36 took a two-coach stopping train at 8-15 a.m. to Berwick. In season they frequently found their way to the East coast resorts of Bridlington and Scarborough. Occasionally they had brief spells of glory, as in December 1931 when No. 1108 was seen on the "Queen of Scots" Pullman train and on another occasion a K3 was put on the "Flying Scotsman" after a failure of the booked engine. York K3's also appeared between Harrogate and Barnard Castle on the "Northern Belle" land-cruise train (see Part 1 of this series, fig. 13). An interesting duty for Gateshead K3's in 1937-39 was on the night train from Newcastle to Marylebone on which the engines worked through to Leicester thrice weekly alternating with B17's from Leicester shed as described on p. 118 of Part 2B.

Transfers between sheds until the 1939 War were not numerous, usually dictated by a change in traffic flow, a decision to use a different class of engine on certain duties, or the allocation of new engines. In 1934 six Armstrong Whitworth-built engines were run-in from Heaton shed and afterwards allocated to Gateshead (2) and Tweedmouth (4), the latter displacing further B16's to York and Leeds. At the same time five K3's built by Robert Stephenson were run-in at Darlington and afterwards allocated to Heaton (4) and York (1); two more, Nos. 1307/22, were placed in store at Gateshead Works for some three weeks before entering traffic at Heaton in January 1935.

In September 1937, after an interval of ten years, Blaydon shed again received three K3's (Nos. 33/8, 46 from Heaton), displacing B16's Nos. 932 to York and 2365/77 to Dairycoates. The K3's at Blaydon were again used for Carlisle workings.

Tweedmouth shed, having first obtained K3's in 1929 for intensive use on goods trains to Tyneside and Edinburgh, suffered a big change in its status in March 1939 when Berwick marshalling yard was closed as an economy measure. Of the seventeen engines then at Tweedmouth, seven went to St. Margaret's, four each to Heaton and York, leaving two at Tweedmouth to cover any failures on the revised through workings between Newcastle and Edinburgh.

In October 1939 Stockton Yard was reopened, having been closed in 1930, and five K3's were sent to the shed there, three from Gateshead and two from Heaton, liberated by new V2 2-6-2's allocated to the Tyneside sheds. Two more K3's went to Stockton in April 1940, but a decrease in traffic there in July 1940 led to four K3's moving to Darlington and being replaced by two J39's and one J21. A further K3 left Stockton in December 1940 for Darlington and the last two left in June 1941 for Blaydon. Other wartime changes led to a greater amount of home-produced ironstone being used at the iron and steel works on Tees-side, instead of imported ore, and in September 1940 four K3's were sent to the Southern Area in exchange for class O4 2-8-0's required to work the ore traffic forward from York. Shortly after, eight more K3's drawn from several N.E. Area sheds were sent on temporary loan to the Southern Area to replace engines on loan to the Great Western Railway. Six more moved from Darlington and Stockton to Blaydon in June 1941 to cover increased Carlisle goods traffic, replacing class Q6 0-8-0's.

Additional construction of V2's allowed seven K3's (Nos. 1101, 1302/8/94/5/6, 3829) to move from the N.E. Area to March in late 1941 and early 1942 (the intention was to transfer ten, but three were cancelled), and another sign of the times was the transfer of three K3's to Leeds (Neville Hill) in January 1943, two of which were required to work petrol trains. The arrival of numerous U.S.A. 2-8-0's in mid-1943 gave rise to another general re-allocation. The American engines allocated to Neville Hill displaced class Q6 0-8-0's to Tees-side, which in turn displaced J39's to Blaydon and these displaced K3's to Heaton and Gateshead.

To handle increased traffic to East Coast ports following the end of the War in Europe, Dairycoates received nine K3's from Darlington in July 1945, the first of the class to be allocated to Hull apart from the short stay by Nos. 1108 and 1119 in 1931. Hull used them to advantage; for instance in 1950 they were regularly seen on the 10-50 p.m. Hull-Mottram and 1-15 a.m. return fast goods. At nationalisation twenty-one were allocated there; the remainder of the North Eastern Region's stock were at Gateshead (9) and Heaton (10). In 1953 Dairycoates had sixteen

double-shifted diagrams taking each engine to two of the following destinations each day:-Doncaster, Leeds, Wath, York, Peckfield Colliery, Bridlington, Gascoigne Wood or Goole. Additional turns were to Doncaster single-shifted, two turns to Colwick and three "Anywhere" engines working to any point ordered by Control. Summer Saturdays brought a complete change. Numerous Hull K3's were to be seen on passenger trains to Bridlington, Filey Holiday Camp and Scarborough. One usually acted as emergency engine at Bridlington each Saturday. Certain goods duties rostered to class O7 2-8-0's during the week were given to K3's on Saturdays when part of the duty involved working a passenger train. In addition to the normal goods train duties, Hull K3's sometimes undertook special train work as on 11th April 1959 when Nos. 61904/22/45 all went through to Bradford (Forster Square) on football excursions. Due to a failure of a class D49 4-4-0 on 27th August 1960, No. 61965 took the "Yorkshire Pullman" from Hull to Doncaster. In their final months of service the Hull K3's were seen on some through specials to Blackpool in the summer of 1962.

Typical Heaton goods workings were three turns to Edinburgh, with a two minute stop at Tweedmouth to change crews. At the same period (1954) Tweedmouth had one goods turn to Edinburgh. Tyneside K3's appeared regularly on Newcastle-Carlisle excursions during 1957-58 and as late as autumn 1960 No. 61930 of Tweedmouth was working Berwick-Newcastle stopping passenger trains. A very unusual duty worked by No. 61984 of Blaydon on 23rd and 24th May 1952 was on the St. Boswells – Tweedmouth branch passenger trains. It was sent to replace a failed class C15 tank and on Sunday 25th May it travelled light to Hawick for the 9-0 a.m. passenger train to Edinburgh.

SCOTTISH AREA

In 1924-25 six new K3's (together with a seventh engine transferred from the N.E. Area) were allocated to the Scottish Area, followed by three new engines in 1930, three in 1935, two in 1936 and three in 1937, making a total of eighteen engines. Due principally to the reorganisation of East Coast goods train working following the closure of Berwick marshalling yard and the reduction in status of Tweedmouth shed, ten K3's were transferred from the N.E. Area to Scotland in 1939-40. Ten more moved to Scotland from the Southern Area in 1942 as part of a redistribution scheme for goods and mixed traffic tender engines agreed between the three L.N.E.R. operating areas after a series of meetings arising from the terrible experiences during the previous winter due to chronic engine shortages. Two schemes were submitted; the Southern Area, calculating its figures on a "train hours" basis, concluded that it needed fifty-eight additional engines – fifty-four from the North Eastern Area and four from the Scottish Area. However, the latter two Areas put forward a joint proposal based on "train miles" worked, asking that 110 engines be taken from the Southern Area – sixty-six to the N.E. Area and forty-four to Scotland. Clearly, whatever decision had been taken, not everyone would have been satisfied!

Of the original Darlington-built batch, Nos. 184/6/8/91/5 went new to Carlisle and No. 200 to Eastfield. This latter engine was exhibited at the British Empire Exhibition, Wembley during the summer of 1925 and was not put into traffic at Eastfield until 4th December although nominally allocated there on 10th April. Carlisle (Canal) also received a further engine in 1925 (No. 32). No.186 moved from Carlisle to Polmont in 1925, to Eastfield by 1928, then back to Polmont by 1932. No. 200 moved from Eastfield to Carlisle in 1931. The Scottish Area received three of the 1930 engines, which were allocated to Carlisle (Nos. 2767/9) and St. Margaret's (No. 2768). By 1932 No. 2768 had moved to Carlisle and No. 2769 to Eastfield. Three of the 1935 engines were allocated to Carlisle (Nos. 2938/9/40) and five of the 1936-37 engines went to St. Margaret's (Nos. 2471/2, 3830/1/2), making the Scottish Area allocation eleven at Carlisle, five at St. Margaret's and one each at Polmont and Eastfield. In 1940 the Eastfield engine was transferred to Sheffield and the Polmont engine to St. Margaret's.

Carlisle K3's were chiefly employed on the Waverley Route working express goods trains to Sighthill (Glasgow), Edinburgh, Polmont and Thornton. The Sighthill train was a lodging turn worked alternate days by the Eastfield engine. The Polmont working was balanced by a train from Falkirk (Grahamston) operated on a lodging basis alternately with the Polmont engine. (This explains the presence of single K3's at Eastfield and Polmont sheds). Carlisle shed also had two lodging turns to Edinburgh, involving early morning departures from Canal yard and evening departures from Edinburgh, always worked by Carlisle engines and men, so requiring two engines and two sets of men per duty each week. Similarly Carlisle always undertook the lodging turn to Thornton. Regular K3 duties from St. Margaret's included the 11-55 p.m. Duddingston-Newcastle (Forth) beer train (by then re-routed via Berwick in both directions and operated entirely by St. Margaret's engines and men), and the 8-35 a.m. Edinburgh-Perth passenger train returning with the 1-0 p.m. goods from Perth via Markinch ("The Whisky"). Very early on, two K3's ran light over the line to Fort William after which the Civil Engineer prohibited their use on the West Highland section. Nevertheless shortly after No. 1855 transferred from Carlisle to Eastfield in May 1946, it was observed entering Crianlarich from the north.

The seven K3's which moved from the North Eastern Area in March 1939 all came from Tweedmouth shed (Nos. 1306/65/8/86/8, 3823/8) and were based at St. Margaret's as were three more which moved in early 1940 (Nos. 1333/89 from Heaton and 1399 from York). At the same time the five K3's already at St. Margaret's (Nos. 2471/2, 3830/1/2, without water pick-up gear) were transferred to Carlisle in exchange for five earlier engines having G.N. tenders with pick-up gear (Nos. 32, 184/91/5, 200). The main employment of the St. Margaret's K3's was on express goods trains between Edinburgh and Newcastle with remanning at Tweedmouth. A further ten K3's moved to St. Margaret's from the Southern Area in 1942 (Nos. 75, 170, 1101/21/33/55/7/62, 1394, 2463), three taken from Doncaster and the rest from March. For varying periods during 1941-44 up to five of the St. Margaret's K3's were allocated to Haymarket. By this time traffic on the East Coast route was extremely heavy, imposing severe demands on the restricted facilities at St. Margaret's. To ease the pressure a new Main Line goods link was formed at Haymarket, which hitherto had been mostly concerned with passenger work, and where the facilities were not being utilised so near to capacity. Demands for train working were so great that engines were working seven days a week, spending as little time as possible on shed. Under these conditions the engines became for all practical purposes "common user", both North Eastern and Scottish Area engines being manned indiscriminately by crews from Gateshead, Heaton, Tweedmouth, St. Margaret's and Haymarket. In addition, K3's from the Southern Area were often pressed into service by the Tyneside sheds for northbound trains. The exceptional circumstances of those

Class K3/2 No. 1954 on an up goods leaving Boston, June 1947.

Unshaded Gill Sans numbers and letters.

Class K3 No. 61979 on a down empty coaching stock train near Stoke summit,
August 1959.

Fig. 135   Class K5 No. 61863 on a class A goods near Boston.

Fig. 136   Class K5 No. 61863 at Hitchin on a train of empty coaching stock.

Fig. 137   Class K4 No. 3441 *Loch Long* at Fort William, 1938.

Nameplate on smokebox side, reversing rod sloping down alongside firebox, connection for Flaman speed recorder on left-hand side, black livery with red lining, Group Standard 3,500-gallon tender with low front.

Fig. 138   Class K4 No. 3442 *The Great Marquess* at Crianlarich on a
Fort William-Glasgow train, August 1938.

Nameplate extended beyond smokebox, mechanical lubricators for cylinders (front) and axleboxes (rear), smokebox door handrail below top hinge strap, door stops as extensions to hinge straps, less sloping outside steam pipe covers than on No. 3441, green livery.

Fig. 139   Class K4 No. 3445 *MacCailin Mór* at Eastfield shed, June 1939.

Two sets of front guard irons.

Fig. 140   Class K4 No. 61995 *Cameron of Lochiel* at Eastfield shed, June 1957.

Odd-shaped cylinder steam pipe cover on left-hand side only, vacuum ejector exhaust pipe drain skirting round nameplate, smokebox door handrail above top hinge strap, door stop mid-way between hinges, B.R. numberplate above handrail, lined black livery with B.R. emblem on tender.

Fig. 141   Class K4 No. 61998 *MacLeod of MacLeod* at Eastfield shed, April 1957.

Guard irons removed from main frames, B.R. numberplate below smokebox door handrail, 3,500-gallon tender with high front.

Fig. 142   Class K4 No. 61995 *Cameron of Lochiel* at Fort William shed, June 1960.

4,200-gallon tender with low front (from class K3), lined black livery with second type of B.R. emblem.

Fig. 143   Class K4 No. 3443 *Cameron of Lochiel* on a down West Highland goods train between
Crianlarich and Tyndrum, 1940.

Snowplough attached to bufferbeam.

Fig. 144   Class K4 No. 3446 *MacLeod of MacLeod* on a westbound goods train at Saughton,
February 1946.

Wartime black livery with lettering "N E" on tender.

Fig. 145   Class K4 No. 1996 *Lord of the Isles* at Fort William, May 1948.

Post-war green livery. Showing bracket for speed indicator.

Fig. 146   Class K4 No. 61995 *Cameron of Lochiel* near Mallaig Junction on a Fort William-Mallaig
train, June 1951.

L.N.E.R. green livery with B.R. number and lettered "L N E R" on tender.

times were recognised to the extent that the L.N.E.R. fitted many engines with a special receptacle in the cab, where a card was kept to record the boiler wash-out dates in view of the fact that engines were liable to be away from their home sheds for long periods. For about two months in August-October 1945 Nos. 32, 188, 1121/35 moved from St. Margaret's to Aberdeen. All four then went south to Doncaster.

During the War the practice of trainmen lodging away from home was suspended by the L.N.E.R. and so the method of goods train working on the Waverley Route was completely re-arranged on the "change-over" principle. Usually St. Margaret's men worked to Hawick where they changed over with Carlisle men. Lodging was not re-introduced for N.B. Section goods working after the War so that changing over continued as the normal method of operating long-distance goods trains. However, two double-trip diagrams were introduced on the Edinburgh-Carlisle section in 1949, Pacifics and V2's being the types usually rostered, but occasionally a K3 would be utilised.

K3's were not normally employed on regular passenger work in the Scottish Area (apart from the Edinburgh-Perth duty mentioned above), but from time to time they appeared on expresses on both the Waverley Route and the Glasgow (via Falkirk) main line. They frequently appeared on Saturdays Only trains (e.g. from Edinburgh to Hawick), and on specials. A Tweedmouth K3 often reached Edinburgh on the 1-8 p.m. stopping train from Berwick, working forward to Corstorphine whence it returned at 6-20 p.m. In 1935 the K3's built by the North British Locomotive Co. were run-in from Eastfield, sometimes being used on a main line goods duty such as the 5-13 p.m. Sighthill-Niddrie before despatch to the Southern Area.

The initial allocation of the Scottish K3's to the Waverley Route will have been noted, and in this connection it should be remembered that this had been a very important N.B.R. main line for through English traffic. On this work the K3's superseded the J37 class, conveying restricted loads on special timings. For many years after Grouping traffic was sent via Carlisle to stations on the former Midland line, including even the London terminus at Somers Town. Perhaps even more surprisingly, traffic for Ancoats (Manchester) continued to be despatched from Glasgow via Edinburgh for transfer to the L.M.S. Western Division at Carlisle (Upperby).

The normal single engine loads (in wagons of goods) for the principal main lines in the Southern Scottish Area, as published in 1928, are set out in the accompanying table.

	K3	J38	J37 & J39	K2
Edinburgh to Berwick	62	60	55	50
Edinburgh to Carlisle	46	44	40	38
Edinburgh to Glasgow (via Falkirk High) ..	79	77	70	67
Edinburgh to High Street (via Bathgate) ..	–	–	40	38
Glasgow to Fort William	–	–	34	31
Edinburgh to Aberdeen	61	59	55	50
Edinburgh to Perth	49	47	43	41

These were "equal to" figures; in practice trains were restricted for operating reasons to 60 wagons.

In general the K3's in Scotland continued on their normal duties after nationalisation, with all twenty engines allocated to St. Margaret's. In 1949 this number was increased to a peak of twenty-four when Nos. 61878/81/97, 61928 were transferred from Gateshead. The only subsequent changes were transfers to Carlisle in 1951 (No. 61916) and Hull in 1957 (Nos. 61857/97). From time to time unusual workings were observed over former L.M.S. lines as on 5th April 1950 when No. 61876 took the 5-55 p.m. Glasgow (Buchanan Street) to Perth passenger train and on 16th April 1953 No. 61911 was on the 4-0 p.m. Aberdeen-Perth. About the same time several other St. Margaret's K3's took turns on Glasgow-Perth (L.M.S.) goods trains, whilst No. 61931 was on the 3-27 p.m. Perth-Waverley. On one occasion both Nos. 61931/83 were seen at Aberdeen having worked goods trains via the East Coast lines.

At nationalisation Carlisle (Canal) had an allocation of seven K3's. During the period that this shed was under Scottish Region control, one engine was acquired from St. Margaret's in 1951 (No. 61916) and one was transferred to Hull in 1957 (No. 61854). In February 1958 the London Midland Region took over permanent responsibility for Canal shed. Subsequent changes were the temporary loan to March in 1959-60 of Nos. 61851, 61937 and the transfer to Woodford in 1959-60 of Nos. 61851/82.

When well maintained the K3's were very fine engines and were highly regarded by the N.B. men. Unfortunately from 1939 onwards their condition deteriorated as a result of discontinuance of regular manning, and the introduction of common-user working between the different operating areas. They never had a nickname of general application in Scotland, but individual engines were often referred to in very uncomplimentary terms, such as "rattlesnake" or "lump of animated iron". This class appeared to suffer from neglect more than most, becoming very noisy and rough. Nevertheless they did a tremendous amount of hard work during the critical years of the 1939-45 War.

Service Stock

Three of the engines which were condemned in September 1962 were retained for a time as stationary boilers. Nos. 61835 and 61912 were at New England and King's Cross respectively, where they replaced K2's on similar duties before them. On the closure of King's Cross to steam, No. 61912 was hauled to Grantham on 15th June 1963 by class A3 No. 60112 *St. Simon.* No. 61943 was at Colwick where it was eventually replaced by class B1 No. 61264 (see Part 2B, p. 150). The boilers in Nos. 61835 and 61943 worked at 100 lb. per sq.in., that in No. 61912 worked at 120 lb. The dates these engines were retained in Service Stock are summarised in the accompanying table.

Engine No.	Stationary Stock from	Stationary Boiler No.	Condemned
61835	9/62	4520	9/63
61912	9/62	4521	3/65
61943	9/62	4522	10/65

Engine Diagrams

Section N, 1/1924.	K3	G.N. engines. Replaced by K3/1 diagram 12/1924.
Section N, 12/1924.	K3/1	G.N. engines with G.N. tender. "Engine 4007 only" added, 12/1936. Replaced by new diagram with altered engine weights, 12/1937.
Section L.N.E., 1936.	K3/1	G.N. engines with 4,200-gallon tender. Replaced by new diagram with altered engine weights, 12/1937.
Section N, 1937.	K3/1	No. 4007 with G.N. tender and engine weights altered to agree with K3/2. Whistle height altered from 13ft. 5in. to 13ft. $3\frac{7}{8}$in.; superheater element diameter corrected from $1\frac{1}{4}$in. to 1.244in., 12/1938. Engine converted to K3/2 and diagram deleted, 12/1939.
Section L.N.E., 1937.	K3/1	G.N. engines with 4,200-gallon tender and engine weights altered to agree with K3/2. Whistle height altered from 13ft. 5in. to 13ft. $3\frac{7}{8}$in.; superheater element diameter corrected from $1\frac{1}{4}$in. to 1.244in., 12/1938. Engines converted to K3/2 in 1939-40 and diagram deleted, 12/1940.
Section N, 12/1924.	K3/2	Engines built at Darlington 1924, with 4,200-gallon tender. Replaced by Section L.N.E. diagram 12/1925.
Section L.N.E., 1925.	K3/2	Engines built at Darlington 1924-25, with 4,200-gallon tender. Boiler tubes diameter corrected from $2\frac{1}{4}$in. to $1\frac{3}{4}$in., 12/1927. Replaced by consolidated K3/2 diagram, 12/1935.
Section L.N.E., 1926.	K3/2	Engines with G.N. tender. Deleted 12/1936 but not replaced until 12/1938.
Section L.N.E., 1929.	K3/3	Engines built at Doncaster 1929, with Westinghouse brakes and vacuum ejector. "or S & VE" added, 12/1932. "W & VE" deleted, 12/1933. Tender weights redistributed, 12/1936. Diagram replaced 12/1937.
Section L.N.E., 1937.	K3/3	Revised diagram with engine weights altered to agree with K3/2. Replaced by combined K3/2 and K3/3 diagram, 12/1938.
Section L.N.E., 1930.	K3/4	Engines built at Darlington 1930. Engines reclassified K3/2 and diagram deleted, 12/1935.
Section L.N.E., 1931.	K3/5	Engines built by Armstrong Whitworth 1931. Engines reclassified K3/2 and diagram deleted 12/1935.
Section L.N.E., 1934.	K3/6	Engines built by R. Stephenson and Armstrong Whitworth 1934-35. Engines reclassified K3/2 and diagram deleted, 12/1935.
Section L.N.E., 1935.	K3/2	Consolidated diagram depicting 4,200-gallon tender, using previous K3/5 engine weights. Distance from pony truck wheels to buffers corrected from 6ft. 3in. to 4ft. 3in.; weight of tender altered from 51 tons to 52 tons, 12/1936. Replaced by combined K3/2 and K3/3 diagram, 12/1938.
Section L.N.E., 1938.	K3	Combined K3/2 and K3/3 diagram depicting 4,200-gallon tender. Note added for alternative Diagram 96A boiler, 12/1946. Class parts discontinued and diagram deleted, 12/1947.
Section L.N.E., 1938.	K3/2	Engines with G.N. tender, revised engine weights. Distance from pony truck wheels to buffers altered from 4ft. 1in. to 4ft. 3in.; length over buffers altered from 57ft. $5\frac{3}{4}$in. to 57ft. $7\frac{3}{4}$in., 12/1939. Note added for alternative Diagram 96A boiler, 12/1946. Class part discontinued and diagram deleted, 12/1947.
1947.	K3	New style diagram depicting G.N. tender; short lap valve details quoted in error.
1947.	K3	New style diagram depicting 4,200-gallon tender.
Not issued, 1945.	K3 Rebuild	New style diagram titled "K3 Rebuild", depicting No. 206 after rebuilding with two cylinders, produced but not officially circulated.
1946.	K5	Previous diagram issued after being retitled K5.

Classification (K3 and K5): Southern Area load class 6; Route availability 8; B.R. power class 6MT.

Summary of K3 and K5 Classes

B.R. No.		1946 No.		1924 No.		Maker	Works No.	Built	Orig. Class Part (a)	Brakes	L.T. Valves fitted	Side Window Cab	Drive	Tender Type Changes (b)	Withdrawn
61800	7/48	1800	5/46	4000	10/25	Doncaster	1509	3/1920	1	V	7/32	6/39	R.H.	GN, GS (10/25)(c)	7/62
61801	2/49	1801	8/46	4001	5/25	"	1513	6/1920	1	V	3/33	2/40	"	GN, GS (5/25)(c)	4/62
61802	5/50	1802	8/46	4002	1/25	"	1514	8/1920	1	V	10/33	5/40	"	GN, GS (2/25)(c)	3/60
61803	5/48	1803	12/46	4003	6/24	"	1515	9/1920	1	V	5/33	12/39	"	GN, GS (1/26)(c)	7/61
61804	10/48	1804	12/46	4006	6/25	"	1516	10/1920	1	V	10/29	4/40	"	GN, GS (6/25)(c)	3/62
61805	2/49	1805	11/46	4004	1/25	"	1517	12/1920	1	V	1/30	11/40	"	GN, GS (5/25)(c)	9/62
61806	2/49	1806	11/46	4005	6/25	"	1520	12/1920	1	V	2/34	11/39	"	GN, GS (2/26)(c)	3/60
61807	5/48	1807	7/46	4007	7/24	"	1522	4/1921	1	V	8/31	8/39	"	GN, GS (1/42)	11/62
61808	5/49	1808	9/46	4008	2/25	"	1526	5/1921	1	V	12/31	3/39	"	GN, GS (9/27)(c)	9/61
61809	3/49	1809	12/46	4009	9/25	"	1529	8/1921	1	V	7/33	10/40	"	GN, GS (2/29)(c)	3/62

B.R. No.		1946 No.		Orig. No.	Maker	Built	Orig. Class Part (a)	Brakes	Steam Reverse Fitted	Steam Reverse Removed	L.T. Valves fitted	Drive	Tender Type Changes (b)	Withdrawn
61810	12/49	1810	9/46	17	Darlington	8/1924	2	V	—	—	3/34	R.H., L.H.(9/35)	GN, GS (3/29)(c)	8/62
61811	11/49	1811	11/46	28	"	8/1924	2	V	12/27	1/35	1/35	R.H., L.H.(1/35)	GN, GS (8/29)(c)	11/62
61812	2/49	1812	11/46	32	"	8/1924	2	V	—	—	1/32	R.H.	GS, GN (3/27)(c)	9/62
61813	10/48	1813	10/46	33	"	9/1924	2	V	—	—	12/34	R.H.	GS	4/62
61814	10/48	1814	10/46	36	"	9/1924	2	V	12/27	12/34	8/35	R.H., L.H.(12/34)	GS	12/61
61815	11/48	1815	8/46	38	"	10/1924	2	V	12/27	8/35	10/34	R.H., L.H.(8/35)	GS	7/60
61816	11/48	1816	5/46	39	"	10/1924	2	V	3/28	10/34	11/34	R.H., L.H.(10/34)	GS	5/62
61817	11/49	1817	4/46	46	"	10/1924	2	V	—	—	4/36	R.H., L.H.(4/36)	GS	9/62
61818	11/49	1818	5/46	52	"	10/1924	2	V	11/27	4/36	1/34	R.H., L.H.(11/34)	GS	3/62
61819	10/48	1819	11/46	53	"	10/1924	2	V	4/28	11/34	9/34	R.H., L.H.(5/37)	GS	12/62
61820	8/48	1820	12/46	58	"	10/1924	2	V	—	9/34	1/31	R.H.	GS	11/62
61821	4/48	1821	5/46	69	"	11/1924	2	V	—	—	2/32	R.H.	GS	9/62
61822	4/50	1822	12/46	73	"	11/1924	2	V	—	—	3/32	R.H.	GS	11/62
61823	10/49	1823	9/46	75	"	11/1924	2	V	—	—	1/34	R.H.	GS	12/59
61824	7/48	1824	9/46	80	"	11/1924	2	V	—	—	1/32	R.H.	GS, GN (3/28), GS (5/42)	7/61
61825	4/48	1825	9/46	91	"	11/1924	2	V	—	—	2/31	R.H.	GS	9/62
61826	8/48	1826	10/46	92	"	11/1924	2	V	—	—	12/32	R.H.	GS	9/62
61827	5/48	1827	6/46	109	"	11/1924	2	V	—	—	1/30	R.H.	GS	9/62
61828	8/48	1828	3/46	111	"	12/1924	2	V	—	—	11/31	R.H.	GS	3/61
61829	3/49	1829	4/46	112	"	12/1924	2	V	—	—	2/33	R.H.	GS	2/62
61830	6/48	1830	4/46	113	"	12/1924	2	V	—	—	12/33	R.H.	GS	11/62
61831	10/48	1831	5/46	114	"	12/1924	2	V	—	—	1/31	R.H.	GS, GN (12/33), GS (5/42)	9/62
61832	12/49	1832	5/46	116	"	12/1924	2	V	—	—	1/33	R.H.	GS	10/62
61833	4/49	1833	5/46	118	"	12/1924	2	V	—	—	11/33	R.H.	GS	9/61
61834	4/48	1834	6/46	120	"	12/1924	2	V	—	—	12/30	R.H.	GS	5/62
61835	1/50	1835	6/46	121	"	1/1925	2	V	—	—	4/33	R.H.	GS	9/62
61836	9/48	1836	5/46	125	"	1/1925	2	V	—	—	4/31	R.H.	GS	2/60
61837	8/49	1837	6/46	126	"	1/1925	2	V	—	—	7/32	R.H.	GN (8/33), GS (12/33)	4/62
61838	9/49	1838	6/46	127	"	1/1925	2	V	—	—	7/33	R.H.	GS	3/60
61839	1/50	1839	1/47	134	"	1/1925	2	V	—	—	10/28	R.H.	GS, GN (3/28), GS (12/33)	1/62
61840	3/49	1840	10/46	135	"	2/1925	2	V	—	—	1/31	R.H.	GS	9/62
61841	9/49	1841	3/46	140	"	2/1925	2	V	New	—	6/31	R.H.	GS, GN (3/28), GS (8/33)	3/62
61842	11/48	1842	8/46	141	"	2/1925	2	V	New	2/31	5/34	R.H.	GS	8/61

Table 1

B.R. No.	(renum.)	1946 No.	(renum.)	Orig. No.	Maker	Built	Orig. Class Part (a)	Steam Reverse Fitted	Steam Reverse Removed	Drive	Tender Type (b)	Rebt. to K5	Withdrawn
61843	5/50	1843	12/46	143	Darlington	2/1925	2	New	3/30	R.H.	GS	—	10/62
61844	12/48	1844	8/46	146	„	2/1925	2	New	7/32	R.H.	GS	—	6/61
61845	12/48	1845	12/46	153	„	2/1925	2	New	11/32	R.H.	GS	—	9/62
61846	3/48	1846	12/46	156	„	2/1925	2	New	6/32	R.H.	GS	—	12/62
61847	12/48	1847	12/46	158	„	2/1925	2	New	8/31	R.H.	GS	—	12/62
61848	3/48	1848	5/46	159	„	3/1925	2	New	3/32	R.H.	GS	—	9/62
61849	8/48	1849	7/46	163	„	3/1925	2	New	5/34	R.H.	GS	—	4/61
61850	10/48	1850	10/46	167	„	3/1925	2	New	2/33	R.H.	GS	—	6/61
61851	9/48	1851	8/46	170	„	3/1925	2	New	12/33	R.H.	GS	—	11/61
61852	3/49	1852	12/46	178	„	3/1925	2	New	7/31	R.H.	GS	—	7/61
61853	12/49	1853	7/46	180	„	3/1925	2	New	6/31	R.H.	GS	—	12/62
61854	11/48	1854	10/46	184	„	3/1925	2	New	1/32	R.H.	GN	—	10/62
61855	5/49	1855	5/46	186	„	3/1925	2	New	7/33	R.H.	GN	—	7/59
61856	2/50	1856	12/46	188	„	3/1925	2	New	7/32	R.H.	GN	—	12/62
61857	9/48	1857	10/46	191	„	4/1925	2	New	2/33	R.H.	GN	—	12/62
61858	9/48	1858	8/46	195	„	4/1925	2	New	11/32	R.H.	GS, GN (6/25)	—	4/61
61859	11/48	1859	3/46	200	„	4/1925	2	New	—	R.H.	GS, GN (3/29), GS (9/62)	—	11/62

Table 2

B.R. No.	(renum.)	1946 No.	(renum.)	Orig. No.	Maker	Built	Orig. Class Part (a)	Brakes	Steam Reverse Fitted	Steam Reverse Removed	L.T. Valves Fitted	Drive	Tender Type (b)	Rebt. to K5	Withdrawn
61860	9/49	1860	3/46	203	Darlington	8/1925	2	S + VE	New	8/31	12/29	L.H.	GS	—	11/61
61861	5/49	1861	3/46	202	„	8/1925	2	S + VE	„	9/30	11/32	„	GS	—	12/62
61862	1/49	1862	4/46	204	„	9/1925	2	S + VE	„	2/31	6/32	„	GS	—	1/62
61863	1/50	1863	3/46	206	„	9/1925	2	S + VE	„	11/30	5/33	„	GS	6/45	6/60
61864	5/49	1864	3/46	207	„	9/1925	2	S + VE	„	5/31	4/32	„	GS	—	9/62
61865	12/48	1865	5/46	208	„	9/1925	2	S + VE	„	4/31	4/32	„	GS	—	6/61
61866	4/48	1866	4/46	227	„	10/1925	2	S + VE	„	5/31	5/31	„	GS	—	10/61
61867	11/48	1867	3/46	228	„	10/1925	2	S + VE	„	5/31	5/31	„	GS	—	11/62
61868	12/48	1868	6/46	229	„	10/1925	2	S + VE	„	11/30	2/32	„	GS	—	8/59
61869	10/48	1869	3/46	231	„	12/1925	2	S + VE	„	11/31	11/31	„	GS	—	12/62

Table 3

B.R. No.	(renum.)	1946 No.	(renum.)	Orig. No.	Maker	Works No.	Built	Orig. Class Part (a)	Drive	Brakes	Withdrawn
61870	6/49	1870	3/46	1300	Doncaster	1711	4/1929	3	W + VE	S + VE (3/32)	7/62
61871	7/48	1871	1/46	1312	„	1712	5/1929	3	W + VE	S + VE (3/32)	12/62
61872	7/48	1872	4/46	1318	„	1713	6/1929	3	W + VE	S + VE (4/33)	12/62
61873	1/49	1873	3/46	1331	„	1714	6/1929	3	W + VE	S + VE (10/31)	5/62
61874	12/48	1874	8/46	1345	„	1715	7/1929	3	W + VE	S + VE (2/32)	5/61
61875	4/48	1875	5/46	1364	„	1716	7/1929	3	W + VE	S + VE (11/31)	12/62
61876	11/48	1876	6/46	1365	„	1717	7/1929	3	W + VE	S + VE (7/33)	9/59
61877	7/49	1877	5/46	1367	„	1718	8/1929	3	W + VE	S + VE (4/33)	7/62
61878	10/48	1878	5/46	1368	„	1719	8/1929	3	W + VE	S + VE (2/32)	8/59
61879	8/50	1879	3/46	1386	„	1720	9/1929	3	W + VE	S + VE (1/32)	6/59
61880	6/49	1880	11/46	1387	Doncaster	1721	10/1929	3	W + VE	S + VE (3/32)	9/62
61881	11/48	1881	11/46	1388	„	1722	10/1929	3	W + VE	S + VE (4/32)	4/60
61882	9/48	1882	9/46	1389	„	1723	10/1929	3	W + VE	S + VE (2/32)	5/60
61883	1/49	1883	11/46	1391	„	1724	10/1929	3	W + VE	S + VE (11/31)	12/62
61884	12/48	1884	8/46	1392	„	1725	11/1929	3	W + VE	S + VE (11/31)	7/62
61885	7/48	1885	2/46	1394	„	1726	11/1929	3	W + VE	S + VE (2/32)	11/59
61886	9/49	1886	9/46	1395	„	1727	11/1929	3	W + VE	S + VE (4/32)	9/62
61887	11/48	1887	9/46	1396	„	1728	11/1929	3	W + VE	S + VE (4/32)	3/62
61888	6/49	1888	10/46	1397	„	1729	12/1929	3	W + VE	S + VE (3/32)	9/61
61889	10/48	1889	7/46	1398	„	1730	12/1929	3	W + VE	S + VE (5/32)	11/62

Summary of K3 and K5 Classes (continued)

B.R. No.		1946 No.		Orig. No.	Maker	Works No.	Built	Orig. Class Part (a)	Brakes	Withdrawn
61890	12/48	1890	9/46	2761	Darlington	—	7/1930	4	S+VE	9/62
61891	10/49	1891	11/46	2762	"	—	7/1930	4	S+VE	9/61
61892	5/48	1892	10/46	2763	"	—	7/1930	4	S+VE	10/62
61893	12/48	1893	10/46	2764	"	—	7/1930	4	S+VE	12/62
61894	8/49	1894	8/46	2765	"	—	7/1930	4	S+VE	10/61
61895	1/49	1895	9/46	2766	"	—	7/1930	4	S+VE	7/62
61896	4/49	1896	11/46	2767	"	—	8/1930	4	S+VE	5/62
61897	9/48	1897	9/46	2768	"	—	8/1930	4	S+VE	12/62
61898	9/48	1898	10/46	2769	"	—	8/1930	4	S+VE	2/59
61899	4/48	1899	1/46	1100	Armstrong Whitworth	1111	3/1931	5	S+VE	12/62
61900	11/49	1900	2/46	1101	"	1112	3/1931	5	S+VE	3/60
61901	2/50	1901	1/46	1102	"	1113	3/1931	5	S+VE	12/61
61902	11/48	1902	2/46	1106	"	1114	3/1931	5	S+VE	7/61
61903	7/48	1903	1/46	1108	"	1115	4/1931	5	S+VE	11/61
61904	5/48	1904	1/46	1117	"	1116	3/1931	5	S+VE	6/61
61905	4/48	1905	1/46	1118	"	1117	3/1931	5	S+VE	11/62
61906	9/48	1906	1/46	1119	"	1118	4/1931	5	S+VE	12/62
61907	12/48	1907	7/46	1121	"	1119	4/1931	5	S+VE	9/62
61908	1/50	1908	1/46	1125	"	1120	4/1931	5	S+VE	1/62
61909	8/48	1909	1/46	1133	"	1121	4/1931	5	S+VE	4/60
61910	12/49	1910	1/46	1135	"	1122	4/1931	5	S+VE	7/62
61911	3/48	1911	3/46	1137	"	1123	5/1931	5	S+VE	11/59
61912	3/48	1912	2/46	1141	"	1124	5/1931	5	S+VE	9/62
61913	11/48	1913	1/46	1154	"	1125	5/1931	5	S+VE	2/62
61914	2/49	1914	1/46	1156	"	1126	5/1931	5	S+VE	8/62
61915	11/49	1915	2/46	1158	"	1127	5/1931	5	S+VE	9/62
61916	7/48	1916	1/46	1162	"	1128	5/1931	5	S+VE	12/60
61917	1/49	1917	1/46	1164	"	1129	5/1931	5	S+VE	11/62
61918	7/49	1918	2/46	1166	"	1130	6/1931	5	S+VE	3/62
61919	3/49	1919	3/46	1302	"	1156	7/1934	6	V	6/61
61920	10/49	1920	3/46	1304	"	1157	7/1934	6	V	9/61
61921	5/48	1921	4/46	1308	"	1158	8/1934	6	V	7/61
61922	5/48	1922	3/46	1310	"	1159	8/1934	6	V	5/62
61923	3/48	1923	3/46	1324	"	1160	9/1934	6	V	4/62
61924	4/49	1924	3/46	1306	"	1161	9/1934	6	V	12/60
61925	5/50	1925	4/46	2934	"	1162	9/1934	6	V	7/61
61926	7/49	1926	1/47	2935	"	1163	9/1934	6	V	4/62
61927	1/49	1927	11/46	2936	"	1164	1/1935(d)	6	V	7/61
61928	5/48	1928	10/46	2937	"	1165	1/1935(d)	6	V	2/60
61929	10/49	1929	3/46	1325	R. Stephenson & Co.	4075	8/1934	6	V	7/62
61930	12/49	1930	4/46	1332	"	4076	9/1934	6	V	12/62
61931	8/50	1931	4/46	1333	"	4077	9/1934	6	V	7/59
61932	11/48	1932	3/46	1339	"	4078	9/1934	6	V	2/62
61933	3/49	1933	11/46	1399	"	4079	9/1934	6	V	9/60
61934	8/49	1934	5/46	1307	"	4081	1/1935(d)	6	V	11/62
61935	4/48	1935	5/46	1322	"	4080	1/1935(d)	6	V	7/62
61936	8/48	1936	7/46	2938	"	4082	1/1935(d)	6	V	11/61
61937	10/48	1937	10/46	2939	"	4083	1/1935(d)	6	V	3/60
61938	4/48	1938	5/46	2940	"	4084	1/1935(d)	6	V	12/61

No.	Date	No.	Date	Builder No.	Builder	Works No.	Built			Withd.
61939	6/49	1939	10/46	2425	N.B. Loco. Co.	24225	8/1935	6	>	11/62
61940	11/48	1940	8/46	2426	,,	24226	8/1935	6	>	5/62
61941	8/48	1941	11/46	2427	,,	24227	8/1935	6	>	7/61
61942	8/49	1942	10/46	2428	,,	24228	8/1935	6	>	9/62
61943	1/50	1943	9/46	2438	,,	24229	9/1935	6	>	9/62
61944	3/48	1944	1/46	2439	,,	24230	9/1935	6	>	2/62
61945	1/49	1945	12/46	2440	,,	24231	9/1935	6	>	6/62
61946	9/48	1946	3/46	2442	,,	24232	9/1935	6	>	8/62
61947	4/48	1947	6/46	2443	,,	24233	9/1935	6	>	3/62
61948	5/48	1948	12/46	2447	,,	24234	9/1935	6	>	4/62
61949	2/49	1949	3/46	2448	,,	24235	9/1935	6	>	11/62
61950	2/49	1950	3/46	2449	,,	24236	9/1935	6	>	11/62
61951	6/49	1951	3/46	2450	,,	24237	9/1935	6	>	12/62
61952	2/50	1952	9/46	2451	,,	24238	10/1935	6	>	3/62
61953	10/49	1953	9/46	2459	,,	24239	10/1935	6	>	9/62
61954	9/49	1954	9/46	2461	,,	24240	10/1935	6	>	5/60
61955	12/48	1955	4/46	2463	,,	24241	10/1935	6	>	9/62
61956	12/49	1956	2/46	2466	,,	24242	10/1935	6	>	9/62
61957	3/49	1957	10/46	2467	,,	24243	11/1935	6	>	9/62
61958	8/48	1958	9/46	2468	,,	24244	11/1935	6	>	5/62
61959	1/49	1959	8/46	2417	Armstrong Whitworth	1270	5/1936	2	>	11/61
61960	12/48	1960	9/46	2429	,,	1271	5/1936	2	>	9/62
61961	4/49	1961	9/46	2445	,,	1272	5/1936	2	>	10/61
61962	10/49	1962	8/46	2446	,,	1273	5/1936	2	>	12/62
61963	8/49	1963	9/46	2453	,,	1274	6/1936	2	>	9/62
61964	12/49	1964	1/46	2455	,,	1275	6/1936	2	>	7/61
61965	4/48	1965	12/46	2458	,,	1276	6/1936	2	>	12/62
61966	11/50	1966	3/46	2465	,,	1277	6/1936	2	>	2/62
61967	6/48	1967		2471	,,	1278	7/1936	2	>	4/61
61968	9/48	1968		2472	,,	1279	8/1936	2	>	10/61
61969	4/48	1969	9/46	2470	Darlington	—	10/1936	2	>	12/62
61970	2/49	1970	11/46	2473	,,	—	10/1936	2	>	11/62
61971	3/48	1971	9/46	2498	,,	—	10/1936	2	>	3/61
61972	12/48	1972	11/46	2499	,,	—	10/1936	2	>	9/62
61973	9/48	1973	11/46	3813	,,	—	11/1936	2	>	11/62
61974	8/49	1974	7/46	3814	,,	—	11/1936	2	>	7/62
61975	4/49	1975	9/46	3815	,,	—	11/1936	2	>	9/61
61976	5/48	1976	9/46	3816	,,	—	11/1936	2	>	1/62
61977	11/48	1977	7/46	3817	,,	—	11/1936	2	>	9/62
61978	9/48	1978	9/46	3818	,,	—	11/1936	2	>	8/61
61979	1/49	1979	7/46	3819	,,	—	12/1936	2	>	10/61
61980	3/49	1980	11/46	3820	,,	—	12/1936	2	>	12/62
61981	11/49	1981	11/46	3821	,,	—	12/1936	2	>	11/62
61982	6/48	1982	8/46	3822	,,	—	12/1936	2	>	9/62
61983	11/49	1983	11/46	3823	,,	—	12/1936	2	>	7/59
61984	6/48	1984	8/46	3824	,,	—	12/1936	2	>	11/62
61985	8/48	1985	4/46	3825	,,	—	1/1937	2	>	12/62
61986	4/48	1986	12/46	3826	,,	—	1/1937	2	>	5/62
61987	1/49	1987	11/46	3827	,,	—	1/1937	2	>	3/62
61988	12/48	1988	11/46	3828	,,	—	1/1937	2	>	11/59
61989	11/48	1989	11/46	3829	,,	—	2/1937	2	>	6/62
61990	5/49	1990	10/46	3830	,,	—	2/1937	2	>	10/60
61991	6/48	1991	10/46	3831	,,	—	2/1937	2	>	5/59
61992	4/48	1992	9/46	3832	,,	—	2/1937	2	>	6/60

(a) The Part 1 engines were included with Part 2 when side window cabs were fitted. From December 1935, Parts 4, 5 and 6 were included with Part 2. Class Parts 2 and 3 discontinued from December 1947.

(b) Tender types:-
GN = Original G.N.R. type with coal rails.
GS = Group Standard.

(c) These dates are not officially confirmed.

(d) Nos. 1307/22, 2936-40 were delivered in 1934 although not sent to traffic until January 1935.

CLASS K4

GRESLEY 5ft. 2in. ENGINES

ENGINES BUILT AFTER GROUPING (1937-39): 3441-6. TOTAL 6.

The West Highland line of the former N.B.R. presented difficult operating problems with its long steep gradients, severe curves and axle load restrictions. Passenger work at Grouping was in the hands of class D34 Glen 4-4-0's, the maximum load between Glasgow and Fort William being 190 tons unaided, but even before Grouping the advent of heavier stock had resulted in some double-heading, usually with two Glens. Under the L.N.E.R. there was an early proposal to use K3's on this line to obviate the need for assisting, though weight restrictions would have barred them from the Mallaig extension. Bridge tests involving K3's were made on the West Highland and as a result the Civil Engineer vetoed the idea entirely.

A proposal appeared in October 1924 for a 2-6-0 with 5ft. 2in. diameter coupled wheels, K3 boiler and three 18in. by 26in. cylinders (see Appendix, drawing 4). The tractive effort would have been 31,182 lb., compared with 22,100 lb. of class D34, and the maximum axle load 19 tons 18 cwt., compared with 20 tons 13 cwt. of class K3. The proposal was not pursued as about this time the G.N. Section loaned fourteen K2's to the N.B. Section, which were found suitable for use on the West Highland line.

Engine Nos.	Maker	Date ordered	No. built	Date
3441	Darlington	10/1936	1	1937
3442-6	,,	2/1938	5	1938*

* Nos. 3445/6 were not sent to traffic until January 1939, although officially put into stock in December 1938.

The K2's were a satisfactory compromise: the engines had more power and greater adhesion than the D34's, and lighter axle loadings than the K3's. In addition, the K2's were being displaced on the G.N. by new K3's and alternative work was being sought for them. The K2's could handle 220-ton passenger trains unaided on the West Highland line, which was an improvement on the D34's, though some double-heading was still necessary. In October 1925 the K2's were permanently transferred to the N.B. Section and for the time being nothing more was heard of the three-cylinder design for the West Highland.

The late B. Spencer, in his paper "The Development of L.N.E.R. Locomotive Design 1923-1941", referred to a proposal for a 2-8-0 passenger engine with 5ft. 2in. diameter coupled wheels for the West Highland. This would have provided the necessary adhesion to increase the tractive effort whilst keeping the individual axle loadings within reasonable limits. The proposal was probably considered in 1934 in the King's Cross drawing office only and no development work was carried out at Doncaster.

Then in September 1934 Gresley asked Doncaster to look into the possibility of increasing the tractive effort of the K2's, either by altering the boiler pressure, the cylinder diameter, or both. It was calculated that by increasing the boiler pressure to 220 lb. per sq.in. and the cylinder diameter to 21in., the tractive effort could be increased to 31,531 lb. This would have reduced the factor of adhesion to 3.7 which Doncaster did not recommend.

At the meeting of the Joint Traffic & Locomotive Committee on 21st February 1935 provision was made in new construction for one new 2-6-0 engine for the West Highland line, though design work had not yet begun. The drawing office at Doncaster made a start on the new design about May 1936 and then proceeded with great haste. The outline drawing appeared in July and showed a return to the 1924 proposal for a 2-6-0 with 5ft. 2in. diameter coupled wheels, but with K3 cylinders, K2 boiler and B17 firebox. The boiler pressure was to remain at 180 lb. per sq.in., providing a tractive effort of 32,939 lb. with an estimated factor of adhesion of 3.92. The construction order was signed on 10th September for one new K4 to be built at Darlington. As authority had not been given to construct an additional engine on the 1936 building programme, the current Darlington order for twenty-one K3's was reduced to twenty.

No. 3441 *Loch Long* entered traffic on 28th January 1937 and differed little from the July 1936 outline drawing. The weight of the engine in working order, the adhesive weight and the maximum axle load were all slightly greater, and the factor of adhesion was 3.94. The engine quickly showed itself capable of handling unaided loads of up to 300 tons between Glasgow and Fort William. However, the working pressure had to be raised to 200 lb. per sq.in. in June 1937 to facilitate faster uphill working, though this reduced the factor of adhesion to 3.54. Its new tractive effort was 36,599 lb.

On 16th February 1938 the Chief General Manager authorised a further five K4's on the 1937 building programme, and the next day Gresley issued the Darlington Works order. No. 3442 was sent into traffic in July 1938 and Nos. 3443-6 in December 1938 and January 1939. These engines all bore names of Scottish clan chiefs. The construction of the class is summarised in the table on page 144.

There were certain differences between the first engine and the remaining five, which will be referred to later. No more K4's were built, which was not surprising on account of the specialised nature of their work. Only on the West Highland line could one expect to make use of a powerful passenger engine with such small diameter coupled wheels. Even so they were not suited to the level stretches of track at the Glasgow end.

In 1945 Thompson rebuilt No. 3445 as a two-cylinder engine to become the prototype of his new class K1 and its subsequent history is described under that class heading. The remaining engines were not rebuilt and they continued to work on the West Highland line in their original form.

In 1959 all the K4's were transferred to Thornton shed when the end for them was clearly in sight. Four were taken out of traffic in October 1961 and the fifth engine, No. 61994 *The Great Marquess,* was withdrawn in the following December. Fortunately, this last engine was purchased by Viscount Garnock, restored and repainted in L.N.E.R. green livery.

L.N.E.R. Renumbering

The engines were allocated numbers 1993-8 under the 1943 renumbering scheme and these were applied in 1946 though in the meantime one of the engines, No. 3445, had been rebuilt to class K1.

Standard L.N.E.R. Dimensions

Cylinders (3)	.. ..	$18\frac{1}{2}'' \times 26''$
Motion	.. ..	Walschaerts/
		Gresley with 8"
		piston valves
Boiler:		
Max. diam. outside	..	5' 6"
Barrel length	..	11' 9" (a)
Firebox length outside	..	10' 0½"
Pitch	.. ..	8' 6½"
Diagram No.	..	110
Heating surface:		
Firebox ..	..	168.0 sq.ft.
Tubes (164 × 1¼")	..	871.1 sq.ft.
Flues (24 × 5¼")	..	382.5 sq.ft.
Total evaporative	..	1421.6 sq.ft.
Superheater (24 × 1.244")	..	310.0 sq.ft.
Total	..	1731.6 sq.ft.
Grate area	..	27.5 sq.ft.
Boiler pressure	..	.. 200 lb./sq.in.(b)
Leading wheels	..	3' 2"
Coupled wheels	..	5' 2"
Tender wheels	..	3' 9"
Tractive effort (85%)	..	36,598.7 lb.(c)
Length over buffers	..	58' 1¼"
Wheelbase:		
Engine ..	..	.. 8' 11" + 7' 6" +
		8' 9" = 25' 2"
Tender ..	..	.. 7' 0" + 6' 0" =
		13' 0"
Total ..	..	48' 7"
Weight (full):		
Engine ..	..	68T 8C
Tender ..	..	44T 4C
Total ..	..	112T 12C
Adhesive	..	57T 18C
Max. axle load	..	19T 17C
Water capacity	..	3,500 gallons
Coal capacity	..	5T 10C

(a) The engine diagram quoted the distance between tubeplates (11' 7⅛"). See under Details.
(b) 180 lb./sq.in. until June 1937.
(c) 32,939 lb. until June 1937.

Details

FRAMES AND RUNNING GEAR

The main frames were 5in. longer at the rear end than in the K3 class. The coupled wheel journal surfaces were 9½in. diameter and 11in. long. The pony truck was similar to that used in the K3's except that its radius swing was 6ft. 7in. instead of 5ft. 11½in. Guard irons were originally fitted to both the main frames and the pony truck frames. In common with a number of other classes, the guard irons were removed from the front end of the main frames during the fifties, as those on the pony truck were better placed and gave adequate protection (cf. figs. 139 and 141).

The outside cylinders were inclined at 1 in 30, whilst the inside cylinder was inclined at 1 in 7.96 to enable the inside connecting rod to clear the leading coupled axle. All three cylinders drove on to the second coupled axle. The steam chests were in the same horizontal plane, with that for the inside cylinder close to the left-hand frame. No. 3441's cylinders were based closely on the latest K3 pattern and perpetuated the elbow joint in the steam pipes with the steam having to negotiate a double right-angle bend after leaving the side of the smokebox before passing through the running plate to the outside cylinders. The joint was hidden from view under the steam pipe casing. The cylinders fitted to Nos. 3442-5 had their steam passages altered so that the elbow joint was eliminated; the steam pipe flange on the outside cylinder was 5in. closer to the frame, so that the steam pipe casing was inclined more vertically (cf. figs. 137 and 138).

Details are not recorded of cylinder changes but it would appear that in May 1942 No. 3443 acquired the left-hand outside cylinder from No. 3441. Its own steam pipe casing would not fit over the steam pipes and one had to be fabricated in a hurry. Its shape resembled that of the earlier V1 steam pipe casing, but it was not identical. For the remainder of its life this engine carried the odd casing on the left side and a normal one on the right (cf. figs. 140 and 142).

The usual Hoffmann combined ball and roller bearings were provided in the fulcrums of the motion levers in front of the cylinders, Skefko ball bearings in the connecting rod cranks and Ransome & Marles roller bearings in the radius link trunnion, radius link foot and all three joints in the combination lever. No. 3444 received brass bushes in place of roller bearings in its valve motion in November 1941 as a wartime expedient. Unlike the K3's which had vertical screw reversing gear, the K4 gear was inclined at a slight angle from the horizontal, with the reversing rod visible alongside the firebox (fig. 137).

The engines had two Wakefield No. 7 mechanical lubricators on the right-hand running plate (fig. 138). That at the front was for cylinder and valve lubrication, whilst the other was for the axlebox journals. Auxiliary oilboxes were provided for the axlebox horn guides. The horns had tapered steel wedges to compensate for wear.

The sanding arrangement was the same as in the latest K3's. The sanders in front of the leading coupled wheels were gravity fed, whilst those in front of the driving coupled wheels were steam-operated. There were no sanders for reverse running. The front sandbox lids were set at an angle to reduce spillage between the frames.

BOILERS

No. 3441's original boiler was constructed of $\frac{5}{8}$in. plate in one tapered barrel ring, having an outside diameter of 5ft. 6in. at the firebox end and 5ft. $4\frac{1}{4}$in. at the front. The smokebox tubeplate was $\frac{3}{4}$in. thick, recessed into the barrel, and the radius of its flange was $\frac{1}{2}$in. The distance between the tubeplates was 11ft. $7\frac{1}{8}$in. No. 3442's original boiler had a barrel which was made of two telescopic parallel rings, the other dimensions being the same with no external difference. The boilers on Nos. 3443-6 were similar to that on No. 3441.

The outer firebox was lightly constructed, with its wrapper plate only $\frac{1}{2}$in. thick. (Extra stiffening plates had to be riveted to the firebox sides after June 1939). The back plate was $\frac{9}{16}$in. thick and the throat plate $\frac{5}{8}$in. The inner copper firebox was constructed of $\frac{9}{16}$in. plate, except for the tubeplate which was 1in. The water space above the foundation ring was $3\frac{1}{4}$in. wide at the front and 3in. at the sides. Similar fireboxes were fitted to the B17's.

The inner firebox was supported by twenty rows of roof stays plus two rows of expansion and sling stays supporting the front end. There were also many transverse stays which supported the outer firebox sides. There were seven hand holes in the firebox sides above the handrails; three on the left and four on the right. The fireboxes had a drop grate section at the front, with the rodding alongside the frames on the right-hand side connected to a screw mechanism in the cab. The ashpan had a front door only.

A 10mm. live steam injector was provided on the driver's (left-hand) side under the footplate and a 9mm. exhaust steam injector on the fireman's side, also under the footplate. The engines had vertical slide regulator valves in the dome, with two pull-out handles in the cab.

A 24-element Robinson superheater was fitted, of the type fitted to the class O2 2-8-0's; cast-iron in the case of No. 3441, cast steel in the later engines. The elements were the standard long-loop type, $1\frac{1}{4}$in. outside diameter and 10 S.W.G. thick (inside diameter 1.244in.). The thickness was changed to 9 S.W.G. (inside diameter 1.212in.) from, officially, November 1944,

though this final change was not recognised on the engine diagram.

A new type of superheater was introduced in September 1940 for renewals in both K4's and O2's, though to what extent they appeared on the former engines is not known. This was the "V" bolt type, requiring elements with ball-jointed (Melesco type) ends, instead of plain ends which were expanded into the header. Whilst the new headers in the O2's were made of cast-iron, the K4 headers were cast steel presumably because of the higher working pressure. There is no reference to any subsequent change to the "Through" bolt type of header which afterwards became standard in, for example, class B1 boilers.

The chimney, which was 1ft. 4in. high, was the same pattern which Gresley had introduced in August 1923 for class O2. The type of chimney was later fitted to class C1 No. 3279 and classes O1 (latterly O3) and O4/5. Thompson also fitted it to classes B1, K1, K1/1 and L1. The blastpipe top had a 5in. diameter orifice. In December 1938 it was agreed that the K4's should be fitted with jumper-top blastpipes but it appears that the work was never carried out.

Spark arresters were fitted to the five remaining K4's in 1947 – Nos. 1994/5/6/8 in April and 1993 in May.

GENERAL

The cab platform extended back and almost filled the gap in the entrance doorway, with the fall plate hinged on the tender front plate. In April-May 1941 the tender fall plates were removed from all six engines and replaced by a 10in.-deep wood platform which projected forward and almost filled the gap in the cab entrance. The cab footboards were shortened and a fall plate was attached to them.

The engines had Flaman speed recorders operated from the coupling rod pin on the trailing axle. The equipment was fitted to Nos. 3441 in August 1937 (on the left-hand side at first, until it was replaced by a new one on the right-hand side in January 1939), 3442 in December 1938 and 3443-6 when new. Their use on engines which worked on the West Highland line may seem surprising but there were numerous and severe speed restrictions throughout its length. The recorders were removed during the War but the support brackets were left in place to the end on the right-hand side (cf. figs. 137 and 147).

The boiler handrails curved round the front of the smokebox. The smokebox door was 4ft. 9in.

diameter with a curvature of 10ft. 2½in. radius and the centres of the hinge straps were 1ft. 3in. apart. Stops were fitted to the hinges to prevent the door from being opened too far (fig. 138). Subsequently, all doors had the alternative form of stop, half way between the two hinges (fig. 140). The handrail on the door was fitted below the top hinge strap at first, but appeared above it latterly (cf. figs. 138 and 140). B.R. cast numberplates were fitted after 1948, usually just above or just below the door handrail, the position varying on different engines as smokebox doors were changed about (cf. figs. 140 and 141). An oddity respecting the doors was the absence of the knob at different times in the case of Nos. 61993/4/6/8 (fig. 147), though this was not an omission restricted to the K4's only.

After being in service a while, the engines were adapted at the front to take miniature snow ploughs (fig. 143). A bracket was fitted to the running plate above the draw-hook and holes were provided along the bottom of the bufferbeam, so that it was then a simple matter to fit the snowplough when the need arose. Dates of fitting of the brackets are as follows:—

Engine No.	Bracket fitted
3441	12/37
3442	11/38
3443	2/40
3444	1/40
3445	2/40
3446	6/39

In September 1945 No. 3441 was fitted to take the wooden bench (known at Cowlairs as the "Engineer's Chair") that was attached to the front bufferbeam. (For illustration, see Part 4 of this series, fig. 38).

Brakes

The K4's had vacuum brakes for engine, tender and train, with two 21in. diameter brake cylinders under the cab. The vacuum ejector exhaust pipe ran horizontally alongside the boiler and entered the smokebox on the driver's side of the engine. Inside the smokebox the pipe curved down and then up again to join the chimney liner. A ⅛ in.-bore copper pipe was fitted to the bend to drain away water which collected. This drain pipe dropped down between the frames behind the middle cylinder to discharge itself under the engine. In the fifties the drain was taken instead from the exhaust pipe just before it entered the smokebox. The drain pipe skirted

round the nameplate, or simply passed over it, passed through a hole in the running plate ahead of the outside cylinder and disappeared from view (fig. 140).

Tenders

The engines were provided with 3,500-gallon capacity tenders, which were adequate for their needs. No. 3441's tender was the low-front type whilst the remaining five engines had the newer high-front type (cf. figs. 137 and 141, see under class J39 for description).

The tenders changed around within the class and the only significant alteration came in 1959. Nos. 61993-6 then acquired 4,200-gallon tenders with straight sides from K3's which were by then being withdrawn (fig. 142 and see Summary). The low-front tender from No. 61993 was then attached to class J39 No. 64926 whilst one of the high-front tenders (that which had been attached to No. 3445 when it was new) was attached to class J38 No. 65911. When No. 61994 was restored to working order as L.N.E.R. No. 3442 after its withdrawal in December 1961, it was given a low-front 3,500-gallon tender (fig. 148).

Maintenance

The K4's were shopped at Cowlairs and the only recorded exception was No. 61998 which had a non-classified repair at Inverurie in March 1960. The minimum mileage expected between heavy repairs was 50,000. Life mileage figures for the five surviving K4's were as follows:—

No.	Mileage
61993	628,153
61994	605,088
61995	575,478
61996	607,323
61998	632,527

Liveries

The first engine was painted lined black before it was sent into traffic (fig. 137), after the usual official photographs had been taken showing it in shop-grey livery. Nos. 3442-6 however were painted in green fully-lined passenger livery (fig. 138), and No. 3441 was brought into line in April 1940.

Wartime conditions caused a change to unlined black with "N E" on the tender (fig. 144). No. 1996 was restored to green livery in July 1947 (fig. 145) followed by No. 1995 in the following November. At nationalisation Nos. 1993/4/8 were still unlined black with "N E" on the tender.

All five K4's received B.R. numbers during 1948, with interesting variations in the method of application. No. 61993 remained unlined black with "N E" on the tender, No. 61994 received B.R. lined black livery with "BRITISH RAILWAYS" on the tender, Nos. 61995/6 retained their green livery including "L N E R" on the tender, whilst No. 61998 acquired L.N.E.R. green livery with "BRITISH RAILWAYS" on the tender (cf. figs. 146 and 147).

Nos. 61993/5/6/8 eventually received B.R. lined black livery and tender emblem, in April, June, July 1952 and February 1953 respectively (fig. 140). No. 61994 also acquired the emblem in December 1952. All the K4's survived long enough to receive the 1956 version of the B.R. emblem (fig. 142).

Names

No. 3441 was named *Loch Long,* which was an extension of the theme used for the K2's which were named after inland lochs. The West Highland line ran along the shores of Loch Long, which however was open at its southern extremity to the Firth of Clyde. Like the K2's, the engine had no splashers but in its case a straight nameplate was provided fitting neatly on the smokebox side (fig. 137).

The other five K4's were given names of Scottish clan chiefs appropriate to the districts served by the West Highland line. Their nameplates too were fitted on the smokebox sides, but such were their lengths that in the cases of Nos. 3442/3/6 they encroached on the boiler clothing plate (fig. 138).

No. 3442 entered service carrying the name *MacCailein Mór,* honouring the Duke of Argyll as head of Clan Campbell, traditionally known by this Gaelic patronymic meaning Great Son of Colin. Within a fortnight it had been renamed in Eastfield shed *The Great Marquess,* sobriquet of the head of the Graham family who became the first Marquess of Montrose, in 1644.

No. 3443 *Cameron of Lochiel* was named after the chief of Clan Cameron.

No. 3444 *Lord of the Isles* honoured the chief of Clan MacDonald, whose ancestors had borne this title until 1493 when it was forfeited to the Scottish crown and thus eventually passed to successive male heirs to the throne of the United Kingdom.

No. 3445 was named *MacCailin Mór* with the spelling altered (see Part 1, fig. 80), though why is not known. Gaelic authorities are by no means unanimous as to the spelling and several renderings have appeared in reference books. Ian Grimble in "Clans and Chiefs" uses the spelling as used on No. 3442's original nameplates, and this is the version quoted in Dwelly's Gaelic Dictionary. This later rendering "MacCailin Mór" is understood to be regarded as quite wrong by Gaelic scholars.

No. 3446 was originally named *Lord of Dunvegan,* honouring the chief of the Dunvegan MacLeods. However the last of the male line had recently died, in 1935, and the new chief, who had succeeded her father in the Barony of Dunvegan, made a successful request for *MacLeod of MacLeod* to be displayed instead, and this change was made on 30th March 1939.

British Railways

The five remaining engines of the class were duly renumbered during 1948, with the addition of 60,000 to their numbers.

Allocation and Work

No. 3441 was allocated in January 1937 to Eastfield shed in Glasgow, at first working on goods trains. Its first appearance on the West Highland line was on 4th March, on goods, and on 15th March, on passenger. On the morning of 31st March it worked from Fort William to Mallaig and back before going on to Glasgow later that day. Soon it was working unaided the 5-50 a.m. Glasgow (Queen Street) – Fort William passenger train and the 1-44 p.m. return. Because of the arduous nature of the route, it had not hitherto been usual practice to make the 244-mile round trip in one day, so that this feature is worth noting. Whilst the engine was capable of handling trains of up to 300 tons without assistance, its full potential could not be realised until it was possible to diagram it with a similar engine or engines, with due regard to maintenance.

In July 1938 No. 3442 arrived at Eastfield. First of all it had to wait for its new nameplates to arrive and its first jobs were a night goods to Bo'ness on 26th July, the 3-30 a.m. goods to Garelochhead on the 28th and a Clydebank-Portobello excursion on the 29th. It then worked a few goods trains to Fort William and on 5th April it appeared on the 9-46 a.m. passenger Fort William-Glasgow. With two K4's now available it was possible to make proper use of their extra power. As trains on the Mallaig extension were not normally double-headed there was no need at that time for K4's to appear on this line. Both engines therefore kept to the Glasgow to Fort William section, where they obviated the need for an assisting engine on the trains they worked. There was then a five month delay before further engines were completed.

Nos. 3443-6 appeared in December 1938 and January 1939 and were also allocated to Eastfield, which at that time was also responsible for the provision of power for its sub-shed at Fort William. There were then three daily diagrams on the West Highland line covered by K4's, two of them goods one way and passenger the other. These were: (1) 5-50 a.m. Glasgow-Fort William passenger, 4-7 p.m. Fort William-Glasgow passenger; (2) 2-5 a.m. Sighthill-Fort William goods, 10-3 a.m. Fort William-Glasgow passenger (engine detached at Cowlairs and train worked into Queen Street by an Incline Pilot); (3) 2-50 a.m. Sighthill-Fort William goods, 1-43 p.m. Fort William-Glasgow passenger. Another K4 duty was soon added to the roster and this involved working the 3-46 p.m. Glasgow-Fort William passenger, returning at 4-30 a.m. on a goods to Maryhill. All of these were lodging turns so that engines were manned alternately by Eastfield and Fort William crews, but from 1940 lodging was abolished and men changed over footplates en route. In October 1939 Fort William gained an allocation of K4's in its own right, receiving Nos. 3443/4. The K4's performed nearly all their work on the line between Glasgow and Fort William although in their early years the Eastfield engines also had a regular goods working on the 5-15 p.m. Glasgow (Sighthill) to Edinburgh (Niddrie).

During the summer months of 1939 there were four passenger trains a day in each direction on the West Highland line, all of them having a restaurant car. When hauled by a K4 they could be loaded to nine vehicles (two more than a K2 could take single handed). The goods train load for a K4 on the Craigendoran Junction-Fort William section was "equal to 37", whilst a K2 could take "equal to 31" and classes J37 and J39 both took "equal to 34".

Leaving Glasgow on a West Highland passenger train there was the stiff climb up Cowlairs Incline to be faced immediately, though there was invariably a banking engine assisting in the rear. Then followed something of a gallop through the north western suburbs and along the banks of the Clyde to Craigendoran, where the West Highland line proper began at little above sea level. Almost exactly 100 miles away was Fort William, at just about the same height above the arm of the sea known as Loch Linnhe. In between there was Corrour summit, 1,347 feet above sea level, roughly $71\frac{1}{2}$ miles from Craigendoran travelling north or only $28\frac{1}{2}$ miles from Fort William in the southbound direction. Most of the gradients were both long and steep. Northbound, for instance, there was an almost unbroken climb, much at 1 in 60, for fifteen miles from Ardlui to the County March summit beyond Tyndrum. Southbound there was the formidable climb from Tulloch to Corrour which involved six miles continuously at 1 in 67, steepening to 1 in 59 over a further mile to the summit.

Superlative climbing ability was essential but also the facility to negotiate the almost continuous curvature of the line, many of the curves being tight. These curves and climbs drastically limited the speeds at which they could be taken, but the K4's were designed with this hard slogging well in mind and they performed this part of their task with no trouble.

What became literally their undoing was the speeds at which they had to run on the 20 miles of level track at the Glasgow end and a comparable $8\frac{1}{2}$ mile stretch alongside Loch Eil. Nut tightening on the middle big-end was a frequent necessity and, on one occasion, the middle connecting rod actually dropped off. The 5ft. 2in. diameter coupled wheels, in combination with Gresley's three-cylinder arrangement, were not ideally suited to the West Highland and maintenance costs rose. The later V4 class, with its 5ft. 8in. diameter coupled wheels, was more popular with the enginemen but it was lacking in power, so that it could be considered more as a rival to the K2's than to the K4's.

The appearance of class B1 4-6-0's on the Glasgow to Fort William line in 1947 resulted in the K4's making regular appearances on the Mallaig extension, on both passenger and goods trains. The 1-0 p.m. from Mallaig could amount to seven coaches with up to eleven fish vans. Another heavy train was the 10-28 a.m. Fort William-Mallaig on Thursdays in the summer of 1948, in connection with a sea excursion. This was a K4 working and on 11th June 1948, for example, No. 1994 worked this train, with eight coaches and three vans. The K4's then became rare on passenger trains between Glasgow and Fort William.

In 1949 the new class K1 2-6-0's started to appear in numbers on the West Highland line. These were a derivative of the K4's and therefore had 5ft. 2in. diameter coupled wheels also, but without the complication of a third cylinder and with it the troublesome big-end. Ex-L.M.S. class 5 4-6-0's then appeared on the line in 1950 though they were slower in establishing themselves. By mid-1954 the policy was to use the Class 5's on the Glasgow to Fort William section and the K1's on the Mallaig extension. From May 1954 therefore, all five K4's were concentrated at Eastfield, and intended to be used on the West Highland line on goods trains only. Reports of K4's on passenger trains on the West Highland thereafter are scanty. On 30th August 1954, both Nos. 61996/8 were on such duties on the Mallaig extension, whilst on 14th July 1956 No. 61995 handled unaided the 8-32 a.m. Fort William-Mallaig, with a 303-ton load.

During 1959 all the K4's were transferred from Eastfield to Thornton, where it was intended to use them on goods trains. Thus ended their love-hate relationship with the West Highland after twenty years or so, though on 18th June 1960 No. 61995 was chartered by the Stephenson Locomotive Society to work the "White Cockade" special, from Glasgow to Fort William and back. The outward journey was over the West Highland whilst the return trip, after the engine had been given attention at Fort William shed to some heated axleboxes, was via the Caledonian route from Crianlarich to Glasgow (Buchanan Street) via Stirling.

Throughout the time that the K4's were closely associated with the West Highland line, they also appeared from time to time on the Edinburgh line. Such an example occurred on 19th July 1941 when No. 3442 worked a Glasgow-Leeds express to Edinburgh with thirteen bogies.

Their range increased after nationalisation (for example, No. 61993 was noted at Tweedmouth shed on 14th July 1955) and they occasionally appeared on former L.M.S. lines. Notable instances in the fifties were: No. 61995 on a Perth-Forfar freight in July 1952, No. 61995 on an excursion from Milngavie to Troon, Prestwick and Ayr in July 1954, No. 61996 on an engineer's train at Dunkeld on the Highland line

in August 1955, No. 61996 on the 9-15 a.m. Perth-Mossend goods in February 1957 and No. 61998 on the 9-0 p.m. Aberdeen-Glasgow freight in February 1958.

Nos. 61993/6 arrived at Thornton in April 1959. For a short time they regularly worked the 1-30 a.m. Thornton-Aberdeen and the 7-30 a.m. Kelty-Aberdeen freight trains, following trouble encountered with W.D. 2-8-0's on such trains as these. The other three K4's were transferred to Thornton in December 1959. This shed treated the K4's as goods engines but on 11th June 1960 No. 61998 appeared on an Edinburgh-Ladybank relief passenger train and the next day it was noted on a Kirkcaldy train. Less than one week later came their swan song when, as already recorded above, No. 61995 made its farewell appearance on the West Highland line. Shortly afterwards, No. 61994 was noted on Carlisle (Kingmoor) shed on 1st August 1960.

The full allocations of these engines are set out in the table below.

No. 3442 "The Great Marquess"

After this engine was withdrawn in December 1961 it was purchased by Viscount Garnock. It was restored to working order and L.N.E.R. livery at Cowlairs Works (fig. 148) after which it worked south to Neville Hill on a special goods train on 29th April 1963. The shed there became its new home for over nine years, during which time it worked a number of enthusiasts' specials. On 3rd October 1964 it revisited its birthplace, Darlington Works, where it was presented with a cabside plaque commemorating the occasion. Probably its most unusual excursion was a rail tour on 12th March 1967 from London (Victoria) to Southampton via Brighton and the South Coast, returning later from Eastleigh to East Croydon, whence the remainder of the journey to Victoria was covered by diesel. On 6th September 1972 No. 3442 was hauled to the Severn Valley Railway, its present home.

No.	Allocation
3441/61993	EFD 1/37, THJ 4/59 (Wdn. 10/61).
3442/61994	EFD 7/38, THJ 12/59 (Wdn. 12/61).
3443/61995	EFD 12/38, FW 10/39, EFD 5/54, THJ 12/59 (Wdn. 10/61).
3444/61996	EFD 12/38, FW 10/39, EFD 5/54, THJ 4/59 (Wdn. 10/61).
3445	EFD 1/39 (Rebuilt 12/45).
3446/61998	EFD 1/39, THJ 12/59 (Wdn. 10/61).

The abbreviations used above for the sheds are as follows: EFD Eastfield, FW Fort William, THJ Thornton. Prior to October 1939 Fort William was a sub-shed under Eastfield.

Engine Diagrams

Section L.N.E.,1937.   With 3,500-gallon tender. Grate length amended, 12/1941. Inner firebox inside length at the top amended, 12/1942.

Not issued, 1959.   With 4,200-gallon tender.

Classification: Route availability 6; B.R. power class 6MT.

Summary of K4 Class

B.R. No.	1946 No.	Orig, No.	Maker	Built	Name	Rebuilt to K1	4,200-gal. tender attached	Withdrawn
61993 5/48	1993 9/46	3441	Darlington	1/1937	Loch Long	–	11/59	10/61
61994 10/48	1994 9/46	3442	,,	7/1938	The Great Marquess (a)	–	9/59	12/61
61995 7/48	1995 9/46	3443	,,	12/1938	Cameron of Lochiel	–	9/59	10/61
61996 11/48	1996 12/46	3444	,,	12/1938	Lord of the Isles	–	11/59	10/61
–	–	3445	,,	1/1939(b)	MacCailin Mór	12/45	–	–
61998 4/48	1998 5/46	3446	,,	1/1939(b)	MacLeod of MacLeod (c)	–	–	10/61

(a) At first named *MacCailein Mór*.
(b) Nos. 3445/6 were included in the stock figures for 1938 although not sent to traffic until January 1939.
(c) Named *Lord of Dunvegan* until March 1939.

ig. 147   Class K4 No. 61998 *MacLeod of MacLeod* on an up class A goods, making a shunt at
Crianlarich, c. 1950.

Retaining bracket for Flaman speed recorder on right-hand side, knob missing from smokebox door, L.N.E.R. green
livery with B.R. number and lettering "BRITISH RAILWAYS" on tender.

g. 148   Class K4 No. 3442 *The Great Marquess* at Worcester, September 1965.

As preserved, with 3,500-gallon tender re-attached. Number on tender bufferbeam (not carried in L.N.E.R. days).

Fig. 149   Class K1/1 No. 3445 *MacCailin Mór* at Doncaster Works, December 1945.

Wartime black livery with lettering "N E" on tender.

Fig. 150   Class K1/1 No. 3445 *MacCailin Mór* on an up goods crossing Welwyn Viaduct, April 1946.

Smokebox door hinge straps 2ft. 0in. apart, no handrail on smokebox door.

Fig. 151   Class K1/1 No. 61997 *MacCailin Mór* at Fort William, June 1954.

Smokebox door with wheel and handle fastening, hinge straps 1ft. 3in. apart, no door knob, lined black livery.

Fig. 152   Class K1 No. 62009 at Ayr, July 1949.

As delivered in lined black livery with "BRITISH RAILWAYS" on tender, raised cover plate on firebox in front of safety valves.

g. 153   Class K1 No. 62064 at Darlington, May 1962.

raised cover plate on firebox, A.W.S. timing reservoir on running plate in front of cab and battery box in front of cab footsteps, tender coal
division plate further forward and made higher.

g. 154   Class K1 No. 2005 at Shildon, August 1975.

As preserved.

Fig. 155   Class K1 No. 62011 on a passenger train with two fish vans leading at Mallaig station, May 1960.

Fig. 156   Class K1 No. 62039 on an up coal train at Cambridge, Chesterton Junction, August 1953.

ig. 157   Class K1 No. 62047 on an up goods leaving York, April 1965.
Fitted with A.W.S.

. 158   Class K1 No. 62052 on a Mallaig-Fort William train at Lochailort station, June 1954.
Stone's electric lighting set with steam generator on right-hand running plate.

CLASS KI/I

THOMPSON REBUILD FROM GRESLEY K4 CLASS

AND

CLASS KI

PEPPERCORN 5ft. 2in. ENGINES

CLASS K1/1 – ENGINE REBUILT AFTER GROUPING (1945): 3445. TOTAL 1.

CLASS K1 – ENGINES BUILT AFTER NATIONALISATION (1949-50): 62001-70. TOTAL 70.

In February 1945 the first outline drawing appeared for the rebuilding of the three-cylinder K4's with Thompson's standard two-cylinder arrangement and a shortened version of his B1 boiler. The rebuilding order for one engine was issued a month later and No. 3445 was returned to traffic rebuilt in the following December.

Coal consumption tests were held in January 1946 between this engine and class J39 No. 2987. The engines worked outwards on the 7-45 a.m. class A goods Ferme Park – New England with empty wagons, and returned with the 1-35 p.m. class A New England – Ferme Park coal train. All the trains were made up to class 6 loadings though class

J39 was normally rated to take class 5 loads. It was considered that neither engine was worked to its maximum capacity but No. 3445 had a greater reserve of power. However, the J39 lost four minutes on one run due to being given a class 6 load. The conclusion was that the K1 was a good substitute for the J39, though its wheelbase was too long to ensure a satisfactory balance on a 50ft. 0in. turntable. Its 3,500-gallon tender was a definite restriction and it was suggested that the 4,200-gallon type should be considered in future, though it was conceded that the extra length would then restrict its use even further due to it requiring a larger turntable. It was suggested that it might be worth while altering the superstructure of the tender top to provide a tender weatherboard by altering the slope of the top of the tender sides, thus providing a clear view when working tender first. The results of these tests are summarised below.

| Date | Engine No. | Load (veh./tons) | | Coal consumption | |
		Outward	Return	(lb./mile)	(lb./ton mile)
15/1/46	3445	64/424	38/708	59.9	0.108
16/1/46	3445	61/404	45/695	59.0	0.109
24/1/46	2987	65/428	44/717	66.2	0.118
25/1/46	2987	64/427	46/752	69.0	0.120

No more K4's were rebuilt and this conversion scheme was eventually endorsed "no action" in February 1949. The prototype No. 3445 at first took the classification K1, which had been vacant since 1937. Then in December 1946 it was reclassified K1/1 in anticipation of the production engines.

The order for the production engines was placed in July 1947 with N.B. Locomotive Co., in advance of the necessary authority which was received on 30th October 1947. The engines were included in the 1948 building programme though

the first ones did not appear until 1949. Meanwhile Thompson had retired and certain modifications were made to the design by Peppercorn, his successor. The most obvious external difference was the shape of the running plate in front of the cylinders, which was cut away on these later engines to give easier access to the steam chests (cf. figs. 149 and 152). 4,200-gallon tenders were provided, which increased both the length over buffers and the total wheelbase, but no special provision was made for running tender first. The construction of the entire class is summarised in the accompanying table.

The K1's proved to be almost as versatile as the B1's and worked anything from colliery trips to express passenger trains, the latter in particular on the West Highland line. No. 61997 was withdrawn in June 1961, preceding the K4's by several months, but the post-nationalisation engines lasted until 1962-67. The last survivor, No. 62005, was sold privately for preservation as L.N.E.R. No. 2005 and, at the time of writing, is at work on the North Yorkshire Moors Railway.

Engine Nos.	Maker	Order No.	Date Ordered	Works Nos.	No. Built	Date
3445	Doncaster	–	March 1945(a)	–	1	1945
62001-70	N.B. Loco. Co. (b)	L982	July 1947	26605-74	70	1949-50

(a) Rebuilding order. For previous history see under class K4.
(b) Queen's Park Works.

Standard L.N.E.R. Dimensions

Cylinders (2 outside)	$20'' \times 26''$
Motion	Walschaerts with $10''$ piston valves
Boiler:	
Max. diam. outside	$5' 6''$
Barrel length	$11' 9''$ (a)
Firebox length outside ..	$10' 1\frac{1}{2}''$(b)
Pitch	$8' 6\frac{1}{2}''$
Diagram No.	116
Heating surface:	
Firebox	168 sq.ft.
Tubes ($141 \times 2''$)	858 sq.ft.
Flues ($24 \times 5\frac{1}{4}''$)	382 sq.ft.
Total evaporative	1408 sq.ft.
Superheater ($24 \times 1.212''$) ..	300 sq.ft.
Total	1708 sq.ft.
Grate area	27.9 sq.ft.
Boiler pressure	225 lb./sq.in.
Leading wheels	$3' 2''$
Coupled wheels	$5' 2''$
Tender wheels	$3' 9''$
Tractive effort (85%)	32,081 lb.

	K1/1	K1
Wheelbase:		
Engine	$8' 11'' + 7' 6'' + 8' 9''$ $= 25' 2''$	$8' 11'' + 7' 6'' + 8' 9''$ $= 25' 2''$
Tender	$7' 0'' + 6' 0'' = 13' 0''$	$7' 3'' + 6' 3'' = 13' 6''$
Total	$48' 6\frac{7}{8}''$	$49' 5''$
Length over buffers ..	$58' 1\frac{5}{8}''$	$59' 10''$
Weight (full):		
Engine	66T 17C	66T 0C
Tender	44T 4C	52T 0C
Total	111T 1C	118T 0C
Adhesive	56T 17C	56T 0C
Max. axle load	19T 14C	19T 4C
Water capacity	3,500 gallons	4,200 gallons(c)
Coal capacity	5T 10C	7T 10C

(a) The engine diagram quoted the distance between tubeplates, $11' 7\frac{1}{8}''$ ($11' 7''$ from December 1950). See under Details.
(b) Alternative figures were quoted on the engine diagram, see under Details.
(c) 3,750 gallons with coal-weighing tender.

Numbering

The prototype No. 3445 was renumbered 1997 in 1946 in the series allocated to the K4's. The production engines appeared after nationalisation and were numbered from 62001 onwards. This entailed the renumbering in mid-1949 of class D31 Nos. 62059/60/72 to 62281/2/3 to clear these particular numbers, though in the event the highest number taken by a K1 was 62070 (see Part 4 of this series, p. 32).

Details

CLASS K1/1

The main frames were the same length as in class K4, with the same wheel spacings. Other principal details which were retained in the rebuilding were the generous 9¾in. diameter by 11in. long coupled axle journals, steel wedges to compensate for wear in the horn gaps and the 4ft. 0in. long bearing springs (fifteen ½in. thick plates). The bufferbeam at the front was 8ft. 5in. wide and had the lower corners cut away. The buffers were the Group Standard pattern, 1ft. 8in. long. Footsteps were provided at the front and a small handgrip was fitted to the running plate above them. No guard irons were provided on the frames, as those on the pony truck were considered better placed and adequate.

The pony truck was redesigned. Whereas the K4, in common with other Gresley classes, had a double swing link suspension arrangement, No. 3445's new truck had spring side control, copied from the Stanier class 8F 2-8-0's (L.N.E.R. class O6). This new arrangement afterwards became standard for classes K5, L1 and V2. An experimental feature of No. 3445's truck was the employment of laminated bearing springs, comprising seven ½in. plates at 2ft. 6in. centres. Similar sets were used in the pony trucks of classes K5, L1 (No. 9000 only) and V2 (seven engines only).

As in class K4, the overall width over the running plate was 8ft. 6in. except alongside the cab where it was 8ft. 9in. However, the height above rail level to the underside of the running plate over the coupled wheels was raised 3 inches to 6ft. 0in.

The cylinders were the type used by Thompson in a number of his classes, in particular the B1's. They were inclined at 1 in 30 and extra ½in. thick liner plates were needed between the cylinders and frames to space their centres 6ft. 8½in. apart so that the type of motion which was used in class K5 could be employed. (The centres were 6ft. 7½in. apart for example in class B1). The

drive was taken by the second coupled axle and the maximum travel of the piston valves at 75 per cent cut-off was 6⅝in.

The engine had two Wakefield No. 7 mechanical lubricators on the left-hand running plate, for the axleboxes, cylinders and valves.

Steam-operated sanding for forward running was applied in front of the driving coupled wheels with gravity fed sanders in front of the leading coupled wheels. For reverse running, steam-operated sanding was applied behind the driving coupled wheels from sandboxes which were fitted to the frame alongside the firebox.

The boiler was a shortened version of the B1 boiler and in fact No. 3445's boiler was constructed at Gorton as a Diagram 100A boiler and immediately afterwards converted at Doncaster to become the prototype Diagram 116. Some of the details were therefore common to both boiler types.

The barrel was constructed from two telescopic rings, $\frac{11}{16}$in. thickness. The rear ring was 5ft. 6in. outside diameter and the front one was 5ft. 4⅝in. The front tubeplate was ¾in. thick, recessed into the barrel, and the radius of the flange was ¼in. From December 1950 replacement tubeplates were ⅞in. thick with 1in. radius flange, reducing the distance between the tubeplates from 11ft. 7⅜in. to 11ft. 7in.

The firebox casing was constructed of $\frac{9}{16}$in. thick steel plate, except for the throat plate which was ⅝in. (increased to $\frac{11}{16}$in. from July 1947). The length of the casing at the bottom was 9ft. 0in., whilst the overall length was 10ft. 1⅛in., against 8ft. 11in. and 10ft. 0½in. respectively in the Diagram 110 boiler (class K4). However, the engine diagram showed the overall length as 9ft. 7¼in., taking this measurement from the front of the firebox tubeplate to the extreme back end of the outer casing. The inner firebox was constructed of $\frac{9}{16}$in. copper plate, but with a 1in. thick tubeplate. The water space above the foundation ring was 3½in. wide at the front and rear, and 3in. at the sides.

The superheater elements were the long return bend type, 1½in. outside diameter and 9 S.W.G. thick (inside diameter 1.212in.). The elements had ball-jointed (Melesco type) ends, which were attached to the header by the "Through" bolt method.

The firebox had a drop grate section at the front. The rodding ran down at an angle on the right-hand side of the firebox from a screw mechanism in the cab to the drop grate shaft. An ordinary ashpan was provided below the firegrate with a front damper door only.

The smokebox door was similar to those fitted to the first ten B1's, 4ft. 5¼in. diameter and 11ft. 0in. radius curvature, with the centres of the hinge straps 2ft. 0in. apart. There was no door handrail at first, as the boiler handrail curved round the top of the smokebox (fig. 150). After nationalisation a variety of doors were noted on No. 61997, all of which were 4ft. 9in. diameter, 6ft. 5¼in. radius curvature, with the centres of the hinge straps 1ft. 3in. apart, as follows: by 1952 – long hinge straps, single door stop instead of projections on the ends of the hinges; by 1954 (fig. 151) – additional handrail, no opening knob, wheel and handle fastening; by 1957 – standard K1 door (see later).

The chimney, 1ft. 4in. high, was the pattern fitted also to the K4's. The blastpipe top had a 5⅛in. diameter orifice, as currently fitted to the B1's.

After rebuilding, No. 3445 retained its original cab with its sides suitably altered to allow for the alteration to the profile of the running plate.

CLASS K1

The frames were the same overall length as in the prototype No. 3445, with certain detail differences. In particular the coupled wheel journals were only 8¾in. diameter by 9in. long and the bearing springs were 3ft. 6in. across their centres (eleven ⅝in. thick plates), which were features of the new class L1 2-6-4 tank engines. The bufferbeam at the front was 7ft. 7½in. wide, with the lower corners cut away deeper than on the prototype (cf. figs. 150 and 157).

The pony truck differed in one respect from that fitted to No. 3445. The latter had laminated bearing springs, which afterwards proved to be unsuitable on the handful of V2's which also had them, and it was decided to return to fitting helical springs instead. History had repeated itself once more, as this was precisely the lesson which Gresley had learned in 1914 after fitting the pony trucks of his early 2-6-0's with laminated bearing springs (see p. 66). The production K1's therefore had coil springs, but the prototype was never brought into line in this respect.

The overall width over the running plate was 8ft. 5½in. except alongside the cab where it was 8ft. 8in. Alongside the cab was a footstep in the curve of the running plate (not provided on No. 3445). The height above rail level to the underside of the running plate over the coupled wheels was the same as No. 3445. The main running plate stopped short in front of the cylinders and there was a platform at a lower level in front of it, the overall width over which was only 7ft. 7½in.

The cylinders were the same pattern as used in the prototype, but with the ½in. liner plates omitted so that the centres were 6ft. 7½in. apart. The axlebox and cylinder lubrication was similar, except that the mechanical lubricator boxes themselves were placed close together (cf. figs. 149 and 152). The sanding gear was also similarly arranged, except that all were now steam-operated and in addition the filler cap above the driving coupled wheel was raised at an angle with a backing plate behind it to avoid sand spilling down between the frames and causing trouble (fig. 153).

The production Diagram 116 boilers differed from the boiler which was fitted in 1945 to No. 3445 in one particular respect. There were thirteen rows of ordinary roof stays, instead of fifteen, and four rows of expansion and sling stays instead of only two. To strengthen the firebox wrapper plate immediately in front of the safety valves on these new boilers, a patch plate was provided which required an alteration to the clothing plate and a raised cover plate above. Later this raised plate was usually absent (cf. figs. 152 and 153).

The firebox had a rocking grate, which was easy to operate from inside the cab. A hopper ashpan was also provided to obviate the need for men to go under the engine to clear out the ashes. The hopper door was opened by operating a key on the right-hand side below the frame. The key was easily lost and in a later arrangement a fixed handle was fitted instead. Trouble was experienced through distortion of the hopper ashpan doors and the apertures were strengthened on Nos. 62014/29/39/63/7 between October 1952 and March 1953, but this made little difference and the experiment was concluded in May 1956. In November 1956 the rocking grate bars were rearranged on No. 62005 to see if this had any effect. They were still in this form after its return from works in February 1961, with the comment that they were giving satisfaction.

Altogether seventy-eight Diagram 116 boilers were constructed, including the one which had been converted from Diagram 100A. The boilers were freely interchangeable between classes K1/1 and K1, but no others. No. 3445 (later 61997) kept its original Diagram 116 boiler until October 1954, after which it was subsequently carried by Nos. 62005 (November 1955 to October 1958), 62027 (November 1958 to May 1963) and 62011 (July 1963 to its withdrawal).

The smokebox door was the later type, introduced on class B1 Nos. 61350 onwards in 1949: 4ft. 9in. diameter, 6ft. 5½in. radius curvature, with the centres of the hinge straps 1ft. 3in. apart. An additional footstep was fitted on the door to assist the fireman when reaching up to the electric lamp on the top of the smokebox. The smokebox seams were welded instead of riveted. The engines all had B.R. smokebox door numberplates when they were delivered. These were fitted just above the top hinge strap, below the lampiron. Smokeboxes were frequently changed in the works, as a result of which odd smokebox doors appeared from time to time. For example Nos. 62016/26/50/8 were noted with longer hinge straps and a centre door stop, Nos. 62008/26 with the footstep absent and No. 62026 with a short horizontal handrail.

The smokebox was fitted with self cleaning apparatus which had a detrimental effect on steaming. Latterly, new blastpipe tops with 4¾in. diameter orifices (instead of 5¼in.) and 2in. shorter in height were generally fitted to the K1's operating in the N.E. Region to improve steaming when fitted with self cleaning smokeboxes.

The production engines had electric lighting sets, with a Stone's steam generator alongside the smokebox on the right-hand running plate in front of the steam pipe. The equipment was recorded as having been removed later from a number of engines, including Nos. 62002/18/33/53/4, and there were no doubt others which lost their equipment in later years.

B.T.H. speed indicating equipment was provided. This was located on the left-hand side of the engine, mounted on a bracket which was attached to the running plate just in front of the cab. Not all the engines had the full equipment when new, though they all had the bracket. In many cases the equipment was later recorded as having been removed, e.g. from Nos. 62002/15.

Brakes

The class was provided with steam brakes for engine and tender with a vacuum ejector for train braking. There was a 10in. diameter steam brake cylinder under the cab. A number of engines latterly received A.W.S. equipment (figs. 153 and 157).

Tenders

The original scheme of February 1945 envisaged either 3,500 or 4,200-gallon tenders

being attached, as circumstances required. The prototype, No. 3445, retained its current 3,500-gallon riveted tender (No. 7570), which was incidentally class K4 No. 3442's original tender and the first one of this type to have the new high front plate. The tender brakes were converted from vacuum to steam but this was virtually the only alteration which was necessary at the time of rebuilding. This tender stayed with No. 61997 until its withdrawal and the only subsequent modification of note was the raising of the division plate at the back of the coal space to prevent spillage around the water filler hole.

The production engines had 4,200-gallon welded tenders (Nos. 3901-70) which were virtually identical to those attached to the last batch of B1's which the N.B. Locomotive Co. built (Nos. 61360-99) with square-end frames and running plate supports (see Part 2B of this series, p. 136).

No. 62001's original tender had been in service only a week when it was damaged in a collision at Balloch. The N.B. Locomotive Co. loaned tender No. 3914 to run with No. 62001 whilst Cowlairs repaired the damage. After the necessary work had been completed, on 19th June 1949, No. 62001 regained its original tender and No. 3914 was returned to its makers to await the completion of No. 62014.

In connection with an experiment to soften the feed water in the tender, two K1's based at March, Nos. 62016/7, had Alfloc tube feeders fitted in January 1952. These were eventually removed in December 1955 and January 1956 respectively.

In the mid-fifties the division plate at the back of the coal space was raised in height and repositioned 1ft. 10½in. further forward to prevent coal spillage around the water filler hole (fig. 153).

From time to time coal weighing tenders from class B1 engines were temporarily attached to K1's, as follows:-

Tender No.
4095   62019 4/52-5/52; 62010 3/54-6/54.
4200   62015 3/52-4/52; 62019 4/52; 62020 4/52.

Ordinary B1 tenders, amongst which were the type with riveted tanks, were also noted attached to K1's from time to time, including:-

Tender No.
4036   62066 1/53-wdl.
4067   62020 5/52-wdl.
4085   62045 4/61-11/63; 62046 11/63-wdl.
4248   62063 1/63-wdl.
4366   62007 8/63-wdl.

Maintenance

After it was rebuilt in 1945, maintenance of No. 3445 was transferred to Doncaster, though it subsequently had three non-classified repairs at Cowlairs in May, October and November 1957. The production engines normally visited Doncaster for repairs, until maintenance of steam engines ceased there in September 1963. The Scottish members of the class also paid occasional visits to Cowlairs for light casual repairs whilst one of them, No. 62012, visited Darlington for a heavy intermediate repair in September 1956.

From September 1963 general maintenance of the class was undertaken by Darlington, ceasing in December 1965 with the repair of No. 62067. During 1966 Cowlairs undertook casual repair work to Nos. 62044/5/59/67. One of these engines, No. 62059, was the last steam engine overhauled at this works. It returned to traffic on 22nd September 1966 after receiving a full repaint, which was most unusual.

Liveries

When No. 3445 was rebuilt it was turned out in unlined black, with the letters "N E" on its tender (fig. 149). It was renumbered 1997 in December 1946. In September 1947 it was again repainted black, but gained in full the letters "L N E R". No. 1997 was taken into British Railways stock and duly had 60,000 added to its number in January 1949, with the inscription "BRITISH RAILWAYS" on the tender and a numberplate fitted to its smokebox door. The engine survived long enough to acquire lined black livery and in turn the two styles of emblems.

Nos. 62001-70 were delivered in one batch in 1949-50, in black livery and fully lined out in red, cream and grey. The first fifty engines originally had "BRITISH RAILWAYS" on their tenders whilst the last twenty engines had the first style of tender emblem (fig. 152), which afterwards appeared on the earlier engines. All acquired the second style in due course.

Allocation and Work

When the prototype K1 appeared in December 1945 it first went to New England where it worked on diagrams usually operated by class K2 and K3 2-6-0's on the lighter goods and coal trains to Hornsey and King's Cross. On occasions it went northwards to Doncaster and even to Sheffield. Trials were conducted in January 1946 between New England and Hornsey in conjunction with the class K5 rebuild No. 206. The K1 then moved on to Blaydon in May 1946 remaining there for two months before going to the Scottish Area at St. Margaret's. From there it was sent to Thornton and Eastfield sheds before returning south in October to Norwich, where it remained until October 1947. It then returned to New England for just over a year, moving on to Eastfield in November 1949. It finally went to Fort William in May 1954 where it remained until withdrawal in June 1961. From December 1945 until November 1949 a Southern Area K2, No. 4639 (61729), was stationed in the Scottish Area in exchange for the K1. During its stay in the south No. 3445, carrying the Gaelic name *MacCailin Mòr,* was often the centre of attraction. On one occasion in May 1946 it appeared on the 2-5 p.m. King's Cross-Cambridge passenger train and the Locomotive Foreman was heard to declare that it was a "new express passenger type"!

Trials with the prototype having been successful, seventy new engines were ordered in 1947 to be eventually allocated between North Eastern Region (40) and Eastern Region (30). Of the former, thirty went to Darlington and ten to Blaydon whilst on the E.R. ten were allocated to Gorton and twenty to March.

All seventy K1's were delivered by the builders from their Queen's Park Works, Glasgow, to Eastfield shed for running-in and acceptance trials over a period of ten months between 20th May 1949 and 29th March 1950. In many cases lengthy periods were spent at Eastfield before despatch to allocated sheds. Apart from the usual local goods and slow passenger duties, some as far as Edinburgh, much use was made of the early K1's on West Highland duties but more remarkable was their appearance on excursions to Ayr on 2nd July 1949 (No. 62009) (fig. 152) and on 16th July (62016). On the Edinburgh road Nos. 62009 and 62015 were seen on the "Queen of Scots" Pullman on 15th and 16th July respectively. On 27th July No. 62019 worked an Officers special from Glasgow to Carlisle and back, via Edinburgh and the Waverley route. No fewer than nine engines (Nos. 62010-6/8/9) were at Eastfield on Thursday 28th July, possibly having been retained to cover extra trains for the Glasgow Fair holidays. In September there were several instances of new K1's taking West Highland passenger trains, as on 10th when Nos. 62027/30 left Queen Street with nine coaches on the 5-50 a.m. to Fort William and in the afternoon No. 62030 returned assisting class B1

No. 61197 on the 2-57 p.m. ex-Fort William. Further afield No. 62043 was at Thornton Junction on 25th October. On 21st November No. 62054 went to Inverkeithing on a goods and three days later No. 62049 had returned from Fort William overnight, very dirty – it had been at Eastfield almost seven weeks! On Saturday 11th February 1950 No. 62067 took a football special from Dumbarton to Stirling. It would appear there were some mechanical troubles with several of the later batch for on 28th March No. 62069, which had been delivered on 20th February, was still working to Fort William but failed to return as booked on the 2-57 p.m. which had class K2 No. 61776 instead. Again on 3rd April No. 62069 failed to return on the 9-57 a.m. from Fort William which was in charge of class K2 No. 61772. There was a considerable gap between delivery of No. 62069 on 20th February and No. 62070 on 29th March.

Nos. 62011-20, the first ten production K1's allocated to the Eastern Region, went to Gorton shed. Little has been recorded about their work during the ten months of their sojourn in the Manchester area. They were observed on the 8-55 p.m. Deansgate-York goods, but were soon replaced by K3's on this duty. In the summer of 1949 K1's appeared on the Saturdays Only holiday trains to the East Coast, e.g. 8-20 a.m. Manchester (Central) – Skegness, and in September No. 62014 was at Scarborough on a relief passenger train from Manchester. The first record of a Gorton K1 at Retford was on 25th September 1949 when No. 62013 passed through on the 7-34 a.m. passenger to Lincoln. This may have been an extension of the 1-15 a.m. Dewsnap-Sheffield goods which Gorton K1's are said to have worked regularly at that time. Afterwards the class was seen frequently on all kinds of goods, coal and empties trains over the former G.C. lines through Retford. Some of their work was on the Cheshire Lines; on 24th September 1949 No. 62020 was on passenger train duties from Stockport (Heaton Mersey) shed and in October it spent two weeks on trials from Liverpool (Brunswick). The latter shed seems to have borrowed No. 62016 on 14th September when it took the 7-30 a.m. Liverpool-Manchester (Central) semi-fast train. For the most part K1's were seen on freight work over the Cheshire Lines and many of them were recorded at Walton shed between September 1949 and April 1950. It was stated that the K1's were eventually banned from working class C fitted freights in the Manchester area. The general opinion seems to have been that they

were not powerful enough for this work, particularly over Woodhead. Consequently the K1's were not considered suitable for the work at Gorton shed and the whole allocation was transferred to March in May 1950 and replaced by a number of K3's and O4's recruited from various Eastern Region depots.

Between August 1949 and March 1950 twenty new K1's (Nos. 62031-40/51-5/66-70) were allocated to March, and were joined in May 1950 by the ten from Gorton. All thirty engines were utilised on the lighter goods and coal trains to and from Temple Mills, Norwich and Ipswich, replacing some of the older 0-6-0 classes. Additionally all the remaining K2's on the G.E. Section were then returned to the G.N. Section. Apart from some very brief loans of three K1's to Cambridge in 1951-52, the March allocation remained intact until five (Nos. 62011/2/31/4/52) left for Scotland in 1952. No more transfers occurred until 1958.

It was customary for a number of March engines to lie over at Stratford at weekends between duties and in the summer months it became usual for them to be borrowed for relief passenger trains on Saturdays, work performed previously by J39 and K2 engines. Such was the demand for the versatile K1's to be used on this passenger work that, in addition to those scheduled to lie over at Stratford, others were kept back on Friday nights with alleged minor defects, such as burned firebars, and the rostered K1 workings back to March were taken by Stratford steam-braked goods engines. Needless to say, the K1's concerned were hard at work the following day on the seasonal passenger trains. Ipswich shed also made use of K1's on Saturdays in the summer. Examples of K1's on passenger work occurred in June 1950 when No. 62031 arrived at Ipswich on the 8-6 a.m. Liverpool Street-Yarmouth express; about the same time Nos. 62015/66 were active on local passenger duties in the Ipswich area. The "Fenman" was taken from Cambridge to Lynn by No. 62034 on 21st August. In 1951 the North Country Continental left Ipswich behind No. 62014 on 4th June and five days later the same engine went through from Liverpool Street to Yarmouth on the 12-25 p.m. (SO) express, reputedly the first K1 to work over the East Suffolk line. At the same period Nos. 62032/40 were seen on Liverpool Street-Clacton Interval services.

During the following summer the same thing happened. For instance on 30th May 1952 No. 62035 took the 2-15 p.m. Cromer express out of Liverpool Street, whilst during July Nos.

62014/36 were noted handling Southend traffic. More passenger workings were recorded in 1953 when extensive use of the class was made at weekends working additional trains on the G.E. Section, and they were similarly used elsewhere. For instance, on 26th May No. 62053 of March took the 8-5 a.m. ex-Cleethorpes through to Manchester, returning on the 5-25 p.m. Manchester-Doncaster special. On the same day No. 62035 passed Guide Bridge on a 7-30 a.m. Brindle Heath-Newmarket horse box special and next day No. 62066 reached Manchester on a flower special from March. The 4-30 p.m. Ipswich-Cambridge slow was taken by No. 62051 on 13th June. In 1955 some were borrowed by Southend shed for summer extras to Liverpool Street whilst on 4th August no fewer than ten March K1's were noted working Clacton trains out of Liverpool Street. In 1957 March K1's worked regularly to York and back on the through expresses from Yarmouth and Colchester and were also used between March and Yarmouth on summer Saturday through trains from the Midlands.

Towards the end of 1958 six of the March K1's were transferred to Stratford and were joined by another in June 1959. Introduction of diesel units then imposed changes in G.E. Section motive power and early in 1960 five K1's left for Frodingham, followed near the year end by four others. Two of these were from Stratford and the rest from March. During 1961 the G.E. Section engines gradually left until by the year end only eight remained, all at March whence they could still be used on workings other than to London. By mid-1962 these had been dispersed, mainly to Doncaster and Retford.

Throughout their life at March the K1's were regular performers on the Ely-Newmarket-Ipswich line where some difficulty was experienced on heavy goods trains when the engines' deficient brake power led to at least two major derailments at Haughley Junction through failure to hold trains on the down grade. One occasion was most dramatic, with bombs from the derailed ammunition train scattered over the line. In 1950 the first recorded appearance of the class on the M. & G. N. Section took place: on 16th March No. 62039 travelled from South Lynn to Melton Constable on a goods and was again seen on 13th October taking the South Lynn-Fakenham goods, on which No. 62038 appeared four days later.

No K1's were allocated to G. C. Section sheds after the ten originally at Gorton had left in May 1950 until 1959 when nine engines (Nos.

62013/4/6/7/8/20/32/3/5) made redundant on the G.E. Section were transferred to Frodingham. In November 1962 No. 62014 moved to Doncaster but the rest stayed at Frodingham until 1963-65. On arrival at Frodingham they were reported to be very run down. Consequently failures were numerous and, as spares were in very short supply, they often lay idle for long periods. In January 1960 they took over from class J11 on the Barnetby Pilots. Three engines were required, working around the clock, marshalling goods traffic and banking on the heavy trains operating in and out of the Frodingham iron and steelmaking complex thirteen miles away. These turns included assisting the ironstone trains from Highdyke and Holton-le-Moor and coke trains from Orgreaves to Frodingham, and steel trains for Immingham and Woodford. The K1's were also used on the Sunday ballast trains in the Barnetby district. On Saturday evenings, at the end of a working week, the three pilot engines were placed at Wrawby Junction, on the site of the one-time locomotive shed. Unless required for maintenance at Frodingham shed, they remained there until midnight on Sunday when a Barnetby crew was assigned to light up and prepare the engines for a fresh week's work. Nos. 62013/6/32 were withdrawn in 1963 and in January 1964 were still at Frodingham shed being used to supply spare parts so that the others could be kept in service. No. 62018 was withdrawn in March 1964 and in January 1965 Frodingham received Nos. 62014/5 from Doncaster and No. 62067 from Retford. At that time there were still three bankers employed at Wrawby Junction but by the following August only Nos. 62017/67 remained in stock. These two went to North Blyth in October, the work by then having been taken over by diesel locomotives.

In September-October 1961 five K1's went to Retford (G. C.) shed from March. These were followed in the first half of 1962 by four more, also from March. At Retford these engines took over duties formerly undertaken by class J6 and J11 0-6-0's, working G. C. Section coal and mixed freights to Lincoln or Immingham and some local colliery trips in the Worksop area. It was not customary for them to work on G. N. line diagrams. Four moved away to Doncaster in November 1962 and, as related above, No. 62067 went to Frodingham but the remaining four were all withdrawn from Retford.

Between January 1961 and November 1962 twelve K1's were allocated to Doncaster. All except Nos. 62014/5, which went to Frodingham in January 1965, were withdrawn from there. As at Retford there was some work available in place of withdrawn J6 and O2 classes but in the main it was only local. Apart from No. 61997 (ex-3445) already referred to earlier, these were the only K1's allocated to the G. N. Section. Nevertheless quite a number of the class managed to appear at the southern end of the system mainly in consequence of the seemingly haphazard control over locomotive workings which was a feature of the fifties. At the end of August 1950 Cambridge used No. 62012 of March on both the 9-25 a.m. and 4-22 p.m. slow passenger trains to Hitchin. More unusual was the sight of No. 62005 of Heaton on a braked goods leaving Doncaster for King's Cross and returning north on the 8-5 p.m. parcels ex-Palmers Green on 5th September. Greater activity by the class was evident in 1953, beginning on 10th March when No. 62014 left Cambridge for King's Cross on the 8-12 a.m. slow passenger and in July other members appeared frequently on the evening pick-up from Cambridge to Hitchin, returning on the 9-37 p.m. Hitchin-Cambridge passenger train. Surprisingly, in the same month there were three recorded occasions of K1's taking the 1-0 p.m. King's Cross-Royston outer suburban train: Nos. 62013, 62070 and 62053 were seen on 11th, 18th and 25th July respectively. On 19th August No. 62034, then at Eastfield shed, was noted on the 11-15 a.m. empty stock from King's Cross to York. Presumably this engine was running-in following overhaul at Doncaster Plant. In the heart of G.N. territory No. 62061 of York passed Boston on 1st March 1958 with a southbound train of empty cattle wagons, returning north two days later on a Highdyke-Frodingham iron ore train. Later, in the London area, a surprising sight on 15th August was No. 62019 from March working the 7-57 p.m. King's Cross to Cambridge Buffet Express.

Early in the morning of 19th November 1958 there was a multiple collision at Hitchin blocking all running lines for several hours. During this time many East Coast expresses were diverted at Peterborough via Ely and Cambridge to Lea Bridge, Stratford and Liverpool Street. The empty stock of the up "Night Scotsman" travelled from Liverpool Street to Hornsey via Palace Gates and Bounds Green behind No. 62066 which later took the 4-39 p.m. Broad Street-Baldock outer suburban train. On the following morning No. 62016 worked the up "Aberdonian" into Liverpool Street. The yard

pilot at Yaxley on 30th January 1959 was No. 62057 of York and next day No. 62070 from March was station pilot at Peterborough North instead of the usual V2. From then on there does not seem to have been any notable use of K1's on the G.N. lines.

The prototype No. 61997 was at Eastfield from November 1949 mostly working on West Highland duties though it also appeared frequently between Glasgow and Edinburgh. More unusually it was on the 12-52 p.m. Waverley-Hawick on 15th August 1953 and on the 7-2 p.m. Waverley-Hawick on 26th March 1955, by which time it was allocated to Fort William! No further K1's were allocated to Scottish sheds until 1952 when five (Nos. 62011/2/31/4/52) arrived at Eastfield from March for use on the West Highland trains in place of the ageing K2's. Nos. 62011/2 quickly moved on to Fort William and in 1954 all five, together with No. 61997, were out-stationed there, working to both Mallaig and Glasgow (fig. 158). These continued working the West Highland passenger and goods duties until 1961. Afterwards they began to move away following replacement by other classes. By the end of 1962 all were withdrawn except Nos. 62011/2 which passed to the North Eastern Region.

The first twenty engines allocated to the North Estern Region were equally divided between Darlington (Nos. 62001-10) and Blaydon (Nos. 62021-30). Later, twenty engines (Nos. 62041-50/6-65) went initially to Darlington, by which time some of the earlier allocation had been redistributed to other sheds.

Darlington's allocation of K1's settled down to fourteen, gradually reducing to eleven by 1962. Many were used to release class B1 4-6-0's from medium distance goods duties. Usually the engines were double-shifted and worked two trips per day to two of the following destinations: York, Heaton, Tyne Dock, Sunderland, Blaydon or Newport. Darlington had one through class C turn to Guide Bridge, normally undertaken by a B16, but No. 62014 was seen on this duty a number of times during 1950. In July and August of the same year several K1's went to Scarborough on special excursions. A severe snowstorm on 20th December 1955 disrupted workings in the West Riding and No. 62062 took the "Yorkshire Pullman" from Harrogate to Leeds that morning.

For the most part Blaydon K1's worked the Carlisle road where they were allowed to take 700-ton loads as against 550 tons by class J39

0-6-0's. Eight double-shifted engines were responsible for fifteen return trips per day between Blaydon and Carlisle (London Road). The second shift on one engine worked to Shildon and Darlington, returning to Norwood. Blaydon K1's also worked some passenger services between Newcastle and Blackhill or Consett, and in July-August 1953 several were used on race specials to Redcar and Stockton. Another passenger service in which Blaydon K1's participated was that between Newcastle and Hawick via Hexham and Reedsmouth. When the Border Counties line was closed on 13th October 1956, the last train from Newcastle at 11-10 a.m. to Hawick was hauled by No. 62022, returning from Hawick at 4-22 p.m. Over the years the Blaydon stud increased to a total of fifteen until dispersal began in 1962 when dieselisation began to make an impression.

Dispersal of the Darlington K1 allocation began in September 1949 when Nos. 62002/3/5/7/10 were transferred to Heaton. Here they were temporarily joined by Nos. 62048/9/50 from November 1950 to early January 1951, and by Nos. 62049/50 again from late January to June 1951. The remaining engines remained at Heaton until July 1952 when they moved on to Blaydon and Darlington. Whilst at Heaton they were noted on goods trains between Tyneside and Edinburgh.

During the first half of 1950 Stockton received eight K1's from Darlington. At the end of the following year this allocation was reduced to six and this number was maintained until Stockton shed closed in June 1959 when all were transferred away, four going to the new depot at Thornaby and two to Low Moor.

Haverton Hill was another early recipient of the K1 class from Darlington, receiving two in January 1951 followed by five more that autumn. Here they replaced Q5's and J27's on the many local trip workings around Tees-side. Five of the Haverton Hill K1's remained until June 1956, when they were transferred to York, but the remaining two stayed one more year.

Northallerton received No. 62044 from Darlington in May 1952 to work the Hawes pick-up goods on the morning shift and to York, thence Darlington (Croft) and back to Northallerton on the late turn. Nos. 62003/59 joined No. 62044 early in 1960 (although No. 62059 only stayed for five months) when a second diagram was introduced for a K1 based at Northallerton. This was to Thirsk and Thirsk Town in the morning and on the second shift to Newport, thence to York and back to Northaller-

ton. Both K1's left Northallerton in March 1963.

York's first allocation of K1's arrived in June 1956 when five engines each from Darlington and Haverton Hill were transferred there. They ranged widely over lines to the south and west of York to Neville Hill, Doncaster, Mexborough, Healey Mills, Normanton and Wakefield, again mostly double-shifted and visiting two of these destinations each day. In addition York had two K1 diagrams to Whitemoor Yard, March, one of which involved a single engine, which did a return trip in the day, and the other which required two engines, each of which performed a round trip in forty-eight hours. As was usual with York engines, the K1's tended to stray from their normal workings. In October 1956 No. 62063 was seen at Killamarsh on a down goods and on 17th the 2-33 p.m. passenger train ex-Cleethorpes arrived at Sheffield behind No. 62046. This engine saw some use over the southern end of the former G.C. main line in August 1957 when it worked the 1-15 p.m. (SO) Brackley-Marylebone passenger train, returning with the 5-0 p.m. to Woodford. Earlier in the month it worked a local from Leicester to Woodford on 3rd August. Two days before that No. 62057 passed Gerrards Cross on a southbound rake of empty Southern Region stock, then on 16th September it left Sheffield on a Cardiff-Newcastle express in tandem with B.R. Standard Cl. 5 4-6-0 No. 73005. This particular class K1 engine saw much more extensive travel in 1965 when it took a Washwood Heath-Stoke Gifford goods train and went on to Cardiff; on 19th August it travelled through from York to Bristol on a goods. Another York engine, No. 62062, passed through Leicester with a southbound goods on the Midland lines on 28th October. In 1966 the York-based engines were working between York and Derby daily. Remarkable too was the sight of No. 62008 from Darlington passing Carstairs with a southbound West Coast main line goods on 2nd March 1966. The class appeared at Scarborough on specials and excursions during the summer months, but usually only at the busiest week-ends. York provided the engines each Saturday to work the Scarborough to Newcastle and Edinburgh trains, which made a double reversal at Malton and used the single line through Gilling to join the East Coast main line at Pilmoor. On one occasion a K1 was provided instead of the usual B1 or V2.

During 1956-57 the lines in the Leeds/Bradford area that were formerly under E.R. and L.M.R. control were transferred to the N.E.R. An early result of this was the stationing of class K1 Nos. 62043/59 at Ardsley shed during the summer months to work specials to coastal resorts. This was repeated in 1959 when Nos. 62005/9 were sent to Ardsley. On August Bank Holiday both were seen at Preston returning eastwards from Blackpool. During the first two weeks of August No. 62009 worked into Blackpool daily from the West Riding. Prior to this both Nos. 62005/6 (the latter a York engine) were at Cleethorpes with excursions from Bradford on 12th July. At the same time as Ardsley housed the above engines, two others (Nos. 62047/65) went from Stockton to Low Moor (an ex-L. & Y. shed) and were also used for coastal excursions. After use at Low Moor these two K1's were transferred to York.

Borough Gardens shed housed No. 62060 for a year from June 1958. Its regular duty began each day with the 7-0 a.m. goods from Park Lane to West Hartlepool returning with the 11-10 a.m. Later in the day it worked the 8-50 p.m. Park Lane-Carlisle (London Road) class D and the 1-30 a.m. class H return, due back at Park Lane at 4-49 a.m.

From 1962 more general use of K1's was made on the N.E.R. and the class was distributed among a number of other sheds where they took over menial duties from withdrawn engines, such as classes J26, J27 and J39. Such sheds were Gateshead, Consett, South and North Blyth. Typical of their work was that at North Blyth, with the engines going out to collieries with trains of empty mineral wagons and returning with loads of coal for shipment at the famous staiths.

From November 1962 until June 1966 Alnmouth had an allocation of K1's, Nos. 62006/21/3/5/30 together with Nos. 62011/2 sent from the Scottish Region being the usual engines. Later No. 62050 replaced 62012, which went to York in September 1964. In addition to goods duties from Alnmouth shed, these engines worked the passenger shuttle service to Alnwick, also to Newcastle.

As they were displaced by diesel locomotives the duties of the K1's decreased in importance. For instance, in 1961 the Darlington engines had only one working to York and one to Heaton: the others were local turns to Crook, Fencehouses, Bishop Auckland, Shildon and Richmond. By 1962 York provided three K1's for engineer's work: one shunting all day in the Engineer's Yard, one shunting in the yard in the morning and delivering material in the afternoon, and the third out all day on permanent way trains. However, in the winter of 1962-63 York still had daily K1 diagrams to Frodingham, Grimsby and Healey Mills.

The North Eastern Region commenced to withdraw the K1's in 1964. From then on there were some moves to sheds which had not previously housed the class: Sunderland, West Hartlepool and Tyne Dock. Neville Hill had No. 62007 from June 1964 until October 1965 when it moved to Sunderland. The last haven for K1's was Tyne Dock shed and when this was closed in September 1967, the remaining engines (Nos. 62011/45/50/60) were withdrawn, with the exception of No. 62005 which had a charmed life.

As far back as May 1960 it is believed to have assisted with the stabling overnight of the Royal Train at Picton and it certainly acted in this capacity on the occasion of the Maundy Thursday visit to Durham in March 1967. It had also partnered the preserved class K4 No. 3442 *The Great Marquess* on the "Whitby Moors Rail Tour" in March 1965, so that it was already something of a celebrity.

In May 1967 it took part in the "Three Dales Rail Tour", from Stockton to Newcastle via Redmire (Wensleydale), Richmond (Swaledale), Westgate-in-Weardale, Eaglescliffe and the coast route. On 12th August 1967 it was exhibited at the Shildon Works Open Day and a week later it was sent to the works of the Hunslet Engine Co. with a view to seeing if its boiler could be transferred to *The Great Marquess*. It then returned to Sunderland for normal work, whilst on 9th September it took over from Castle class 4-6-0 No. 7029 *Clun Castle* at King Edward Bridge on a special from Peterborough to Newcastle. Later that day it was sent light to Holbeck shed on permanent transfer. This former Midland shed had no work for it but it was handy for the nearby works of Hunslet Engine Co., if the proposed boiler exchange materialised.

The engine was officially withdrawn on 30th December 1967, as the last of its class and the last steam engine in the Eastern Region. This was not the end of the story as just before Christmas the I.C.I. North Tees works at Port Clarence had suffered a major breakdown in its steam-raising plant. No. 62005 was towed to Port Clarence and for almost six weeks it provided steam continuously to the works. Pure water was brought in by road tanker to avoid the need to wash out the boiler, and coal came in by road too. West Hartlepool supplied the fireman. Thus at the time of its official withdrawal it was probably working harder than ever before in its life! The I.C.I. eventually overcame their troubles and No. 62005, now withdrawn, was returned to Leeds, where it was to spend a few more years in store at Neville Hill awaiting a decision on its future.

The accompanying table shows the numbers at each shed at: (i) 31st December 1950, when the full number of engines had been delivered, and (ii) at the end of 1960 before withdrawal commenced.

Allocation at 31st December	1950	1960
March	30	11
Stratford	–	5
Frodingham	–	9
Heaton	8	–
Blaydon	10	15
Darlington	14	11
Northallerton ..	–	2
Stockton	8	–
Thornaby	–	2
York	–	10
Eastfield	1	–
Fort William ..	–	6

No. 2005

No. 62005 was in store at Neville Hill shed for a considerable time pending a decision as to whether or not its boiler could be transferred to the preserved K4, No. 3442 *The Great Marquess.* Had this taken place then no doubt the rest of the engine would have been cut up. To prevent this unhappy possibility the engine was eventually purchased in 1972 by The 45428 Stanier Class 5 Locomotive Society Ltd. who promptly donated

it to the North Eastern Locomotive Preservation Group, with a view to its ultimate appearance in full working order on the North Yorkshire Moors Railway.

The engine was hauled to Thornaby shed where it was gradually restored. It was painted in L.N.E.R. apple green livery, typical of the immediate post-war period when so many classes were so honoured except, unfortunately, any K1's. However, it was felt fitting that this survivor, a fine example of late L.N.E.R. design, should at last acquire the dignity of resplendent L.N.E.R. green livery in the Doncaster tradition. Every effort was made to check that the lining out followed late L.N.E.R. styling, which was a creditable performance by a band of enthusiasts (fig. 154). After restoration, No. 2005 ran in steam from Thornaby shed to Grosmont and on to the North Yorkshire Moors Railway.

In recent years, in addition to putting in some good work on the N.Y.M.R., it has proved to be a very reliable engine maintained by a devoted team of volunteers.

Engine Diagrams

1946.	K1/1.	No. 3445 rebuilt in 1945.
1946.	K1.	Diagram issued for production engines, Nos. 62001-70, which appeared after nationalisation.

Classification: Route availability 6; B.R. power class 6MT.

Summary of KI/I and KI Classes

B.R. No.	1946 No.	Orig. No.	Built as K4 Darlington	Rebuilt Doncaster	Name	Class part	Withdrawn
61997 1/49	1997 12/46	3445	1/1939	12/45	*MacCailin Mór*	1*	6/61

* Class part introduced December 1946.

No.	Maker	Works No.	Built	Withdrawn	No.	Maker	Works No.	Built	Withdrawn
62001	N.B.Loco.Co.	26605	5/1949	4/67	62036	N.B.Loco.Co.	26640	9/1949	10/63
62002	,,	26606	6/1949	10/66	62037	,,	26641	9/1949	12/64
62003	,,	26607	6/1949	6/65	62038	,,	26642	9/1949	10/63
62004	,,	26608	6/1949	12/66	62039	,,	26643	9/1949	12/63
62005	,,	26609	6/1949	12/67	62040	,,	26644	10/1949	1/65
62006	,,	26610	6/1949	9/66	62041	,,	26645	10/1949	4/67
62007	,,	26611	6/1949	9/67	62042	,,	26646	10/1949	7/67
62008	,,	26612	6/1949	12/66	62043	,,	26647	10/1949	7/65
62009	,,	26613	6/1949	11/64	62044	,,	26648	10/1949	7/67
62010	,,	26614	6/1949	10/65	62045	,,	26649	10/1949	9/67
62011	,,	26615	5/1949	9/67	62046	,,	26650	10/1949	2/67
62012	,,	26616	7/1949	5/67	62047	,,	26651	10/1949	3/65
62013	,,	26617	7/1949	10/63	62048	,,	26652	10/1949	6/67
62014	,,	26618	7/1949	6/65	62049	,,	26653	10/1949	6/65
62015	,,	26619	7/1949	7/65	62050	,,	26654	10/1949	9/67
62016	,,	26620	7/1949	7/63	62051	,,	26655	11/1949	1/65
62017	,,	26621	7/1949	2/67	62052	,,	26656	11/1949	12/62
62018	,,	26622	7/1949	3/64	62053	,,	26657	11/1949	12/63
62019	,,	26623	7/1949	7/64	62054	,,	26658	11/1949	12/64
62020	,,	26624	8/1949	1/65	62055	,,	26659	11/1949	12/64
62021	,,	26625	8/1949	10/66	62056	,,	26660	11/1949	5/65
62022	,,	26626	8/1949	9/66	62057	,,	26661	11/1949	5/67
62023	,,	26627	8/1949	6/67	62058	,,	26662	12/1949	8/64
62024	,,	26628	8/1949	2/67	62059	,,	26663	12/1949	2/67
62025	,,	26629	8/1949	4/67	62060	,,	26664	12/1949	8/67
62026	,,	26630	8/1949	7/67	62061	,,	26665	12/1949	12/64
62027	,,	26631	8/1949	3/67	62062	,,	26666	1/1950	5/67
62028	,,	26632	8/1949	11/66	62063	,,	26667	1/1950	9/64
62029	,,	26633	8/1949	10/64	62064	,,	26668	1/1950	9/65
62030	,,	26634	8/1949	8/65	62065	,,	26669	1/1950	3/67
62031	,,	26635	8/1949	12/62	62066	,,	26670	1/1950	1/65
62032	,,	26636	8/1949	9/63	62067	,,	26671	2/1950	1/67
62033	,,	26637	8/1949	1/65	62068	,,	26672	2/1950	1/64
62034	,,	26638	9/1949	12/62	62069	,,	26673	2/1950	1/64
62035	,,	26639	9/1949	7/65	62070	,,	26674	3/1950	1/65

Appendix

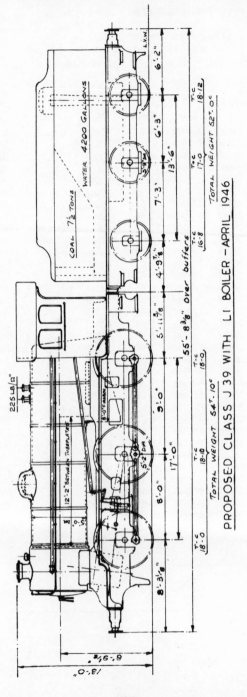

PROPOSED CLASS J39 WITH L1 BOILER - APRIL 1946

166

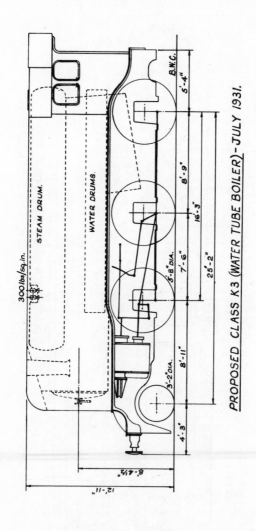

PROPOSED CLASS K3 (WATER TUBE BOILER) – JULY 1931.

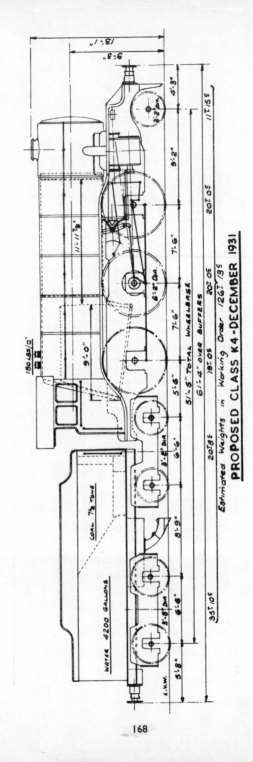

PROPOSED CLASS K4 - DECEMBER 1931

Estimated Weights in Working Order 126T 13S

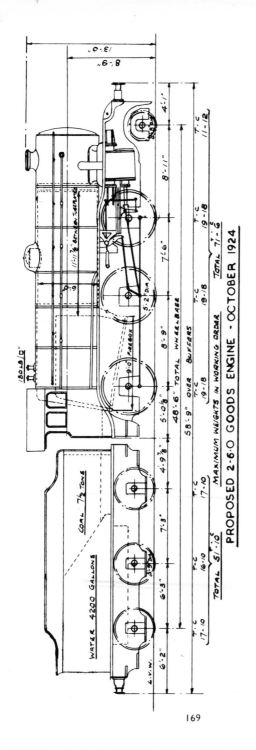

PROPOSED 2-6-0 GOODS ENGINE - OCTOBER 1924

169

4

ACKNOWLEDGEMENTS

This Part is mainly the work of Messrs. M. G. Boddy, E. Neve, D. F. Tee and W. B. Yeadon, with assistance from Messrs. E. V. Fry and W. Hennigan. Thanks are also due to Messrs. B. W. Calvert, J. M. Edgson and L. V. Wood for preparing the line drawings and others who have so willingly helped with information and advice.

Acknowledgement of Illustrations:-
T. G. Hepburn (Figs. 1, 2, 5, 8, 14/5, 24, 36, 41, 57/8/9, 61/2/3/7/8/9, 71, 83/8, 92, 108/18/9/20/2/38/47), E. V. Fry (Figs. 4, 30/1, 158), N. Fields (Figs. 6, 109), P. H. Groom (Figs. 7, 47, 112/29), C. J. L. Romanes (Fig. 9), R. D. Stephen (Fig. 10), J. L. Stevenson (Figs. 11, 140/4), E. R. Wethersett (Figs. 12, 37/9, 134), T. J. Edgington (Figs. 13, 148), J. D. Darby (Figs. 16, 85, 121), L.N.E.R. (Figs. 17/8, 28, 89, 91/6/7/8, 101/49), H. C. Casserley (Figs. 19, 49, 52/4), L. Hanson (Figs. 20, 79, 100/53), S. J. Rhodes (Fig. 21), J.M. Craig (Figs. 25, 90), W. J. Reynolds (Fig. 26), W. Potter (Figs. 27, 42, 95), R. J. Buckley (Figs. 32/4, 78, 114/23/7), J. Robertson (Figs. 33, 115), W. L. Good (Figs. 35, 64, 73, 93/4, 105), E. Woods (Figs. 38, 133), W. Rogerson (Figs. 43/4/5, 103/26), H. N. James (Fig. 46), J. P. Wilson (Figs. 50/1/3, 77, 128), Dr. I. C. Allen (Fig. 55), J. T. Rutherford (Figs. 70, 139), C. L. Kerr (Figs. 72, 143), A. G. Ellis (Fig. 74), A. R. Goult (Figs. 75, 155), P. J. Hughes (Fig. 76), F. R. Hebron (Figs. 80/1/2/4, 116), D. M. C. Hepburne-Scott (Figs. 86, 159), W. H. Whitworth (Figs. 99, 104), Armstrong Whitworth (Fig. 102), K. R. Pirt (Fig. 111), T. A. Greaves (Fig. 113), H. G. Tidey (Fig. 117), L. R. Peters (Figs. 130/2/56), J. F. Henton (Figs. 131/42), L. Perrins (Fig. 135), D. W. Law (Fig. 136), A. C. Cawston (Fig. 137), G. W. Goslin (Fig. 145), E. D. Bruton (Fig. 146), C. L. Turner (Fig. 150), A. King (Fig. 157).

Figs. 3, 4, 23, 30, 44/5, 60, 103/7/10/24/6/41/50/1/4/8 are by courtesy of Photomatic, Figs. 9, 29, 125 of L.G.R.P., Figs. 10/7, 28, 102 of National Railway Museum, York (Crown copyright), Figs. 12, 37/9, 40 of Ian Allan Ltd., Figs. 26, 117 of Real Photographs, Fig. 65 of L.P.C., Fig. 70 of J. Robertson, Esq., Figs. 80/1/2/4/6, 104/59 of B. Stephenson, Esq., Fig. 87 of Lens of Sutton, Fig. 143 of W. Potter, Esq. T. G. Hepburn's photographs are reproduced by courtesy of B. Stephenson, Esq.